Whose Sacrifice Is the Eucharist?

Whose Sacrifice Is the Eucharist?

The Offering of Christ and His Church in Catholic and Methodist Theology

by
Stephen B. Sours

Foreword by Edgardo Colón-Emeric

The Catholic University of America Press
Washington, D.C.

The paper used in this publication meets the minimum requirements of
American National Standards for Information Science—Permanence of
Paper for Printed Library Materials, ANSI Z39.48-1992

∞

Cataloging-in-Publication Data is available from the Library of Congress

ISBN: 978-0-8132-3808-1
eISBN: 978-0-8132-3800-8

In Memory of Geoffrey Wainwright
Theological Mentor and Lover of the Church

Contents

Abbreviations

BCP	*Book of Common Prayer*
BEM	*Baptism, Eucharist and Ministry*
CCC	*Catechism of the Catholic Church*
CE	*Church of England*
CSS	*The Christian Sacrament and Sacrifice* (John Wesley)
EE	*Ecclesia de Eucharistia*
EP	*Eucharistic Prayer*
FWS	*Faith We Sing*
GIRM	*General Instruction of the Roman Missal*
HAP	*Hymns and Psalms*
HLS	*Hymns on the Lord's Supper* (John Wesley and Charles Wesley)
LG	*Lumen gentium*
MC	*Mirae Caritatis*
MD	*Mediator Dei*
MEC	*Methodist Episcopal Church*
MF	*Mysterium Fidei*
PL	Patrologia Latina
SC	*Sacrosanctum Concilium*
SS	*Sunday Service*
STF	*Singing the Faith*
UMC	United Methodist Church
UMH	*United Methodist Hymnal*
WMC	World Methodist Council

Foreword

Edgardo Colón-Emeric

For over a decade, I have participated in national and international Methodist-Roman Catholic dialogues. In response to Christ's prayer "that they may all be one" (Jn 17:21), the goal for these dialogues is "full communion in faith, mission, and sacramental life" (Nairobi, 20). Since 1967, round after round of ecumenical dialogue has advanced growth in mutual understanding and recognition of the measure of communion already shared by Methodists and Catholics. When I describe these dialogues to my students, I use terms like rigorously intellectual, spiritually rich, historically honest, joyfully hopeful, and keenly painful. Fifty-plus years of ecumenical dialogue have been fruitful and offer cause for celebration. However, the persistent signs of imperfect communion are also cause for lament and longing. These signs are particularly evident at the time of Holy Communion.

When Methodists and Catholics gather for dialogue, we do not only sit and discuss, we also worship. On one occasion, our joint commission met at a retreat center outside Atlanta, Georgia. The United-Methodist-run facility was wonderfully hospitable. Not only did they provide excellent meeting, dining, and sleeping facilities, they also opened their chapel for our worship services. There, Methodists and Catholics took turns preaching and presiding. The arrangement was not without its challenges. First, the retreat center staff never could understand why Catholic priests must use wine and not grape juice for the celebration of Holy Communion. Second, the Eucharistic celebration made visible our ecclesial division, as some received both body and blood of Christ and others only a blessing. The pain of imperfect communion was compounded by the setting. Here I was, a Methodist receiving a blessing from a Catholic priest celebrating in a Methodist chapel, using a Methodist chalice and paten, consecrating bread and wine procured, even if with puzzlement, by Methodists.

In a divided Christianity, the Eucharist is a sign of communion and contradiction. The pain and puzzlement experienced at that ecumenical gathering in Atlanta is felt in the daily life of mixed marriages, parochial schools, and the church's rites of passage. Full communion in the sacramental life of the church calls for full communion in its witness in the world and full communion in the articles of faith. In other words, the ecumenical journey is not simply paved by warm hearts and generous spirits (important though these are) but through theological exploration of disputed doctrines. This is where the present book comes in.

It is with great joy that I introduce Stephen Sours's *Whose Sacrifice is the Eucharist? The Offering of Christ and His Church in Catholic and Methodist Theology*. This book does not present quick fixes or easy answers to the challenges of eucharistic hospitality and intercommunion. Instead, it engages in careful, patient theological inquiry that advances doctrinal convergence on a disputed question, namely the relation of Christ's sacrifice to the Eucharistic celebration. Stephen Sours and I are both graduates of Duke Divinity School. Hence, in order to introduce Stephen Sours's book, I believe it would be helpful to introduce the school that formed his theology.

First, theology at Duke Divinity School is rooted in a Methodist identity and is ecumenical in scope. From its founding in 1926, Duke Divinity presented itself as a Methodist school that would be not narrowly denominational but broadly catholic. Differently stated, it was ecumenical because it was Methodist. Being catholic with a little "c" belongs with its birthright. John Wesley could be sharply polemical, but his theological vision was strongly ecumenical, as seen in his sermon *Catholic Spirit*, his *Letter to a Roman Catholic*, and his promotion of Catholic figures as exemplars of holiness. The commitment to an ecumenical, Wesleyan theological vision at Duke is evident in many ways. Here I name two. On the one hand, through its work on the critical edition of *The Works of John Wesley*, Duke Divinity has been a key source in the revival of Wesley's theology. On the other hand, one of its most illustrious deans, Robert Cushman, was one of the official Protestant Observers at the Second Vatican Council and, along with Albert Outler, an interpreter of its importance for Methodists. To this day, theological studies at Duke are pursued with an ear to what the Spirit is saying to the church catholic and for the sake of its theological, liturgical, and missional renewal.

Second, the ecumenical way of theology at Duke Divinity was exemplarily embodied by Geoffrey Wainwright, to whom Stephen Sours dedicates this book. The impact of this renowned Methodist theologian on the ecumenical movement is remarkable. He worked alongside the Catholic Jean-Marie Tillard and the Orthodox John Zizioulas in drafting key portions of the World Council of Churches' statement *Baptism, Eucharist, and Ministry* (1992), perhaps the high watermark of multilateral ecumenical dialogues. His legacy to the Methodist Roman Catholic International Commission, which he co-chaired for twenty years (1991–2011), is just as weighty. For example, it was under his leadership that the World Methodist Council affiliated itself with the Joint Declaration on the Doctrine of Justification of the Lutheran World Federation and the Roman Catholic Church, a first in ecumenical work. Wainwright was a mentor to generations of theologians. He introduced his students to the scandal of church disunity, the ecumenical imperative, the theological depth of the Wesleyan heritage, and the centrality of liturgy. It is no accident that Methodist-Catholic reports include citations from John Wesley's writings and Charles Wesley's poetry. Wainwright's thought foregrounds the doxological dimension of theology, the intertwining of *lex orandi* and *lex credendi*, praise and confession. Incidentally, the meeting in Atlanta was the last Geoffrey Wainwright attended, but his legacy endures. When Sours considers the doctrinal significance of Charles Wesley's hymns such as "Victim Divine," he is following in the footsteps of Wainwright.

Third, theology at Duke Divinity advances unity by embracing *ressourcement*. Tradition matters at Duke. It is common at this school to bring the founder of Methodism and the angelic doctor into dialogue for the sake of deepened doctrinal understanding. Stephen Sours's pairing of Wesley and Aquinas joins and extends the work of other alums: Stephen Long's *John Wesley's Moral Theology* and Kenneth Loyer's *God's Love through the Holy Spirit*, and my own *Wesley, Aquinas, and Christian Perfection*. At the risk of being overly self-referential, a few words about my own work may elucidate the value of this approach. In my work, I examined the doctrine of Christian perfection, a doctrine that had not previously been ecumenically explored in depth. A close reading of the teachings of John Wesley on Christian perfection next to those of Thomas Aquinas revealed many convergences: the importance of beatitude, the centrality of love and the other virtues, the universality of the call to perfection, and the social character of holiness. In light of these convergences, I proposed that the theological approaches of Aquinas and Wesley should be seen as largely complementary. To put it another way, reading Aquinas can help Methodists become more Wesleyan. Indeed, it was because of my work on these topics at Duke that I was invited to join the Methodist-Catholic International Commission that met in Atlanta.

I am proud to present Stephen Sours as a Duke Divinity theologian. He is Methodist; he is ecumenical; he is dialogical. In the spirit of theology at Duke as embodied by Wainwright, he harvests the work of the ecumenical dialogues. He attends to the significant convergences that these have achieved in sacramental theology while pointing to areas in need of further exploration, such as theological anthropology, which incidentally was one of the main topics of discussion at the Methodist-Catholic meeting in Atlanta. Sours looks to the liturgy as lived theology that can resource Methodist doctrinal development. The gap between Methodist worship practice and official statements can become a springboard for movement toward full communion. Sours's engagement with Thomistic theology and Catholic teaching can help Methodists understand their own theology and practices better. For instance, in many Methodist congregations, pastors offer altar calls to discipleship and invite "sinners to the gospel feast," to quote one of Charles Wesley's eucharistic hymns. These two invitations are often disconnected in practice. However, to speak of an altar is to speak of priest and sacrifice. Sours helps us connect these in fresh ways.

In sum, it is my hope that Sours's call for a more generous exchange of gifts among Methodists and Catholics on the doctrine of the sacrifice of the Eucharist will be ecumenically fruitful. The achievement and celebration of convergence on this topic would hasten the day when Methodists and Catholics fully share in Holy Communion for the sake of the church's mission in the world. On that day, the celebration of a Catholic Eucharist in a chapel at a Methodist retreat center would be not a painful reminder of division but a sign of the kingdom.

Acknowledgments

A book on the eucharist should be filled with thanksgiving, and this one certainly is. Numerous institutions, groups, and individuals have been instrumental in helping me with this project, and without them I would never have managed to see it to completion.

The faculty and administration at Huntingdon College are not only colleagues, but also friends, and they foster a genuine collegiality that helps us live out our motto of Faith, Wisdom, and Service. Among Methodist scholars, the network of John Wesley Fellows regularly inspires my intellect and nourishes my spirit. It is a wonderful embodiment of the Wesleyan connection. A special thanks goes to Asbury Theological Seminary for supporting and organizing the Wesleyan Studies Summer Seminar. This month-long fellowship was invaluable in providing the time, resources, and relationships to bring this work to fruition. I am also indebted to the Huntingdon library staff for all their research assistance and to Katy P. for her ace editing skills.

No academic couple ever had two sets of parents who were more supportive than ours, and no four children ever had grandparents who looked out for them the way theirs do. Our families have championed our cause, and they have supported our endeavors in every conceivable way. We never would have made it even half this far without them. What a blessing it is to have a spouse who is a fellow scholar. Sarah not only understands the demands of research and writing, but she also values their contribution to the church and academy. In supporting and encouraging me, she has undertaken countless sacrifices, and I am profoundly grateful.

Randy Maddox and Reinhard Huetter were vital in directing this research. I cherish the knowledge and skills they have given me. Their influence is ongoing, and their words are always filled with wisdom. I am deeply appreciative of their mentorship. Ecumenical theologians will recognize in this book the strong influence—both in content and method—of Geoffrey Wainwright. Most of my theological formation took place under his training, and it would be impossible to express how richly his teaching has shaped me theologically. My gratitude for his work is tremendous, and I dedicate this book to his memory.

Whose Sacrifice Is the Eucharist?

Introduction
Why Eucharistic Sacrifice?

Eucharistic sacrifice is both a doctrine of the church and a sacramental practice. Doctrinally, it explains in what manner the sacrament is a sacrifice, or at least its sacrificial dimension; liturgically, it refers to the offering that is made in the church's celebration of the eucharist—that is, who and what is offered and by whom. Eucharistic sacrifice raises a series of complicated questions. Was the Last Supper a sacrifice or in any way sacrificial? What is the relationship between the Supper, the cross, and the eucharist? What is the relationship between the different actors—Christ, the Holy Spirit, the ordained minister, and the congregation/church—in the eucharist? While eucharistic sacrifice developed in the early and medieval church without causing division, it quickly became a central point of controversy at the Reformation.

As a result, Protestant churches largely abandoned the doctrine of eucharistic sacrifice—sometimes even abandoning the language of offering—or severely truncated its scope, subjecting it to rigid qualifications. Due to their reading of patristic sources and to their own Anglican heritage, John and Charles Wesley maintained a doctrine of eucharistic sacrifice uncharacteristically stronger than many Protestant traditions of their day; however, after the death of the Wesleys, Methodism followed suit with the traditional Protestant skepticism of eucharistic sacrifice, and it maintained this position until the second half of the twentieth century. This diminishment in eucharistic theology, however, in no way accurately describes the practice or the theology of the Wesleys, since a theology of eucharistic sacrifice figured prominently in the theology and hymnody of early Methodism. Nor does it accurately describe the current eucharistic prayers of British and United Methodism, since these churches have gone a long way in recovering eucharistic sacrifice in their recent liturgical revisions through their participation in the ecumenical movement and in a recovery of their Wesleyan origins.

The rapprochement between churches in the twentieth century cannot be highlighted and celebrated too often: the growth of the ecumenical movement, the Second Vatican Council, and the liturgical movement, for example, have all served to bring divided traditions closer together. The document *Baptism, Eucharist and Ministry* (*BEM*) stands as a product and an instrument of the ecumenical movement for the noteworthy convergences to which it bears witness and that it has succeeded in garnering around these fundamental elements of the church's life.[1] Throughout this new concord, Catholic theology has remained relatively consistent in its theology of eucharistic sacrifice.[2] From the Methodist side, however, despite the recovery of eucharistic sacrifice prominently confessed in the current Great Thanksgivings, official teaching on the doctrine remains underdeveloped.

Methodists have been enthusiastic participants in the ecumenical movement since its inception—commonly regarded as beginning with the 1910 Edinburgh Conference on World Mission—and subsequent creation of the World Council of Churches in 1948. Indeed, intra-Methodist ecumenism among global Methodist bodies began in 1881 in London with the creation of the Ecumenical Methodist Conference. In 1951 this conference became the World Methodist Council (WMC) and began meeting every five years in different locations around the world. Today, the WMC consists of eighty member churches in 138 countries totaling 80 million people.[3] One of the many objectives and tasks of the WMC is to represent the Wesleyan/Methodist traditions in global ecumenical dialogue. (Individual Methodist bodies also engage in bilateral ecumenical dialogues, such as those, for example, that British and United Methodists have with Catholics in Britain and America.) The WMC has (or has had) ecumenical engagements with several global partners: the World Lutheran Federation, World Alliance of Reformed Churches, Anglican Communion, Orthodoxy, Salvation Army, and Roman Catholicism. The WMC–Roman Catholic Church (WMC–RCC) dialogue has continued fruitfully since 1967. It is the WMC's longest-running dialogue, as well as "theologically the most mature of Methodism's bilateral conversations."[4] Kenneth Cracknell and Susan White summarize global Methodism's current ecumenical methodology: "In the twentieth century the search for visible unity became more urgent when Methodist theologians on both sides of the Atlantic came increasingly to the sobering conclusion that Methodists were not equipped with an ecclesiology, or doctrine of the

---

1. World Council of Churches, *Baptism, Eucharist, and Ministry*, Faith and Order Paper No. 111 (Geneva: World Council of Churches, 1982).

2. See, for example, Pope Pius XII, *Mediator Dei* (November 20, 1947); Pope Paul VI, *Mysterium Fidei* (September 3, 1965); Vatican II, *Lumen Gentium* (1964); and John Paul II, *Ecclesia de Eucharistia* (April 17, 2003), not to mention the scores of books by individual theologians. Unless otherwise specified, Vatican documents can be accessed at www.vatican.va.

3. "What Is Methodism?," World Methodist Council: https://worldmethodistcouncil. org/about-us/, accessed May 10, 2023.

4. David M. Chapman, "Methodism and the Future of Ecumenism," in *The Oxford Handbook of Methodist Studies*, ed. William J. Abraham and James E. Kirby (New York: Oxford University Press, 2009), 455.

church, adequate to sustain their communion in separation from the rest of Christianity."[5]

From the beginnings of its dialogues with Catholics, Methodism has held in tension its own history alongside its ecumenical impulses: on the one hand, Methodists do not have a history of "issuing a comprehensive doctrinal statement on the eucharist," and even while Methodist "practice and theology often fall short" of the Wesleys' hymns, they remain the benchmark for Methodist eucharistic theology;[6] while on the other hand, Raymond George—British Methodist theologian and ecumenist—formulated the phrase: "Methodists accept that whatever is properly required for the unity of the whole of Christ's Church must by that very fact be God's will for his Church."[7] The statement, of course, turns on the understanding of the words "properly required." Even though United Methodists and Catholics "view the eucharist as a type of sacrifice, and both view Holy Communion as the communion of the church,"[8] nevertheless, the United Methodist–Roman Catholic document *Eucharistic Celebration* states, "The role played by the church in the offering of this sacrifice remains a problem. The answer to the question 'Who offers what?' is far from clear. . . . The two churches do not have doctrinal agreement about the specific sense in which the offering of the church is the full offering of Christ."[9]

5. Kenneth Cracknell and Susan J. White, *An Introduction to World Methodism* (New York: Cambridge University Press, 2005), 252.

6. *Growth in Understanding*, 51. World Methodiast Council-Roman Catholic dialogues from the 1970s–90s are found in Harding Meyer and Lukas Vischer, eds., *Growth in Agreement: Reports and Agreed Statements of Ecumenical Conversations on a World Level*, 2 vols. (Geneva: World Council of Churches, 1984). Individually: Meyer and Vischer, *Growth in Agreement* (1971), *Growth in Understanding* (1976), *Towards an Agreed Statement on the Holy Spirit* (1981), *Towards a Statement on the Church* (1986), *The Apostolic Tradition* (1991), *The Word of Life: A Statement on Revelation and Faith* (1996). Additionally: World Methodist Council–Roman Catholic Church, *Speaking the Truth in Love: Teaching Authority among Catholics and Methodists* (Lake Junaluska, NC: World Methodist Council, 2001), and World Methodist Council (WMC)–Roman Catholic Church (RCC), *The Grace Given You in Christ: Catholics and Methodists Reflect Further on the Church* (Lake Junaluska, NC: World Methodist Council, 2006). References from the dialogues are given by paragraphs.

7. David M. Chapman, *In Search of the Catholic Spirit: Methodists and Roman Catholics in Dialogue* (Peterborough: Epworth Press, 2004), 147.

8. United Methodist Church–United States Conference of Catholic Bishops, *Through Divine Love: The Church in Each Place and All Places* (2005), 144; web document: https://www.usccb.org/resources/Through-Divine-Love-the-Church-in-Each-Place-and-All-Places.pdf.

9. United Methodist Church–United States Conference of Catholic Bishops, *Eucharistic Celebration: Converging Theology—Divergent Practice* [United Methodist-Roman Catholic Dialogue, 1981], in *Building Unity: Ecumenical Dialogues with Roman Catholic Participation in the United States*, Ecumenical Documents 4, ed. Joseph A. Burgess and Jeffrey Gros (New York: Paulist Press, 1989), 316. To the question "Who offers what and how?," see Kathryn Nichols, "The Theology of Christ's Sacrifice and Presence in Charles Wesley's Hymns on the Lord's Supper," *Hymn* 39 (1988): 19–29.

Thankfully, however, these latter citations from United Methodist–Catholic dialogues do not adequately express the degree of convergence achieved after *BEM*, nor do they articulate in detail the nature of the questions still remaining.

If Catholics and Methodists are ever fully to realize the communion that they seek, then convergence on the two churches' teachings on eucharistic sacrifice will be paramount. The 2006 statement of the Roman Catholic–World Methodist Council dialogue recognizes that sacramental theology and ecclesiology mutually inform one another, and it sets the agenda for future dogmatic theological investigation. *The Grace Given You in Christ: Catholics and Methodists Reflect Further on the Church* intentionally builds on two previous statements and their attention to ecclesiology and doctrinal consensus.[10] Both sides rejoice that each party recognizes the other as church to some degree,[11] but the text lists "major issues" awaiting resolution: the relationship between eucharistic fellowship and ecclesial unity; the nature of the ordained minister as president of the eucharist; the specifics of Christ's eucharistic presence; and the sacrificial nature of the eucharist and its meaning as a sacramental memorial of Christ's saving death and resurrection.[12] Eucharistic sacrifice is a discrete systematic topic, even while it relates to other facets of eucharistic theology as a whole: especially the presence of Christ in the eucharist; the theology of ordained ministry; *epiclesis*, *anamnesis*, and eschatology; atonement theology; and the degree to which the eucharist is understood not just as a sign of but as a means toward Christian unity. These related doctrines are considered only at points where they bear directly on the discussion of eucharistic sacrifice at hand. An in-depth treatment of this latter issue at the level of bilateral ecumenical dialogue is the focus of this book, and the place to begin is to recognize how recent Catholic-Methodist dialogues frame eucharistic sacrifice within the context of a shared sacramental theology.[13]

10. WMC-RCC, *Grace Given You in Christ*, Preface, referring to *Towards a Statement on the Church* (1986) and *The Apostolic Tradition* (1991).

11. WMC-RCC, *Grace Given You in Christ*, 7, 144.

12. WMC-RCC, *Grace Given You in Christ*, 94, 155.

13. For the most complete history and analysis of Catholic-Methodist relations, see Chapman, *In Search of the Catholic Spirit*. See, too, David Carter, "Can the Roman Catholic and Methodist Churches Be Reconciled? (Conference Given at the Centro Pro Unione, November 1999)," *Ecumenical Trends* 31, no. 1 (2002): 1–9, and Geoffrey Wainwright, "The Ecumenical Scope of Methodist Liturgical Revision," in *Liturgical Renewal as a Way to Christian Unity*, ed. J. F. Puglisi and Horace T. Allen (Collegeville, MN: Liturgical Press, 2005), 35–59.

The Sacramental and Anthropological Context of Eucharistic Sacrifice

In signaling the need to reconsider eucharistic sacrifice, the dialogue explicitly invokes two related ecclesiological foci. First, it notes that the sacrifice of the Mass "became obscured in Protestant thought and life instead of simply being reformed of [its] excesses."[14] The topic of eucharistic sacrifice, therefore, cuts to the heart of each church's self-identity and the theological articulation of its raison d'être: for while Protestant liturgies historically reflect the rejection of all but the faintest sacrificial dimension, Catholic eucharistic theology has always maintained that the eucharist is a sacrifice, yet it has done so quite cognizant of charges that the Reformation brought upon it, as the Council of Trent attests. Second, the desire for convergence on eucharistic sacrifice serves the stated goal of the Methodist-Catholic dialogue—namely, "full communion in faith, mission, and sacramental life."[15] In other words, because Methodism commits itself to unity at the same time that it knows itself to be only a part of the Body of Christ, it imposes on itself (in keeping with John Wesley's example) a hermeneutic of charity with respect to its dialogue partners. It therefore seeks not to defend a doctrinal confession forged in division but, for the sake of unity, to strive to accept as much of the doctrines of other churches as it can. If Methodism takes seriously this hermeneutic of seeking to integrate its Wesleyan heritage into the greater church catholic, it should bear fruit in its ecumenical dialogues, especially with Roman Catholics, and especially around such a historically contentious topic as eucharistic sacrifice.

The Grace Given You in Christ directs much of its attention to the similarities and differences between the two churches with respect to the relationship between ecclesiology and sacramental theology, with close attention naturally given to the eucharist. Significantly, any discussion of convergence within sacramental theology emerges from the shared conviction of the centrality of sanctification and from the common confession that in the power of the Holy Spirit Christ's members continue to share in the paschal mystery of the incarnate Son.[16] The means by which believers participate in this mystery come both by doing acts of mercy and by attending to the means of grace. Thus, the sacramental life of the church lies at the heart of its conformity to the

---

14. WMC-RCC, *Grace Given You in Christ*, 130.

15. WMC-RCC, *Grace Given You in Christ*. 98. See, too, United Methodist Church, *The Book of Discipline* (Nashville: United Methodist Publishing House, 2016), "Ecumenical Commitment," #105.

16. WMC-RCC, *Grace Given You in Christ*, 17 and 52.

image of its Lord: "Conformity with Christ . . . means entering into the glory of Trinitarian love by the way of suffering characteristic of the paschal mystery."[17] Consequently, the church also participates with its head in this divine modality of salvation. "The idea of a sacrament is ideally suited to holding together internal and external, visible and spiritual, and both Catholics and Methodists have begun to speak of the church in a sacramental way."[18]

Wesley consistently rejected attempts to exchange the mediating communion of the Lord's Supper for unmediated communion with Christ.[19] The dialogues regularly emphasize commonalties surrounding sacramental theology, and following overtures laid down in earlier sessions, the 1996 and 2006 dialogues treat this convergence in detail.[20] Based on the biblical confession of Christ as the "mystery of our religion" (1 Tm 3:16), both churches see the incarnation of the Son as the "primary sacrament," since he is "both the sign of our salvation and the instrument by which it is achieved." Although Methodists do not speak quite so strongly as Catholics, both confess the sacramental nature of the church as the Body of Christ, "the instrument for extending the divine offer as widely as the scope of God's eternal purpose for humankind." The sacraments, then, exist as "instances of the divine Mystery . . . instituted by Christ and made effective by the Spirit" as the means by which "the Saviour continues his words and actions among us."[21]

The Grace Given You brings together more closely the two churches' sacramental convergence and the consequences this might have for eucharistic theology. The agreement that the sacraments are instituted and ordered by the Lord is a crucial one. Even though Trent clearly affirmed this, Reformation polemics often attacked medieval sacramental theology for locating the institution and distribution of grace in the authority of the priest rather than with the risen Lord. Wesley was adamant that any power in the sacraments derived from Christ's authority and the Spirit's power.[22] It places the sacramental nature of the church in its pneumatological and trinitarian context; reiterates the ecclesial dimension of the eucharist; teaches the complementary relationship between word and sacrament; and expresses Methodist openness to

17. *Word of Life*, 110.

18. WMC-RCC, *Grace Given You in Christ*, 102; see Randy Maddox, "Social Grace: The Eclipse of the Church as a Means of Grace in American Methodism," in *Methodism in Its Cultural Milieu*, ed. Tim MacQuiban (Oxford: Applied Theology Press, 1994), 131–60.

19. Randy Maddox, *Responsible Grace: John Wesley's Practical Theology* (Nashville: Kingswood, 1994), 193.

20. See *The Apostolic Tradition*, 88–91; *Speaking the Truth in Love*, 52–61; *Toward a Statement on the Church*, 9.

21. *Word of Life*, 94–98.

22. WMC-RCC, *Grace Given You in Christ*, 134.

receiving historic apostolic succession.[23] It confidently and forthrightly signals a trajectory to pursue in light of the current agreement on sacramental theology: "This agreement between Catholics and Methodists on the need for 'graced, free and active participation in God's saving work' lies at the very heart of the possibility of our moving towards a common understanding of the nature and mission of the Church which makes use of concepts associated with 'sacramentality.'"[24]

Furthermore, the theological convergence between Methodists and Catholics with respect to the effective sacramental mediation of grace derives in large part from shared convictions concerning theological anthropology, and it is in this area of sacramental theology specifically from which further convergence on eucharistic sacrifice must come. Shared anthropological presuppositions between the two churches have received less attention than their shared sacramental convictions, although with respect to eucharistic sacrifice they are no less significant.

From the Methodist side, for example, while Randy Maddox concentrates more on Wesley's doctrines of justification, sanctification, and perfection than on eucharistic sacrifice, he gives special mention to Wesley's conception of human cooperation in the *via salutis*. As to the charges against Wesley in his own time that he preached salvation by works, and to the historians' debate of whether Wesley was a synergist, Maddox says, "If synergism is understood as simply the preservation of a role for grace-empowered human co-operation in salvation, then it too reflects a concern of Wesley's understanding of Prevenient Grace." Maddox notes that while "co-operant grace," if properly understood, rightly describes Wesley's teaching, he prefers the term "responsible grace": a double entendre on the fact that humans respond to God's grace at the same time that they are created to act responsibly with respect to it.[25] Ole Borgen also calls attention to Wesley's cooperative anthropology concerning justification and sanctification, even though he does not make the connection between Wesley's anthropology and eucharistic sacrifice. He notes, as Maddox does, that for Wesley faith is the "condition" of justification and sanctification at the same time that it is the instrument of sanctification. Wesley liked to talk of "faith working by love," and he understands that God gives grace by means and sacraments.[26]

23. WMC-RCC, *Grace Given You in Christ*, 76–83,103, 104, 106, 112.

24. WMC-RCC, *Grace Given You in Christ*, 77.

25. Maddox, *Responsible Grace*, 92. Maddox points to Wesley's sermon on Philippians 2:12–13, "On Working Out Our Own Salvation," as his classic statement.

26. Ole E. Borgen, *John Wesley on the Sacraments: A Theological Study* (Nashville: Abingdon Press, 1972), 202–8.

The Grace Given You in Christ capitalizes on this shared anthropology and connects it directly with the potential for greater convergence:

> Catholics are at one with Methodists in their understanding that holiness entails conversion and transformation, being "changed from glory into glory." Bearing in mind the controversy at the Reformation between Catholics and Protestants regarding cooperation with grace, it is of immense significance that Catholics and Methodists stand together on this matter. Methodists believe, as Catholics do, that we truly cooperate with God's grace and participate in God's life. . . . There are foundations here for a serious shared exploration of the idea of sacramentality.[27]

The dialogue gestures toward, but does not explicitly extend, the implications of cooperation and sacramental theology to eucharistic sacrifice. In this study, I intend to build off this foundation by advancing an exploration into the sacrificial dimension of the eucharist from an anthropological perspective, both Christ's and ours. The cooperative way of salvation bears directly on the deep commonalities between Methodists and Catholics in sacramental theology and on the prospects of convergence on eucharistic sacrifice.

An Overview of the Argument

Now, after five decades of productive ecumenical dialogue, Catholics and Methodists seek to discern the points of convergence and divergence between them on this controversial doctrine. In short, where do Catholics and Methodists agree and disagree on eucharistic sacrifice? This book is a work of systematic theology that draws from the insights of several related fields: liturgical theology, historical theology, sacramental theology, ecclesiology, and ecumenism.

Chapter 1 serves to elucidate the state of affairs between the two churches with an investigation into what Catholics and Methodists have shared with each other to date in ecumenical dialogue. They have raised the issue of eucharistic sacrifice in their bilateral dialogues and in ecumenical discussions that have taken place at the multi-lateral level—namely, through their involvement in *Baptism, Eucharist, and Ministry* and their responses to it. The churches' comments in these venues set the stage for subsequent chapters. In *The Grace Given You in Christ*, the Catholic delegation even offers a trajectory for investigating eucharistic sacrifice:

> Vatican II taught that through the sacraments, and most especially by Baptism and the eucharist, we are "united in a hidden and real way to

27. WMC-RCC, *Grace Given You in Christ*, 123.

Christ in his passion and glorification." In other words, we are sacramentally united with Christ, as his body, in the great single act of his sacrifice, by which he entered into glory. There can never be any repetition of that act. . . . Nevertheless, the eucharist truly has a sacrificial character because Christ is really present there in the very act of his supreme self-gift to his Father. The sacramental presence of Christ himself is at once the sacramental presence of his sacrifice also, because the Christ who is present is he who has entered the sanctuary once and for all bearing his own blood to secure an eternal redemption (Heb 9:12). He now lives forever, exercising a perpetual priesthood, making intercession for us. Catholics regret any impression they may have given of a repetition of Christ's sacrifice in the Mass, but they also reject the overreaction which denies a sacrificial character to the eucharist.[28]

In chapters 2, 3, and 4, I seek to listen carefully to the traditioning voices of Thomas Aquinas and John Wesley, who provide instances of detailed teaching on eucharistic sacrifice. Aquinas's theology must be understood within his teaching on broader concepts, such as religion, justice, corporate worship, theological anthropology, and the sacraments, and his thought continues to exert its influence in contemporary Catholic teaching. Although the richness of Wesley's eucharistic theology was largely overlooked in nineteenth-century Methodism, his theology of eucharistic sacrifice—especially his Christology of Jesus' eternal and heavenly priesthood—anticipates significantly the convergence that the liturgical and ecumenical movements have achieved on this topic. Methodism has indeed returned to Wesley as an authoritative figure in its own sacramental renewal, yet only a handful of contemporary Methodist theologians have explored Wesley's theology of eucharistic sacrifice in detail, and fewer still from an ecumenical perspective.

In chapters 5 through 8, I address the ecclesiological dimension of eucharistic sacrifice. In recent decades, Catholic and Methodist churches have circulated official teaching on eucharistic sacrifice and made significant revisions to their eucharistic liturgies. An analysis of these texts demonstrates how each church currently articulates its doctrine of eucharistic sacrifice and celebrates it liturgically. This analysis then allows for an assessment of the current degree of convergence between the two churches on eucharistic sacrifice.

What emerges over the course of this investigation is the conviction not only that Methodists can fully affirm the doctrine of eucharistic sacrifice adumbrated previously, but that an even deeper convergence exists between the two churches, one based on a shared doctrine of Christ's eternal Priesthood

---

28. WMC-RCC, *Grace Given You in Christ*, 131.

and another on a shared theological anthropology that embraces the notion of humanity's graced participation in God's saving work. This participation is at once individual and corporate, so that ultimately both churches understand eucharistic sacrifice to be the action of offering the *totus Christus*—the whole Christ, head and body—in thanksgiving to God the Father.

The conclusion is that, first, Methodism has begun to recover a strong doctrine of eucharistic sacrifice, and greater attention to its Wesleyan heritage can only strengthen it further. Second, the two churches share more on eucharistic sacrifice than is frequently appreciated; indeed, Methodism should recognize in Catholicism a doctrine and a liturgy with which it can fully agree. Third, eucharistic sacrifice necessitates a clearly formulated ecclesiology, which is a topic in the dialogues where Catholics can continue in love to provoke Methodists to deeper reflection. Convergence on eucharistic sacrifice, if recognized by both churches, would constitute a significant step forward on the path to full communion between them.

CHAPTER 1

Eucharistic Sacrifice in Catholic-Methodist Dialogues and *BEM*

The purpose of this chapter is to assess the current state of affairs between Catholics and Methodists with respect to eucharistic sacrifice; that is, what have Catholics and Methodists actually shared with each other (at the ecclesial level) concerning their official beliefs and practices of eucharistic sacrifice? This exchange has taken place in two principal venues: bilateral dialogues—chiefly at the international level between the Catholic Church and the World Methodist Council (RC-WMC)—and multilateral dialogues, particularly *BEM*. While individual rounds of the bilateral dialogues have cursorily addressed the topic of eucharistic sacrifice, they did not yet engage the doctrine directly until 2011. *BEM*, on the other hand, addressed eucharistic sacrifice in much more detail, as did the Catholic and Methodist responses to *BEM*. Each of these venues is considered in roughly chronological order, and an assessment of the official comments by Catholics and Methodists in these dialogues will set the stage for our investigation in subsequent chapters.

The question of eucharistic sacrifice in Catholic-Methodist international dialogues has an interesting history. Right from the beginning, the topic was addressed in the first two rounds of dialogue. Commonalities and differences were enumerated, but a sustained investigation was not pursued, perhaps wisely, as the dialogue was not sufficiently mature to tackle such a controversy-laden doctrine as eucharistic sacrifice. The greater need was to establish agreement (or at least convergence) on more fundamental issues, which the dialogues from the 1980s and 1990s succeeded in doing. When the two churches recognized their agreement on certain fundamentals of sacramental theology (*The Grace Given You in Christ*, 2006), the step was not far to considering more closely many of the subtleties of eucharistic theology, including its sacrificial dimension.[1] The eucharist chapter of the 2011 dialogue *Encoun-*

---

1. For an accounting of these dialogues, see Geoffrey Wainwright, "An Ecclesiological Journey: The Way of Methodist-Roman Catholic International Dialogue," *Ecclesiology* 7 (2011): 50–70.

tering Christ the Saviour: Church and Sacraments discusses eucharistic sacrifice directly. Without being comprehensive, it identifies areas of agreement and suggests a way forward for further research. Not surprisingly, though, it is precisely at the level of each church's many doctrinal subtleties where apparent disagreement and (more commonly) misperception set in.

Early Explorations

The first two dialogues consider the topics of real presence, memorial, communion with Christ, and sacrifice. Despite the remarkable brevity with which they discuss these topics, they are surprised to uncover an "astonishing measure of agreement," even though the churches diverged on the usage of the language of sacrifice. *Growth in Agreement* (1971) lists points of agreement and disagreement associated with these three topics, but ironically lists no disagreement on eucharistic sacrifice. Areas of agreement include:

1. "The eucharist is the celebration of Christ's full, perfect and sufficient sacrifice, offered once and for all, for the whole world."
2. "It is a memorial which is more than a recollection of a past event. It is a re-enactment of Christ's triumphant sacrifice and makes available for us its benefits."
3. "For this reason Roman Catholics call the eucharist a sacrifice, though this terminology is not used by Methodists."
4. "In this celebration we share in Christ's offering to [*sic*; of?] Himself in obedience to the Father's will."[2]

Growth in Understanding (1976) elaborates the issues previously raised, commenting again on the "measure of agreement" and on the lack of any "points of disagreement":

1. Affirmation of Christ's complete and perfect sacrifice offered only once for all. It is a memorial in which Christ is present with his benefits. "Re-enactment" language is diminished.
2. By sacrifice, Methodists intend: (a) Christ's unique sacrifice; (b) our pleading of that sacrifice; (c) our offering of a sacrifice of praise; (d) the holy and living sacrifice of self in union with Christ.
3. Catholics concur, and they offer another meaning: the church offers the sacrifice of the Mass in "all ages . . . as making present in a sacramental way the same sacrifice." Methodists "prefer" not to use sacrifice

---

2. *Growth in Agreement*, 83–85.

in this way, but use instead the language of "intercession," so that our union with his sacrifice is our "only plea."[3]

With respect to item number one, the history behind the use (and then disuse) of "re-enactment" language in the dialogues is interesting, although unclear. It was perhaps introduced as a way of explaining the recovery of the concept of *anamnesis*, and perhaps it was then dropped because Methodists feared that it was too suggestive of the repetition of the cross (the perennial Protestant fear). If this was the case, then the change was understandable in the early stages of the dialogue. Significantly, though, as a part of its liturgical revisions (which took place after these initial dialogues) in which the liturgy sacramentally "re-enacts" the fourfold action of Christ as a repetition of the Last Supper, both British and United Methodism reappropriates the concept of "re-enactment" as the chief hermeneutic for structuring the liturgy. Although the use of the word is not common among Methodists, James White exemplifies how they understand the term: "Every time we 'do this' we thankfully show forth what God has done in Christ and continues to do. It is a practice older than the written gospels and epistles and directly in line with Christ's use of the Passover occasion to combine reenactment and presence in a new covenant."[4]

The dialogues claim that concerning sacrifice, the principal differences are not doctrinal, but largely language and emphasis. Three other Protestant observations exist with respect to the Catholic teaching of Christ's same sacrifice in the eucharist. First, Catholics often use the terminology of "eucharist" and "Mass" interchangeably, whereas at least until *BEM* and perhaps even now, Methodists associate the eucharist with The Great Thanksgiving and not the whole Sunday worship service. When Methodists celebrate the eucharist on Sunday morning, they refer to the worship as a Service of Word and Table; *BEM* defines this as "eucharist" (E 27). Thus, the Protestant critique that in the Mass the meal overshadows the Word no longer holds when "eucharist" refers to the whole service of Word and Table. The Reformers, Wesley, and the near-universal majority of Protestants certainly see Sunday worship as a making present in all ages the sacrifice of Christ, primarily through preaching. That the Reformers' theology of the preached Word is itself an act analogous to a sacrament, and that Protestants have perpetuated the sacrifice of the cross through the ages in preaching, only serves to express the degree of convergence that has become expressed in practice through the liturgical movement.

3. *Growth in Understanding*, 62–67. See Wainwright, "Ecumenical Scope," 40–45.

4. James White, "Function and Form of the Eucharistic Prayer," *Reformed Liturgy and Music* 16, no. 1 (Winter 1982): 20.

Second, Wesley and the Reformers insisted on the need for believers to gather corporately, both because they were duty-bound to *give* God the glory due his name and in order to receive the benefits of divine grace through prayer and the *hearing* of the preached Word. The anthropology implicit in this Protestant conviction has much in common with the Catholic theology of a corporate sacrifice: the necessity of making an offering in the form of a liturgical rite by the Body of Christ, not because God needs it, but for the church's sake. As we will see, Wesley makes this connection explicit in his affirmation that the eucharist is a sacrifice.

Third, Catholic reference to the Mass (Word and Table) as a propitiatory sacrifice loses much of its offense in light of the fact that the eucharist (*BEM*), or Word and Table (UMC), entails confession, repentance, and pardon. What could Methodists imagine occurs at Word and Table other than that the Lord— through his promise at the Supper—reconciles a community of believers estranged to him by sin through repentance (itself at least an intellectual work) and grants communion with him? And what could this communion be? Followers of Wesley can say that the propitiatory sacrifice is the eternal intercession of our High Priest in which he grants sacramental communion with him through his real presence in the bread and wine, a communion that is a participation in the propitiation of the cross and that is yet another step on the road to sanctification that finds its end in perfection (i.e. deification).

Subsequent dialogues do not delve into eucharistic theology to this degree until, after three decades of discussion and post-*BEM*, *The Grace Given You* outlines eucharistic issues requiring further dialogue. Both sides share a host of affirmations on what the eucharist is: a sign, instrument, and sacrament ultimately presided over by Christ; a fresh hearing of God's Word; a deeper communion with the "saving mystery of Christ"; a new "encounter" with Christ—really present—at the "heart of the church"; an anointing with the Holy Spirit, which is a fuller transformation into Christ's body; a commission to witness to Christ; and a foretaste of the heavenly banquet.[5] Methodists recognize many potential gifts that closer unity with Catholics may yield, and not least among them is a "more developed theology of the eucharist."[6] At the same time, they mutually wish to discuss further the "nature and validity" of the eucharistic president, the "precise meaning" of sacramental memorial,[7] the metaphysics of Christ's real presence, and the relation between the eucharist

---

5. *Grace Given You in Christ*, 93–94; see 155.

6. *Grace Given You in Christ*, 111.

7. For agreement on *anamnesis*, see United Methodist Church–United States Catholic Conference, *Thirty Years of Mission and Witness* (Washington, DC: United States Catholic Conference, 2001), 21.

and ecclesial unity. More specifically—and in recognition of Methodism's explicit efforts to move past the Reformation divisions—the Catholic side invites more attention to the topics of sacrifice and priesthood. The seriousness with which it raises these topics is suggested by the fact that these are the only topics of eucharistic theology for which it offers a line of investigation.

In paragraphs 130–31 of *The Grace Given You*, the Catholic side reiterates and interprets *Lumen gentium* (7) that in the eucharist "we are 'united in a hidden and real way to Christ in his passion and glorification.' In other words, we are sacramentally united with Christ, as his body, in the great single act of his sacrifice, by which he entered into glory." This historic action occurred once and for all and is never repeated (Heb 10:10). What makes the eucharist sacrificial, especially when all churches profess the "once and for all" character of Jesus' crucifixion? In short, his real presence: "The eucharist truly has a sacrificial character because Christ is really present there in the very act of his supreme self-gift to his Father. The sacramental presence of Christ himself is at once the sacramental presence of his sacrifice." Christ present in the eucharist is the same Christ present on the cross. The work Christ achieved on the cross he now offers as the glorified high priest to the Father in heaven. J. Ernest Rattenbury interprets Wesley in like fashion and agrees in this instance with the Catholic critique that the Reformers went too far in dismissing all sacrificial overtones in the eucharist.[8] The dialogue continues: "In the sense outlined above, [Catholics] endorse the statement of the Lima text of the World Council of Churches' Faith and Order Commission that the eucharist is 'the sacrament of the unique sacrifice of Christ, who ever lives to make intercession for us.'" The Catholic recourse to *BEM*'s use of *intercession* is both significant (for the convergence it marks) and confusing, because *BEM*'s use of the language of intercession—as a term chosen to garner ecumenical support that the word "sacrifice" would not—is one of the very few elements in *BEM* on the eucharist that the original Catholic response finds inadequate. In both the early and latest rounds of dialogue, therefore, the Catholic delegation clearly expresses eucharistic sacrifice to consist of the *real presence* of Christ in the sacramental *memorial* of his saving sacrifice, which he gives through his heavenly, priestly *intercession* in union with his ecclesial body.

The paragraphs treating eucharistic sacrifice in the dialogues may be few, but their concision can be misleading, for they actually raise a wide array of key topics that direct the scope of inquiry for the following chapters. Their shared affirmations are noteworthy. For Catholics and Methodists, then, the eucharist is grounded in the uniqueness of Christ's self-sacrifice on the cross

---

8. J. Ernest Rattenbury, *Thoughts on Holy Communion* (London: Epworth, 1958), 70–71.

and sustained by Hebrews' Christology of his eternal heavenly intercession as high priest. Christ exercises this office in the eucharist both as its president and as self-gift—i.e., the glorified One who perpetually offers himself to the Father on our behalf and to his body as spiritual food. Because Jesus is the same yesterday, today, and forever, the forgiveness that he announced at the Supper and that he won on the cross are offered to those who unite with him in communion. This is the nature of eucharistic *anamnesis*: Christ himself extends the benefits of his sacrifice every time it is celebrated; this benefit is simply Christ himself. Believers' reception of Christ entails the conviction of a theological anthropology that holds that just such a reception is neither passive, nor merely intellective, nor sufficient as a sacrifice of praise; rather, the reception of Christ entails the self-offering of believers themselves as living sacrifices who, through the bread and wine, become partakers in the body and blood of Christ.

To be sure, important differences remain. Unmentioned so far is the action of offering the eucharistic elements to God as a thank-offering. Additionally, in the early dialogues, the Catholic side broached the complex issue of the relationship between the Supper, the cross, and the eucharist, noting that the eucharist makes "present in a sacramental way the same sacrifice"; however, it did not develop the doctrine further. Coupled with the latest dialogue that emphasizes the priestly ministry of Christ based on Hebrews, the two brief paragraphs (thirty years apart) echo some of the principal dogmas of Trent, thereby attesting to a diachronic fidelity to Catholicism's teachings. Finally, and quite significantly, the Catholic side initiates what must be a concurrent discussion alongside that of sacrifice—namely, eucharistic presidency and the ordained ministry. Again, faithful to Trent, it unites priesthood and sacrifice: "Catholics believe that, as there is only one sacrifice, so there is also only one priest, namely Christ. Those who are called 'priests' are *only ever representatives* of Christ the priest in the midst of the priestly people."[9]

The question of priestly orders cannot satisfactorily be pursued here, but as this topic is the second one for which the Catholic side suggests a line of investigation, a study focused on ministry would certainly complement this one on sacrifice. Just a couple of remarks here must suffice. First, explicit attention to sacrifice and priesthood should be welcomed by Methodists, since previous Catholic-Lutheran and Catholic-Anglican documents on eucharistic sacrifice that have elided the question of priesthood have been critiqued by the magisterium for precisely this oversight.[10] Second, the line of investigation that the Catholic side opens up proffers a close relationship between the for-

---

9. *Grace Given You*, 132, emphasis added.

10. See Chapter 1 of David Power, *The Sacrifice We Offer: The Tridentine Dogma and Its Reinterpretation* (New York: Crossroad, 1987).

mulations of *Sacrosanctum concilium* and *Lumen gentium* with *BEM*. Thus it says, "'Vatican II taught that every liturgical celebration is 'an action of Christ the Priest and his Body' (SC §8), and that there are two proper sharings in this one priesthood within the Church, which are 'ordered to one another,' namely the royal priesthood of all the faithful and the ministerial priesthood of those faithful who are called and ordained to represent Christ himself in the midst of his people, acting in the name and person of Christ to effect the eucharistic sacrifice and offer it to God in the name of all people (*LG* §10)." The ministerial priesthood "represents" Christ, and it cites the use of "representation" from *BEM*'s ministry chapter: "Catholics welcome the statement of the Lima text that ordained ministers are 'representatives of Jesus Christ to the community,' and they value its further statement that ordained ministers 'may appropriately be called priests because they fulfill a particular priestly service by strengthening and building up the royal and prophetic priesthood of the faithful through word and sacraments.'"[11] Should the magisterium encourage this association between Vatican II and *BEM*, then more convergence may exist on the question of ordained ministry between Methodists and Catholics than has heretofore been perceived. David Carter interprets the function of the priest/minister, the sign of ordination, and the language of "representative" in a similar manner as the aforementioned Catholic contribution, but David Power interprets some of John Paul II's comments as an elevation of the ministerial priesthood that goes beyond what the Council of Trent defined.[12] Clearly this topic warrants further independent investigation.

The question of priesthood and the citation from *Lumen gentium* indirectly raises an issue as old as Luther's rejection of the Mass—that is, does Christ only give himself to his church for spiritual food as a testament of the forgiveness of sins while the faithful in turn offer themselves as a living sacrifice; or does the church, through the ministry of the priest and along with its risen Lord, offer Christ's body and blood to the Father for the forgiveness of sins? These are among the many questions raised in the RC-WMC dialogues, the answers to which we will pursue.

Eucharistic Sacrifice in *Baptism, Eucharist, and Ministry*

Both Catholic and Methodist theologians—along with delegates of dozens of other member churches—contributed to the text of *BEM*, and what is more, *BEM* and the RC-WMC dialogue share the same methodology.

---

11. *Grace Given You*, 132; see *BEM*, 11 and 17.

12. David Carter, "Can the Roman Catholic and Methodist Churches Be Reconciled?," 6–8; Power, *The Sacrifice We Offer*, 25.

That is, both parties have sought to avail themselves of the fruits of the liturgical and ecumenical movements in order either to get behind historic controversies or to look at them afresh so that divided Christians may once more be united in one visible body for the sake of Christ and the church's witness to the world.[13] Furthermore, the fact that in the 2006 dialogue Catholics reference *BEM* approvingly on sacrifice and ministry as a direction for convergence with Methodists means that what *BEM* expounds bears directly on the potential for future doctrinal agreement.

BEM is "simply unparalleled in its attempt to state agreements and convergences."[14] For a multilateral ecumenical document it is unique. As the result of decades of dialogue, *BEM* is the high-water mark for ecumenical convergence at the same time that it has become the basis of inspiration for liturgical revision and catechesis among numerous churches.[15] Wainwright notes the unique status that churches have accorded *BEM* because of the history behind it, its approved methodology, and the widespread convergence it achieved. The text called member churches not simply to acknowledge where they agreed with the document, but to articulate how they can "recognize" (i.e., receive) "the faith of the Church through the ages," even where that entails a willingness on their part to be corrected by it.[16]

13. *BEM*, Preface, 4.

14. John Reumann, *The Supper of the Lord: The New Testament, Ecumenical Dialogues, and Faith and Order on Eucharist* (Philadelphia: Fortress, 1985), xi.

15. Geoffrey Wainwright, "Ecumenical Convergences," in *The Oxford History of Christian Worship*, ed. Geoffrey Wainwright and Karen B. Westerfield Tucker (New York: Oxford University Press, 2006), 745. The history of *BEM* has been amply documented and need only be referenced here; see Geoffrey Wainwright, "Word and Sacrament in the Churches' Responses to the Lima Text," *One in Christ* 24, no. 4 (1988): 304–27; Geoffrey Wainwright, *Baptism, Eucharist and Ministry: A Liturgical Appraisal of the Lima Text* (Rotterdam: Liturgical Ecumenical Ctr Trust, 1986); Max Thurian and Geoffrey Wainwright, *Baptism and Eucharist: Ecumenical Convergence in Celebration*, Faith and Order Paper No. 117 (Geneva: World Council of Churches, 1983); Geoffrey Wainwright, "Any Advance On "BEM"? The Lima Text at Twenty-Five," *Studia liturgica* 37, no. 1 (2007): 1–29; Geoffrey Wainwright, "The Lima Text in the History of Faith and Order," *Studia liturgica* 16, no. 1–2 (1986): 6–21. See also Horton Davies, *Bread of Life and Cup of Joy: Newer Ecumenical Perspectives on the Eucharist* (Grand Rapids, MI: Eerdmans, 1993); especially chapter 3, "The Eucharist as Sacrifice." For an appraisal and engagement with the Lima liturgy, see Thomas F. Best, Dagmar Heller, and World Council of Churches, *Eucharistic Worship in Ecumenical Contexts: The Lima Liturgy and Beyond* (Geneva: WCC, 1998), and Kenneth W. Stevenson, "Eucharistic Sacrifice—an Insoluble Liturgical Problem," *Scottish Journal of Theology* 42, no. 4 (1989): 469–92. And for the more administratively inclined, John Deschner, Günther Gassmann, and World Council of Churches Commission on Faith and Order, *Baptism, Eucharist & Ministry 1982–1990: Report on the Process and Responses*, Faith and Order Paper No. 149 (Geneva: WCC, 1990).

16. Wainwright, "The Lima Text in the History of Faith and Order," 20.

A sacrificial dimension permeates the chapter as a whole, and an understanding of this broader perspective will initially be helpful.[17] The chapter consists of three parts, and *BEM*'s treatment of eucharistic sacrifice is, not surprisingly, primarily concentrated in its section on *anamnesis*.

I. The Institution of the Eucharist
II. The Meaning of the Eucharist
    A. Eucharist as Thanksgiving to the Father
    B. Eucharist as Anamnesis or Memorial of Christ
    C. Eucharist as Invocation of the Spirit
    D. Eucharist as Communion of the Faithful
    E. Eucharist as Meal of the Kingdom
III. The Celebration of the Eucharist

The chapter expresses at least three ecumenical gains that were widely celebrated by the churches and that characterize the document as a whole. First, the chapter acknowledges its debt to the liturgical reform movement and argues that church doctrine, practice, and convergence are all interrelated: "The best way towards unity in eucharistic celebration and communion is the renewal of the eucharist itself in the different churches in regard to teaching and liturgy."[18] Second, the eucharist is essentially a trinitarian event, and the chapter's outline—based on the Nicene Creed and its concentration on Christology and soteriology—highlights this fact. "It is the Father who is the primary origin and final fulfillment of the eucharistic event. The incarnate Son of God by and in whom it is accomplished is its living centre. The Holy Spirit is the immeasurable strength of love which makes it possible and continues to make it effective."[19] Third, in a further attempt at liturgical convergence, the chapter teaches that churches should not pit Word and Table—i.e., preaching and eucharist, against one another, but should see them as integrated and inseparable. "Since the *anamnesis* of Christ is the very content of the preached Word as it is of the eucharistic meal, each reinforces the other. The celebration of the eucharist properly includes the proclamation of the Word."[20]

17. See Geoffrey Wainwright, "The Eucharist in the Churches' Responses to the Lima Text," *One in Christ* 25, no. 1 (1989): 53–74; see, too, the responses of individual churches to the Eucharist chapter in Max Thurian, *Churches Respond to BEM* (Geneva: World Council of Churches, 1986), vols. 1–6.

18. *BEM*, E 28.

19. *BEM*, E 14; see Geoffrey Wainwright, "The Ecumenical Rediscovery of the Trinity," *One in Christ* 34, no. 2 (1998): 95–124.

20. *BEM*, E 12; see Owen F. Cummings, *Eucharistic Doctors: A Theological History* (Mahwah, NJ: Paulist Press, 2005), 26–27.

Moving through the flow of the chapter, we see that Christ's sacrifice necessarily defines the eucharist's institution. Citing the Passover memorial, the meal of the Covenant on Sinai (Ex 24:9–11), Jesus' numerous fellowship meals, the eschatological Supper of the Lamb (Rv 19:9), the Last Supper, and primarily the Supper narratives, it begins by saying, "The Church receives the eucharist as a gift from the Lord . . . its celebration continues as the central act of the Church's worship."[21] The eucharist conveys the love Jesus has toward his disciples "to the end" (Jn 13:1). The text stresses the continuity, through Christ, between the Supper and the eucharist. This is important because Protestant polemics have sometimes denied that Jesus celebrated the first eucharist at the Supper. (They still deny that Jesus constituted the apostles as priests in this sacrificial meal.) Moreover, the text appears to have taken a page from Trent's playbook with its delicate treatment of how the Last Supper relates to Christ's sacrifice on the cross: "In his last meal, the fellowship of the Kingdom was connected with the imminence of Jesus' suffering . . . the last meal celebrated by Jesus was a liturgical meal employing symbolic words and actions."[22] It neither affirms nor denies anything with respect to the salvific efficacy of the Supper. The meaning of the eucharist also derives immediately from the person and work of Christ:

> The eucharist is essentially the sacrament of the gift which God makes to us in Christ through the power of the Holy Spirit. Every Christian receives this gift of salvation through communion in the body and blood of Christ. In the eucharistic meal, in the eating and drinking of the bread and wine, Christ grants communion with himself. God himself acts, giving life to the body of Christ and renewing each member. In accordance with Christ's promise, each baptized member of the body of Christ receives in the eucharist the assurance of forgiveness of sins (Mt 26:28) and the pledge of eternal life (Jn 6:51–58).[23]

As thanksgiving to the Father, the eucharist is "proclamation and a celebration," "the great sacrifice of praise," "the benediction (*berakah*)," and the "great thanksgiving to the Father for everything accomplished in creation, redemption and sanctification."[24] In addition to praise and thanksgiving, the eucharist also consists of the church's prayers, which it offers on behalf of the whole world. The church's intercession relies squarely on its Lord's: "Christ unites the faithful with himself and includes their prayers within his own inter-

21. *BEM*, E 1.
22. *BEM*, E 1.
23. *BEM*, E 2.
24. *BEM*, E 3–4.

cession so that the faithful are transfigured and their prayers accepted."[25] Finally, although not cited, Irenaeus's influence emerges with the teaching that the "bread and wine, fruits of the earth and of human labour, are presented to the Father in faith and thanksgiving." Following him, the offering of the elements unites the orders of creation and redemption, such that "the eucharist thus signifies what the world is to become: an offering and hymn of praise to the Creator."[26] An alternate interpretation of the offering, one that construes divine transcendence and theological anthropology as agents of actions in competition—i.e., if one is "first," the other must be "second," and it is the "first" action that determines the meaning and telos of the act in question—is precisely what I seek to problematize in this study. Both the Wesleys and Catholics understand theological anthropology in such a way that they can speak of the eucharist as a sacrifice of the church and still maintain the sufficiency of Christ's once for all sacrifice.

One of the reasons that the church came to refer to the eucharist as a sacrifice was its observation that the Christ who gave himself to the Father on the cross was the same one who gives himself to the church in the sacrament. Based on this notion of identity, the entire sacrificial memorial of the eucharist, in which Christ is really present, relies on the work of the Holy Spirit. "The Spirit makes the crucified and risen Christ really present to us in the eucharistic meal, fulfilling the promise contained in the words of institution."[27]

In addition to uniting word and sacrament, as well as liturgy and practice, the sections on "Communion of the Faithful" and "Meal of the Kingdom" reunite the often yet unwarranted separation of theology and ethics around the notion of justice, which demands sacrificial discipleship. The church's embodiment of justice derives from the Spirit-empowered imitation of Christ's sacrificial love for the world.[28] "The eucharist involves the believer in the central event of the world's history. As participants in the eucharist, therefore, we prove inconsistent if we are not actively participating in this ongoing restoration of the world's situation and human condition."[29] Participation in

---

25. *BEM*, E 4.

26. *BEM*, E 4. Max Thurian refers to Irenaeus and Hippolytus when he stresses the desirability, indeed necessity, of the offertory in "The Eucharistic Memorial, Sacrifice of Praise and Supplication," in Max Thurian and World Council of Churches Commission on Faith and Order, *Ecumenical Perspectives on Baptism, Eucharist and Ministry*, Faith and Order Paper No. 116 (Geneva: World Council of Churches, 1983), 102. Complementarily, Cummings cites Justin Martyr and Hippolytus, *Eucharistic Doctors*, 23–24, 31. See, too, Thurian's influential book *L'Eucharistie: mémorial du Seigneur, sacrifice d'action de grâce et d'intercession* (Neuchatel: Delachaux et Niestlé, 1959).

27. *BEM*, E 14.

28. See Reumann, *Supper of the Lord*, 162.

29. *BEM*, E 20.

the cross means reconciliation and sharing, the rejection of injustice, such as racism, and the endeavor to maintain just economic and political systems. This participation takes liturgical expression in acts such as the mutual forgiveness of sins, intercession, table fellowship, and taking the elements to the sick and imprisoned. Strong consensus is found in the idea that sacrificial participation in the cross overflows from the church to the world: "Reconciled in the eucharist, the members of the body of Christ are called to be servants of reconciliation among men and women, and witnesses of the joy of resurrection."[30]

Under the third part of the chapter, the "Celebration of the eucharist," the text makes a vital distinction with respect to eucharistic presidency. "In the celebration of the eucharist, Christ gathers, teaches and nourishes the Church. It is Christ who invites to the meal and who presides at it. He is the shepherd who leads the people of God, the prophet who announces the Word of God, the priest who celebrates the mystery of God. In most churches, this presidency is signified by an ordained minister."[31] In seeing Christ as the true celebrant of the eucharist, the chapter draws heavily on Hebrews' teaching that speaks of Christ as the great high priest forever interceding on behalf of his people, uniting their prayers with his own and sanctifying them in his Spirit. In this respect, too, it aligns with Trent's teaching that in the Mass it is really Christ offering through the ministry of the priest. At the same time, however, it does not advance Trent's theology that through the priestly ministry the body and blood of Christ are offered to the Father for the forgiveness of sins.[32]

The crux of the discussion on eucharistic sacrifice takes place in the section on *Anamnesis*, or "Memorial of Christ," at the heart of the eucharist chapter. Consistent with many of the anaphoras of the early church, and indeed with Paul's theology that the congregation's sacrificial meal is itself a proclamation of Christ's sacrifice, the text incorporates its teaching on Christ's sacrifice under the topic of memorial. It says, "The eucharist is the memorial of the crucified and risen Christ, i.e., the living and effective sign of his sacrifice, accomplished once and for all on the cross and still operative on behalf of all humankind."[33] By the concept of memorial, the text deepens the relationship between the eucharist and Christ's sacrifice, in fact, by integrating Christ's passion with his whole incarnation and ministry: "Christ himself with all that he has accomplished for us and for all creation (in his incarnation, servanthood,

---

30. *BEM*, E 24.

31. *BEM*, E 29.

32. See the "Ministry" chapter, 14 and 17.

33. *BEM*, E 5. Wainwright grounds both Paul's theology and the Supper institution in the theology of Israel's Passover memorial; "Eucharist in the Churches' Responses to the Lima Text," 64.

ministry, teaching, suffering, sacrifice, resurrection, ascension, and sending of the Spirit) is present in this *anamnesis*, granting us communion with himself."[34]

It is within this framework of *anamnesis* that the chapter tackles the historically most controversial topic of eucharistic sacrifice. Already the text prepares for the key paragraph by the affirmation that Christ's sacrifice entails not just the cross but his resurrected and pneumatologically mediated presence. As Davies notes, sacrifice must entail "the recognition that his entire life of obedience to the Father and his continuing intercession in heaven for all is an everlasting sacrifice."[35] *BEM* never calls the eucharist a sacrifice, nor does it say (as Trent does) that in the eucharist a sacrifice occurs; instead, it speaks rather of the eucharist as the sacramental memorial of Christ's unique sacrifice. Thus, the paragraph reads:

> Representation and anticipation are expressed in thanksgiving and intercession. The church, gratefully recalling God's mighty acts of redemption, beseeches God to give the benefits of these acts to every human being. In thanksgiving and intercession, the Church is united with the Son, its great High Priest and Intercessor (Rom 8:34; Heb 7:25). The eucharist is the sacrament of the unique sacrifice of Christ, who ever lives to make intercession for us. It is the memorial of all that God has done for the salvation of the world. What it was God's will to accomplish in the incarnation, life, death, resurrection and ascension of Christ, God does not repeat. These events are unique and can neither be repeated nor prolonged. In the memorial of the eucharist, however, the Church offers its intercession in communion with Christ, our great High Priest.[36]

The committee included a commentary to this paragraph that seeks further convergence.

> It is in light of the significance of the eucharist as intercession that references to the eucharist in Catholic theology as "propitiatory sacrifice" may be understood. The understanding is that there is only one expiation, that of the unique sacrifice of the cross, made actual in the eucharist and presented before the Father in the intercession of Christ and of the Church for all humanity. In the light of the biblical conception of memorial, all churches might want to review the old controversies about "sacrifice" and deepen their understanding of the reasons why other traditions than their own have either used or rejected this term.[37]

---

34. *BEM*, E 6.
35. Davies, *Bread of Life*, 77.
36. *BEM*, E 8.
37. *BEM*, E 8, Commentary.

The sacrifice of Christ is the basis upon which those united to him can offer themselves as living and holy sacrifices (Rom 12:1; 1 Pt 2:5), so that through the eucharist the sacrifice of the body is joined with the sacrifice of its head: "United to our Lord and in communion with all the saints and martyrs, we are renewed in the covenant sealed by the blood of Christ."[38]

On the one hand, the text clearly seeks to safeguard the salvific uniqueness of the cross while making it effective in all times and places. It does this through *anamnesis*, in which—analogous to how each Jewish generation is incorporated into Israel's deliverance through the Passover memorial—the church beseeches that those benefits of the cross, i.e. the one expiation, be made actual in each eucharistic celebration. As Wainwright summarizes, "The Lima text employs the general principle [of *anamnesis*] as a means of confessing and conceiving the presence and sacrifice of Christ in the eucharist which undercuts later Western controversies on the issues."[39] This union between Jesus' priestly intercession and the body's self-offering is the locus of communion, forgiveness, and sanctification, or in short, of salvation.[40] On the other hand, this is the dynamic by which the commentary interprets the Catholic theology of propitiatory sacrifice. Absent from either the text or the commentary, however, is a consideration of Trent's teaching on the necessity of a priestly ministry through whom Christ as priest offers his body and blood to the Father.

Consonant with some early fathers such as Justin Martyr, Hippolytus, and Irenaeus, the eucharist is an offering to God in thanksgiving for the gift of creation and redemption.[41] It recalls Jesus' ministry of fellowship and hospitality to sinners even while it serves as a foretaste of the final banquet. In imitation of Christ and by his grace through the Spirit, it requires that believers live sacrificially toward one another and the world in reconciliation, service, and justice. And most centrally, through the minister and the elements, the eucharist commemorates and proclaims Christ's passion. It is a sacrificial meal because it is presided over by the crucified and risen Lord whose whole person and work—both heavenly and earthly—reveal the true nature of sacrifice: as Christ says to his Father, "See, I have come to do your will" (Heb 10:9). This meal offers communion between Christ and the faithful, and it signifies the self-offering of the faithful to God. It now remains to be seen how the Catholic and Methodist churches have responded to this teaching.

---

38. *BEM*, E 11. See Wainwright, "Eucharist in the Churches' Responses to Lima," 58–59, 66–67.

39. Wainwright, "Lima Text in the History of Faith and Order," 16.

40. *BEM*, E 2.

41. See Cummings, *Eucharistic Doctors*, 23–24, 31.

Catholic and Methodist Responses to BEM

Although Methodist churches historically trace their roots to the revival led by John and Charles Wesley and seek to maintain a continuity of practice and doctrine with them, they are, at the same time, variegated bodies from diverse, global settings. Consequently, Methodist churches vary widely on how they interpret their Wesleyan heritage with their own unique situations. Thus, unlike Roman Catholicism, which can expound a unified and authoritative teaching, Methodist churches neither approach dogmatic issues with one mind nor speak officially with one voice. Here we consider how Catholic and Methodist churches have responded to *BEM* with respect to eucharistic sacrifice.[42]

The two Methodist responses from Germany evince a Lutheran perspective that is critical of the methodology of *BEM* and its theology of eucharistic sacrifice.[43] Both traffic in dualisms: they pit *sola scriptura* over against ecclesial tradition, and as a result, this position renders them highly critical of *BEM*'s sacramental theology. Both feel that *BEM*'s language of sacrament and sign is uncritical, which leads to sacramentalism that impedes the free work of Christ. To them, *BEM*'s "objective" and "institutional" bent tends toward "formal religion" and obscures the central concept of soteriology, and this despite *BEM*'s deliberate attempts to disavow this position.[44] Positively, the responses welcome the rite's grounding on the biblical narratives and on Christ, the uniqueness of the cross, the unity between word and sacrament, and Christ's real presence.[45]

To be expected, perhaps, is that several of the criticisms focused on sacrifice. Both think that the use of the term "eucharist," almost to the exclusion of others, overly privileges the anthropological aspect away from "God's

---

42. For discussions that are broader in scope, see the complete responses by individual churches in Thurian, *Churches Respond to BEM*. See, too, Michael A. Fahey and Catholic Theological Society of America, *Catholic Perspectives on Baptism, Eucharist and Ministry* (Lanham, MD: University Press of America, 1986); Geoffrey Wainwright, "The Roman Catholic Response to Baptism, Eucharist and Ministry: The Ecclesiological Dimension," in *A Promise of Presence*, ed. David Noel Power, Michael Downey, and Richard N. Fragomeni (Washington, DC: Pastoral Press, 1992), 187–206; Geoffrey Wainwright, "Methodism through the Lens of Lima," in *Sunday Service of the Methodists*, ed. Karen B. Westerfield Tucker (Nashville: Kingswood Books, 1996), 305–22.

43. The Evangelical-Methodist Church: Central Conference in the German Democratic Republic (EMC: GDR), and the Evangelical-Methodist Church: Central Conference in the Federal Republic of Germany and West Berlin (ECM: FRG) in Thurian, *Churches Respond*, 4:167–71 and 173–82, respectively. Henceforth, references to official church responses found in Thurian are listed by volume and page number.

44. *Churches Respond to BEM*, 4:167–68 and 4:174.

45. *Churches Respond to BEM*, 4:160 and 4:176.

action in Christ," again contrary to *BEM*'s emphases.[46] The EMC: GDR thinks that the eucharist (1) as "Thanksgiving to the Father" (including the offering of the elements to God in thanks), (2) as the "*anamnesis* of Christ" (including the offering of self and the sacrifice of praise), and (3) as "offering on behalf of the whole world," with its focus on reconciliation and justice (in sum nearly half the chapter!), "surpasses the meaning of the Lord's Supper as it is established by Christ." The reply demonstrates a rather truncated interpretation of Christ's institution and a rather sweeping criticism of *any* notion of sacrifice, and both are based on a rather brief rationale: "During the Lord's supper we are always the ones who receive, and never those who make offerings."[47]

Similarly, the criticisms of the EMC: FDR revolve almost exclusively around notions of sacrifice. It, too, cannot accept in the eucharist any sense of offering, whether as a sacrifice of praise on "behalf of the whole creation" (E 4), or as intercession in communion with Christ (E 8), or as a "representative act of thanksgiving and offering on behalf of the whole world" (E 20).[48] So restrictive is this position toward eucharistic sacrifice that, in effect, it risks severing the body from its head. This hermeneutic makes it nearly impossible for the church to be faithful to Jesus' memorial command in the Supper to "do this in memory of me" when it is strictly prohibited from *doing* anything at all, including the clearly biblical exhortation to offer itself as a living sacrifice for the sake of the world. Lacking, too, is any sense of Christ and his church as the *totus Christus* that acts in unity, despite the fact that this image is prominent in the Wesleys' *Hymns on the Lord's Supper*.

The United Methodist Church, Central and Southern Europe echoes similar methodological concerns. It finds *BEM*'s formulation of "the faith of the Church through the ages" to place too much emphasis on tradition at the expense of the individual's and the church's immediate standing before God as the *creatura verbi divini*. This emphasis fosters a "sacramentalist" stance that tends to overshadow the necessity of a personal encounter with God and the "new birth."[49] These fears are carried over in its assessment of the eucharist chapter, even though it finds it to be the "most well-balanced" of the document. The response also prefers the term "Lord's Supper" to "eucharist," with all that the word historically implies. Overall, its concerns do not highlight questions of sacrifice, but instead ones of theological anthropology. The sacramentalist emphasis of *BEM*, it thinks, risks objectifying salvation in the rite apart from God's actions and the believer's response: "Salvation is not depend-

---

46. *Churches Respond to BEM*, 4:170 and 4:178.
47. *Churches Respond to BEM*, 4:170–71.
48. *Churches Respond to BEM*, 4:179.
49. *Churches Respond to BEM*, 2:201.

ent on the Lord's supper. The gift of salvation demands a personal response in repentance and commitment to Christ."[50] But *BEM* states clearly, "While Christ's real presence in the eucharist does not depend on the faith of the individual, all agree that to discern the body and blood of Christ, faith is required" (E 13). At one point, the response seems to speak of *BEM*'s portrayal of the eucharist as some rite external to the life of faith: it disagrees with the affirmation from E 1 that the eucharist is the "central act of the Church's worship" because "for us the presence of Christ is central—a presence which is experienced in the proclamation of the word, the celebration of the Lord's supper, and other acts of worship."[51] Yet this is precisely how *BEM* defines the eucharist, as Word and Table and acts of worship where Christ is present (E 27). Like the Methodist responses from Germany, this response fixates on its own lingering fears of ritual and fails to appreciate how *BEM* strives to recast the eucharist in a manner that transcends historic stereotypes, misunderstandings, and divergent practices.

The brief report from the small Methodist Church of Southern Africa strikes a different tone. The response notes that Methodism often finds itself caught between its two founding traditions of the Reformation and its Anglo-Catholic heritage. Analogously, it notes with appreciation *BEM*'s attempt to move away from polemic and caricature and toward an honest assessment of the current state of affairs. Its reaction to the eucharist chapter is highly positive. It affirms *BEM*'s words on Christ's real presence that avoid "crass materialism"; the emphasis on the *epiclesis* and the Holy Spirit; its emphasis on community, justice, and reconciliation; the eschatological dimension; and the definition of "eucharist" that encompasses the whole rite of Word and Table. With respect to sacrifice, it finds the teaching on *anamnesis* especially valuable as a way of maintaining the uniqueness of the cross with its "continued effect in the present" and the link between thanksgiving, intercession, and self-offering. It singles out the line from E 12 that the *anamnesis* of Christ is the "very content of the preached word as it is of the eucharistic meal." It states, "This linking of preaching and sacrament is useful in removing the bogey of a repeated sacrifice and helping us to grasp the concept of a past event being recalled in such a way as to have continuing effects in the present."[52] Contrary to the aforementioned responses, this response does not exhibit a fear of sacramentalism or lingering old controversies, and it expresses a willingness to receive tentatively the ecumenical gains exemplified in *BEM*.

---

50. *Churches Respond to BEM*, 2:205.
51. *Churches Respond to BEM*, 2:205.
52. *Churches Respond to BEM*, 2:238–39.

The response of the Methodist Church in Ireland is brief but offered against the backdrop of its Wesleyan heritage. It notes that Wesley underscored the call to frequent communion and the eucharist's eschatological dimension while denying a possible interpretation of the E 15 commentary that leaves open the option for transubstantiation. Concerning sacrifice, it approves the section on *anamnesis* and sacrifice as "a corrective to the possible misunderstanding of the idea of the priest offering a meritorious sacrifice," and E 13's emphasis on faith "helps to counter an *ex opere operato* view of the sacrament."[53] Although it does not explain what it understands by meritorious sacrifice or *ex opere operato*, the response does not suggest a fear that *BEM* remains trapped in a detrimental sacramentalism.

The Methodist Church (UK) submitted one of the most extensive and serious responses to *BEM* from among all the Methodist contributions. Its tone is appreciative and collegial, even cordial at points. It has a deep appreciation for its Wesleyan origins, yet realizes that any contemporary theology must now be done in conversation with other churches.[54] The response is as interested in questions of theological method and perspective as it is in particular doctrinal questions.[55] On the eucharist chapter, the response is most concerned in raising questions about how best to understand Christ's "unique" presence in the eucharist (E 13) vis à vis other modes of his presence in other means of grace, and to explain why it is not possible, institutionally, for Methodists to celebrate the eucharist on a weekly basis. It attributes the liturgical and ecumenical movements with reinvigorating a deeper appreciation for and continued interest in the eucharist, as represented in its recent liturgical revisions and congregational worship.[56] It warmly welcomes the ecumenical formulation of *anamnesis* and finds the section on eucharistic memorial to be a "major point of reconciliation among Christians" and a prominent theme within Methodism's theology and hymnody (although it does not cite the collection of *Hymns on the Lord's Supper*).[57] The response does not signal any difficulties with the sacrificial dimension of the eucharist as advocated in *BEM*.

The United Methodist Church's response to *BEM* is thoroughly positive. It is not troubled by the (necessary) recourse to tradition in *BEM*'s method and doctrinal formulations, and it concurs with the goal of visible unity, expressed in one eucharistic fellowship, which undercuts the "denominational model."[58]

---

53. *Churches Respond to BEM*, 2:233.
54. *Churches Respond to BEM*, 2:210–11.
55. *Churches Respond to BEM*, 2:212–19.
56. *Churches Respond to BEM*, 2:222–24.
57. *Churches Respond to BEM*, 2:215.
58. *Churches Respond to BEM*, 2:191.

The UMC response sees the name "Wesleyan" as denoting its "genuinely ecumenical, evangelical, apostolic, and catholic" heritage that it seeks to share with other churches.[59] Nowhere is this more applicable than in the early Wesleyan/Methodist conjunction of eucharistic piety and fervent preaching, for the Wesleys' sermons and hymns attest to a "substantial eucharistic theology." It admits that Methodists lost this unity of Word and Table, but that the liturgical and ecumenical movements have "forced Methodists to rediscover their own history, [and] they have been amazed at the richness of it."[60]

The section on the eucharist could hardly be more receptive, even down to praising its "lofty, doxological, and eschatological" language. It admits that its practice has fallen short of the church's historical witness and has privileged the pulpit over the altar. Moreover, the response shares none of the anti-sacramentalist predilections of some of its sister churches but agrees with *BEM*'s emphasis on the eucharist: "As BEM rightly shows, the eucharist is 'the central act of the Church's worship' because it effectively unites word and sacrament. God's effectual word is there revealed, proclaimed, heard, seen and tasted."[61] The response then proceeds to affirm nearly every other aspect of the chapter on eucharist: the trinitarian scope; the *epiclesis* and work of the Spirit; the eschatological meal of the kingdom; the integrity of the rite as a whole and its frequent celebration; the rite as the locus of reconciliation with God; the moral imperatives of justice stemming from the eucharist; and the relationship of eucharistic fellowship and visible church unity.[62]

On the question of sacrifice, the response makes two affirmations. First, and in marked contrast to the continental European Methodist concerns, it concurs with *BEM*'s and Thurian's appropriation of Irenaeus and the patristic gesture of offering the elements as a means of uniting God's grace in creation and redemption. In fact, it makes the additional observation of highlighting the eucharistic imperative for justice as an integral component to this unity. "The bread and wine intrinsically remind us of their natural origin and their manufacture by persons involved in the economic and political realities of society. The meal of the coming kingdom is also for today's time in the world. The elemental themes of community, justice, forgiveness, reconciliation and peace are woven into the eucharistic action and crowned by God's love for all humankind."[63]

Second, what the Council of Bishops finds ecumenically noteworthy is the way *BEM* uses the concepts of *anamnesis* and *epiclesis* to stress the primacy

---

59. *Churches Respond to BEM*, 2:179.
60. *Churches Respond to BEM*, 2:187.
61. *Churches Respond to BEM*, 2:188.
62. *Churches Respond to BEM*, 2:189–92.
63. *Churches Respond to BEM*, 2:192.

of Christ's agency and presence in the eucharist. It affirms *BEM*'s formulation of *anamnesis*: "*anamnesis* (memorial, remembrance, representation) means that past, present, and future coincide in the sacramental event. All that Jesus Christ means in his person and redemptive work is brought forth from history to our present experience, which is also a foretaste of the future fulfillment of God's unobstructed reign. . . . All this we find explicitly taught by John and Charles Wesley."[64] Consistent with the history we have traced thus far, the UMC response closely relates *anamnesis* and the question of sacrifice:

> Throughout Christian history the concept of the sacrificial and atoning death of Jesus Christ has been closely related to the sacrifice of worshipping Christians in the context of the Lord's supper. . . . As Wesleyans, we are accustomed to the language of sacrifice; and we find BEM's statements to be in accord with the church's Tradition and with ours. The uniqueness of Christ's sacrifice, once for all, is a critical matter. *BEM*'s assertion that 'God does not repeat' the sacrificial life, death and resurrection of Christ removes the cause of past disputes.[65]

Catholics should welcome the affirmation that the "cause of past disputes" has been removed. Unlike other Methodist responses—either critical or silent—the UMC could hardly receive *BEM*'s eucharist chapter and its paragraphs on sacrifice more positively. The affirmation is also significant because it suggests what the bishops (following *BEM*) understand the dispute historically to entail—namely, the repetition of Christ's sacrifice. While accusations of Christ's re-crucifixion in the Mass have been a part of Protestant criticism, this notion has enjoyed more traction within popular piety than in dogmatic theology. Trent does not take up the matter directly, nor was it among the principal criticisms of the Reformers, who were more concerned with agency in the eucharist, priestly power, the relationship to penance, the role of the laity, and questions related to the elements, their reception, and Christ's presence. If the question were simply whether the cross is ever repeated, then it never would have turned into a dispute needing resolution, for Catholicism has never officially taught that eucharistic sacrifice was based on Christ's repeated crucifixion. Although the UMC understands "the cause of past disputes" to refer too narrowly to Jesus' re-crucifixion, nevertheless, its acceptance of E 8, in conjunction with the rest of the eucharist chapter, makes its response to *BEM* by far the most approving of all the Methodist responses.

---

64. *Churches Respond to BEM*, 2:188.
65. *Churches Respond to BEM*, 2:189; see E 8 and commentary.

The report sees *BEM* as an essential component in future dialogues, which has in fact taken place. It pledges to teach elements of *BEM* that United Methodism had left obscured, to continue to reinvigorate its Wesleyan eucharistic practice, and to provide education to all age levels in the churches.[66] This pledge has to a significant degree been fulfilled, since within Methodism frequency of and appreciation for eucharistic practice has increased in recent decades, due in part to the fact that its Great Thanksgiving bears the marks of the ecumenical and liturgical movements' influence.

The Roman Catholic Response

The Roman Catholic response is also highly favorable. It reaffirms Catholicism's commitment to visible unity and sees *BEM* as "a stage along the way" that might be further advanced the more individual churches can affirm *BEM*. The response distinguishes the methodology of *BEM* from a Catholic approach to the same issues by requesting that ecclesiology, the controlling dogma, come to the center of the ecumenical discussion, under which it then locates the issues of sacramentality, discerning the apostolic tradition, and church authority.[67] Not surprisingly, the Catholic response to *BEM* is offered through this ecclesial hermeneutic; nevertheless, with respect to the eucharist, it approves almost the entire chapter. Under *General Appreciation* and *Particular Comments* it commends the text on the following issues:

- The trinitarian dimension centered on Christ and the sacrifice of the cross.
- The use of scripture and sources in tradition, including respect for the ancient liturgy.
- The complementary yet diverse roles played by each person of the Trinity.
- The church's role in making intercession and memorial.
- The emphasis on corporate sanctification, mission, and eschatology.
- The institution of the eucharist by the Lord in the power of the Spirit.
- The affirmation that Jesus is both host and meal.
- The description of the eucharist as gift, sacramental meal, and memorial by signs.[68]

Its response to the "meaning of the eucharist" is more nuanced, yet the affirmations largely continue.

---

66. *Churches Respond to BEM*, 2:190–91.
67. *Churches Respond to BEM*, 6:4–8.
68. *Churches Respond to BEM*, 6:16–17.

- It agrees that the eucharist is the sacramental gift of Christ really present in the power of the Holy Spirit through the bread and wine, and that this gift is "salvation"; it wishes the language of "participation" were used (even though *BEM* uses it elsewhere).[69]
- It appreciates the "thanksgiving" to the Father for the work of salvation and forgiveness (associated with penance) in Christ.
- The Church's sacrifice of praise is well stated, although a closer association with the agency of Christ would improve it. Three times in one paragraph it says that the eucharistic prayer is chiefly the thanksgiving of Jesus to the Father that the church receives and with which it associates itself.[70] With the repeated insistence that the eucharist is "first and foremost the thanksgiving of Jesus Christ to the Father," the Catholic response clarifies that the one who offers the body and blood to the Father is Jesus himself, which is an offering in which the church participates sacramentally. It is clearly comfortable with the theological anthropology of cooperation.
- It approves of the theology in which the church offers the "first fruits of the earth."[71]
- That the eucharist always has to do with both the whole church and each local congregation corresponds with Catholic ecclesiology.[72]
- *BEM*'s articulation of Christ's real presence, the *epiclesis*, and the emphasis on the words of institution correspond to Catholic doctrine.[73]

The response agrees with the definition of *anamnesis*. Thus, United Methodists, Catholics, and *BEM* are of one accord concerning the meaning and significance of eucharistic memorial. The church's act of memorial at the same time accompanies Christ's priestly work.

- *Anamnesis* correctly links the sacrifice of the cross to the present: "The sacrifice of the eucharist [not *BEM*'s words] is one in which the sacrifice of the cross is represented to the end that its saving power be applied here and now for the salvation of the world."
- *Anamnesis* is also the appropriate context for relating the sacrifice of the cross with his real presence in the eucharist, where he is, again, "host of the meal from the outset."

69. *Churches Respond to BEM*, 6:17.
70. *Churches Respond to BEM*, 6:18.
71. *Churches Respond to BEM*, 6:18; see E 4.
72. *Churches Respond to BEM*, 6:19–20.
73. *Churches Respond to BEM*, 6:21.

- Because Christ is the principal agent, the eucharist is a remembrance of past events, a real participation now, and a promise of future glory. (The UMC response uses "memorial" in precisely this fashion, noting that the "tenses" of *anamnesis* are representation, participation, and anticipation.)
- *BEM* rightly notes that the *anamnesis* of Christ is both the content of the preached Word and the eucharistic meal, and thus the two are neither conflated nor divided from one another.[74]

BEM intentionally avoids any language of sacrifice with the exception of reference to Christ's sacrifice on the cross. It asks whether its definitions of *anamnesis* and *intercession* can suffice: the Catholic response accepts much of the use of *intercession* but requires the word *sacrifice*. Yet here is where some confusion sets in. The Catholic understanding of *sacrifice*—articulated in dialogue with Methodists with reference to *BEM*—as Christ's real sacramental *presence* in which he exercises his priestly *intercession* proves insufficient here. This proves even more interesting in light of the fact that the *BEM* response predates the dialogue's citation of it. Why would a Catholic dialogue use as an acceptable definition the formulation from *BEM* (which Methodists already accepted) that the Catholic *BEM* response did not fully endorse?

- *BEM* (E 8) uses *intercession* to refer both to Christ's heavenly work as High Priest and the church's communion with Christ. The Catholic response agrees and refers to this spiritual and sacramental communion with Christ's real presence as "the commemorative active presence of the sacrifice of Christ." It does not use *sacrifice* with respect to Christ's priestly office in heaven. Initially, it appears that *intercession* is an acceptable term.
- *BEM* meets Catholic teaching by relating *intercession* and *participation*, since the eucharist is an "offering made to the Father by the whole Christ, head and body."
- At this point, though, and contrary to the dialogues, intercession is deemed "insufficient to explain the sacrificial nature of the eucharist." All are agreed that historic events are not repeated, but because as High Priest Christ "is the crucified and risen Lord, his offering of self on the cross can be said to be 'made eternal.'" *Intercession*, however, does not do justice to this work. Likewise, *intercession* does not sufficiently describe the propitiatory effects of the cross. Also, *intercession* does not sufficiently describe the role of the church in union with Christ, so the

74. *Churches Respond to BEM*, 6:19–20.

language of the self-offering of the church should be used to correspond to Christ's eternal self-offering.[75]

It appears, then, that *intercession* is an acceptable term, to a degree, but is not sufficient to capture the scope of the eucharistic rite. These elements of the Catholic response, therefore, suggest a particular line of investigation to pursue in more detail, but a few comments are in order here.

First, a question of language. In terms of *intercession*, which the response prefers to call the *self-offering* of the church, it immediately recognizes that E 9–11 conveys this sense. With respect to the church's action and Christ's, the Catholic response does not clearly express how, in its opinion, *intercession* differs from *self-offering* (or sacrifice), nor does it fill in the content of *self-offering*, except to say that it is the work of the cross made eternal without a historic repetition. But *BEM* says exactly this, and it is a point of ecumenical agreement (at least with Methodists). As the early Methodist-Catholic dialogue remarked, the difference turns largely on the choice of language, while the concept that the different words describe is the same. Anscar Vonier uses the language of sacrifice similarly to *BEM* and Hebrews: "Heaven has no sacrifice, but is the consummation of all sacrifices. Sacrifice belongs to the period of faith and hope, where things are seen in a dark manner. . . . Christ's Priesthood is eternal, not because the sacrifice is everlasting, but because the consummation of the sacrifice is eternal."[76]

Second, to take a specific instance, consider how the response uses these terms:

> Christ first offered himself sacramentally to the Father in the eucharist, in a sacrifice that actualizes the redemption of humanity. If he now offers himself as a means of sacramental communion to the faithful, it is to allow them to associate themselves with his self-offering to the Father. Only insofar as Christ offers himself to the Father in the sacrificial action *of the church's liturgy* do the elements become sacrament of his self-offering to the communicants. . . . [*BEM*] does not say unambiguously that the eucharist is in itself a *real sacrifice, the memorial* of the sacrifice of Christ on the cross.[77]

This is a highly circumscribed use of language. Previously, the response approved *BEM*'s use of *intercession* as it refers to the church's union with Christ's primary agency in thanksgiving and prayer. As *BEM* suggests,

75. *Churches Respond to BEM*, 6:19–20.

76. Anscar Vonier, OSB, *A Key to the Doctrine of the Eucharist* (Westminster, MD: Newman Press, 1951), 261–63.

77. *Churches Respond to BEM*, 6:21–22; emphasis added.

however, with the words *consummation* and *intercession*, the "movement" of the eucharistic celebration is not only unidirectional from the church through Christ to the Father. Yes, the Spirit unites the Body to the Head in intercession, thanksgiving, prayer, and self-offering, but the Spirit also really gives the Head to the Body as spiritual food. The Catholic response notes the corporate and liturgical (i.e., sacrificial) action of the church as it participates in the eucharist, but what does it envision the glorified and impassible Christ in heaven to be "doing" if not what *BEM* says—that is, consummating, interceding, mediating, and being present sacramentally as host and meal? Does *self-offering* or *sacrifice*, once it is filled out, provide yet more content? Do all churches that concur with the content of *BEM*'s eucharist chapter need to use the language of self-offering or sacrifice to affirm the reality of the "commemorative active presence of the sacrifice of Christ?"

The logic of the Catholic response runs, briefly, like this: at the Last Supper Jesus instituted a sacrificial meal/rite, and the eucharist is a sacrifice in that the church continues it (a memorial representation); at the Supper he also offered himself (or began to do so) as a sacrifice, and in the eucharist he continues to do so: i.e., to offer himself sacramentally (and here even the Catholic response uses the language of self-offering rather than sacrifice, which it uses to describe the church's action). But because the church remembers and celebrates his sacrificial meal, it still offers a sacrifice, a memorial of the cross. In these texts the sacrificial language of the eucharist derives from its liturgical, commemorative, and memorial qualities and from the fact that the rite is offered (anthropologically).[78] That is to say, in the eucharist the church as Body participates in a sacramentally analogous way to the Head, in thanksgiving, prayer, intercession, and self-offering. Anthropologically, Catholic theology calls the latter aspect *sacrifice*, especially as it relates to the Body's liturgical expression. With the one word *intercession*, *BEM* affirms the same reality Christologically as Catholicism does with *self-offering* and anthropologically as Catholicism does with *sacrifice*. The Catholic response, therefore, insists on particular theological language and content in formulating carefully what occurs sacrificially in the eucharist, both Christologically in Christ's priestly office and his "making eternal" the unique sacrifice of the cross and anthropologically in the church's liturgical action of self-offering. Wainwright says hopefully, "Further exploration of the category of '*anamnesis*' employed by *BEM* may help to show that due recognition of the uniqueness of Christ's work and an acknowledgment of the sacrificial character of the eucharist may not be so contradictory as historical controversies have made them out to be."[79]

---

78. See Vonier's chapter, "The Eucharistic Liturgy," 241–49.

79. Wainwright, "Eucharist in the Churches' Responses to Lima," 59.

By and large, we have seen that the most contentious issues associated with eucharistic sacrifice relate to questions of theological anthropology: i.e., what is the nature of human agency in the rite—its purpose and its goal; what, if anything, does the church's liturgy (its divine service) accomplish or effect; and what is the relationship between the Last Supper, the eucharist, and the sacrifice of the cross? Furthermore, the most promising area of agreement for Methodists and Catholics lies in *BEM*'s Christology—i.e., its emphasis on the presidency of Christ in his priestly office in the eucharist. *BEM* seeks to bring the anthropological and Christological together with the concept of *anamnesis* and sacramental memorial and the language of intercession. While the language of intercession is insufficient for Catholics (and for Wesley), the emphasis on Christ's priesthood and *anamnesis* accords with Catholic teaching that the eucharist is a sacramental representation of Christ's sacrifice, presided over by Christ himself.

Overall, the Catholic response to *BEM* on the eucharist is both substantive and ecumenically favorable. It affirms nearly the entire chapter and sees it as a benchmark for future ecumenical dialogues, inviting other churches to affirm as much of the chapter as they can. In the case of Methodist churches, their level of affirmation varies widely, with the German churches affirming little and the United Methodists affirming much. With respect to sacrifice more specifically, the Catholic response expressed an unwillingness—historically conditioned no doubt—to jettison the language of sacrifice, even when *BEM* sought to express the conceptual equivalent in other words. Again with Methodism, what the German churches criticize most strongly—also historically conditioned—is the degree of human agency (tradition, participation, the elements, self-offering) that the chapter advocates. United Methodism and British Methodism respectively affirm or do not oppose the role of self-offering in *BEM*.

Encountering Christ the Saviour: Church and Sacraments (2011)

The 2011 bilateral dialogue builds on a foundation of four decades of Catholic-Methodist ecumenical engagement. With the shared teaching on eucharistic theology and humanity's free, graced participation in God's economy of salvation laid down in *The Grace Given You in Christ*, the 2011 dialogue proceeds to tackle the topics of baptism, eucharist, and ministry.[80] Nearly thirty years after *BEM*, these topics are fitting, since the 2011 dialogue relies on the insights of *BEM* at key points, the first of which is the primacy of Christ as the one who presides over the church's sacraments in the exercise of his priestly office.

---

80. World Methodist Council–Roman Catholic Church, *Encountering Christ the Saviour: Church and Sacraments* (Lake Junaluska, NC: World Methodist Council, 2011).

The text begins with a beautiful reflection from Philippians 2:1–11 on the paschal mystery of Christ's death and exaltation, and chapter 1 is a penetrating exposition of Christ's once-for-all atoning sacrifice that lies at the heart of the church's life, mission, and witness. The Christian life—individual *and* corporate—is marked by a profound identification and imitation of the Lord: "I want to know Christ and the power of his resurrection and the sharing of his sufferings by becoming like him in his death, if somehow I may attain the resurrection from the dead" (Phil 3:10–11).[81] Christ's *kenosis* and self-sacrifice, culminating on the cross, establish his priestly office and serve as a common Christological framework for further exposition on the sacraments: "Christ and his sacrifice and his victory are one and inseparable."[82] This approach—gleaned from the insights of *BEM*—is a vital one, because it identifies the Triune God as the principle agent in the church's sacramental liturgy. "This sacrificial self-giving of Christ is something 'made flesh' once-for-all in human history on the cross, but the innermost reality of Christ's 'Grand Oblation' is an eternal mystery at the very heart of the Holy Trinity."[83] While chapter 1 notes the ecclesial context of the sacraments and some of the differences that obtain between Catholics and Methodists, it also underscores their common conviction that baptism and eucharist are among the chief means by which Christians enter into communion with Christ's death and resurrection. The sacraments, therefore, bear a sacrificial character in their form, their enactment, and their telos.

Chapter 3, on the eucharist, begins by drawing from the shared eucharistic theology enumerated in *The Grace Given You in Christ* and by recommending the Wesleyan *Hymns on the Lord's Supper* as an authoritative theological resource that can advance the conversation. This is the first time these hymns have been used extensively in the dialogues, and they are a focus of our investigation in chapter 4. Christ's presence and sacrifice are key topics in the chapter, and they mutually inform one another: "The one crucified, risen and ascended is the host of his Supper and is present there [in the elements] in the fullness of his being, both human and divine."[84] The chapter makes recourse to four important concepts in its discussion of eucharistic sacrifice: Christ's priestly office, *anamnesis*, Augustine's doctrine of the *totus Christus*, and our participation with Christ.[85]

81. *Encountering Christ the Saviour*, 14.

82. *Encountering Christ the Saviour*, 14.

83. *Encountering Christ the Saviour*, 103.

84. *Encountering Christ the Saviour*, 78.

85. The chapter also discusses the nature of Christ's real presence and the pneumatological and eschatological dimensions of the eucharist, but they are not the focus here.

Christ is the true priest of the eucharist, and any priestly offices and actions in the church derive their authority and direction from him. The vision from Hebrews 7–10 and Revelation 5 of Christ's unchanging, heavenly intercession on our behalf shapes the sacrificial nature of the eucharist. "Catholics and Methodists are united in understanding the 'offering' and 'pleading' of Christ's unique sacrifice—of his blood—as fundamental to his heavenly intercession"; likewise, "When the risen Christ is present, he comes as the one whose body was given for us, whose blood was poured out for us, the one who has given his life as a ransom."[86]

Basal to sacramental theology is the idea that what Christ accomplished in his earthly ministry is available to subsequent generations because God transcends time and space. The concept of *anamnesis* as a dynamic and active memorial of the cross—developed extensively by *BEM* and received widely by the churches—plays a central role in this chapter. "It is the risen, ascended and exalted Christ who meets us in the eucharist, and he comes to us with the past and future made present in himself."[87] Christ's passion is never repeated, but the sacramental memorial of his passion is: "The eucharist is the celebration of Christ's full, perfect and sufficient sacrifice, offered once and for all, for the whole world. It is a memorial which is not a mere calling to mind of a past event or of its significance, but the Church's effectual proclamation of God's mighty act in Christ. In this celebration we really share in Christ's offering of himself in obedience to the Father's will."[88] Thus, the eucharist is not a new sacrifice in addition to the cross (as the Catholic side stresses with references to Trent); rather, it is the celebration in which the reconciling power of the cross is given to the believer for forgiveness and healing.

The ecclesial dimension of the eucharist comes to the fore in the self-evident observation that it is the church that celebrates the memorial of her Lord, coupled with the fact that Christ's sacrifice to the Father and his heavenly intercession is "for us." Augustine's doctrine of the *totus Christus*, with Christ as the head and the church as his body, is also prominent in Wesley's theology. In the act of making memorial, the eucharist incorporates Christ's body into his self-offering: "The risen Lord, united with the Church as head to his body, presents his saving sacrifice before the Father, and his members receive the fruits of that sacrifice in faith."[89] At the same time, though, eucharistic sacrifice entails much more than the church just "receiving the fruits" in faith: individuals and the church also make an offering (in fact,

---

86. *Encountering Christ the Saviour*, 99, 102.
87. *Encountering Christ the Saviour*, 101.
88. *Encountering Christ the Saviour*, 93.
89. *Encountering Christ the Saviour*, 91.

offerings) in union with Christ's eternal priesthood. "When we ask the question 'Who offers the eucharistic sacrifice?' our answer together as Methodists and Catholics is 'Christ our Head united with his Body, the Church.'"[90]

The text stresses the church's active and participatory role in offering the eucharistic sacrifice, and this common affirmation is already significant with respect to this divisive doctrine. The dialogue identifies sacrificial elements that Methodists readily affirm: offering spiritual sacrifices (1 Pt 2:5), offering oneself as a living sacrifice (Rom 12:1), offering a sacrifice of praise, good works, and sharing (Heb 13:15–16).[91] The chapter goes one step further, in fact, and unites the concepts of priesthood, *anamnesis*, and *totus Christus* in addressing the action of offering the eucharist as a sacrifice. "Because of this God-given unity of head and body, Catholics would readily echo the Wesley hymns in saying that in the eucharist the Church in Christ 'presents' Jesus' death and 'offer[s] up the Lamb to God,' and that therefore 'We . . . with thy sacrifice ascend.' Our sacrifice is united to Christ's sacrifice, and in Christ we 'plead,' 'present,' and 'offer' that one sacrifice of Christ to the Father."[92] This is indeed a strong statement on sacrifice, likely much stronger than most Methodists would anticipate, yet it is Wesley's theology.

With this joint affirmation in place, the text does not go on to probe in detail what Catholics and Methodists mean by "offering that one sacrifice of Christ" and how this offering is enacted in the liturgy. How does each tradition understand this concept and action? Do Methodists, for example, understand "pleading" as synonymous with "offering"? Do Catholics? Is pleading a disposition of the heart or a ritual enactment, or both? The chapter begins and ends by suggesting that the ideas of "memorial" and "pleading" can encompass much of what eucharistic sacrifice entails and that the language of "pleading" and "offering" can be reconciled.[93] But the Catholic response to *BEM* was that *anamnesis* does not go far enough with respect to sacrifice, and neither is "pleading" the same as "offering." The text does not address related issues of sacrifice, such as the sacrificial nature of the Last Supper; the relationship between the Supper, the cross, and the eucharist; and the legitimacy of offering the elements to God in sacrifice.

All the same, the dialogue is correct that it has laid a "firm foundation for further common reflection and agreement" on eucharistic sacrifice, and

90. *Encountering Christ the Saviour*, 114.

91. *Encountering Christ the Saviour*, 96.

92. *Encountering Christ the Saviour*, 117. The text quotes hymn 125:2: "With solemn faith we offer up, and spread before thy glorious eyes, the only ground of all our hope, that precious bleeding sacrifice."

93. *Encountering Christ the Saviour*, 74, 124, 132.

the recognition that both churches offer the one sacrifice of Christ to the Father is a significant breakthrough. It is also correct that Wesley's *Hymns on the Lord's Supper* is an invaluable resource for ongoing study. The dialogue ends by pointing the way in which this study can move forward: "Both Catholics and Methodists can fruitfully ponder more deeply what it means to come to the eucharist, to be drawn by Christ himself into his life, death and resurrection, and [especially] to enter the movement of his self-offering to the Father."[94] This is the direction of investigation in the following chapters.

94. *Encountering Christ the Saviour*, 131.

CHAPTER 2

Eucharistic Sacrifice in the Theology of Thomas Aquinas

In chapters 2, 3, and 4, the focus shifts away from Catholic and Methodist responses on the topic of eucharistic sacrifice in contemporary ecumenical dialogue and turns now to a careful reading of two key figures, Thomas Aquinas and John Wesley. From a systematic and historical perspective, the selection of these two should not be surprising: both Aquinas and Wesley stand as principal traditioning voices within their respective churches—i.e., each has been recognized by later generations of his community as expressing the church's faith in decisive (and sometimes authoritative) ways. Not only do contemporary Catholic and Methodist theologians regularly appeal to Aquinas and Wesley for theological warrant, but the Catholic magisterium has received Aquinas's thought in ways analogous to the elevation of Wesley's doctrines by Methodist churches. In short, the thought of both continues to shape Catholic and Methodist teaching, and for this reason, what each one writes with respect to eucharistic sacrifice merits our careful attention.

Whereas we will see that Methodism's fidelity to Wesley's eucharistic faith and practice is marked primarily by discontinuity—although the current United Methodist Great Thanksgiving happily reverses this trend—the degree of continuity between Aquinas and twentieth-century Catholic teaching remains high. Jean-Pierre Torrell, for example, has done much to highlight Aquinas's thought as a traditioning voice in Catholic theology and to demonstrate the timeliness and relevance of continued attention to his work.[1] Concerning eucharistic sacrifice, therefore, Aquinas proves advantageous for several reasons: (a) his work is relevant in light of the ongoing renaissance of his theology; (b) his role in the formulations of the Council of Trent renders

---

1. Among Jean-Pierre Torrell's many publications on Aquinas, see *Nouvelles Recherches Thomasiennes* (Paris: J. Vrin, 2008); *Aquinas's Summa: Background, Structure, and Reception*, 1st ed. (Washington, DC: The Catholic University of America Press, 2005); *Saint Thomas Aquinas*, vol. 1, *The Person and His Work* (Washington, DC: The Catholic University of America Press, 1996); and *Saint Thomas D'aquin, Maître Spirituel: Initiation 2* (Paris: Cerf, 1996). Torrell also calls attention to Nicholas M. Healy, *Thomas Aquinas: Theologian of the Christian Life*, Great Theologians Series (Burlington, Vt.: Ashgate, 2003), and Thomas F. O'Meara, *Thomas Aquinas, Theologian* (Notre Dame, IN: University of Notre Dame Press, 1997).

41

him historically significant;[2] and (c) his theology anticipates much of the Reformation critique of eucharistic sacrifice, yet without the atmosphere of polemics, distrust, and schism. An analysis of Aquinas's teaching, therefore, will offer a way to understand deeply the teachings of Vatican II and contemporary papal encyclicals in chapters 5 and 6.

It will first be helpful to state the scope and outline of this chapter. The primary goal, ultimately, will be to explicate clearly Aquinas's teaching, which will aid not only in interpreting contemporary Catholic teaching, but in rendering Wesley's thought more intelligible. Because I argue for a convergence between Catholics and Methodists on eucharistic sacrifice—in part based on agreement between Aquinas and Wesley—my exposition will naturally seek to raise questions or emphasize facets of Aquinas's thought that are germane to the contemporary ecumenical discussion. Consequently, we will seek to read Aquinas and Wesley on their own terms; nonetheless, we will do so through a certain pair of lenses.[3]

The events of Sinai (Exodus 24) and Passover hold together Israel's practice of communal meal and the richness of covenantal sacrifice, which Christ in his Pasch both fulfills and transforms as Israel's Temple, and which the church continues in the eucharist as the body of Christ.[4] To be sure, not all contemporary Catholic theologians follow Aquinas's thought, and Matthew Levering engages in a heated intra-Catholic debate over the proper interpretation of eucharistic sacrifice.[5] Arguing for continuity between Israel, Aquinas, Trent, and contemporary magisterial Catholic teaching (especially John Paul II), Levering comments that with the possible exception of von Balthasar,

2. See Liam Walsh, "Sacraments," in *The Theology of Thomas Aquinas*, ed. Rik Van Nieuwenhove and Joseph Peter Wawrykow (Notre Dame, IN: University of Notre Dame Press, 2005), 328; see Vonier, *Key to the Doctrine*, chapter 15, "S Thomas and the Council of Trent on the Oneness of the Christian Sacrifice."

3. See Richard Schenk, "'Verum sacrificium' as the Fullness and Limit of Sacrifice in the Sacramental Theology of Thomas Aquinas: Historical Context and Current Significance," in *Ressourcement Thomism: Sacred Doctrine, the Sacraments, and the Moral Life; Essays in Honor of Romanus Cessario*, ed. Reinhard Huetter and Matthew Levering (Washington, DC: The Catholic University of America Press, 2010), 169–207.

4. Matthew Webb Levering, *Sacrifice and Community: Jewish Offering and Christian eucharist*, Illuminations, Theory and Religion (Malden, MA: Blackwell, 2005), 50–68.

5. For example, Robert J. Daly, SJ, *Sacrifice Unveiled: The True Meaning of Christian Sacrifice* (New York: T. and T. Clark, 2009); Edward J. Kilmartin, SJ, *The Eucharist in the West: History and Theology*, ed. Robert J. Daly, SJ, (Collegeville, MN: Liturgical Press, 1998); David Power, *The Eucharistic Mystery: Revitalizing the Tradition* (New York: Crossroad, 1992); Louis-Marie Chauvet, *Symbol and Sacrament: A Sacramental Reinterpretation of Christian Existence*, trans. Patrick Madigan and Madeleine Beaumont (Collegeville, MN: Liturgical Press, 1995); Joseph Martos, *Deconstructing Sacramental Theology and Reconstructing Catholic Ritual* (Eugene, Ore.: Resource, 2015).

"mainstream academic twentieth-century Catholic eucharistic theology distanced itself from the Jewish (and Catholic) mode of communion in and through sacrifice."[6]

At the same time, he clarifies his use of terminology by using the words *sacramental*, *cultic*, *sacrificial*, and *liturgical* synonymously. The church's eucharist is certainly a doxological act, but it must also uphold the sacrificial dimension of humanity's redemption from sin and communion with God that Christ's passion completes. Those theologians and traditions that move away from this essential sacrificial dimension Levering charges with "'eucharistic idealism': the linear-supersessionist displacement of the Jewish mode of embodied sacrificial communion by spiritualizing accounts of eucharistic communion with God."[7] Insofar as he critiques Hegel, Schleiermacher, Calvin, and Luther, he implicitly implicates Protestantism—or at least large portions of it—as well. We will see that although Wesley was a champion of the Reformation as he understood it, his theology of eucharistic sacrifice does not fall under the charge of "eucharistic idealism." Levering brings these themes together with a programmatic statement of Aquinas's theology of eucharistic sacrifice:

> Through sacramentally sharing in Christ's sacrifice, the Church herself becomes sacrificial, imbued with radical love. The eucharist, as a communion of love in and through Christ's sacrifice, involves learning cruciformity as members of Christ's sacrificial Body. As such, the eucharist fulfills Israel's mode of sacrificial worship, in which sacrifice and communion are inextricably integrated. . . . Union with Jesus Christ in the sacramental-sacrificial liturgy of the eucharist is both a sharing in Christ's sacrificial fulfillment of Torah and Temple and a contemplative participation in the trinitarian life of the divine Word.[8]

Additionally, Aquinas locates eucharistic sacrifice within a larger theological discourse of sacrifice. This discourse entails several considerations: the function of sacrifice in religion; the epistemological need for ritual; the necessity of worship as a function of the virtue of justice and the role of sacrifice therein; the singularly redeeming event of Christ's sacrifice; the sacraments as a modality of God's work of salvation and deification; the presence of Christ in the eucharist; the relationship of the eucharist to the Last Supper and the Cross; the sacramental representation of Christ's passion; and the eucharistic sacrifice as the church's participation in the sacrifice of Christ. An understanding of the larger context of sacrifice in Aquinas, therefore, will

6. Levering, *Sacrifice and Community*, 25.
7. Levering, *Sacrifice and Community*, 8.
8. Levering, *Sacrifice and Community*, 26–28.

facilitate an accurate exposition of his theology of eucharistic sacrifice. Thus, this chapter begins broadly and narrows systematically in focus.

Worship—Religion—Epistemology

The celebration of the eucharist is the chief act of the church's worship, the act toward which all human acts (including the worship of Israel) are directed. Liam Walsh quotes Aquinas approvingly: "The common good of the whole Church is contained substantially in the sacrament of the eucharist." Walsh continues, "The eucharist, then, is the sacrament in which the eschatological fullness proper to the sacramental economy is most fully realized and manifested. There is nothing further to be done when one has received the eucharist."[9] Aquinas's theology of worship (broadly conceived) and ritual, along with his broadly Aristotelian epistemology, greatly inform his understanding of eucharistic sacrifice. At the same time, sacrifice plays an important role within these concepts.

According to Aquinas, God ordained the ceremonial precepts of the Old Law, including the institution of ceremonial sacrifices, for the purposes of directing the mind away from idolatry toward divine worship and of foreshadowing Christ. Right from the beginning, Christ's passion thoroughly shapes Aquinas's understanding of sacrifice. Old Testament sacrifices had the pedagogical and epistemological functions of directing, teaching, and signifying, and Christ's passion had the function of redemption: "[God] wished [sacrifices] to be offered to him, in order to prevent idolatry; in order to signify the right ordering of man's mind to God; and in order to represent the mystery of the redemption of man by Christ."[10] While discussing the sacraments of the Old Law, he writes, "Consequently the chief sacrifice is that whereby Christ Himself *delivered Himself to God for an odor of sweetness* (Eph 5:2). And for this reason all the other sacrifices of the Old Law were offered up in order to foreshadow this one individual and paramount sacrifice,—the imperfect forecasting the perfect."[11] Here Aquinas cites Ephesians 5:2: "Christ loved us and gave himself up for us, a fragrant offering and sacrifice to God"; it is one of two key texts that shapes his understanding of sacrifice, Christ's passion, and eucharistic sacrifice. The second is Romans 3:25: "whom God put forward as a sacrifice of atonement by his blood."

---

9. Walsh, "Sacraments," 360. See John P. Yocum, "Sacraments in Aquinas," in *Aquinas on Doctrine: A Critical Introduction*, ed. Thomas Weinandy, Daniel Keating, and John Yocum (New York: T. and T. Clark, 2004), 159–82.

10. *ST* I-II, q. 102, a. 3, ad 1; see q. 102, a. 1–q. 102, a. 4, and q. 102, a. 6.

11. *ST* I-II, q. 102, a. 3.

Some sacrifices of Israel foreshadowed the manifold benefits of Christ's passion more directly than others: thus circumcision signifies baptism as an act of consecration, purification rituals provide cleanliness and expiation, and the paschal banquet signifies the passion: "Christ our pasch is sacrificed" (1 Cor 5:7).[12] Sinai, Yom Kippur, and Passover are focal points of Israel's sacrificial theology because these sacrifices bring together the many requirements of humanity's right worship with God, a relationship whose true end between Creator and creature is justice. Aquinas can talk about the sacrifices of Israel as sacraments because they are material signs that point beyond themselves and that carry divine power. They do not, however, bear justifying or sanctifying grace, and their power of expiation is of a highly qualified sort; sacrifices expiate sin through faith in Christ's passion: "not that those carnal sacrifices had of themselves the power of expiating sin; but that they signified that expiation of sins which was to be effected by Christ, and of which those of old became partakers by protesting their faith in the Redeemer."[13] Aquinas argues that through its sacrifices and its faith, God made Israel a partaker in Christ's redemption. Not just Israel, then, but all humanity is also ordained to participate in God's salvation. The duty of worship extends beyond Israel and the church to all creatures: "It belongs to human right ordering to give thanks to the Creator. . . . Liturgy is first of all the human mode of offering something to the divine Benefactor, in accord with the natural law."[14]

What is the relationship between Israel's sacrifices and the church's sacraments; why, under both dispensations, is ritual necessary; and why does Aquinas narrate so positively the function of sacrifice? His questions on religion and sacrifice (*ST* II-II, q. 81 and 85) both offer answers and direct the discussion toward Christ's passion, the church's sacraments, and ultimately the eucharist. Religion, in its broadest sense, refers to the relationship of the creature to the Creator, "for it is He to whom we ought to be bound as to our unfailing principle," and it entails both ritual acts and acts of service to widows and orphans.[15] Aquinas rejects the ideas of his objector to dichotomize between "cultic" sacrifices and acts of mercy and justice; he names both sacrifice, since both direct the believer toward right worship: "Every virtuous deed is said to be a sacrifice, insofar as it is done out of reverence of God."[16] In a noteworthy answer on the external act of religion that clearly anticipates his sacramental

12. See *ST* I-II, q. 102, a. 5, and a. 5, ad 2.

13. *ST* I-II, q. 102, a. 5, ad 4.

14. Matthew Levering, "Aquinas on the Liturgy of the Eucharist," in Weinandy, Keating, and Yocum *Aquinas on Doctrine*, 185.

15. *ST* II-II, q. 81, a. 1, and q. 81, a.1, ad 1.

16. *ST* II-II, q. 81, a. 4, ad 1.

theology, he brings together the Creator-creature relationship, the epistemological need for ritual, and the relationship of ritual to faith (reverence):

> We pay God honor and reverence, not for His sake (because He is of Himself full of glory to which no creature can add anything), *but for our own sake*, because by the very fact that we revere and honor God, our mind is subjected to Him. . . . Now the human mind, in order to be united to God, needs to be guided by the sensible world. . . . Wherefore in the Divine worship it is necessary to make use of corporeal things, that man's mind may be aroused thereby, as by signs, to the spiritual acts by means of which he is united to God. *Therefore the internal acts of religion take precedence of the others and belong to religion essentially, while its external acts are secondary, and subordinate to the internal acts.*[17]

As John Yocum summarizes, "The sacraments of both the Old Law and the New Law are ordained to the fulfillment of the human duty of religious reverence: worship."[18] Through sacramental signs, God leads humanity into deeper knowledge of the divine.

Aquinas reiterates these ideas when he turns to sacrifice directly (*ST* II-II, q. 85). His response demonstrates on three levels that the kind of sacrifice we make corresponds to how God has constituted us as creatures. He begins by saying, "Natural reason tells man that he is subject to a higher being, on account of the defects which he perceives in himself, and in which he needs help and direction from someone above him." First, he says, sacrifice belongs of the order of nature: "Now the mode befitting to man is that he should employ sensible signs in order to signify anything, because he derives his knowledge from sensibles. Hence it is a dictate of natural reason that man should use certain sensibles, by offering them to God in sign of the subjection and honor due to Him," which is "what we mean by a sacrifice."[19] Second, the believer is able to recognize his or her interior self-offering as the sacrificial movement of the soul: "A sacrifice is offered in order that something may be represented. Now the sacrifice that is offered outwardly represents the inward spiritual sacrifice, whereby the soul offers itself to God according to Ps 50:19, *A sacrifice to God is an afflicted spirit.*"[20] Third, sacrifice is rightly associated with the virtue of religion because it is performed in reverence to God: "The very

17. *ST* II-II, q. 81, a. 7 (emphasis added).

18. Yocum, "Sacraments in Aquinas," 160; see Liam G. Walsh, "The Divine and the Human in St. Thomas's Theology of Sacraments," in *Ordo Sapientiae et Amoris*, ed. Carlos Josaphat Pinto de Oliveira (Fribourg, Switzerland: Universitätsverlag Freiburg Schweiz, 1993), 321–52.

19. *ST* II-II, q. 85, a. 1.

20. *ST* II-II, q. 85, a. 2.

fact that we wish to cling to God in a spiritual fellowship pertains to reverence for God: and consequently the act of any virtue assumes the character of a sacrifice through being done in order that we may cling to God in holy fellowship."[21] Aquinas also offers a more technical definition of sacrifice, which, like his understanding of religion, anticipates both Christ's passion and the eucharist: "A 'sacrifice,' properly speaking, requires that something be done to the thing which is offered to God, for instance animals were slain and burnt, the bread is broken, eaten, blessed, [and Jesus' body is scourged, raised up, and pierced]. The very word signifies this, since 'sacrifice' is so called because a man does something sacred."[22]

Levering helpfully relates sacrifice to worship and justice: "Sacrifice of one's own will to the Creator-God, a sacrifice or self-offering that is signified by the visible sacrifice, constitutes the fundamental act of justice."[23] This perspective significantly reorients justice away from an exclusively juridical notion of transgression and restitution—i.e., a punishment that humanity must undergo in the face of divine anger. Instead, Aquinas sees justice as giving to one what is due, so that what creatures owe their Creator is right worship. Justice names this relationship rightly ordered, and sacrifice names the enactment of this right worship, both ethically and liturgically. "Justice is thus never extrinsic to the relationship of God and creatures," like sin; rather, "Justice describes in a theologically specific way a central aspect of God's 'presence' to his people."[24] Notice, too, Levering's careful ascription of agency: justice "describes" God's "'presence' to his people." Justice is a relationship in which God is present, rather than a penalty, or punishment, or commodity that needs to be exchanged—although a just relationship may sometimes entail this dimension. Furthermore, God is not present passively, but actively. God wills justice with Israel, the church, and all creation, and actively seeks to enact it. As Walsh puts it, "Concretely, sacraments are the events in which the divine gift of salvation, realized eschatologically in Christ and the Spirit, is actually given to humans and received by them."[25]

Notably absent from these citations is any sense that human actions, either cultic or virtuous, effect any change on the part of God; they effect change on the human side in that they both direct the mind and body to right worship of God and to just service of others. Whatever power of expiation cultic sacrifices carry resides ultimately in the work of Christ. God does not

---

21. *ST* II-II, q. 85, a. 3, ad 1.
22. *ST* II-II, q. 85, a. 3, ad 3.
23. Levering, "Aquinas on the Liturgy of the Eucharist," 187.
24. Levering, *Sacrifice and Community*, 72.
25. Walsh, "Divine and the Human," 328.

need our worship, although Aquinas teaches that right worship that honors God alone as Creator and Savior is the duty of the creature and is therefore pleasing to God. Christian worship does function as a means of rightly ordering the creature to the Creator, yet the institution of justice ultimately resides in God's initiation and decree.

Aquinas deepens his teaching on religion and sacrifice when he expounds his doctrine of Christian sacraments, especially the eucharist, but one cannot move from Passover to eucharist by passing over the sacrificial dimension of Christ's passion and priesthood, for the conjunction of sacrifice and justice culminate in Christ's passion. In his understanding of Christ's passion as a sacrifice and of eucharistic sacrifice, Aquinas focuses on how God is present in Christ, who in his humanity alone is able to offer to God the Father the perfect offering of himself in all his being, which—as the right worship between God and humanity—is the fulfillment of justice.

Priesthood and Humanity in the Sacrifice (Passion) of Christ

Aquinas's understanding of Christ's priesthood owes a great deal to his understanding of Christ's passion and vice versa; the topics of sacrifice, and to some extent the eucharist, pervade these questions. Jesus is a priest because he fulfills the office of one who mediates between humanity and God, and the mediating function he fulfilled was one of reconciliation. Citing Mal 2:7, Heb 5:1, 2 Pt 1:4, and Col 1:19, he says: "The office proper to a priest is to be a mediator between God and the people. . . . He reconciled the human race to God. . . . Therefore it is most fitting that Christ should be a priest."[26] Just as the sacrament-sacrifices of the Old Law precede yet are qualified by Christ's passion, so also his priesthood follows yet transcends all other orders of priests. Christ's priesthood is *sui generis* because he mediates by the reconciling sacrifice of himself; citing Ephesians 5:2, Aquinas notes that by his sacrifice, Christ is both priest and victim. Denis Chardonnens considers Christ's priesthood in its eucharistic dimension: "The double role of the priest [as intermediary between God and humanity] has been assumed by Christ in a perfect and unique manner, and it grounds the descending and ascending nature of his mediation."[27]

Aquinas reminds the reader of the three reasons that require sacrifice—remission of sin, perseverance in grace, and right order with God—and notes that their realization derives from Christ's humanity: "Christ himself, as man,

26. *ST* III, q. 22, a. 1.

27. Fr. Denis Chardonnens, OCD, "Éternité du sacerdoce du Christ et effet eschatologique de l'eucharistie," in *Revue Thomiste* 99 (1999): 160; my translation.

was not only priest, but also a perfect victim, being at the same time victim for sin, victim for a peace-offering, and a holocaust."[28] Aquinas orders his answer of Christ as priest and victim around two other citations (in addition to Eph 5:2 and Rom 3:25) that permeate his comments on sacrifice: "As Augustine says: 'Every visible sacrifice is a sacrament, that is a sacred sign, of the invisible sacrifice.' Now the invisible sacrifice is that by which a man offers his spirit to God, according to Psalms 50:19: 'A sacrifice to God is an afflicted spirit.'" Note how in Aquinas's epistemology, sign, sacrament, and ritual harmonize the often irreconcilable tension between faith and ritual on the one hand and justice and worship on the other. Aquinas speaks of Christ's priesthood and victimhood as a doxological offering: Christ realizes the requirements of sacrifice, because "whatever is offered to God in order to raise man's spirit to Him, may be called a sacrifice," and Christ raises the believer's spirit to its end in deification—i.e., "the perfection of glory."[29] Additionally, Aquinas's words on Christ's death reflect a balancing of perspectives that have prompted modern sensibilities to offer a distorted theology of the crucifixion as something other than a sacrifice: he holds both that the slayers of Christ's humanity commit an egregious sin, even while the One whose will is also the Father's will perfectly offers himself to God, even unto death.[30]

The expiation of Christ's passion is explicitly eucharistic in scope. The effect of Christ's priesthood is the expiation of sin, and Aquinas again follows (and cites) Augustine, who enumerates the four aspects of every sacrifice: the gift, the giver, the recipient, and the beneficiary, and who says, "The same one true Mediator reconciling us to God by the sacrifice of peace, was one with him to whom it was offered, united in himself those for whom he offered it, at the same time offered it himself, and was himself that which he offered."[31] Aquinas ends this question with an explicit reference to the eucharist when he teaches that Christ's priesthood does not exist for his own benefit, but for humanity's. Eschatologically, those with God will eternally require the "consummation" of Christ's passion, the deifying virtue of which "endures for ever."[32] In history, the faithful regularly participate in Christ's priesthood and passion: in the Old Law the priest sprinkled the blood of the sacrifice, and in the New Law the church more excellently follows Melchizedek when it offers

---

28. *ST* III, q. 22, a. 2.

29. *ST* III, q. 22, a. 2.

30. *ST* III, q. 22, a. 2, ad. 1 and 2. Aquinas's eschatological note of perfection in glory is prominent in Levering's work; see "Aquinas on the Liturgy of the Eucharist," 184, 186. For a profound reflection on Christ's death as sacrifice, see David Bentley Hart, *Beauty of the Infinite: The Aesthetics of Christian Truth* (Grand Rapids, MI: Eerdmans, 2003), 346–94.

31. *ST* III, q. 22, a. 3, ad 1.

32. *ST* III, q. 22, a. 5, ad. 1 and 2.

bread and wine.[33] Christ's mediating priesthood in the eucharist directs humanity toward its ultimate end, namely God.[34]

When Aquinas discusses Christ's passion directly—its causes, effects, benefits—it is clear that for him this singularly saving event within history is what gives the familiar themes of worship, justice, appeasement, and sacrifice their primary signification; in addition, he relates the universal work of Christ to personal application by means of "faith and the sacraments of faith," thus preparing the way for his treatise on the sacraments, culminating in the eucharist.[35] The way Aquinas approaches these questions (*ST* III, q. 46–49) offers a miniature hermeneutic both for interpreting the causes and effects of Christ's death and for how theology can use language to talk about this unique event. This hermeneutic and method will prove pivotal when he uses these same words in the sacramental context of the eucharist. To be sure, Aquinas is concerned with much more than hermeneutics; he is concerned with the church's dogma. But Christ's passion is at the center of both: at the same time that it is primarily God's salvation of humanity, it functions methodologically in Aquinas's thought as the pivotal event that illuminates what certain words mean and how they should be used. As David Berger notes, "The original image of all sacrifices and the sole source which makes all human sacrifice meritorious is Christ's sacrifice."[36]

Christ did not need to suffer, as if the passion represented the only solution to the problem of sin that God confronted; instead, Christ's passion was a redemptive act to which Jesus the Son voluntarily elected to submit for the sake of humanity.[37] Christ's passion became the fitting event and cornerstone in God's providential and sovereign ordering of salvation history.[38] Christ's passion was a fitting display of God's justice and mercy, since it freed humanity from sin and made satisfaction for its sin, satisfaction humanity itself could never make.[39] Van Nieuwenhove demonstrates that, following Anselm's *Cur*

---

33. *ST* III, q. 22, a. 6, ad 2.

34. Chardonnens, "Éternité du sacerdoce du Christ et effet eschatologique de l'eucharistie," 159.

35. For a more thorough development of Aquinas's theology of Christ's passion, see Rik Van Nieuwenhove, "Bearing the Marks of Christ's Passion: Aquinas' Soteriology," in Van Nieuwenhove and Wawrykow, *Theology of Thomas Aquinas*, 277–302.

36. David Berger, *Thomas Aquinas & the Liturgy*, 2nd ed. (Naples, Fla.: Sapientia Press of Ave Maria University, 2005), 68.

37. See Van Nieuwenhove, "Bearing the Marks," 279–80.

38. For a discussion on the notion of *conveniens* in Aquinas's theology, see Paul Gondreau, "The Humanity of Christ, the Incarnate Word," in Van Nieuwenhove and Wawrykow, *Theology of Thomas Aquinas*, 258–62.

39. *ST* III, q. 46, a.1, ad 3.

Deus homo, Aquinas qualifies the meaning of satisfaction, thereby excluding any sense of penal substitution or vindictive justice. He does this by drawing attention to the Pauline notion of the Body; by separating satisfaction and suffering from punishment; and by associating satisfaction and suffering, but not punishment, with Christ's passion.[40] Indeed, because he is the ultimate arbiter of forgiveness, God could have forgiven humanity apart from requiring satisfaction without any breach of justice: "just as anyone else, overlooking a personal trespass, without satisfaction, acts mercifully and not unjustly."[41] Nevertheless, Christ's passion was most suitable for several reasons: the display of God's love, the example of obedience, the meriting of justifying grace, and the overthrow of the devil.[42] For Aquinas, Christ's passion has an essentially sacrificial element; he cites Ephesians 5:2 and now Romans 5:10: "'We are reconciled to God by the death of His Son,' insofar as Christ's death was a most acceptable sacrifice to God."[43] Once again, Aquinas's thought exhibits no tension between the Son and the Father with respect to the divine work of redemption: "Christ as God delivered Himself up to death by the same will and action as that by which the Father delivered Him up; but as man He gave Himself up by a will inspired of the Father. Consequently there is no contrariety in the Father delivering Him up and in Christ delivering Himself up . . . and consequently we give praise to both."[44]

Far from applying a definition of appeasement or sacrifice from the philosophy of religion to the work of Christ, Vonier states, "The Christian sacrifice stands by itself with its own rites, and we know best what a sacrifice really is from the inspired literature of our Scriptures."[45] He defines Christ's sacrificial passion similarly to Aquinas: "The sacrifice is a mode of divine worship which is absolute, in the sense that God alone may be honoured in such a mode,"[46] and in the case of Christ (as was sometimes prefigured under the Old Law), his sacrifice entailed the loss of life. He notes the unavoidable intertextuality between Exodus 29:25 and Ephesians 5:2, as well as the ritual and doxological element of sacrifice in which the victim "sends up to heaven a

40. Van Nieuwenhove, "Bearing the Marks," 288–91. On satisfaction and justice, see Levering, *Sacrifice and Community*, 81.

41. *ST* III, q. 46, a. 2, ad 3.

42. *ST* III, q. 46, a. 3.

43. *ST* III, q. 47, a. 2.

44. *ST* III, q. 47, a. 3, ads 2–3. Gérard Remy, "Le Christ Médiateur dans l'oeuvre de Saint Thomas D'aquin," *Revue Thomiste* 93 (1993); on this topic, see especially his sections "L'amour de Dieu et le sacrifice du médiateur selon la *Somme*," 194–96, and "Le Christ médiateur et prêtre en tant qu'homme," 214–17.

45. Vonier, *Key to the Doctrine*, 159.

46. Vonier, *Key to the Doctrine*, 160.

perfume of sweetness which is pleasing to the Lord God Almighty."[47] This idea runs throughout the Old Testament and is fulfilled by Christ at his passion. Vonier follows Aquinas in that a theory of sacrifice external to a biblical notion of justice is not applied to Christ's passion; rather, Christ fulfills the just worship of sacrifice between humanity and God. Thus, Vonier says, "Christ's death on the cross was truly a ritual act, as it was done at the time, in the manner, with the circumstances, ordained by the Father, and foreshadowed by all the ancient sacrifices. To make of the crucified Christ anything less than a victim, in the ceremonial sense of the word, is to bring down his death to the human plane."[48]

Aquinas's doctrine becomes even clearer when he discusses the means and effects of Christ's passion. Modern notions of atonement frequently stumble over the word *hilasterion* (propitiation, expiation, appeasement) in Romans 3:25 (see 1 Jn 2:2; *ST* III, q. 48, a. 2) because they pit the Father's demand for "justice" against the Son's "forgiveness" and conceive of the cross as a penal transference of wrath from the heavenly judge onto the unfortunate victim. Aquinas's hermeneutic, however, exhibits no such modern predilection because he attends closely to how Christ perfects and transcends such concepts as sacrifice, appeasement, and propitiation (whether in scripture or the church's teaching): "A sacrifice properly so called is something done for that honor which is properly due to God, in order to appease Him . . . and this voluntary enduring of the passion was most acceptable to God, as coming from charity. Therefore it is manifest that Christ's passion was a true sacrifice."[49] Aquinas's trinitarian theology and Christology serve as the foundation for his theology of the Incarnation and the effects of Christ's passion for humanity (and for the sacraments, below).

> Christ's passion, according as it is compared with His Godhead, operates in an efficient manner: but insofar as it is compared with the will of Christ's soul it acts in a meritorious manner: considered as being within Christ's very flesh, it acts by way of satisfaction, inasmuch as we are liberated by it from the debt of punishment; while inasmuch as we are freed from the servitude of guilt, it acts by way of redemption: but insofar as we are reconciled with God it acts by way of sacrifice, as shall be shown farther on [q. 49].[50]

47. Vonier, *Key to the Doctrine*, 162.

48. Vonier, *Key to the Doctrine*, 164; see Levering, "Aquinas on the Liturgy of the Eucharist," 189.

49. *ST* III, q. 48, a. 3. See Colman O'Neill, *Sacramental Realism: A General Theory of the Sacraments* (Chicago: Midwest Theological Forum, 1998), 90–91.

50. *ST* III, q. 48, a. 6, ad 3.

He employs medicinal metaphors with equal frequency as he does juridical ones, thereby juggling plates that Western theology dropped at the time of the Reformation.[51]

Specifically, Christ's sacrifice reconciles humanity to God. It does so in two ways: first, by way of taking away sin so that humanity is no longer God's enemy; second, by way of appeasement: "Christ's voluntary suffering was such a good act that, because of its being found in human nature, God was appeased for every offense of the human race with regard to those who are made one with the crucified Christ in the aforesaid manner [baptism]."[52] Here again, Aquinas's hermeneutic should be noted: just as in Christ's passion when the Godhead is neither divided, nor does the Father demand the death of Christ on account of humanity's sins, neither, too, do sacrifice and appeasement signify that the slaughter of one victim in place of another assuages the wrath of an angry deity. He asserts, "Christ is not said to have reconciled us with God, as if God had begun anew to love us, since it is written [Jer 31:3], 'I have loved thee with an everlasting love.'"[53] Christ's sacrifice—on behalf of humankind— appeased the Father by corresponding to the order of justice because of the fervor of his charity and the depth of his obedience in his self-offering. Thus, for Aquinas, Christ's passion fulfills words like sacrifice and appeasement, and it also gives form to words like worship and justice: "The source of hatred [i.e., human sin] was taken away by Christ's passion, both through sin being washed away and through compensation being made in the shape of a more pleasing offering."[54] Levering notes, "On the cross, Christ perfectly fulfills the order of justice between human beings and God by offering in charity the perfect sacrifice to God, the perfect act of worship or liturgy."[55]

Christ's passion embodies the perfect sacrifice even as it embodies the perfect doxological and liturgical act. This is a point that contemporary Protestant theology does not sufficiently appreciate. On the one hand, the effects of Christ's passion do not stop at his ascension, since his sacrifice is the medicine for past, present, and future sin; on the other hand, the universal scope of God's salvation requires personal application.[56] For Aquinas, the sacra-

51. *ST* III, q. 49, a. 1, ad 3; the sacraments are a spiritual medicine: III, q. 60, a. 1. On Aquinas's "use of medicinal metaphors," see Van Nieuwenhove, "Bearing the Marks," 282– 84, 296. On Wesley's construal of the cross and sanctification as medicinal, see Maddox, *Responsible Grace*, 62, 91, 112, 121, 144–46.

52. *ST* III, q. 49, a. 4.

53. *ST* III, q. 49, a. 4, ad 2.

54. *ST* III, q. 49, a. 4, ad 2.

55. Levering, "Aquinas on the Liturgy of the Eucharist," 188.

56. Chardonnens, "Éternité du sacerdoce du Christ": "the effect that Christ's Passion worked in the world, the eucharist works in us"; 168, my translation.

ments apply the effects of Christ's liturgical act (as head) to his body—namely, the church: "Now by Christ's passion we have been delivered not only from the common sin of the whole human race, both as to its guilt and as to the debt of punishment, for which he paid the penalty on our behalf; but, furthermore, from the personal sins of individuals, who share in his passion by faith and charity and the sacraments of faith."[57] Commenting on Aquinas and Hebrews 9, Vonier ties together this section's themes of Christ's priesthood, his sacrificial passion, and the eucharist: Hebrews demonstrates "the sacrificial nature of the passion of Christ, and, above all, the sacrificial nature of the pouring out of the Blood. This latter feature in Christ's passion seems to be the supreme sacerdotal act, and no doubt it is there we must find the essence of the great Christian sacrifice."[58]

Christ's Sacrifice and the Sacraments

The transition from the effects of Christ's passion to the celebration of the church's sacraments follows logically for Aquinas not only as a result of his epistemology, but because his doctrines of Christology and sacrament reinforce one another. Because the sacraments derive their power from Christ's passion, and because through them the efficacy of Christ's passion is applied to us, the sacraments in general also necessarily have a sacrificial dimension. When he speaks of the sacrificial nature of Christ's passion, he says, "Even Christ's passion, although denoted by other figurative sacrifices, is yet a sign of something to be observed by us."[59] As Van Nieuwenhove notes, "In this general sense, the whole life, death, and resurrection of Christ acquire sacramental status: they signify our salvation in him. Conversely, the sacraments in the strict sense are signs of the salvific efficacy of Christ's redeeming work."[60] As John Saward writes, "The Son is thanksgiving in his very person, 'the Father's substantial eucharist.'"[61] When Aquinas turns directly to his sacramental theology, his remarks are thoroughly commensurate with his teaching that Christ's incarnation and passion are themselves sacramental. In addition, it immediately continues his discussion of sacrifice, adapted to a sacramental mode.

---

57. *ST* III, q. 49, a. 5. On the importance of faith, see Remy, "Le Christ Médiateur," 204–6. The role of faith on the part of the believer and/or the priest runs throughout question III, q. 49 on Christ's passion and questions III, q. 73–83 on the eucharist.

58. Vonier, *Key to the Doctrine*, 175.

59. *ST* III, q. 48, a. 3, ad. 2.

60. Van Nieuwenhove, "Bearing the Marks," 293. See, too, Gondreau, "Humanity of Christ," 260.

61. Quoted in Aidan Nichols, OP, *The Holy Eucharist: From the New Testament to John Paul II* (Dublin: Veritas, 1991), 121.

He approvingly cites Augustine's line "The visible sacrifice is the sacrament, i.e. the sacred sign, of the invisible sacrifice," which is the interior sacrifice of the heart by faith.[62] "Consequently a sacrament properly so called is that which is the sign of some sacred thing pertaining to man; so that properly speaking a sacrament, as considered by us now, is defined as being the 'sign of a holy thing so far as it makes men holy.'"[63] Sacraments consist of a signification that is past, present, and future: "the very cause of our sanctification, which is Christ's passion; the form of our sanctification, which is grace and the virtues; and the ultimate end of our sanctification, which is eternal life."[64] Moreover, a crucial element—and one of prime importance with respect to eucharistic sacrifice—is that God has ordained the sacraments to bear witness to the drama of Christ's salvation of humanity; they attest both to the locus of human salvation and to the manner in which God saves. He writes, "In the use of the sacraments two things may be considered, namely, the worship of God, and the sanctification of man: the former of which pertains to man as referred to God, and the latter pertains to God in reference to man."[65]

The celebration of sacraments, and supremely the eucharist, is at once a divine, saving event as much as it is a sacrificial human act of worship.[66] From the human side, sacramental worship is the free, uncoerced act that the creature owes to God; from the divine side, the effect of this act, which is implied in the cause that the sacraments signify, is the divine gift of grace. As Vonier notes, "The sacrament, remaining a sacrament, may be a worship as much as a sanctification; in fact, it is more truly a sacrament through the worship of God than through the sanctification of man."[67] In the liturgical worship of the church, the priest plays a pivotal role, for "the minister of a sacrament acts in the person of the whole Church, whose minister he is; while in the words uttered by him, the intention of the Church is expressed";[68] and at the

---

62. *ST* III, q. 60, a. 1, on the contrary.

63. *ST* III, q. 60, a. 2. On Aquinas's achievement of relating this theology of divine sanctification via material signs to his theological anthropology of the human person as necessarily composed of body and soul, see Berger, *Thomas Aquinas & the Liturgy*, 52–57. For more on Aquinas's anthropology, although without reference to its relationship to ritual and liturgy, see Gilles Emery, "The Unity of Man, Body and Soul in St. Thomas Aquinas," in *Trinity, Church, and the Human Person: Thomistic Essays* (Naples, FL: Sapientia Press of Ave Maria University, 2007), 209–36.

64. *ST* III, q. 60, a. 3; see also III, q. 61, a. 4.

65. *ST* III, q. 60, a. 5; see also III, q. 63, a. 1.

66. On the manner in which Aquinas relates his notions of sign, instrumental causality, Christ's passion, and the church's cultic worship, see Liam G. Walsh, *The Sacraments of Initiation: Baptism, Confirmation, Eucharist* (London: Geoffrey Chapman, 1988), 31–32.

67. Vonier, *Key to the Doctrine*, 46–47.

68. *ST* III, q. 64, a. 8, ad 2.

same time "because the priest is the appointed intermediary between God and the people; hence as it belongs to him to offer the people's gifts to God, so it belongs to him to deliver consecrated gifts to the people."[69] Nowhere is this more the case than in the eucharistic celebration: in the prayers of the Mass he represents the church, but in the consecration of the elements, the words are Christ's, which the Lord speaks through the priest who stands in *persona Christi*.[70] In his explanation of the manner in which God incorporates the church into the divine life—or, the manner in which the church participates in the life of the Trinity—the themes of epistemology, faith, and instrumentality predominate questions III, q. 60–64.

Aquinas has already laid much of the foundation concerning the first two themes, which only need brief mention here, but when he turns from Israel's sacraments to the church's, his account deepens. He dedicates the entirety of question III, q. 61 to answering the question of whether or not sacraments are necessary for salvation, and they are—although not apart from faith or as works righteousness: "Christ's passion is a sufficient cause of man's salvation," he writes, "but it does not follow that the sacraments are not also necessary for that purpose: because they obtain their effect through the power of Christ's passion; and Christ's passion is, so to say, applied to man through the sacraments according to the apostle: 'All we who are baptized in Christ Jesus, are baptized in his death.'"[71] In article two, he says, "Man's nature is the same before and after sin, but the state of his nature is not the same. Because after sin, the soul, even in its higher part, needs to receive something from corporeal things in order that it may be perfected: whereas man had no need of this in that [pre-fallen] state."[72]

The originality in Aquinas's sacramental theology, it is widely remarked, lies in his hermeneutic of instrumental causality that unites the believer's epistemology and faith, on the one hand, with the benefits of Christ's passion and God's conferral of grace, on the other. Paul Gondreau argues that precisely this hermeneutic allows Aquinas thoroughly to maintain the full humanity of the incarnate Word—the Word functioning as the principal cause and Jesus' humanity as the instrumental cause of salvation.[73] Van Nieuwenhove

---

69. *ST* III, q. 82, a. 3.

70. *ST* III, q. 82, a. 7, ad 3; III, q. 78, a. 1; and III, q. 64, a. 1.

71. *ST* III, q. 61, a. 1, ad 3.

72. *ST* III, q. 61, a. 2, ad 2. In addition to question III, q. 61, see III, q. 60, a. 4–5. See Vonier, *Key to the Doctrine*, 23–24, and Yocum, "Sacraments in Aquinas," 165–66.

73. Gondreau, "Humanity of Christ," 263–64; see Chardonnens, "Éternité du sacerdoce du Christ," 173. For an extended treatment on the relationship between the Trinity, causality, and human activity in Aquinas's sacramental theology, see Walsh, "Divine and the Human," 335–45.

concurs: "Since Christ's humanity is the instrument of his divinity, all of Christ's acts and sufferings work instrumentally in virtue of his divinity bringing our salvation" (see III, q. 64, a. 3), and Yocum states, "The humanity of Christ is not an instrument in creation, but is the divine instrument for the restoration of humanity, and that work extends to the sacraments as the acts of human agents subordinated to the incarnate Son of God."[74] For Aquinas (and for Wesley), God's grace—principal and instrumental—effects what it signifies. God's grace as a principal cause comes directly from God's power, "since grace is nothing else than a participated likeness of the Divine Nature," and "man is made a member of Christ through grace alone,"[75] because "God alone can enter the soul wherein the sacramental effect takes place."[76] Yet, the sacraments are not merely signs, and he cites Pauline texts on baptism that demonstrate instrumental causality, for water "cleanses the body, and thereby, inasmuch as it is the instrument of the divine power, cleanses the soul: since from soul and body one thing is made."[77]

A key passage from III, q. 62, a. 5 relates the sacrifice of Christ's passion to the instrumental grace of the sacraments, with specific reference to the eucharist and his two central verses, Romans 3:25 and Ephesians 5:2. The power of Christ's passion is the divine power in the sacraments: "Now the principal efficient cause of grace is God himself, in comparison with whom Christ's humanity is a united instrument, whereas the sacrament is as a separate instrument. Consequently, the saving power must needs be derived by the sacraments from Christ's Godhead through his humanity." Reiterating that sacraments are for forgiveness and divine worship, he continues, "Likewise by [the satisfaction of] his passion he inaugurated the rites of the Christian religion by offering 'himself—an oblation and a sacrifice to God' (Eph 5:2). Wherefore it is manifest that the sacraments of the Church derive their power specially from Christ's passion, the virtue of which is in a manner united to us by our receiving the sacraments."[78] The blood and water from Christ's side on the cross thus signify baptism and eucharist, in which the believer participates by faith:

74. Van Nieuwenhove, "Bearing the Marks," 294; Yocum, "Sacraments in Aquinas,"171. See Vonier, *Key to the Doctrine*, 28–29, 38–40, 70; and Berger's sections on the instrumental causality of the incarnation (*Thomas Aquinas & the Liturgy*, 64–67) and the sacraments (73–79); and Walsh, *Sacraments of Initiation: Eucharist*, 47–48. Van Nieuwenhove: "Since Christ's humanity is the instrument of the divinity, his flesh is 'vivifying' both in the eucharist and in the resurrection," ("Bearing the Marks," 295). Aquinas's entire sacramental theology drives toward this end.

75. *ST* III, q. 62, a. 1.

76. *ST* III, q. 64, a. 1.

77. *ST* III, q. 62, a. 1, ad 2; see Gal 3:27 and Ti 3:5.

78. *ST* III, q. 62, a. 5.

Christ dwells in us "by faith." Consequently, by faith Christ's power is united to us. Now the power of blotting out sin belongs in a special way to his passion. And therefore men are delivered from sin especially by faith in his passion, according to Rom 3:25: "Whom God hath proposed to be a propitiation through faith in his blood." Therefore the power of the sacraments which is ordained unto the remission of sins is derived principally from faith in Christ's passion.[79]

Thus, with respect to Christ's sacrifice—and following Aquinas's commentary on Hebrews 9–10, Levering affirms, "There is only one sacrifice, Christ's, through which human beings receive true communion in the forgiveness of sins."[80]

Eucharistic Sacrifice:
Sacramental Representation and Ecclesial Participation

The eucharist is the culmination of the church's sacramental life: "Since the whole mystery of our salvation is comprised in this sacrament, therefore is it performed with greater solemnity than the other sacraments."[81] Aquinas's teaching of transubstantiation and assent of faith in the real presence of Christ ground his sacramental theology and account for the significance and the veneration he accords the eucharist. As a sacrament, the eucharist is not only an effective sign of Christ's passion that bestows grace, but the eucharist is unique because it also "contains something which is sacred absolutely, namely, Christ's own body."[82] Moreover, since the eucharist is celebrated in memory of Christ's passion, it is not surprising that the sacrificial nature of Christ's reconciling work and the church's participation in that reconciliation figure prominently in Aquinas's eucharistic theology. He says, "The eucharist is the sacrament of Christ's passion according as a man is made perfect in union with Christ who suffered . . . so the eucharist is termed the sacrament of charity, which is the bond of perfection (Col 3:14)."[83] Thus, the effects of Christ's passion, which the eucharist commemorates, entail charity, perfection, and union with Christ.

Aquinas's words demonstrate how theology may properly use the word *sacrifice* in more than one way in reference to different events, a subtlety that was missed by both Catholics and Protestants at the Reformation.[84] With

---

79. *ST* III, q. 62, a. 5, ad 2.

80. Levering, *Sacrifice and Community*, 84.

81. *ST* III, q. 83, a. 4.

82. *ST* III, q. 73, a.1, ad 3.

83. *ST* III, q. 73, a. 3, ad 3; questions III, q. 73, 79, and 83 attend chiefly to this dimension.

84. Francis Clark, *Eucharistic Sacrifice and the Reformation*, 2nd ed. (Oxford: Blackwell, 1967), 100–101; see, too, his discussion of a similar mistake by Catholic theologians in chapters 18 and 20.

respect to its historic significance, the eucharist is called a sacrifice because "it is commemorative of our Lord's passion, which was a true sacrifice."[85] His treatment of the eucharist is methodologically consistent with his treatment of the Passover (with the caveat that the former gives grace and contains Christ): both are sacraments, both are sacrifices, and both rely on Christ's sacrifice for their signification and efficaciousness. Aquinas's objector notes that, technically, each sacrament entails a sacred act, so that either all or none deserve the name sacrifice. Aquinas clarifies: "This sacrament is called a 'Sacrifice' inasmuch as it represents the passion of Christ; but it is termed a 'Host' inasmuch as it contains Christ, who is a 'host' [sacrifice, victim] of sweetness [Eph 5:2]."[86] Elsewhere he follows Jerome, noting that Christ is both "guest and banquet, is both the partaker and what is eaten."[87]

Along these same lines Aquinas offers another nuance to eucharistic sacrifice: not only is the sacrament of the eucharist called a sacrifice, but also "the celebration of this sacrament is called a sacrifice": first, because it "is an image [like a painting] representing Christ's passion, which is his true sacrifice"; secondly, because of its effect, "by this sacrament, we are made partakers of the fruit of our Lord's passion."[88] Aquinas sees Christ's passion symbolized throughout the liturgy, as he knew it, which he expounds over the course of question III, q. 83. The ability of the rite to represent Christ's passion derives from the sacrificial aspect of the sacrament (because it contains Christ's own body), as attested to by the organization of his treatise in which the first nine questions focus on the sacrament itself. The distinction, therefore, between the sacrament and the rite should by no means be pressed. Levering remarks, "The 'representation of our Lord's passion' is the sacrifice, and the 'participation of its fruits' is our communion in charity with Christ and each other. . . . It is our offering of Christ's sacrifice that enables, in the sacrament of the eucharist, our sharing in its fruits of ecclesial unity and communion."[89] Thus the sacrament's representation of Christ's sacrifice and the church's participation in it emerge as two inseparable themes. Historically, contention over eucharistic sacrifice has revolved around the sacrificial dimension of the sacrament rather than the liturgy as a whole. It is an achievement that *BEM* defined the eucharist as the whole liturgy that includes Word and Table, even though in popular Protestant imagination and

85. *ST* III, q. 73, a. 4.
86. *T* III, q. 73, a. 4, ad 3.
87. *ST* III, q. 81, a. 1, on the contrary.
88. *ST* III, q. 83, a. 1.
89. Matthew Levering, "John Paul II and Aquinas on the Eucharist," *Nova et Vetera* 3 no. 3 (2005): 651–52.

parlance the eucharist still refers almost exclusively to the sacrament. Could it be that Protestantism's practice of privileging the Word in its Sunday liturgy was a contributing factor for why it lost sight of the sacrificial dimension of the whole liturgy?

Sacramental Representation

For Aquinas, Christ's self-offering on the cross is the "fulfillment and transformation of Israel's sacrificial liturgy," which leads Levering to ask, "What kind of sacrifice, however, is the eucharist?"[90] With respect to the different aspects of the eucharist—i.e., as sacrament, reality and sacrament, and reality—Aquinas discusses four of Israel's sacrifices. As to the sacrament, Melchizedek's offering is the "chief figure"; as to reality and sacrament, which is "Christ crucified," it is the day of atonement; and as to the reality, which is the effect, the chief figure is the manna, which as corporeal refreshment and growth is analogous to the spiritual needs of the soul. Now, "the paschal lamb is the chief figure of this sacrament, because it represents it in every respect": first, it consists of unleavened bread; second, the immolation of the lamb was a figure of Christ's passion, which the eucharist represents; and third, the effect of Passover was to preserve Israel from death and to deliver it from captivity.[91] For Aquinas, therefore, the paschal lamb is the chief figure of both Christ's passion and the eucharist:

> Without faith in the passion there could never be any salvation, according to Rom 3:25: *Whom God hath proposed to be a propitiation, though faith in his blood.* It was necessary accordingly that there should be at all times among men something to show forth our Lord's passion; the chief sacrament of which in the Old Law was the Paschal Lamb. Hence the Apostle says (1 Cor 7): *Christ our Pasch is sacrificed.* But its successor under the New Testament is the sacrament of the eucharist, which is a remembrance of the passion now past, just as the other was figurative of the passion to come. And so it was fitting that when the hour of the passion was come, Christ should institute a new sacrament after celebrating the old.[92]

With this last comment, Aquinas teaches that the power of the eucharist to represent Christ's passion derives from the institution of the sacrament by the Lord himself.

90. Levering, *Sacrifice and Community*, 82

91. *ST* III, q. 73, a. 6; see III, q. 73, 1.

92. *ST* III, q. 73, a. 5. See Peter M. Candler, "Liturgically Trained Memory: A Reading of Summa Theologiae III.83," *Modern Theology* 20, no. 3 (2004): 423–45: "Figures, for Aquinas, analogically participate in the realities which they represent" (432).

What specifically, then, is sacramental representation? In questions III, q. 73 and III q. 83 Aquinas speaks of the eucharist in terms of *commemoration, representation, remembrance, memorial, image, pattern,* and *recollection* of Christ's passion. While some words like *memorial* and *remembrance* remind the believer of the past, the word *representation,* in the sense of re-presentation, evokes more strongly Aquinas's intentions. On the spectrum from *similitude* to *exemplary cause* to signification, *representation* falls between the latter two. *Similitude* is too strong, since the eucharist is not for Aquinas a real, historic, re-crucifixion of Christ; and *signification* is too weak, since Christ is really present in a way that a character in a painting metaphysically is not. In effect, the language of *imago repraesentativa* (q. 83, a. 1, ad 2) of the eucharistic celebration reasserts its sacramental quality. Sacrificial representation is therefore completely qualified by and incorporated within the definition of sacrament.[93] As Humbrecht summarizes, "There is clearly, therefore, a mode of representation proper to the eucharist such that the unique immolation of Christ is represented in his celebration, and because of this we are rendered participants in the effects of this salvific immolation, because the sacramental immolation participates itself in the virtue of the immolation of Calvary."[94]

While *representation* carries the sense of sacramental reality, it is broader than what Aquinas means when he says that the sacrament contains Christ (i.e., his real presence), with the term *contain* being more precise (*Christus contentus*).[95] If *representation* denotes the modality of Christ's presence, what specifically is the nature of his real presence? How is Christ actually present; is there a strict one-to-one correspondence between the sacramental imaging and Christ's person—in other words, is Christ really present as crucified? Vonier begins his detailed exposition by clearly ruling out of bounds what must not be maintained. He vigorously denies any "ultra-realist" position that puts "Christ's self first, the sacrifice and the sacrament after," and he notes, "The immolation itself never causes a new state, either in Christ's Person or in Christ's Body and Blood," because what is immolated are the material signs that signify Christ's body and blood. The eucharist, therefore, is neither a historic prolongation of Christ's passion, nor is it a re-crucifixion of Christ's humanity,[96] because Christ's body

---

93. Thierry-Dominique Humbrecht, "L'eucharistie, 'représentation' du sacrifice du Christ, selon saint Thomas," *Revue Thomiste* 98 (Juillet–Septembre 1998): 360–61, 369, 378; Humbrecht sees Aquinas making an analogy with the word *image* between the Word's representation of the Father as his image and the rite's imaging of Christ's passion (369); see Vonier, *Key to the Doctrine,* 55–60.

94. Humbrecht, "L' eucharistie," 371, my translation.

95. Humbrecht, "L' eucharistie," 373.

96. Vonier, *Key to the Doctrine,* 108–9, 115, 135–37, 261; Humbrecht agrees with Vonier on what the eucharist is not: Humbrecht, "L' eucharistie," 364–65, 378.

is not present in the sacrament the way a created body is present in a place; nor does Christ come to be in the sacrament through a process of local motion, because Christ's resurrected and ascended body remains in heaven.[97] His resurrected body, therefore, is not scattered across many altars, nor broken at each fraction, nor—just to be clear—is his body masticated in its proper species, but spiritually, i.e. sacramentally, eaten in the species of bread and wine.[98]

Sacramental presence differs from the presence of created reality as a result of divine transcendence and power: "But in Christ, being in himself and being under the sacrament are not the same thing, because when we say that he is under this sacrament, we express a kind of relationship to this sacrament."[99] Delineating how Christ is not present in the sacrament provides space for Aquinas to demonstrate how he is. Aquinas offers a counterfactual thought experiment to illustrate how "Christ's body is substantially the same in this sacrament, as in its proper species, but not after the same fashion."[100] Christ celebrated the first eucharist at the Last Supper, and when he consecrated the elements he gave himself to the disciples as spiritual food, just as he continues to give himself to the church, and he gave his passible body to the disciples in an impassible manner, analogous to his self-gift on the cross.[101] On the other hand, had one of the disciples celebrated or reserved the eucharist while Christ was on the cross or in the tomb, the body of Christ alone would remain under the bread and the blood alone under the wine, and his soul would not have been present, because at Christ's passion his body, blood, and soul were each separated from one another.[102] Upon his resurrection, though, his body, blood, and soul are reunited—even while they were never separated from his divine nature—and he is never to die again.[103] "Sacramental representation," therefore, neither "brings Christ's passion into the present" nor "returns Christ's glorified body to its state on the Cross." Instead,

---

97. See III, q. 75, a. 1, ad 3; q. 75, a. 2; and "Hence in no way is Christ's body locally in this sacrament" (III, q. 76, a. 5); "the accidents of Christ's body have no immediate relationship either to this sacrament or to adjacent bodies" (q. 76, a. 6); see Vonier, *Key to the Doctrine*, 88.

98. See Levering, "Transubstantiation," in *Sacrifice and Community*, 115–67, and Reinhard Hütter, *Aquinas on Transubstantiation: The Real Presence of Christ in the Eucharist* (Washington, DC: The Catholic University of America Press, 2019).

99. *ST* III, q. 76, a. 6.

100. *ST* III, q. 81, a. 4.

101. *ST* III, q. 81, a. 3; see John Paul II, *Ecclesia de eucharistia*, Encyclical Letter, April 17, 2003, 3–4; hereafter *EE*. For reflections on how the priest speaks *in persona Christi*, see Vonier, *Key to the Doctrine*, 141, 151, 234, 240, 248, and Aidan Nichols, "The Holy Oblation: On the Primacy of Eucharistic Sacrifice," *Downside Review* 122, no. 429 (2004): 266–69.

102. *ST* III, q. 76, a. 2, and III, q. 81, a. 4.

103. Rom 6:9; 1 Cor 15; see Vonier, *Key to the Doctrine*, 131–33.

Christ "draws the present into his heavenly reality . . . it is we, not Christ, who are changed by the sacrament of the eucharist."[104] Thus, it is the living and glorified Christ—concomitantly with the Godhead—who makes himself present to his church in the eucharist by way of the separate presentation of the body and the blood signifying his sacrifice on the cross.[105]

Aquinas clearly differentiates the grace of baptismal forgiveness from that of eucharistic forgiveness, in part, no doubt, based on the Bible's clear differentiation: "The sacrament of baptism is directly ordained for the remission of punishment and guilt: not so the eucharist, because baptism is given to man as dying with Christ, whereas the eucharist is given as by way of nourishing and perfecting him through Christ."[106] Even while he draws numerous comparisons with baptism throughout III, q. 73–83 (e.g., the reception of grace, incorporation with Christ, ecclesial unity), nevertheless, he makes an important distinction between them. Through baptism God returns the now-justified sinner to friendship with God; it is a one-time, drastic restoration from darkness to light, from death to life. Through the eucharist, God empowers the sojourner on the way to perfection, or deification; it is the daily nourishing meal in which the believer sacramentally feasts on Christ by faith who strengthens the soul.[107]

The relationship between sign and grace is similar in both baptism and eucharist (real presence not withstanding); the former is sacramental rebirth, and the latter is sacramental sacrifice. No one posits, for example, that in dying and rising with Christ at baptism Christ actually dies and rises again; so also at the eucharist, Aquinas does not teach that Jesus is re-crucified. A sacrament is essentially an efficacious representation: baptismal representation yields justification and adoption; eucharistic representation yields spiritual sustenance and deeper bonds of cruciformity and friendship with God: "In both we have nothing else than a representation—in the technical sense of the word—of Christ's death and its application to the individual soul."[108] In different ways, both sacraments represent Christ's passion, and (again in different ways) both

104. Levering, *Sacrifice and Community*, 91–92. See Candler, "Liturgically Trained Memory": "The radical implication here is that by re-narration of the historical event in liturgical time, we take part in the very event we commemorate. Thus memory is transformed from noetic recall into the performance of participation in the divine" (433).

105. *ST* III, q. 76, a. 1, ad 1. See Stepan Martin Filip, "*Imago Repræsentativa Passionis Christi*: St. Thomas Aquinas on the Essence of the Sacrifice of the Mass," *Nova et Vetera* 7, no 2 (Spring 2009): 405–37.

106. *ST* III, q. 79, a. 5, ad 1.

107. *ST* III, q. 73, a. 1; III, q. 73, a. 6, ad 1. *BEM* makes the same distinction between the two sacraments.

108. Vonier, *Key to the Doctrine*, 140; see John Paul II, *EE*, 11–12.

bestow effects of its saving grace. Note here how Vonier, faithful to Aquinas, maintains the complementary emphases between the importance of an individual's assent of faith in perceiving the presence of Christ and believing in his salvation and of the essential supra-subjective aspect of Christ's real presence and transubstantiation, which he elsewhere affirms.[109]

Aquinas's teaching on Christ's real presence inspires Vonier to remark on the representative nature of the eucharistic sacrifice that is commensurate with Humbrecht (in a manner that a Wesleyan can fully affirm). The sacramental representation is the memorial, indeed even the monument, of Christ's passion without it being a re-crucifixion.[110]

> As the eucharistic Body and Blood are such a complete representation of the broken Son of God on Calvary, they are also the most immediate and complete contact of the soul with all the saving power of Golgotha. So it can be said that in the eucharistic sacrifice Christ is truly immolated, because the immolation of Christ on Calvary [signified by the elements] is brought home to us in such a realistic manner. At Mass we do not say that Christ is immolated anew in the eucharistic sacrifice, for this would mean a substantial process of disintegration in the very Person of Christ such as he is now, a thing not to be admitted. But we say that he is immolated, because the Calvary immolation is represented so truly, and is applied so directly, through the eucharistic Body and Blood.[111]

Ecclesial Participation

In exploring the significance of sacramental representation, we have already alluded to the church's participatory role in Christ's sacrifice and noted that these two concepts cannot be entirely separated. What is more, they are in fact two aspects of the same event. Yet once we have understood the nature of Christ's presence and agency in the eucharist through sacramental representation, it is likewise essential to understand the church's agency through participation, as well. The term *ecclesial participation* seeks to denote, therefore, this complex of activity and agency: how the church's agency participates in Christ's priesthood; the relationship of the church's sacrifice to Christ's; the corporate nature of human agency as the body of Christ; as well as the fruits of this unity and participation. For Aquinas, the eucharist is a sacrifice not only because it represents Christ's passion, but because the church offers it. Put another way,

---

109. See, too, Humbrecht, "L' eucharistie," 384–85.

110. Vonier, *Key to the Doctrine*, 123, 138–39.

111. Vonier, *Key to the Doctrine*, 125–26; see Levering, "John Paul II and Aquinas on the Eucharist," 653.

in order to receive the effects of Christ's reconciliation, the church must become a partaker of Christ's sacrifice, and this the church does through sacramental representation. "The Church's offering of Christ's sacrifice, her sharing in Christ's holy sacrificial act, culminates in her reception of, or communion in, the sacrifice. . . . When the Church sacramentally represents Christ's sacrifice, she receives what she has sacramentally represented."[112]

Aquinas develops the relationship between sacramental representation and ecclesial participation by placing his discussion within the enactment of the church's liturgy.[113] For instance, in question III, q. 79 concerning the effects of the eucharist, he says, "In this sacrament we may consider both that from which it derives its effect, namely, Christ contained in it, as also his passion represented by it; and that through which it works its effect, namely, the use of the sacrament, and its species."[114]

Now the effects of the eucharist derive directly from Christ's passion, whose "power" works in the eucharist and is ordered to three purposes: (1) primarily "for securing our eternal heritage" (III, q. 79, a. 2, "attaining eternal glory"); (2) "for justifying grace, which is by faith according to Romans 3:25"; and (3) "for removing sins which are the impediments to both of these [former] things."[115] Complementarily, because Christ is contained in the eucharist, the sacrament gives grace in accordance with Christ's presence: (1) by coming into the Christian sacramentally, the eucharist gives life and grace, just as Christ did in coming into the world; (2) as food nourishes the body, the eucharist works also in the spiritual life "by sustaining, giving increase, restoring, and giving delight"; (3) one loaf and one cup come from many grains and grapes; thus, the eucharist is a "sign of unity" and "bond of charity."[116] In addition to the fact that the eucharist is a sacrifice because it contains Christ and represents Christ, by which the church shares in Christ's sacrifice, the use that the church and individuals make of the eucharist in offering it also shapes its sacrificial character and its effects.

---

112. Levering, "John Paul II and Aquinas on the Eucharist," 652.

113. Candler investigates how Aquinas understands the liturgy of the entire Mass as "an image representing Christ's sacrifice" ("Liturgically Trained Memory," 427), and he seeks to unpack the theological significance of Aquinas's commentary on the liturgy in question 83.

114. ST III, q. 79, a. 2; see Walsh, *Sacraments of Initiation*, 242–43. Bruce Marshall shows how Aquinas's teaching that the sacrament represents Christ's passion and contains Christ is central to his theology of sacrifice; Marshall, "The Whole Mystery of our Salvation: Saint Thomas Aquinas on the Eucharist as Sacrifice," in *Rediscovering Aquinas and the Sacraments: Studies in Sacramental Theology*, ed. Matthew Levering and Michael Dauphinais (Chicago: Hillenbrand, 2009), 47–57.

115. *ST* III, q. 78, a. 3.

116. *ST* III, q. 79, a. 1.

In the Last Supper, Christ gives himself to the apostles under the species of bread and wine. Yet this self-gift is far more than a fellowship meal or a mere memorial. Christ interprets his impending death as an expiatory sacrifice—pure self-offering to the Father—made on behalf of others. By representing the separation of his body and blood in bread and wine and by giving himself to his followers through them, Christ instituted the sacrificial (i.e., cultic) meal of the New Covenant and provided a means of incorporating the church in his redeeming work, which culminated in the cross.[117] The Last Supper, then, is a sacrifice because it participates in the redemption of Christ's cross, and the eucharist is the church's ongoing participation in Christ's saving work. "At the Last Supper, Christ can consume his own body and blood only if his eucharistic body and blood are present through sacramental representation. Christ is present at the Last Supper in two modes, his natural mode and his sacramental mode."[118]

In Catholic teaching, therefore, the faithful who partake of the eucharist find themselves in essentially the same relationship with Christ as did the apostles in the Last Supper, with the only chief difference that the resurrected and ascended Lord gives himself to his disciples through the ministry of the church's priesthood rather than by his own hands.[119] "The priest's consecration of the sacrament constitutes a sacrificial offering that is both Christ's sacrifice and the Church's sacramental-sacrificial sharing in Christ's sacrifice."[120] Thus, the church is not a passive recipient that only receives divine grace; rather, it is active in offering the eucharist—in obedience to Christ's command to "Do this . . . "—and thereby unites with Christ's priesthood in the eucharist.

If Protestantism has failed to appreciate the liturgical, cultic (and even doxological) facets of Christ's cross, as suggested, the same may be said in a related fashion of the Last Supper and its use in the church. Catholic theology attests to continuity—from the patristics through Aquinas and Trent to John

117. Levering, *Sacrifice and Community*, 84–85: "In offering his sacrificial body and blood to his disciples at the Last Supper, he witnesses to the sacramental mode in which he makes his sacrifice present to his Church . . . he instructs the Church to perform a liturgical action."

118. Levering, "John Paul II and Aquinas on the Eucharist," 651. See *ST* III, q. 81, a. 1, ads 2–3. Levering borrows the language of "sacramental representation" from John Paul II; see *EE*, §11.

119. *ST* III, q. 82, a. 1: "Such is the dignity of this sacrament that it is performed only as in the person of Christ."

120. Levering, *Sacrifice and Community*, 91; see Candler: "Christ is the identity leant to the priest and people, and Christ is the end towards which they are ordained"; "Liturgically Trained Memory," 428. See, too, Guy Mansini, "Representation and Agency in the Eucharist," *Thomist* 62 (1998): 499–517.

Paul II—in its teaching on this point.[121] The question of agency in the sacraments quickly became a point of contention among the Reformers that, in part, led them to reject the eucharist as a sacrifice. In his distinctive way, we will see that Wesley—far from denying sacrificial agency of the church in the eucharist—insists that in order for the church to receive God's grace, it must make a sacrifice.[122]

The relationship between the effects/fruits of the eucharist and its use comes through most clearly when Aquinas responds to the question of whether or not the eucharist benefits people other than the recipients. Since sacraments are ordered for the benefit of those who receive them, e.g. baptism, and since the eucharist is also a sacrament, initially it appears that the answer would be in the negative.[123] The eucharist differs from other sacraments, however, because it is also a sacrifice: "Receiving is of the very nature of the sacrament, but offering belongs to the nature of sacrifice."[124] It is this dimension as a sacrifice that makes the eucharist beneficial for partakers and non-partakers alike.[125] Consequently, when Aquinas answers the original question in the affirmative, his answer is two-fold:

> For, it has the nature of a sacrifice inasmuch as in this sacrament Christ's passion is represented, whereby Christ "offered himself a Victim to God (Eph 5:2), and it has the nature of a sacrament inasmuch as invisible grace is bestowed in this sacrament under a visible species. So, then, this sacrament benefits recipients by way both of sacrament and of sacrifice, because it is offered for all who partake of it. . . . But to others who do not receive it, it is beneficial by way of sacrifice, inasmuch as it is offered for their salvation.[126]

A sacrifice offered for the benefit of others? Read in isolation, Aquinas's answer might appear open to the Reformers' critiques concerning sacrifice; however, in its larger context, it becomes clear that in no way is Aquinas proposing an additional sacrifice independent of Christ's sacrifice. On the one hand, we have just seen how Aquinas understands the church's eucharist to be a continuation of the Last Supper and the means by which partaking and offering go together. Indeed, Aquinas also understands the church's use of the eucha-

---

121. While Benedict XVI and Francis have taught and preached on the eucharist, John Paul II's is the last encyclical to treat eucharistic sacrifice in great detail.

122. Clark, *Eucharistic Sacrifice*, 108. See Walsh, "Divine and the Human," 342; see, too, his treatment of "sacramental causality," in *Sacraments of Initiation*, 61–64.

123. *ST* III, q. 79, a. 7, ob 1.

124. *ST* III, q. 79, a. 7, ad 3.

125. See Schenk's section, "Thomas and the Sacrifice of the Mass," 189–92.

126. *ST* III, q. 79, a. 7.

rist—i.e., to offer it sacrificially for others, to imitate obediently Jesus' action and command at the Last Supper. The eucharist is a sacrament and a sacrifice—received and offered by some, and offered for others—inasmuch as "our Lord expressed both ways, saying (Mt 26:28, with Lk 22:20): *Which for you*, i.e. who receive it, *and for many*, i.e. others, *shall be shed unto the remission of sins.*"[127]

At the same time, we have also seen how Aquinas's anthropology and his theology of religion and sacrifice are constitutive of right worship, and how this has come together in the eucharist in his concepts of sacramental representation and participation. Aquinas is, himself, aware that the idea of a sacrifice that benefits others might be misunderstood: if the eucharist were effective in others besides the recipient, the objection goes, "A man might happen to acquire grace and glory and forgiveness of sin without doing or receiving anything himself, through another receiving or offering this sacrament."[128] This objection, though, illustrates that it misconceives the relationship both between the individual and the church and between the church and its head, because the eucharist as sacrifice is embedded within the sacramental practice of the church and not apart from it.[129] Aquinas corrects this misconception in two ways.

First, he appeals to the practice of the church (and cites the liturgy in his response) by noting that the eucharistic sacrifice is not imposed upon the non-recipient in some materially causal fashion; rather, what the church in fact does is pray for its members: "Prayer is made for many others during the celebration of this sacrament; which would serve no purpose were the sacrament not beneficial to others."[130] Second, the one for whom the eucharist is offered and who benefits from the church's prayers must also be united to Christ, similar to the way in which the universal work of Christ requires an individual's faithful response. "As Christ's passion benefits all . . . whereas it produces no effect except in those who are united with [it] through faith and charity, so likewise this sacrifice, which is the memorial of our Lord's passion, has no effect except in those who are united with this sacrament through faith and charity."[131]

What occurs, therefore, in the eucharistic sacrifice is an intensification of the flame of charity and the bond of unity between Christ, the church, and the individual. Catherine Pickstock remarks, "Regarding the Mystery insofar as it is an oblation, the people's praise in singing the Offertory is now realized

---

127. *ST* III, q. 79, a. 7; see III, q. 78, a. 3, ad 8: "[Jesus] says expressly, *for you*, the Jews, *and many*, namely the Gentiles; or, *for you* who eat it, and *for many*, for whom it is offered."

128. *ST* III, q. 79, a. 7, ob 2.

129. Walsh, *Sacraments of Initiation*, 241–42.

130. *ST* III, q. 79, a. 7, on the contrary.

131. *ST* III, q. 79, a. 7, ad 2.

as they imitate in turn the mimetic performances of the choir or priest, for, as Aquinas says, this expresses the joy of the offerers."[132] Aquinas highlights the centrality of desire in uniting with Christ in the eucharist on the part of the individual at several points. Sometimes it is to note that the individual's disposition toward, or desire for, the eucharist is an extension of his or her desire for Christ[133]; or to note the continuity between the "ancient sacrifices" of the "men of old" and the eucharist on the basis of desire[134]; or to adjudicate between the prayers of the church and those of a wicked priest[135]; or to reflect on the fervor of charity in the individual's reception of the eucharist in conjunction with medieval penitential practices[136]; or to affirm that the individual "can be changed into Christ, and be incorporated in him by mental desire, even without receiving this sacrament."[137] In short, to offer the eucharist in sacrifice is the means, externally and in sign, by which the church shares internally in the sacrifice of Christ by faith and charity. Thus, when St. Paul writes, "Are not they that eat of the sacrifices, partakers of the altar?" (1Cor 10:18), Aquinas paraphrases Augustine's interpretation: "Now whoever offers sacrifice must be a sharer in the sacrifice, because the outward sacrifice he offers is a sign of the inner sacrifice whereby he offers himself to God."[138] Commenting on Aquinas's anthropology of the unity between body and soul, and following Catherine Pickstock's theology of gift, Levering remarks, "In such receiving (communion in his body and blood), we receive a *sacrificial offering*, and thus our reception itself belongs to the movement of sacrificial offering."[139]

Thus, the church's sacrifice of the eucharist is not a sacrifice independent of Christ's sacrifice, but it is a participation in Christ's priestly, sacrificial office.[140] As the recapitulation and fulfillment of humanity's right relationship

132. Catherine Pickstock, "Thomas Aquinas and the Quest for the Eucharist," *Modern Theology* 15, no. 2 (1999): 171. See Candler, "Liturgically Trained Memory," 429, 439–40; Levering, "John Paul II and Aquinas on the Eucharist," 648, and references to Aquinas's questions III, q. 79, a. 1, ad 2; III, q. 81, a. 1, ad 3; and III, q. 83, a. 1, ad 2. Wesleyans can appreciate here the relationship between the eucharist and sanctification.

133. *ST* III, q. 79, a. 2, ad 2.

134. *ST* III, q. 83, a. 4, ad 8.

135. *ST* III, q. 82, a. 6.

136. See Romanus Cessario, *Christian Satisfaction in Aquinas: Towards a Personalist Understanding* (Lanham, MD: University Press of America, 1982), 44–47, 252–54.

137. *ST* III, q. 73, a. 3, ad 2; see III, q. 80, a. 1; q. 80, a..1, ad 3; q. 80, a. 2; and Levering, *Sacrifice and Community*, 109–10.

138. *ST* III, q. 82, a. 4.

139. Levering, *Sacrifice and Community*, 176; see Catherine Pickstock, *After Writing: On the Liturgical Consummation of Philosophy*, Challenges in Contemporary Theology (Malden, MA: Blackwell, 1998).

140. Marshall, "Whole Mystery of our Salvation," 58.

to God who reconciles humanity to God by his pure self-offering, Christ remains in the eucharist both victim and priest, the one who offers and the one offered. Citing Augustine again, he writes:

> Sins are commemorated in the New Law, not on account of the inefficacy of the priesthood of Christ, as though sins were not sufficiently expiated by Him: but in regard to those who either are not willing to be participators in His sacrifice, such as unbelievers, for whose sins we pray that they be converted; or who, after taking part in this sacrifice, fall away from it by whatsoever kind of sin. The Sacrifice which is offered every day in the Church is not distinct from that which Christ Himself offered, but is a commemoration thereof. Wherefore Augustine says (De Civ. De. x, 20): "Christ Himself both is the priest who offers it and the victim: the sacred token of which He wished to be the daily Sacrifice of the Church."[141]

Levering notes, "Certainly Christ is the one who offers the sacrifice of himself, both on Calvary and in the sacrament of the eucharist . . . the Church, led by her priests, offers up his sacrifice in, with, and through him. Thus Christ's sacrifice becomes the Church's sacrifice, as the Body is conformed to the Head."[142]

Aquinas's teaching on Christ's priestly ministry in the eucharist leads Berger to contend that understanding the liturgy as "true act" of the church's high priest is essential to counter the "unbridled subjectivity" currently besetting the Catholic theology of the liturgy by showing the relevance of Aquinas's insight on these matters in contemporary authoritative texts such as *Mediator Dei*, *Sacrosanctum Concilium* (no. 7), and the new *Catechism of the Catholic Church* (no. 1069).[143] Christ's presidency in the eucharist is theologically the most satisfactory way of explaining the relationship between the atonement of Christ's passion and God's saving work in humankind: "Christ himself, as the eternal high priest and head of his mystical body, continues in the rite of his Church that worship of God and atonement which culminates in his sacrifice on the cross and which turned his entire life into service to God."[144]

---

141. *ST* III, q. 22, a. 3, ad 2. In his question on the Rite of the eucharist, Aquinas cites Ambrose to the same effect: III, q. 83, a.1, ad 1.

142. Levering, *Sacrifice and Community*, 166.

143. Berger, *Thomas Aquinas & the Liturgy*, 72

144. Berger, *Thomas Aquinas & the Liturgy*, 70; see his section "Liturgy as a Real Act of the Eternal High Priest," 69–73. Wesley and his interpreters make precisely the same comment. See, too, Liam Walsh, "Liturgy in the Theology of St. Thomas," *Thomist* 38 (1974): 580: "the first thing a theologian should say about liturgy is that it is the action of God."

Conclusion:
Aquinas's Theological Synthesis and Ecumenical Prospect

Aquinas's theology of eucharistic sacrifice demonstrates an exceptionally broad synthesis in his thought across a wide range of topics. In order to put his teaching on eucharistic sacrifice in proper perspective, it was necessary to understand his thought on such questions as religion, sacrifice, worship, justice, Christ's priesthood and passion, and the sacraments. Additionally, we have had to consider in more detail the paired concepts of divine and human agency; the eucharist as sacrament and sacrifice; the believer's interior sacrifice of the heart and the church's exterior sacrifice of the liturgy; and sacramental representation and ecclesial participation.

Eucharistic sacrifice, according to Aquinas, consists of several aspects that can be enumerated discretely, but that in fact come together as a comprehensive whole. Anthropologically, humanity communicates through signs, and when this communication occurs between humanity and God, these signs become sacraments—i.e., signs of a sacred reality that they represent. For the church, its sacraments not only represent a sacred reality, but they also effect what they represent because Christ is really present working through them.[145] Thus, Jesus instituted the eucharist not for God's sake, but for the church's, as the means by which the Lord in his wisdom extends the saving work of his passion to all times and places by representing his death in the separation of his body and blood signified in the eucharistic species of bread and wine, and as the means by which those united to Christ testify bodily to their interior sacrifice—the sacrifice of the heart—as they offer themselves to God as living sacrifices. Soteriologically, the passion—as a sacrificial and liturgical act—and the eucharist that commemorates it satisfy God's order of justice because Christ alone as humanity's representative and mediator can offer himself to the Father in love, thereby recapitulating and fulfilling God's purpose and goal for humankind. And eschatologically, because Jesus remains forever the priest and victim of the eucharist, and because the eucharistic sacrifice is a sacramental participation in what it commemorates—namely, Christ's sacrifice—the members of Christ's body are conformed to his cruciform likeness through the deifying power of his Spirit in whom they are united to the Triune God. In sum, "Christ as priest enables believers to share in his sacrifice, that is, to share in himself. All become

---

145. Benoît-Dominique de la Soujeoule makes this clear: "The Importance of the Definition of Sacraments as Signs," in *Ressourcement Thomism: Sacred Doctrine, the Sacraments, and the Moral Life; Essays in Honor of Romanus Cessario*, ed. Reinhard Huetter and Matthew Levering (Washington, DC: The Catholic University of America Press, 2010), 128–29.

sharers in the one sacrifice, sharers in the justice of the one priest and victim, sharers in the reconciliation and deification that Christ, the incarnate Son, accomplishes"[146]

Roch Kereszty highlights the significance of Aquinas's theology for contemporary ecumenical dialogue. He sketches, historically, three ways in which theology has expressed the relationship between Christ's sacrifice and church's eucharistic sacrifice. First, "Christ is the ultimate subject of each eucharistic sacrifice of the church," who does not repeatedly offer himself, but in whose unique sacrificial self-offering the church participates sacramentally. Second, the church—and not Christ—is the subject of the eucharistic sacrifice, which offers Christ repeatedly in each Mass. Third, in "reference to the historical sacrifice," nonetheless, "Christ posits a new sacrificial act . . . or endures a new sacrificial act" with each eucharistic sacrifice.

Antiochene theology in the East (represented by Chrysostom and his notion of *anamnesis*) and Augustine's theology in the West of the daily sacrament (*sacramentum quotidianum*) in which the church "learns to offer herself through it," characterize the first position. Aquinas's theology follows theirs.[147] The second position—represented by the medieval and pre-Reformation era in which theology separated Christ's real presence and the Mass's sacrificial character in which the church offers Christ repeatedly—"makes Luther's protest quite justifiable." Post-Tridentine theories fall into the third scenario and raise as many questions as they seek to answer. He concludes:

> Only in the biblical and patristic renewal of the twentieth century did Catholic theologians and the magisterium rediscover the thanksgiving and praise dimension of the eucharist; only then did they re-apply and deepen the Thomistic notion of sacramental sacrifice. In each and every Mass not only are the offerer and the victim the same Christ who offered himself on the cross, but the one and the same act of His self-offering is participated in by the church. Thus understood, the Mass does not add a new sacrifice of Christ to his perfect historical self-offering. The additional newness of each and every Mass consists in a church community's sacramental and existential participation in Christ's perfect once-and-for-all sacrifice.[148]

146. Levering, "Aquinas on the Liturgy of the Eucharist," 191. See Schenk's section, "Thomas on the True Priest of the Eucharist and His Concelebrants," 193–96.

147. Roch Kereszty, "The Eucharist of the Church and the One Self-Offering of Christ," in *Rediscovering the Eucharist: Ecumenical Conversations*, ed. Roch A. Kereszty (New York: Paulist Press, 2003), 247.

148. Kereszty, "Eucharist of the Church," 249.

Both Berger and Kereszty highlight the influence of Aquinas's position on contemporary Catholic documents, and these will be considered in more detail in chapter 5. At the same time, the significance of this "biblical and patristic" position, in which the church participates in the priestly ministry of Christ who makes available the grace of his passion in all times and places in the eucharist, extends beyond Catholic theologians and the magisterium. Ecumenically, as a result of the liturgical and ecumenical renewal movements of the twentieth century, *BEM* sought to identify convergence on the eucharist by emphasizing the anamnetic aspect of the church's celebration as a response to the risen Christ's agency and presidency, although *BEM* was unable fully to adumbrate the sacrificial dimension of the common patristic tradition. More in keeping with Aquinas and unlike *BEM*, John Wesley—the key traditioning voice in Methodism—was not so constrained. His theology of eucharistic sacrifice is based on the biblical revelation of Jesus the great high priest—the same yesterday, today, and forever—who administers the sanctifying grace of his passion through the eucharist and whose sacrifice the church commemorates by offering to the Father the signs of the Lord's death.

CHAPTER 3

John Wesley's Theological Anthropology and Sacramental Theology

In this chapter and the next we examine closely John Wesley's theological anthropology and his theology of eucharistic sacrifice, analogously to chapter 2, in which we considered Thomas Aquinas's thought on the same topic. As a founder of Methodism and a principal traditioning voice throughout its history, Wesley developed a theology that not only has contributed to the theological legacy of his followers, but more importantly, continues to inform and shape the theology and lives of contemporary Methodist theologians and churches. To be sure, John Wesley (even when joined with his brother Charles) is not the only source of theological inspiration for contemporary Methodism, as the different and sometimes divergent responses to *BEM* demonstrated in chapter 1. Nonetheless, the influence of his theology upon Methodism remains inestimable.

Two helpful works by Owen Cummings and Randy Maddox serve to highlight the motivation and methodology, respectively, behind this chapter. Owen Cummings includes John Wesley in his historical survey of some of the church's key eucharistic theologians.[1] In and of itself, this is not surprising. But what is surprising, at least to some (and perhaps also to Wesley himself),[2] is the connection he makes between Wesley's theology of eucharistic sacrifice (based on Daniel Brevint and select hymns from Charles) and Catholic teaching on the Mass as a sacrifice. Citing the Catholic catechism, Cummings enumerates a threefold rationale behind this teaching: (1) the eucharist is "the making present and the sacramental offering [of Christ's] unique sacrifice"; (2) "it re-presents [makes present] the unique sacrifice of the cross"; which means (3) that the eucharist "applies the fruit of that sacrifice to the participants."[3] Cummings is right that Wesley indeed espouses these three views, and thus on the topic of sacrifice he writes, "There does not appear to be any great doctrinal distance between Wesley and the *Catechism* on these

---

1. Cummings, *Eucharistic Doctors.*
2. Throughout the chapter, reference to "Wesley" means John Wesley.
3. Cummings, *Eucharistic Doctors*, 222.

points."[4] Yet while Cummings's analysis makes important connections on eucharistic sacrifice, its chief contribution—because of its brevity—is to motivate further discussion: what is the relationship between "these points" of eucharistic sacrifice and the doctrine as a whole (i.e. are they the same, or does the doctrine entail more); and how do these affirmations by Wesley that agree with Catholic teaching relate to the rest of his writing on eucharistic sacrifice and with the *Hymns on the Lord's Supper*?

According to Randy Maddox, John Wesley's prominence as a theologian (even among Methodists) has in fact grown significantly in recent decades.[5] Maddox traces the period of roughly a century and a half from the time of Wesley's death to the 1960s, during which time Wesley's status as a theologian suffered neglect, marginalization, and distortion (and this at the hands of his followers).[6] In the last half-century, however, Maddox stresses that "Wesley's model of theological activity" has received an increasingly "positive reevaluation"—i.e., as one cast more from the mold of an Anglican divine than a continental Protestant scholastic, and not just as a "folk theologian," either, but one with unique practices of mission, evangelism, and holiness that derive from theological emphases of grace and soteriology. In this light, Maddox argues, when Wesley is evaluated on his own terms, he emerges as a figure who can serve as an "exemplary model" and a "theological mentor for his contemporary descendants."[7] Geoffrey Wainwright makes a similar argument for the Wesleyan/Methodist tradition: calling the Wesleys "our progenitors in the Gospel, our senior evangelists, our doctrinal guides, our spiritual advisors, our classic hymnographers."[8] Such is the intent of these chapters: namely, a recovery of Wesley's theology of eucharistic sacrifice that might serve as a model for both his contemporary Methodist descendants and the church universal.

---

4. Cummings, *Eucharistic Doctors*, 222. Teresa Berger, too, notes that the "texts show amazing convergence at this point"; Berger, "'Finding Echoes': *The Catechism of the Catholic Church and the Hymns on the Lord's Supper*," in *Hymns on the Lord's Supper: 250 Years; Papers Presented at the Sixth Annual Meeting of the Charles Wesley Society, October 1995, the Divinity School, Duke University, Durham, North Carolina*, Charles Wesley Society (Madison, NJ: Society, Archives and History Center, Drew University, 1996), 2:66.

5. Randy Maddox, "Reclaiming an Inheritance: Wesley as Theologian in the History of Methodist Theology," in *Rethinking Wesley's Theology for Contemporary Methodism*, ed. Randy L. Maddox and Theodore Runyon (Nashville: Kingswood, 1998), 213–26.

6. Maddox, "Reclaiming an Inheritance," 220–23.

7. Maddox, "Reclaiming an Inheritance," 224–26.

8. Geoffrey Wainwright, "'Our Elder Brethren Join': The Wesleys' *Hymns on the Lord's Supper* and the Patristic Revival in England," in *Worship in Eighteenth-Century Anglicanism and Methodism: Papers presented at the fifth annual meeting of The Charles Wesley Society, October, 1994, Princeton, New Jersey*, Charles Wesley Society (Madison, NJ: Society, Archives and History Center, Drew University, 1996), 1:30.

The primary focus is John Wesley's theology of eucharistic sacrifice, so that related doctrines such as justification, atonement, or the sacraments at large cannot be treated directly. Because the focus is on John rather than his brother, I do not offer an extended engagement with Charles Wesley's eucharistic theology, as Daniel Stevick has done so well.[9] Instead, my engagement with the *Hymns on the Lord's Supper*—along with some of John Wesley's key sermons and his notes on the Bible—serve to complement the primary text, which is Wesley's *The Christian Sacrament and Sacrifice*.[10] This is a common arrangement for theologians working on Wesley's eucharistic theology, since these two texts "remained the Wesleys' principal statement of their sacramental doctrine and spirituality," and nothing in the hymns contradicts anything in John's text.[11] As Cummings remarks, "It is not possible to separate the eucharistic theology of John Wesley from the eucharistic hymnody of his brother, Charles . . . there can be no doubt that John was most closely associated with the theological sentiments and convictions set forth in the verses."[12] Furthermore, because John Wesley published nine editions of the volume in his lifetime under both names, Rattenbury regards it as the true expression and "authoritative statements" of Methodist eucharistic theology.[13]

Before turning to consider in detail what Wesley says on eucharistic sacrifice in *The Christian Sacrament and Sacrifice*, it will first be helpful to place this topic within a broader anthropological and sacramental context. We have seen that at the Reformation, Trent, and in responses to *BEM*, some of the primary points of contention turned on the issue of how we participate in God's sal-

---

9. Daniel B. Stevick, *The Altar's Fire: Charles Wesley's Hymns on the Lord's Supper, 1745 Introduction and Exposition* (Peterborough: Epworth, 2004).

10. The *Hymns on the Lord's Supper* (*HLS*)—166 hymns in all—were published under the names of both John and Charles, with a preface of John's *The Christian Sacrament and Sacrifice* (*CSS*) extracted from Daniel Brevint's work of the same title. They may be found in J. Ernest Rattenbury, *The Eucharistic Hymns of John and Charles Wesley: To Which Is Appended Wesley's Preface Extracted from Brevint's Christian Sacrament and Sacrifice Together with Hymns on the Lord's Supper* (London: Epworth, 1948). Citations are referenced by chapter and paragraph, with modernized stylistic revisions for capitalization and italicization. Facsimile edition: John Wesley and Charles Wesley, *Hymns on the Lord's Supper* [facsimile of the first edition] (Madison, NJ: Charles Wesley Society, 1995); *HLS* is also available online through the Center for Studies in the Wesleyan Tradition, Duke Divinity School: https://divinity.duke.edu/initiatives/cswt/charles-published-verse.

11. Stevick, *Altar's Fire*, 3–5.

12. Cummings, *Eucharistic Doctors*, 218–19.

13. J. Ernest Rattenbury, *The Evangelical Doctrines of Charles Wesley's Hymns*, 3rd ed. (London: Epworth, 1954), 63. See Borgen, *John Wesley on the Sacraments* (26–28), who follows Rattenbury, Williams, Bowmer, Outler, and George on this point. Maddox also concurs; Maddox, *Responsible Grace*, 203. Henry R. McAdoo: "The hymns are in fact a faithful reproduction in verse of the theology of *The Christian Sacrament and Sacrifice*"; McAdoo, "A Theology of the Eucharist: Brevint and the Wesleys," *Theology* 97 (1994): 251.

vation, and, more contentiously still, what role individuals (such as priests) and material objects (such as the sacramental elements) play in this regard. This chapter begins with an analysis of two pairs of sermons that provide the broader context (soteriological, sacramental, and anthropological) for understanding Wesley's theology of eucharistic sacrifice. The first pair, "The Scripture Way of Salvation" and "On Working Out Our Own Salvation," elucidates Wesley's theology of grace and how, soteriologically, believers must actively receive that grace. The second pair, "The Means of Grace" and "The Duty of Constant Communion," relates Wesley's insights on the mystery of divine-human agency more specifically to his consistent teaching that salvation comes from God via those instruments divinely instituted to convey saving grace, at the heart of which lies the church's daily sacrifice, the eucharist.[14]

"The Scripture Way of Salvation"

In this sermon Wesley focuses on the way of salvation according to his reading of scripture—i.e., the whole process of what God does in the life of the believer, from prevenient grace and the turning of the conscience to sanctifying grace and the believer's transformation in holiness. Maddox refers to this sermon as Wesley's "classic mature articulation of his soteriology" and notes that for Wesley, salvation has an immediate, progressive, and eschatological scope in which the believer is delivered from the penalty of sin, the plague of sin, and the presence of sin.[15] Attention to God's grace predominates, under which Wesley considers more closely the questions: (I) what is salvation, (II) what is faith, and (III) how are we saved by it? This particular sermon represents the seasoned Wesley's chief exposition on this topic.

I. Salvation. Consistent with his convictions that in divine-human agency neither God nor the believer overpowers or crowds out the other and that God is the primary agent who preveniently initiates salvation in people in such a way as to require their receptive cooperation, Wesley portrays salvation in a way that highlights God's sovereignty while incorporating a role for faith. Consistent with his emphasis on sanctification, he insists that the word *salvation* is not merely synonymous with going to heaven, but refers to what God does here and now in people's lives. Salvation thus "spoken of might be extended

---

14. Citations from Wesley's sermons are from *The Works of John Wesley*, Bicentennial Edition: "Scripture Way of Salvation" (no. 43, vol. II); "On Working Out Our Own Salvation" (no. 85, vol. III); "The Means of Grace" (no. 16, vol. 1); "The Duty of Constant Communion" (no. 101, vol. III); *The Works of John Wesley*; begun as "The Oxford Edition of the Works of John Wesley" (Oxford: Clarendon, 1975–1983; continued as "The Bicentennial Edition of the Works of John Wesley" (Nashville: Abingdon, 1984–); 23 of 35 vols. published to date.

15. Maddox, *Responsible Grace*, 143.

to the entire work of God, from the first dawning of grace in the soul till it is consummated in glory."[16] Properly understood, the earliest stirrings of salvation include not only the drawing of the Father, the enlightenment of the Son, and the convictions of the Spirit on the divine side, but also on the human side what he calls "natural conscience." While God's creatures usually "stifle" and "deny" the presence of prevenient grace, holiness will increase if it is received.[17] Notice that Wesley denies humanity's capacity to exist in a pure state, removed from grace. He also affirms that even what moral bearings seem to originate from within are really the result of the presence of grace.

He considers salvation under the aspects of justification and sanctification, and how they frame the Christian life. Wesley defines justification as pardon, forgiveness, and our acceptance with God, or being "born again, born from above, born of the Spirit."[18] The cause of this right relationship with God is "the blood and righteousness of Christ" and all he has "done and suffered for us." The effects of Christ's work in the faithful are peace, hope, and joy.[19] It is significant that in the definitions of the cause and effect of justification Wesley does not mention the believer's faith. Justification is not something he or she achieves by faith; rather it names the relationship that God has rightly reordered with those who believe. Sanctification begins at justification, since the relational change of the latter necessarily results in a real change in the believer: "We are inwardly renewed by the power of God," which is an event that begins a process of transformation into Christlikeness.[20] Reflecting on his experience and those of many Methodists, he teaches that while the young, newly justified believer may feel free from the power of sin, yet before long "temptations return and sin revives, showing it was but stunned before, not dead," so that now the "two principles" of sin and holiness contend against each other in the Christian.[21] By the Spirit, as the believer is able to live "more and more dead to sin, we are more and more alive to God."[22] The end of sanctification is perfect love: "It is love excluding sin; love filling the heart, taking up the whole capacity of the soul."[23]

---

16. Wesley, "Scripture Way of Salvation," I.1.

17. Wesley, "Scripture Way of Salvation," I.2.

18. Wesley, "Scripture Way of Salvation," I.4.

19. Wesley, "Scripture Way of Salvation," I.3.

20. Wesley, "Scripture Way of Salvation," I.4.

21. Wesley, "Scripture Way of Salvation," I.6.

22. Wesley, "Scripture Way of Salvation," I.8.

23. Wesley, "Scripture Way of Salvation," I.9. See Maddox, *Responsible Grace*, 165; and Randy L. Maddox, "A Change of Affections: The Development, Dynamics, and Dethronement of John Wesley's Heart Religion," in *"Heart Religion" in the Methodist Tradition and Related Movements*, ed. Richard B. Steele (Lanham, MD: Scarecrow, 2001), 18.

II. Faith. The salvation that begins and ends with God is not, as we have seen, something that simply happens *to* the believer as some purely extrinsic cause; rather it is received responsively through the faith of the believer. Wesley moves on quickly to define the "faith through which we are saved," and finally to answer the question of *how* the believer is saved—i.e., justified and sanctified—through this faith. He follows the description of faith given in Hebrews 11:1, but once again is careful to stress that God is the primary cause of faith: "[Faith] implies both a supernatural evidence of God and of the things of God, a kind of spiritual light exhibited to the soul, and a supernatural sight or perception thereof."[24] "Thus for Wesley," Maddox writes, "faith both 'is worked' by love and 'works' by love."[25] The power of the Holy Spirit lies behind both of these capacities to become convinced of and to discern God's ways in the world. What faith allows the believer to do in particular is to see that the reconciling work of God in the world and in the individual Christian comes through Christ's sacrificial self-giving, and then to "receive him in all his offices, as our Prophet, Priest, and King."[26]

III. How we are saved. As to *how* the believer is saved through faith, Wesley treats justification and sanctification with essentially the same hermeneutic. He recognized that his emphasis among the Methodists on repentance and good works—and his frequent linking of them to justification and sanctification—had provoked the accusations of Pelagianism and works righteousness from his critics. This final section keeps this dynamic in view. He begins quite strongly:

> I answer, faith is the condition, and the only condition, of justification. It is the condition: none is justified but he that believes; without faith no man is justified. And it is the only condition: this alone is sufficient for justification. Everyone that believes is justified, whatever else he has or has not. In other words: no man is justified till he believes; every man when he believes is justified.[27]

Maddox's reading of Wesley is instructive: "Thus, faith is not portrayed by Wesley as an inherent human ability which we exercise in order to attain justified status. It is much more properly a 'gift' that is graciously evoked in our lives by the pardoning overtures of God."[28] If this is so, what then does Wesley make of the clear scriptural command for repentance and good works?

---

24. Wesley, "Scripture Way of Salvation," II.I.

25. Maddox, *Responsible Grace*, 174–75.

26. Wesley, "Scripture Way of Salvation," II.2.

27. Wesley, "Scripture Way of Salvation," III.1.

28. Maddox, *Responsible Grace*, 173.

Are not these necessary for justification? Can one hope to be justified without them? He replies, "God does undoubtedly command us both to repent and to bring forth fruits meet for repentance; which if we willingly neglect we cannot reasonably expect to be justified at all."[29] How does Wesley harmonize the apparent disconnect between his comments that faith alone is the only condition of justification and that repentance and good works are also necessary for it?[30] He makes three interrelated points.

First, the average Christian is not the paradigmatic example of how the believer relates to God; instead, it is the thief on the cross, who had only faith, and who best exemplifies the true nature of justification. Thus, repentance and fruits meet for repentance are necessary "if there be time and opportunity for them."[31] Clearly for most Christians, the absence of immediate death renders them necessary. Second, how does this sanctification that is perfected in love occur, gradually or instantaneously? Wesley allows that the former may be the experience of some, in the sense that they cannot name a precise instant when "sin ceases to be";[32] however, he argues that the ordained occurrence is properly instantaneous, in the sense that the work is God's alone independent of what the believer may do. Third, where does Wesley exhort the believer to look for God's instantaneous work of sanctification but "in all those 'good works' whereunto thou art 'created anew in Christ Jesus'"?[33] These are works of piety and mercy, the former consisting of prayer, the Lord's Supper, searching the scriptures, and fasting and abstinence; the latter of feeding the hungry, clothing the naked, visiting the prisoner, etc.

A critical distinction for Wesley, therefore, is the recognition that divinely ordained works of piety and mercy are not the wrongheaded works of "thus or thus" that the Christian believes must be done in order to merit or achieve sanctification. In fact, just the opposite: attending to works of piety and mercy is how the believer seeks the sanctification that God alone can give. "This is the repentance, and these the fruits meet for repentance, which are necessary to full sanctification. This is the way wherein God hath appointed his children to wait for complete salvation."[34] Maddox explains, "Rather, God has chosen to allow a place for our participation, both before and after our justification—

29. Wesley, "Scripture Way of Salvation," III.2; the same holds true for sanctification, III.5.

30. Kenneth J. Collins helpfully places Wesley on the Protestant landscape in relation to Lutherans and Reformed; Collins, *The Theology of John Wesley: Holy Love and the Shape of Grace* (Nashville: Abingdon, 2007), 156–57.

31. Wesley, "Scripture Way of Salvation," III.2; see Maddox, *Responsible Grace*, 149.

32. Wesley, "Scripture Way of Salvation," III.18.

33. Wesley, "Scripture Way of Salvation," III.18.

34. Wesley, "Scripture Way of Salvation," III.10.

not as a means of meriting salvation, but as a 'condition' that upholds our integrity within the relational process of saving grace."[35] The role of the Lord's Supper, then, is a particular work of piety whereof believers avail themselves as they seek in faith the sanctification God gives through the Supper:

> Let thy blood, by faith applied the sinner's pardon seal,
> Speak us freely justified, and all our sickness heal:
> By thy Passion on the tree let all our griefs and troubles cease:
> O remember Calvary, and bid us go in peace.[36]

Thus, what might appear as an inconsistency in Wesley's thought on the nature of faith (or belief) between the thief on the cross and the more common life of Christian discipleship—in the sense that the former did nothing but believe and the latter are called to repentance and good works—turns out to be quite consistent indeed. For the concept of faith (or belief) for Wesley does not mean simply intellective assent to doctrine, nor does that of works mean simply any action or deed. Works, used negatively by Wesley, name the expression of a disordered relationship with God whereby the individual (Christian or otherwise) seeks to realize justification or sanctification by one's own agency through particular actions (in some instances these might even be the sacraments themselves). Faith, on the other hand, names the disposition of the believer as he or she recognizes that only God can justify and sanctify, just as works meet for repentance name (soteriologically speaking) not so much an action as the nature of that action—which must be perceived in faith—where divine and human agency intersect. "One thing more is implied in this repentance, namely, a conviction of our helplessness, of our utter inability to think one good thought, or to form one good desire; and much more to speak one word aright, or to perform one good action but through his free, almighty grace, first preventing us, and then accompanying us every moment."[37] One does not sanctify oneself by the sacraments or by feeding the hungry; instead, it is through the believer's use of these means of grace that the Holy Spirit brings sanctification. Faith, for Wesley, is the correlate of grace.

35. Maddox, *Responsible Grace*, 150–51.

36. *Hymns on the Lord's Supper*, 20:3. Hymn citations in this chapter come from *The Hymns on the Lord's Supper* (*HLS*). The four verses of hymn 20 move from (1) anamnesis, (2) atonement and liberation, (3) pardon, justification, and healing, (4) and perfection. For other hymns that discuss the *ordo salutis* as realized (fully or in part) through the eucharist, see 10:1; 15; 37; 83.

37. Wesley, "Scripture Way of Salvation," III.8.

"On Working Out Our Own Salvation"

This sermon comes late in Wesley's life (1785) and represents his most careful reflection on the mystery of divine and human agency from within the framework of God's way of salvation. Based on Philippians 2:12–13—"Work out your own salvation with fear and trembling, for it is God that worketh in you, both to will and to do of his good pleasure"—he seeks carefully to resolve an apparent twofold contradiction (which he caricatures): if God works in us, why do we need to work; and if God works in us, what work is there that we can do.[38] First, how it can be that God and the believer both work at the same time, together, in the life of the believer toward the same end; and second, on what grounds can Paul legitimately exhort his readers to work out their own salvation when it is properly God alone who can forgive and save? Additionally, one cannot help but hear in this sermon yet another defense of Wesley's soteriology, a hallmark of which was his consistent rejection of irresistible grace and limited atonement, or stated positively, his consistent affirmation of the participatory (i.e., responsible) nature of God's prevenient grace. Wesley saw in the Bible a greater emphasis on the believer's restored "capacity of spiritual life" and union with God, with the end being made partakers of the divine nature, than he did on Christ's imputed righteousness. For him, we are "pardoned in order to participate" in the "recovery of the Likeness of God."[39] He treats the text in three parts: first, God is the one who works in the believer; second, the "improvement" the Christian is to make of this by "working out your own salvation"; and third, the "connection" between the two: God works—"therefore," work out your salvation.

Wesley gives a clue to how he seeks to resolve these apparent contradictions in his introduction: "Having proposed the example of Christ, the Apostle exhorts them to secure the salvation which Christ hath purchased for them." Thus, on a prior and transcendent level, salvation refers to what Christ has already purchased, while on the immediate and human level, "working out your own salvation," as Wesley sees it, is a means of "securing" this salvation. His construal clearly allows for divine and human agency, yet with respect to salvation, they are of a qualitatively—therefore complementary rather than competing—different mode from each other. Does this construal also hold true for the nature of the work that Paul describes God continuing to do in the lives of the believers at the same time that they secure the salvation worked by Christ? That is, does Wesley's

38. Wesley, "On Working Out Our Own Salvation," III.1.
39. Maddox, *Responsible Grace*, 168.

conception of divine-human agency apply to sanctification just as it does to justification?

This question is what Wesley addresses in part one of his sermon. He sets the direction of his entire sermon by noting from the beginning that as it relates to God's activity, the phrase "of his good pleasure" serves to "remove all imagination of merit from man, and gives God the whole glory of his own work," thereby eliminating any cause for boasting or confidence in inherent goodness on humanity's part, and attributing everything to God's grace and mercy.[40] Wesley notes that God's willing and doing in the life of the believer may refer to the states of inward and outward religion, although he decides that it is more likely to mean, "God breathes into us every good desire, and brings every good desire to good effect."[41] By this Christians must know that any glory or boasting must be done in the Lord, since they "know and feel that the very first motion of good is from above, as well as the power which conducts it to the end."[42] God, therefore, is the one who begins, accompanies, and completes the course of holiness in the life of the believer in accordance with the salvation "purchased" by Christ.

In the second part, Wesley explains how the gift of salvation—which includes both forgiveness and holiness—that comes solely from God working in the believer also necessitates Paul's exhortation to "work out your own salvation," since he understands the "work" of the Christian believer to fall within this horizon.[43] Salvation begins with God's prevenient grace, which consists both of the desire to please God and the "first slight, transient conviction of having sinned against him." Prevenient grace, though, entails merely a "tendency toward life," just the "beginning of deliverance." This initial stumbling and groping gains more clarity and is "carried on by 'convincing grace,'" or what Scripture calls repentance, which is a "farther deliverance from the heart of stone." Only at this point, after convincing grace, does the Christian "experience the proper Christian salvation, whereby 'through grace' we 'are saved by faith,' consisting of those two grand branches, justification and sanctification." Justification is salvation from the "guilt of sin" and restoration to the "favour of God," and sanctification is salvation from the "power and root of sin" and restoration to "the image of God." This salvation is both instantaneous and gradual, commencing at the "moment we are justified," then continuing gradually in holiness from a mustard seed, when "at another instant the heart is cleansed from all sin, and filled with pure love to God and man,"

40. Wesley, "On Working Out Our Own Salvation," I.1.
41. Wesley, "On Working Out Our Own Salvation," I.2.
42. Wesley, "On Working Out Our Own Salvation," I.4.
43. Wesley, "On Working Out Our Own Salvation," II.1.

yet still then increasing in greater Christ-likeness until one achieves "the measure of the stature of the fullness of Christ."[44]

Wesley then raises and answers the question: how and by what steps are Christians to work out their own salvation? As to the how, they are to do so "with the utmost earnestness of spirit" as servants of a loving master;[45] and as to what steps, they are—"by the grace already given"—to flee from evil and to learn to do good. Notice once again how Wesley orders the divine-human relationship: believers are to flee evil and do good by the grace they already have if they "desire that God should work in [them] that faith whereof cometh both present and eternal salvation."[46] Once again, faith is not a purely human intellective act that people blindly muster on their own, the pious being more successful than others; rather, like hope and love, it is a divine virtue that God works in the Christian life in cooperation with the believer. Wesley's construal of faith, analogous to repentance, is also an advantageous counterbalance to Protestantism's frequent portrayal (albeit unintentional, yet nonetheless real) of faith as that disposition that the faithful generate and that causes justification. While Protestantism does not intentionally go so far as to make faith a meritorious work with which one justifies oneself, it all the same frequently speaks of it as a goal (or standard) to which one must raise oneself in the hope that one will then be justified. The consequence of removing God as the one who works faith in the believer is frequently an ongoing despair at not having "enough" faith, coupled with a recurrent fear that one is not justified—and thus the cycle continues. Rob Staples argues that Wesley's sacramental theology, which emphasizes the objective work of God, is a vital counterbalance to the "danger of experience"—i.e., the tendency to elevate the subjective, internal disposition to the highest authority.[47]

How, then, do believers cooperate with God? By relying on the means of grace. The means he lists sometimes vary, but in this sermon he enumerates good works, works of piety and mercy, family and private prayer, public and private Bible study, the Lord's Supper "at every opportunity," Christian conversation, denying worldly pleasures that distract from the kingdom, and a readiness to take pleasure in God that may well be "grievous to flesh and blood."[48] Thus, the full answer to the question of how and by what steps

44. Wesley, "On Working Out Our Own Salvation," II.1. See Maddox's discussion of justification and sanctification in Wesley's soteriology in *Responsible Grace*, 172.

45. Wesley, "On Working Out Our Own Salvation," II.3.

46. Wesley, "On Working Out Our Own Salvation," II.4.

47. Rob L. Staples, *Outward Sign and Inward Grace: The Place of Sacraments in Wesleyan Spirituality* (Kansas City, Mo.: Beacon Hill Press of Kansas City, 1991), 32–39.

48. Wesley, "On Working Out Our Own Salvation," II.4.

Christians are to work out their own salvation is for them fervently to avail themselves of the means that God has ordained for them "to secure" the work of grace that God has begun preveniently in them.

> Our helpless unbelief remove, and melt us by thy pard'ning love,
> Work in us faith, or faith's increase, the dawning, or the perfect peace.[49]

Contrary to the position of "flesh and blood" cited earlier, which states that since God works, then human working is either superseded, impractical, unnecessary, or superfluous, Wesley concludes his sermon in part three by bringing the ability and the necessity of human cooperation yet again under the horizon of God's initiating agency. Wesley maintains, "First, God works; therefore you can work. Secondly, God works; therefore you must work."[50] As Wainwright comments, "It is by virtue of God's work for us and in us that we are enabled and obliged to 'co-operate' with God (2 Cor 6:1)."[51] Theodore Runyon puts the matter strongly: "The Reformation's fear that good works rival faith is, from Wesley's standpoint, groundless, for in the divine-human synergy made possible by the restoration of the image, works express faith and reflect the divine life through the indwelling and energizing Spirit."[52] Not only is there no contradiction in Wesley's mind between God's work and the believer's work, it is in fact quite the opposite: "If [God] did not work it would be impossible for you to work out your own salvation."[53] Moreover, everyone is like Lazarus to the degree that they have been called to come out from death to life and, in a faint and inchoate manner, have been given the means to do so. All people need God to work in them if they are to work out their own salvation, but none can make excuse for not working by blaming God for not yet working in them. "For allowing that all the souls of men are dead in sin by nature, this excuses none, seeing there is no man that is in a state of mere nature." Everyone has received, to a greater or lesser extent, some degree of divine illumination in the form of "natural conscience," which he calls prevenient grace. "So that no man sins because he has not grace, but because he does not use the grace which he hath."[54]

49. *HLS*, 76:3.

50. Wesley, "On Working Out Our Own Salvation," III.2.

51. Geoffrey Wainwright, "The Healing Work of the Liturgy," in *Immersed in the Life of God: The Healing Resources of the Christian Faith; Essays in Honor of William J. Abraham*, ed. Paul Gavrilyuk, Douglas Koskela, and Jason Vickers (Grand Rapids, MI: Eerdmans, 2008), 66. He uses Wesley's sermon as a hermeneutical key to how the church participates in the liturgy.

52. Theodore Runyon, *The New Creation: John Wesley's Theology Today* (Nashville: Abingdon, 1998), 57.

53. Wesley, "On Working Out Our Own Salvation," III.3.

54. Wesley, "On Working Out Our Own Salvation," III.4.

Wesley offers a catena of scripture citations (from the Gospels, Paul, and Hebrews), the point of which is to reinforce his assertion that because God works in the faithful, they must also be about the business of working out their own salvation.[55] They must be "workers together with him," and they must "labour, by every possible means, to 'make our own calling and election sure.'"[56] Far from seeing God's work in competition to human work in the way of salvation, Wesley affirms in this sermon that in different ways both divine and human agency are required in salvation—the former essential from beginning to end, and the later reliant upon God's free and unmerited grace for its cooperative role. This sermon reflects Wesley's rejection of both Moravian quietism and Pelagian tendencies. Furthermore, it reflects his affirmation both that God alone is the One who forgives and saves, and that—following the clear witness of the Gospels and the whole of the New Testament—the human person is a genuine moral agent who is united in love to God by grace and who participates with God in a life of holiness. Wesley brings these themes together in this way:

> Therefore inasmuch as God works in you, you are now able to work out your own salvation. Since he worketh in you of his own good pleasure, without any merit of yours, both to will and to do, it is possible for you to fulfil all righteousness. It is possible for you to "love God, because he hath first loved us," and to "walk in love," after the pattern of our great Master. We know indeed that word of his to be absolutely true, "Without me ye can do nothing." But on the other hand we know, every believer can say, "I can do all things through Christ that strengtheneth me."[57]

"The Means of Grace"

The two previous sermons demonstrate Wesley's construal of the mystery of divine-human interaction in the way of salvation, and in this sermon, "The Means of Grace," he explicates in more detail the concrete practices by which the people of God receive saving grace. Wesley's intention here is to protect his followers from those quietists who regard external ordinances as unnecessary, obsolete, and sometimes even spiritually dangerous.[58] In refuting this position, Wesley remains consistent in his theological anthropology throughout these sermons, and this one takes us a step closer to putting his theology of eucharistic sacrifice into its proper anthropological context. Maddox under-

55. Wesley, "On Working Out Our Own Salvation," III. 8.
56. Wesley, "On Working Out Our Own Salvation," III.7.
57. Wesley, "On Working Out Our Own Salvation," III.5.
58. John C. Bowmer, *The Sacrament of the Lord's Supper in Early Methodism* (London: Dacre, 1951), 39–46.

scores Wesley's twofold rationale behind the necessity of the sacraments based on his anthropology: first, the "purified and strengthened tempers" that were the basis of one's sanctification depended upon God's grace given in the means for their transformation; second, the believer's use of the means as a practice in order to develop certain virtues.[59] His theology of the means of grace functions in service of his soteriology, and the sacraments in particular are ordained by God and given to the faithful for the purpose of aiding our "infirmities" and our "weaknesses" of perceiving the ways of God.[60]

His first move is to defend his terminology ("means of grace") and his teaching about it on the basis of its usage within the Christian tradition, beginning with the universal practice of the "apostolical church," which he believed as a matter of course firmly held to the "outward means" as "channels of [God's] grace," and continuing up to the practice of the Church of England of his day.[61] God instituted the means of grace by which Christians receive preventing, justifying, and sanctifying grace; the "chief of these" are prayer, searching the scriptures, and the Lord's Supper. Wesley accepts the classical definition of a sacrament as the outward sign of an inward and spiritual grace, but he also notes that this ordained mode of revelation and grace-filled mediation corresponds to the human constitution.[62] For Wesley, the sacraments are tailored to the way, anthropologically, creatures receive grace. In response to misconstruals of Catholic theology (based on stereotypes that he accepted), he is careful to teach that the sacraments are no mere mechanistic means of procuring grace apart from faith, nor should they be devalued by elevating the immediacy of internal experience over created means.[63] More positively, God instituted the means to serve the end of religion—namely, to further the knowledge and love of God.[64] His theology is strongly trinitarian: the power in the means comes only from the Holy Spirit, and the grace they convey derives solely from the atoning merit of Christ.[65] "We allow farther that the use of all means whatever will never atone for one sin; that it is the blood of Christ alone whereby any sinner can be reconciled to God; there being no other propitiation for our sins, no other fountain for sin and uncleanness."[66]

59. Maddox, *Responsible Grace*, 200–201.

60. Borgen, *John Wesley on the Sacraments*, 52.

61. John Wesley, "Means of Grace," I.1.

62. Wesley, "Means of Grace," II.1.

63. Staples, *Outward Sign and Inward Grace*, 99–100.

64. Wesley, "Means of Grace," II.2.

65. Wesley, "Means of Grace," II.3. See Geoffrey Wainwright, "Wesley's Trinitarian Hermeneutics," *Wesleyan Theological Journal* 36, no. 1 (2001): 7–30.

66. Wesley, "Means of Grace," II.4. See Staples, *Outward Sign and Inward Grace*, 101–2. Wesley, *OT Notes*: Ex 16:34: "Christ himself is the true manna, the bread of life, of which that

The sacred true effectual sign thy body and thy blood it shews,
The glorious instrument divine thy mercy and thy strength bestows.[67]

If instruments thy wisdom chuse, thy grace confers their saving use;
Salvation is from God alone. . . .
We banquet on immortal food, and drink the streams of life divine.[68]

Contrary to some Protestants, but in concert with Aquinas, Wesley sees no contradiction in the dual affirmation that Christ alone is the cause of atonement and that this grace is mediated to believers by instituted, external means.[69]

After defending his theology underlying the centrality of the means of grace, Wesley next considers their function in the way of salvation and refutes some common objections to his teaching. He argues not only that grace is mediated to creatures through created means, but also that the faithful offer worship to God via these means (what he also calls "works of piety"). It is no coincidence, therefore, that those divine actions that he labels "means of grace" he also refers to—from the human perspective—as "works of piety." In these instances, both God and humankind act in the same event and toward the same end, yet not in a competitive manner. His theological anthropology—often implicit in his argumentation—underlies his notion of the purpose of the means of grace for sacramental mediation. Wesley constructs the following imaginary dialogue: *I know that salvation is a gift from God, but how do I receive it? By believing. Yes, but what does this belief look like? It is done by waiting upon God. And what does this waiting entail? It consists of using the means of grace.*[70]

Wesley states that a proper theology of the means of grace derives from what he considers to be a straightforward reading of the clear teaching of the Lord and of the witness of scripture.[71] He takes each of the three chief means in turn. First, Wesley insists that to "receive any gift from God," the means of prayer is an "absolutely necessity."[72] Second, "all who desire the grace of God are to wait for it in 'searching the Scriptures.'"[73] Third, the teaching of

---

was a figure, John 6:49, 50, 51. . . . Christ in the word is to be applied to the soul, and the means of grace used"; see Ex. 24:6; Wesley, *Explanatory Notes upon the Old Testament,* 3 vols. (Bristol: Graham and Pine, 1760–62; many later reprints).

67. *HLS,* 28:2.

68. *HLS,* 61:3.

69. See Borgen, *John Wesley on the Sacraments,* 183, 198.

70. Wesley, "The Means of Grace," II.7. See Collins on this point, *Theology of John Wesley,* 257–60; Kenneth J. Collins, "John Wesley and the Means of Grace," *Drew Gateway* 56, no. 3 (1986): 31.

71. Wesley, "Means of Grace," II.8.

72. Wesley, "Means of Grace," III.1–6.

73. Wesley, "Means of Grace," III.7.

the Apostle Paul ("Ye do show forth the Lord's death till he come"; 1 Cor 11: 23–26) provides the warrant for the Lord's Supper as a means of grace: "Ye openly exhibit the same by these visible signs, before God, and angels, and men; ye manifest your solemn remembrance of his death, till he cometh in the clouds of heaven."[74] Moreover, Paul's theology of eucharistic *koinonia* (the bread and wine are a communion in the body and blood of Christ; 1 Cor 10:16) is essentially a concise understanding of the means of grace. In Wesley's trinitarian formulation:

> Is not the eating of that bread, and the drinking of that cup, the outward, visible means whereby God conveys into our souls all that spiritual grace, that righteousness, and peace, and joy in the Holy Ghost, which were purchased by the body of Christ once broken and the blood of Christ once shed for us? Let all, therefore, who truly desire the grace of God, eat of that bread and drink of that cup.[75]

Wesley's formulation that by eating and drinking the elements God can transmit grace "into our souls" aligns with Aquinas's remark that the grace of God touches the person by "spiritual contact."[76] The key point to note in this regard is that the means of grace become instruments of both divine and human agency in the way of salvation.

> Jesu, my Lord and God bestow all which thy sacrament doth shew,
> And make the real sign a sure effectual means of grace,
> Then sanctify my heart and bless, and make it all like thine.[77]

> Draw near ye blood-besprinkled race, and take what God vouchsafes to
>   give;
> The outward sign of inward grace, ordain'd by Christ himself, receive:
> The sign transmits the signified, the grace is by the means applied.[78]

This observation was lost on some of Wesley's detractors, as is evidenced by two common critiques: first, that one cannot use the means of grace without trusting in them—i.e., as opposed to trusting in God; and second, that using the means of grace is nothing other than seeking salvation by works. His rebuttal to these critiques proves to reinforce his theological anthropology as

---

74. Wesley, "Means of Grace," III.11.

75. Wesley, "Means of Grace," III.12.

76. See Bowmer, *Sacrament of the Lord's Supper*, 171, and Runyon, *New Creation*, 110.

77. *HLS*, 66:1.

78. *HLS*, 71:1. It is by the Holy Spirit's power that these means are indeed effectual: 30:4; 72:1–2; 75:3.

it brings together concisely his understanding of faith, trust, belief, waiting, works, and the means of grace.[79]

Wesley asserts that one should not stop using the means of grace for fear of trusting in them and distrusting the grace of God, since to do so would be to disobey the scriptures. On the contrary, trusting in the means consists of looking for the blessings of God in them (because they both signify and convey Christ's atonement) and "believing that if I wait in this way I shall attain what otherwise I should not. . . . I will believe that whatever God hath promised he is faithful also to perform. And seeing he hath promised to bless me in this way, I trust it shall be according to his Word."[80] Additionally, the means of grace cannot be confused with salvation by works because by this phrase Paul intends either to try to be saved through Israel's cultic law or to achieve salvation on the basis of one's own deeds "by the merit of our own righteousness. But how is either of these implied in my waiting in the way God has ordained, and expecting that he will meet me there because he has promised so to do?"[81] Neither of these ideas approximates Wesley's theology of the means of grace.

Consider, for example, the latent epistemology of hymns 30:4, 8, and 54:3, the union of matter, faith, and grace, and the suggestion of participation in the divine life. Rattenbury writes that this hymn "expresses with great emphasis Charles Wesley's zeal for the Sacrament and the need of its restoration as a daily sacrifice."[82]

> The tokens of thy dying love, O let us all receive,
> And feel the quick'ning Spirit move, and *sensibly* believe. . .
> Now, Lord, on us thy flesh bestow, and let us drink thy blood,
> Till all our souls are fill'd below with all the life of God.
>
> Saviour, thou didst the mystery give that I thy nature might partake,
> Thou bidst me outward signs receive, one with thyself my soul to make,
> My body, soul and spi'rit to join inseparably one with thine.

Thus, Wesley's whole theology of divine human agency utterly precludes either of these interpretations and exemplifies the believer's cooperative role in salvation properly ordered in faith. Ultimately, Wesley puts his faith in God because he believes that "through the merits and sufferings and love of his

---

79. Bowmer, *Sacrament of the Lord's Supper*, 115.

80. Wesley, " Means of Grace," IV.1.

81. Wesley, "Means of Grace," IV.2. See Wesley's comments in his *OT Notes*, Isaiah 12:3, and his *NT Notes*, Titus 3:4–5; Wesley, *Explanatory Notes upon the New Testament*. London: Epworth, 1976.

82. Rattenbury, *Eucharistic Hymns*, 143.

Son," it is God who is faithful.[83] Wesley's theology of grace and of divine-human agency attests to a consistent adherence to the classical systematic hermeneutic that, in the order of knowing, we perceive the created order and move conceptually to the transcendent, while in the order of being, God's preventing grace always comes before, directing one's thoughts and deeds toward their end, which is perfect love in communion with Christ. By working out their own salvation through the means of grace, believers are not seeking to prove their self-earned sanctification. Nor is their use of the means of grace an instance of some version of semi-Pelagianism.[84] Instead, by the grace of God they are responding—in their embodied and divinely ordered way—to receive the faith that God works in them and through which they are saved.

"The Duty of Constant Communion"

Of all the means of grace, Wesley most valued the eucharist, and his eucharistic fervor significantly shaped the Methodist revival. While the question of sacrifice figures little in this sermon, it nonetheless stands as one of his strongest statements on the centrality and necessity of the eucharist in the Christian life. Wesley has two interests in this sermon: first, to explain the very basics of what the Lord's Supper is and why every believer should receive it at every opportunity; and second, to refute some of the more common objections with which he had to contend. The nature of the sermon is more didactic and exhortative than it is a sustained theological mediation on the meaning of the eucharist. In this regard it does not compare to *The Christian Sacrament and Sacrifice*. Its value, however, is to exemplify theologically Methodism's eucharistic piety as a sacramental practice that accompanied its evangelical preaching. His teaching in this sermon should be read within the context of his more encompassing theology of divine-human agency and the eucharist as a means of grace.[85]

Wesley's text for his sermon is Luke 22:19: "Do this in remembrance of me," and as the "plain command of Christ," the Christian is duty bound to "receive the Lord's Supper as often as he can." The bread and wine, as "signs" of the Lord's body and blood, both unite believers who share this faith in common and serve as a perpetual memorial of the Lord's death. In addition

83. Wesley, "Means of Grace," IV.2.

84. Wesley's sacramental convictions do not contradict Trent's nuanced treatment of *ex opere operato*; see Power, *Sacrifice We Offer*, 29–31, 41, 45, and 49.

85. Susanne Johnson, "John Wesley on the Duty of Constant Communion: The Eucharist as a Means of Grace for Today," in *Wesleyan Spirituality in Contemporary Theological Education*, ed. Hal Knight, Paul W. Jones, and Roberta C. Bondi (Nashville: Division of Ordained Ministry UMC, 1987), 25–46.

to obedience to the Lord's command, an equally significant reason for celebrating constantly is to receive the "benefits" that it brings.[86]

The principal benefit of the eucharist is the "forgiveness of our past sins and the present strengthening and refreshing of our souls."[87] Wesley emphasized that upon believers' pardon by God, they are given the power by the Holy Spirit to begin living holy lives.[88] Despite the witness of the Spirit with the believer's spirit, worldly temptations persist and sometimes even triumph in the Christian's life. What better means, therefore, "of procuring pardon from him than the 'showing forth the Lord's death,' and beseeching him, for the sake of his Son's sufferings, to blot out all our sins"? Notice once again that, for Wesley, Christians must act in order to receive God's grace, and that their action in no way competes with God's action of grace in their hearts. In concert with his theology of the means of grace, Wesley is not troubled in the slightest that the celebration of the eucharist will detract from the unique atoning work of Christ. Indeed, it is only because the eucharist is so closely associated with the atonement of the "Son's sufferings" that it can "procure pardon." Furthermore, while Wesley sometimes speaks of "showing forth the Lord's death" as a way for Christians to remember Christ's passion and to proclaim it, in this context the eucharist is a "showing forth" of the Lord's death to God the Father with the end of receiving forgiveness. The eucharistic elements are signs before God, not in a feebly anthropomorphic fashion, but in a way that demonstrates that we are "convinced of having sinned against God."[89]

Wesley continues with a slight shift in emphasis and image. God's gifts of pardon and power are not purely theoretical assertions. The truth of the Lord's teaching in scripture is experienced in the eucharist, which "confirms to us the pardon of our sins by enabling us to leave them." In the eucharist the faithful receive not only forgiveness but spiritual food. "This is the food of our souls: this gives strength to perform our duty, and leads us on to perfection," which entails "strength to believe" and "to love and obey God." This spiritual sustenance also bears an eschatological aspect—i.e., the "refreshing [of the soul] with the hope of glory."[90]

Finally, Wesley refutes several common objections to constant communion, whether they are made on the grounds of pragmatism, feelings of unworthiness, fear of diminishing the heightened emotionalism of rare communion,

86. Wesley, "Duty of Constant Communion," I.1–2.
87. Wesley, "Duty of Constant Communion," I.2.
88. Maddox, *Responsible Grace*, 168, 199–201.
89. Wesley, "Duty of Constant Communion," I.2.
90. Wesley, "Duty of Constant Communion," I.3.

or of a lack of perceived effect.[91] None of these objections convince him, for Wesley can conceive of no good reason not to obey the Lord's plain command or to forsake so great a heavenly mercy. To reject the duty of constant communion is tantamount to "renouncing your baptism," since participation in the Lord's Supper is nothing less than a regular ratification of the believer's covenantal promises of baptism.[92] In effect, for Wesley, constant communion is the liturgical norm for the Christian, and Sunday worship without it is the anomaly. The believer who desires to be in Christ should equally desire to commune with Christ: "If you resolve and design to follow Christ you are fit to approach the Lord's table."[93] Why, instead, would anyone not rush to the eucharist, since "God offers you a pardon for all your sins . . . [and to] deliver your soul from death"?[94]

The preceding four sermons demonstrate Wesley's theology of the mystery of divine-human agency, especially with respect to the believer's participation and the role of the eucharist in the *ordo salutis*. Wesley's distinctive emphases on God's prevenient grace, sanctification, and salvation in this life, and the necessity of the means of grace—with the eucharist at the center— further demonstrate that for him no competition or coercion exists between God and humankind, not even when our reception of God's grace requires us to act. An understanding of this relationship between Creator and creature is essential in order to understand correctly Wesley's teaching on eucharistic sacrifice. The language of eucharistic sacrifice often troubles Protestants, as *BEM*'s delicate wording so clearly attests; however, in *The Hymns on the Lord's Supper*, Wesley speaks of sacrifice without scruple. For him, the theology of sacrifice takes on different, yet related, connotations in different contexts, and he is exceedingly careful to clarify these distinctions. In chapter 4, we focus on interpreting Wesley's theology of eucharistic sacrifice.

91. Wesley, "Duty of Constant Communion," II.2–19.
92. Wesley, "Duty of Constant Communion," II.12.
93. Wesley, "Duty of Constant Communion," II.14.
94. Wesley, "Duty of Constant Communion," II.7.

CHAPTER 4

John Wesley's Doctrine of Eucharistic Sacrifice in *The Hymns on the Lord's Supper* and *The Christian Sacrament and Sacrifice*

With Wesley's theological anthropology and sacramental theology in place, we are now in a position to consider closely the sacrificial character of Wesley's eucharistic theology. For Wesley, as with *BEM* and Thomas Aquinas, the sacrificial dimension of the eucharist is not limited to the words of institution, the *anamnesis*, and the offertory, even while it is concentrated there. In Wesley's *The Christian Sacrament and Sacrifice* and *Hymns on the Lord's Supper* different facets of sacrifice permeate these texts. In order to discern most clearly this dimension of his eucharistic theology, therefore, it will be best to follow closely the thread of the argument, highlighting how sacrifice is woven throughout. One of the central arguments of this book is that Wesley's theology of eucharistic sacrifice provides valuable resources for Methodists attending to contemporary ecumenical concerns.

In *The Christian Sacrament and Sacrifice*, Wesley never lays out specifically the mystery of divine and human agency that he expresses in his sermons, but it is everywhere implicit. It is, in fact, the theological rationale that allows him to insist on the necessity of the eucharist as a sacrifice without worrying that he is detracting from the uniqueness of the cross. Remarkably, while *The Christian Sacrament and Sacrifice* is more didactic and devotional than systematic, Wesley nevertheless succeeds at touching on nearly all the main points of discussion related to eucharistic sacrifice. After a brief introduction, the text is divided into two sections, the first on the eucharist as a sacrament, and the second as a sacrifice. Wesley follows Brevint's eight section headings in his extract, and the hymns are reorganized slightly:[1]

---

1. Throughout her study of Wesley's eucharistic theology, Lorna Khoo notes Wesley's strong reliance on Brevint, as well as those areas where Wesley diverges from him; Khoo, *Wesleyan Eucharistic Spirituality: Its Nature, Sources, and Future* (Adelaide: AFT, 2005).

<table>
<tr><td>Christian Sacrament and Sacrifice</td><td>Hymns on the Lord's Supper (##)</td></tr>
<tr><td>I. Nature of the Sacrament</td><td>I. Memorial: Christ's Death (1–27)</td></tr>
<tr><td>II. As a Memorial</td><td>II. Sign and Means of Grace (28–92)</td></tr>
<tr><td>III. Sign of Present Graces</td><td>III. Pledge of Heaven (93–115)</td></tr>
<tr><td>IV. Means of Grace</td><td>IV. As It Implies a Sacrifice (116–127)</td></tr>
<tr><td>V. Pledge of Future Glory</td><td>V. Sacrifice of Our Persons (117–157)</td></tr>
<tr><td>VI. Commemorative Sacrifice</td><td>VI. After the Sacrament (158–166)</td></tr>
<tr><td>VII. Sacrifice of Ourselves</td><td></td></tr>
<tr><td>VIII. Sacrifice of our Goods</td><td></td></tr>
</table>

The brief first section introduces the "Nature of this Sacrament," and in doing so, makes two main points that are elaborated over the course of the text. First, the eucharist consists of a twofold movement of agency between God and humankind. Both the Lord and his church play a role—albeit an asymmetrical and unequal one—in the eucharistic celebration: "At the holy table the people meet to worship God, and God is present to meet and bless his people."[2] Neil Alexander follows Henry McAdoo in emphasizing this theme of the "intersection of heaven and earth" and notes that among seventeenth-century writers Brevint develops it most prominently. In fact, Brevint's "retrieval of eucharist as sacrifice" is predicated upon this theme, which runs throughout Wesley's text.[3] The noncompeting agencies in the liturgy correspond to the noncompeting presence of grace in Wesley's theological anthropology. Second, and similar to Aquinas, God has prepared the church for understanding the dynamics of this mystery by giving in the Old Testament and the life of Israel the sacrifices that served as a figure to the eucharist—namely, the Levitical cult and Passover: "So that the holy sacrament, like the ancient Passover, is a great mystery, consisting both of sacrament, and sacrifice; that is, of the religious service which the people owe to God, and of the full salvation which God hath promised to his people."[4] Sacrifice, then, is an intrinsic duty (for Aquinas, recall, it is the fulfillment of justice) that demarcates how we as creatures are related to God our Creator.

2. *CSS*, I.1.

3. J. Neil Alexander, "'With Eloquence in Speech and Song': Anglican Reflections on the Eucharistic Hymns (1745) of John and Charles Wesley," in *With Ever Joyful Hearts*, ed. J. Neil Alexander and Marion J. Hatchett (New York: Church Pub., 1999), 251–53. See McAdoo, "Theology of the Eucharist," 246–48; Henry R. McAdoo and Kenneth Stevenson, *The Mystery of the Eucharist in the Anglican Tradition* (Norwich: Canterbury, 1995), 156; Kenneth W. Stevenson and Richard Holloway, *Covenant of Grace Renewed: A Vision of the Eucharist in the Seventeenth Century* (London: Darton, Longman and Todd, 1994), 101–5.

4. *CSS*, I.1.

The Lord's Supper as It Is a Sacrament

Wesley next, in sections II through V, proceeds to explicate the nature of the eucharist as a sacrament. These sections relate to one another based on the aspect of time (although there is considerable thematic overlap between them), and on how Wesley's Christology sees Christ in his priestly office at once to transcend and to unite these aspects of time: thus, section II (past: a memorial of the passion of Christ), sections III and IV (present: a sign and a means of grace), and section V (future: a pledge of future glory).

> O might the sacred word set forth our dying Lord,
> Point us to thy sufferings past, present grace and strength impart,
> Give our ravish'd souls a taste, pledge of glory in our heart.[5]

Anamnesis

The purpose of the Last Supper, like that of the Passover to future generations of Israelites, was to serve as "a holy memorial and representation of what he was about to suffer."[6] As a continuation of the Supper, the eucharist serves the same function of signifying Christ's passion and reminding the church of it, as St. Paul teaches: "So at our Holy Communion, which sets before our eyes Christ our Passover who is sacrificed for us . . . eating this bread, and drinking this cup, ye do shew forth the Lord's death."[7] What Wesley means by such terms as *memorial* and *remembrance*, however, requires careful attention, for he stresses that the proper exercise of faith that sees the Lord's sacrifice represented in the sacrament is "not the bare remembrance of his passion; but over and above, to invite us to his sacrifice, not as done and gone many years since, but as to grace and mercy, still lasting, still new, still the same as when it was first offered for us."[8] The content of Christ's intercession that Wesley emphasizes here is one of priestly self-offering (i.e., Christ himself), and Wesley relies heavily on the Christology found in the Letter to the Hebrews as a way of adjudicating the tension between the church's memorial of Christ's completed historic passion and its reality as "still new, still the same." Don Saliers notes, "To remember what God has done—if we pray with the Bible—carries the astounding claim that what God said and did, God still says and does."[9] Wesley writes,

5. *HLS*, 53:2.
6. *CSS*, II.2.
7. *CSS*, II.3.
8. *CSS*, II.7.
9. Don Saliers, *Worship and Spirituality*, 1st ed. (Philadelphia: Westminster Press, 1984), 21; see Johnson, "John Wesley on the Duty of Constant Communion," 31.

The sacrifice of Christ being appointed by the Father for a propitiation that should continue to all ages; and withal being everlasting by the privilege of its own order [Heb 7:11], which is an unchangeable Priesthood [7:24]; and by his worth who offered it, that is, the blessed Son of God; and by the power of the eternal Spirit [9:14], through whom it was offered: it must in all respects stand eternal, the same yesterday, today, and for ever [13:8].[10]

In his Christology, Wesley is intent on maintaining the biblical truth that Jesus Christ is the same yesterday, today, and forever, at the same time as maintaining the gospel truth that the sacrifice of Jesus in his death and resurrection is the soteriological center of the Trinity's saving work. Wesley is not regularly one for overt metaphysical speculation, but his preaching, teaching, and hymnody reflect that he has not failed to reflect on the concept of Christology and time. Indeed, the way in which he relates time-bound humanity to God's unchangeableness Borgen calls Wesley's "Eternal Now": the effect of Christ's suffering and atonement touches all times and places.[11]

Thou Lamb that suffer'dst on the tree, and in this dreadful mystery
Still offer'st up thyself to God, we cast us on thy sacrifice,
Wrapt in the sacred smoke arise, and cover'd with th'atoning blood.

For us he ever interceeds, his heaven-deserving Passion pleads
Presenting us before the throne; we want no sacrifice beside,
By that great offering sanctified, one with our head, for ever one.[12]

Live our eternal priest by men and angels blest!
Jesus Christ, the crucified, he who did for all atone,
From the cross where once he died now he up to heaven is gone.

He ever lives, and prays for all the faithful race;
In the holiest place above sinners' advocate he stands,
Pleads for us his dying love, shews for us his bleeding hands.[13]

This understanding of the eucharist as the perpetual application of the atoning work of the cross under the priestly agency of Christ is by no means

10. *CSS*, II.7. See Wesley's commentary on Heb 7–9 and 1 Tm 2:5.

11. Ole E. Borgen, "No End without the Means: John Wesley and the Sacraments," *Asbury Theological Journal* 46 (1991): 67–68; see Kathryn Nichols, "The Theology of Christ's Sacrifice and Presence in Charles Wesley's Hymns on the Lord's Supper," *Hymn* 39, no. (1988): 23; and Bowmer, *Sacrament of the Lord's Supper in Early Methodism*, 173–80.

12. *HLS*, 117:1–2. See Nichols, "Theology of Christ's Sacrifice and Presence," 21.

13. *HLS*, 118:1–2; 84:3: "Jesus, master of the feast, the feast itself thou art"; see 5:1 and 14:2.

antithetical to Trent's. Even while Wesley limits the language of propitiation to Christ's passion alone, the effect of the eucharist is nonetheless propitiatory. Moreover, his comment on the role of the ministerial office approaches Trent a bit closer: "And when I look on the minister, who by special order from God distributes this bread and this wine, I conceive, that thus God himself hath given his Son to die; and gives us still the virtue of his death."[14] Wesley implies that God has ordained the (Anglican) priesthood with the liturgical function of representing the presidency of Christ at the Last Supper, although there is no sense that the priest (apart from the laity) has any share in Christ's eternal, bodily self-offering before the Father. Additionally, from Wesley's perspective, the sovereignty of the Son of God—and therefore his ability to be Lord of creation at all times and in all places—is in no way diminished by the events of Jesus' earthly life and passion. The inexorable flow of time does not impede the Lord as he gives the grace of his atonement to the church in the eucharist.

> All the distance of time and countries between Adam and me doth not keep his sin and punishment from reaching me, any more than if I had been born in his house. Adam descended from above, let Thy blood reach as far, and come as freely to save and sanctify me as the blood of my first father did both to destroy and to defile me.[15]

> The instruments that bruis'd him so were broke and scatter'd long ago,
> The flames extinguish'd were, but Jesu's death is ever new,
> He whom in ages past they slew doth still as slain appear.[16]

> Dies the glorious cause of all, the true eternal Pan,
> Falls to raise us from our fall, to ransom sinful man . . .
> Lives our head, to die no more: power is all to Jesus given,
> Worship'd as he was before th' immortal King of heaven.[17]

Although Max Thurian did not turn to Wesley in drafting *BEM*'s chapter on the eucharist, it is nevertheless important to note that Wesley's notion of memorial and of a Christology indebted to Hebrews has much in common with the direction taken in twentieth-century ecumenical dialogues on the eucharist and the convergence that they have achieved. Borgen understands memorial as a "dynamic drama of worship" where believers are sacramentally caught up into God's "eternal now," and Horton Davies comments that an

14. *CSS*, II.5.
15. *CSS*, II.9.
16. *HLS*, 3:2.
17. *HLS*, 21:5, 8.

understanding of memorial as the "actualization of sacrifice by Christ the eternal High Priest and Intercessor" based on the Christology of Hebrews has facilitated the ecumenical convergence on eucharistic sacrifice.[18]

If the anamnetic character of the eucharist functions effectively to render present the grace of Christ's sacrifice, it does so because God has "fitly chosen" the bread and wine to be a "figure" that powerfully "represents" the broken and bruised body of Christ.[19] Wesley's atonement theology is rich, as the range of atonement language in *HLS* 31 and 87 attests, for example: salvation, rest, cooling shadow, redemption, washing, pardon, sanctification, purity, release, apply the blood, relieve, cleansing, and casting out.[20] On the one hand, the eucharist as memorial brings to the present the satisfaction that Christ made in his passion, but on the other hand, and as a sign of present graces, he agrees with Aquinas that the eucharist is heavenly food that provides spiritual nourishment for the journey of the Christian life. The eucharist functions as a "continual supply of strength and grace" in order to "sustain that spiritual life" that is the result of the work of Christ.[21] Yet Wesley stresses that "both these blessings are inseparable"—i.e., that this twofold work of Christ—satisfaction and sanctification, or pardon and cleansing—work together for the good of the believer.[22]

> Jesus is the Truth foreshewed by these figures. He was the true Passover when he died upon the cross, and he feeds from heaven, by continually pouring out his blessings, the souls he redeemed by pouring out his blood. Thus the sacrament alone represents at once both what our Lord suffered and what he still doth for us. . . . In the sacrament are represented both life and death; the life is mine, the death my Saviour's.[23]

Section IV has several functions. First, it repeats the previous claims that the past and present dimensions of the eucharist are more than a "bare memo-

18. Borgen, *John Wesley on the Sacraments*, 86–94, 183; Davies, *Bread of Life and Cup of Joy*, 77.

19. *CSS*, III.1–2.

20. John R. Tyson makes a similar observation about Charles Wesley's hymnody in general; Tyson, "Charles Wesley's Theology of Redemption: A Study in Structure and Method," *Wesleyan Theological Journal* 20, no. 2 (1985): 7–28.

21. *CSS*, III.3.

22. The literature has come to recognize that in their eucharistic theology Aquinas and Wesley incorporate much more in their doctrine of atonement than simply a juridical pardoning—e.g., pneumatology, cleansing, healing, nurturing, and deification. See Maddox, *Responsible Grace*, 94–108, 119–24, 197–200; Jean-Pierre Torrell, *Saint Thomas D'aquin, Maître Spirituel: Initiation 2*, 203–32; Berger, "Finding Echoes," 67; Geoffrey Wainwright, *Eucharist and Eschatology* (London: Epworth, 1971), 56–57; Wainwright, "Our Elder Brethren Join," 10–11, 26–27.

23. *CSS*, III.5–6. See Wesley's *OT Notes* on Dt 16:6; cf. 1 Cor 5:8.

rial or representation," and it corroborates Wesley's theology of the instrumental mediation of grace through divinely appointed means. The eucharist as a sign not only represents Christ's passion, but it is a "means of communicating the blood there represented and remembered to every believing soul!"[24] John Bowmer underscores the Wesleys' emphasis in this regard: "For it is not too much to say that for them it was the highest form of devotion and the most comprehensive act of worship the church could offer"; a preaching service was not the "supreme spiritual exercise. On the other hand, the Lord's Supper was completely satisfying."[25]

Second, this section introduces an aspect of Christ's sacrifice that will become more prominent under the treatment of the eucharist as a sacrifice—namely, its participatory nature in the body and blood of Christ. Wesley values the eucharist so intensely "because I hope to find him there," and he again cites Paul's teaching: "The cup of blessing, which we bless, is it not the communion of the blood of Christ?"[26] He continues: "And thus his body and blood have everywhere, but especially at this sacrament, a true and real presence."[27] To the extent that it relates to sacrifice, Wesley's theology of Christ's presence in the eucharist bears mentioning.

Eucharistic Presence

With the exception of clearly excluding a purely memorialist theology on the Protestant side, Wesley is difficult to pin down on his theology of presence, since his theology has affinities with the numerous positions ranging from Luther to Calvin, Cranmer, and the Non-Jurors. His notes on the New Testament indicate that he reads the words of institution figuratively—i.e., he understands Jesus' gift of bread and wine as signs and memorials of the new covenant.[28] On the Catholic side, he clearly denies transubstantiation, at least as he understands it, as "grossly absurd, to suppose that Christ speaks of what he then held in his hands as his real, natural body."[29] It is not Catholic teaching, however, that Jesus held his *natural* body in his hands at the Last Supper, but that he communicated himself to the apostles *sacramentally* via the elements. (For example, *HLS* 63:2: "No local Deity we wor-

---

24. *CSS*, IV.1.

25. Bowmer, *Sacrament of the Lord's Supper in Early Methodism*, 188@-89. See *HLS* 42:3–4; 1:2; 11:1; 62; 91:3.

26. *CSS*, IV.1.

27. *CSS*, IV.5.

28. *NT Notes*, Mt 26:26; Mk 14:24.

29. Wesley, *Doctrine of Original Sin*, Part II, III.13, in *Works of John Wesley*, Bicentennial ed., 12:261. See Staples, *Outward Sign and Inward Grace*, 215–16.

ship, Lord, in thee.") At the same time, the elements are, for him, effective signs that communicate what they signify—namely, forgiveness by the sacrifice of Christ through communion with him.[30] And while he affirms Christ's real presence in the eucharist,[31] he denies the presence of Christ's human nature in the elements, despite the implication of the citation just shown. Apparently an admission of Christ's bodily presence would have led inextricably to transubstantiation.[32]

> We need not now go up to heaven to bring the long-sought Saviour down,
> Thou art to all already given: thou dost ev'n now thy banquet crown,
> To every faithful soul appear, and shew thy real presence here.[33]

> O the depth of love divine, th' unfathomable grace!
> Who shall say how bread and wine God into man conveys?
> *How* the bread his flesh imparts, *how* the wine transmits his blood,
> Fill his faithful people's hearts with all the life of God!

> Let the wisest mortal shew how we the grace receive:
> Feeble elements bestow a power not theirs to give:
> Who explains the wondrous way? How thro' these the virtue came?
> These the virtue did convey, yet still remain the same.[34]

The debate gets interesting, especially when Catholic theologians interpret Wesley. On the one hand, Cummings argues that the reference to "No local deity" and the denial of language that seems to confine God to a place attests to a lack of understanding of Catholic teaching on transubstantiation; on the other, he cites *HLS* 153 with its language of flesh and blood as the sacramental presence as "just what the Catholic doctrine was designed to say" and wonders just how different the Wesleys and Catholics really are on this point.[35]

---

30. The doxological language of eating Christ's flesh and drinking his blood are instances of metonymy—e.g., 30:8; 33:2; 42:4; see Borgen, *John Wesley on the Sacraments*, 61n42.

31. See, too, *HLS* 30:2; 33:1–3; 39:1; 92:1–6. Charles's theology of memorial and presence shares much with John; see Nichols, "Theology of Christ's Sacrifice and Presence," 26–28; Stevick, *Altar's Fire*, 8–11, 30–38; Steven T. Hoskins, "Eucharist and Eschatology in the Writings of the Wesleys," *Wesleyan Theological Journal* 29, no. (1994): 76.

32. See Borgen's helpful discussion, in *John Wesley on the Sacraments*, 58–69; Bowmer, *Sacrament of the Lord's Supper in Early Methodism*, 17–20, 25–28; and Staples, *Outward Sign and Inward Grace*, 220–21.

33. *HLS*, 116:5.

34. *HLS*, 57:1–2.

35. Cummings, *Eucharistic Doctors*, 220.

Father, thy feeble children meet, And make thy faithful mercies known;
Give us thro' faith the flesh to eat, And drink the blood of Christ thy
    Son;
Honour thine own mysterious ways, Thy sacramental presence shew,
And all the fullness of thy grace, With Jesus, on our souls bestow.

Elsewhere, Cummings goes somewhat further, arguing that not only Wesley's but also Borgen's understanding of transubstantiation is lacking, and he cites John Todd to the effect that although they believed they have denied transubstantiation, they have in fact brought "the whole doctrine back in other language."[36] With respect to sacrifice, however, there is no such confusion: Cummings compares the *Catechism* with hymns 122 and 140 and concludes that there is no "great doctrinal distance" between them.[37]

At least this much seems fair to say: because of the polemics of his day, Wesley did not know enough about what he denied to describe it accurately and therefore was not able to appreciate fully how much his theology of presence shared with Catholic theology. Nonetheless, we are left with a curious scenario: Wesley and some of his Methodist interpreters think he denies transubstantiation, while his Catholic readers believe him to affirm it. Clearly, like the topic of ministerial ordination, eucharistic presence calls for further, independent attention.

Instead, Wesley's position is often characterized as a kind of virtualism (or receptionism), which affirms that Christ is really present (and not just in faith) through the Spirit in the believer's act of partaking of the bread and wine, but denies any corporeal presence in or change of the elements. Wesley does not easily fit into continental European paradigms because his primary influences are Anglican, but he aligns more closely with Luther and Calvin (over against Zwingli) in affirming the real presence of Christ (in his divinity) in the eucharist. In addition to transubstantiation, Wesley also denies Luther's teaching of consubstantiation and instead seems more closely to approximate Calvin's theology of Christ's real presence pneumatologically mediated in the act of receiving the bread and wine.[38] Like many in the Anglican tradition, the Wesleys were content to leave the mode of Christ's presence and his working a mystery.

---

36. Owen F. Cummings, "John Wesley and Eucharistic Ecclesiology," *One in Christ* 35, no. 2 (1999): 147–48. Compare Wesley's comments on transubstantiation in his treatise *Popery Calmly Considered* (1779), IV.5; 14:229@-30.

37. Cummings, *Eucharistic Doctors*, 222.

38. Staples, *Outward Sign and Inward Grace*, 224–28. See Maddox, *Responsible Grace*, 203–4. For a discussion of Wesley's theology of the words of institution, the consecration of the elements, the sanctifying role of the Spirit, and the epiclesis, see Borgen, *John Wesley on the Sacraments*, 72–76.

God incomprehensible shall man presume to know,
Fully search him out, or tell his wondrous ways below?
Him in all his ways we find; *how* the means transmit the power
Here he leaves our thought behind, and faith inquires no more.

How he did these creatures raise and make this bread and wine
Organs to convey his grace to this poor soul of mine,
I cannot the way descry, need not know the mystery,
Only this I know, that I was blind, but now I see.[39]

Christ's Self Sacrifice

One paragraph in this section stands out in particular as a summary of
how Wesley understands the eucharist as a sacrament. In language that goes
beyond *BEM*'s judicious use of "intercession," Wesley understands Jesus'
heavenly priestly office as one of perpetual self-offering before the Father:

> This great and holy mystery communicates to us the death of our
> Blessed Lord, both as offering himself to God, and as giving himself to
> man. As he offered himself to God, it enters me into that mystical body
> for which he died, and which is dead with Christ: yea, it sets me on the
> very shoulders of that Eternal Priest, while he offers up himself, and
> intercedes for his spiritual Israel.[40]

And by means of the eucharist, the body receives from its head both the
"communion of his sufferings" and all the "graces and glories" that its head
can give. Not only is Christ the Host and Feast of the meal, he is also the
Priest and the Victim. Rattenbury notes, "The work of Calvary, if a finished
work in the sense that Christ dying once would die no more, was still unfin-
ished; He was not dead, but risen, ascended at God's right hand. The High
Priest was the Lamb of God, raised up from the dead to be the Great Shepherd of the Sheep. He is the Priest-Victim."[41] Borgen agrees and says, "In
sacrament, God is the giver; in sacrifice, man is the giver . . . the latter is wholly
dependent on the former. . . . The whole question of 'sacrifice' in connection
with the Lord's Supper turns around Christ's 'Priestly Office.'"[42] Because sacrifice is essentially a human act directed toward God the Father for the purposes of reconciliation (Rom 5:10), eucharistic sacrifice and Jesus' human
nature are intrinsically related. Just as Jesus' full humanity is necessary for our

39. *HLS*, 59:1–2.
40. *CSS*, IV.7.
41. Rattenbury, *Eucharistic Hymns*, 103.
42. Borgen, *John Wesley on the Sacraments*, 237.

full redemption, resurrection, and glorification, so one essential feature of eucharistic sacrifice—Christologically and anthropologically—is that the church's sacrifice is made in union with Jesus, whose divine-human self-offering eternally makes atonement between humanity and God.

> O thou eternal victim slain a sacrifice for guilty man,
> By the eternal Spirit made an offering in the sinner's stead,
> Our everlasting priest art thou, and plead'st thy death for sinners now.
>
> Thy offering still continues new, thy vesture keeps its bloody hue,
> Thou stand'st the ever slaughter'd Lamb, thy priesthood still remains
>   the same,
> Thy years, O God, can never fail, thy goodness is unchangeable.[43]

Wesley concludes the paragraph by making some careful distinctions between the types of Christ's sacrificial self-offerings in the Supper and on the cross, just as the Council of Trent was careful to leave undefined the nature of Christ's self-sacrifice at the Last Supper and to specify that the sacrifice of the eucharist did not add to the cross but relied upon it, based on Christ's priesthood in each.

> As he offers himself to man, the Holy Sacrament is, after the sacrifice for sin, the true sacrifice of peace-offerings, and the table purposely set to receive those mercies that are sent down from his altar. Take and eat; this is my body which was broken for you; and this is my blood, which was shed for you.[44]

Notice that while Wesley reserves the language of "sacrifice for sin" (and "propitiation," II.7) for Christ's passion, he still refers to Christ's self-offering at the Last Supper and the eucharist—between which he makes little or no distinction—as a sacrifice. Rattenbury is more astute than many Protestants with respect to Catholic teaching on sacrifice, since he recognizes that the eucharist is not "a repetition of the sacrifice of Calvary," but that the "Mass is a repetition of the Last Supper. . . . It is not the sacrifice of Calvary that is made again, but the same sacrifice that was made at the Last Supper that is made again, with the difference that then the crucifixion was in the future and now it is in the past."[45] Furthermore, he notes how in Catholic theology the sacrifice of the Mass relies on three interrelated convictions: (1) the Last

---

43. *HLS*, 5:1–2.
44. *CSS*, IV.7.
45. Rattenbury, *Thoughts on Holy Communion*, 107.

Supper was itself a sacrifice (as was Jesus' death, Catholics add), (2) at which Jesus constituted the apostles as priests, and (3) at which he transubstantiated the elements of bread and wine. Rattenbury flatly denies all three of these, and earlier he lauds the Reformers for having dislodged the Protestant eucharist from medieval Catholic sacerdotal control and celebrates how the Anglican divines, and especially the Wesleys, have restored the dimension of thanksgiving and joy from the early church.[46] However, while Wesley does disagree with the latter two Catholic convictions on the Last Supper—namely, the priesthood and transubstantiation, he differs from Rattenbury in that he speaks here of the Last Supper and the eucharist as sacrifices.

Borgen does not always discern these distinctions as clearly as Rattenbury. He reasons from a view of the eucharist that is overly fixed. For him, the eucharist has a downward dimension (from God to humanity) and a Godward dimension (from humanity to God), and these dimensions must not be confused.[47] In the Godward dimension, he denies that the eucharist is the "same sacrifice," which he assumes to mean Calvary rather than the Lord's Supper; first, the "believer receives the benefits of Christ's sacrifice," and then Christ's sacrifice, "already received," is "'set forth' before the Father as a pleading sacrifice together with the offering up of 'self.'" He conceptualizes eucharistic sacrifice as moving "both ways" between God and humanity, but such that these ways must be entirely distinct, the church's self-offering necessarily following its reception.[48] The conceptualization of the eucharist as directional is helpful—indeed necessary—in many respects, but Wesley's achievement is that in his eucharistic theology these directions intersect on the altar and in the elements and are, in fact, united in Jesus, who is both sacrificially God and human and sacrificially priest and victim. Christ unites the church's offering to his such that the two coincide and are in fact one. It is not that the church receives Christ's sacrifice and then offers its own; rather, in the eucharistic sacrifice, the church receives Christ's sacrifice as it offers its own.

Interestingly, as an offering from Christ to humankind, Wesley calls the sacrament "the true sacrifice of peace-offerings," thereby reversing the typical agency of peace-offering as that which people offer to God. Unfortunately, he does not expound this image, for in addition to the eucharist as an application of the propitiation of the cross and essential spiritual food, the idea of it as a gesture of peace from the Creator to creatures is one particularly rich in potential.

46. Rattenbury, *Thoughts on Holy Communion*, 60–64.

47. Borgen, *John Wesley on the Sacraments*, 238–41.

48. Borgen, "No End Without the Means," 81. Similarly, see Paul S. Sanders, "Wesley's Eucharistic Faith and Practice," *Anglican Theological Review* 48, no. 2 (1966): 169–70.

Jesus is the risen and glorified Lord even while he is always the Lamb slain from the foundation of the world. The work of the Word incarnate perfectly corresponds to the person of the Son before the Father, and the nature of this work controls our language of Jesus' intercession. As Borgen notes, "Christ's priestly office also involves a never-ending offering of himself before God: he always appears in the presence of God for us. He died once, but he also ever lives and intercedes perpetually for us, by continually representing to his Father his sacrifice as present."[49]

> He dies, as now for us he dies! That all-sufficient sacrifice
> Subsists eternal as the Lamb, in every time and place the same,
> To all alike it co-extends, its saving vertue never ends.

> He lives for us to interceed, for us he doth this moment plead,
> And all who could not see him die may now with faith's interior eye
> Behold him stand as slaughter'd there, and feel the answer to his prayer.[50]

The Lord's Supper as It Is a Sacrifice

In the final three sections, Wesley treats the eucharist in its overtly sacrificial dimension, first, as it is a "commemorative sacrifice," and then as it is a sacrifice of ourselves and our goods.

Commemorative Sacrifice

Anthropologically, humankind is made for sacrifice: "There never was on earth a true religion without some kind of sacrifices."[51] In this first sentence, Wesley goes beyond the formulation of *BEM* in a way that must trouble the German Methodist responses to *BEM*, for unlike them, he is not convinced that at the eucharist the church only receives and offers nothing. The question for Wesley, instead, is what kind of sacrifice God's people will offer. Before the time of Christ, non-Jews did not fully understand Israel's sacrifices, and yet not even Israel's Levitical sacrifices "could ever take away sin, but in dependence on that of Jesus Christ. . . . The Holy Communion alone brings together these two great ends, atonement of sins, and acceptable duty to God, of which all the sacrifices of old were no more than weak shadows."[52] The sacrifice of Christ stands over against all other sacrifices. Therefore, by its "infinite value," its "infinite virtue," and its "infinite worth," his offering is unique and never

49. Borgen, *John Wesley on the Sacraments*, 45.
50. *HLS*, 140:1–2; see 84:3.
51. *CSS*, VI.1.
52. *CSS*, VI.1.

needs repeating (see Heb 10:1–18). Here is another instance where Wesley distinguishes himself from the Continental Reformers. Laurence Landini writes how Biel's theology—which did not recognize the "infinite salvific value" of the eucharistic sacrifice—influenced Luther and the Continental Reformers.[53]

Excursus: Old Testament Sacrifices and Christ's Sacrifice

How does Wesley understand Israel's sacrifices and worship—especially the Passover memorial of the Exodus and the Day of Atonement—in light of Christ's once and for all sacrifice? By and large, he follows Hebrews 8–10 in reading the Old Testament typologically and Christologically.[54] His previous reference to Christ the true Passover and his comments immediately previous entail two important observations.

First, numerous key people, events, and sacrifices in Israel's history function figurally to prepare (and in retrospect explain) the person and work of Christ. Not surprisingly, a concentration of types that prefigure Christ is located in Exodus and Leviticus.

> —The paschal lamb is a type of Christ and the Passover a type of the Christian feast (Ex 12:3).[55]
> —Israel prefigures the church (Ex 16:4).
> —The mercy seat is a type of Christ's propitiation (Ex 25:18).
> —Aaron, the office of the high priest, his garments, and his ministry are types of Christ (Ex 28:15).
> —Aaron's consecration, the blood and oil of the sacrifice, and the altar signify Christ's sacrificial atonement and his anointing by the Spirit; consecration of priests means that all believers are priests, charged with offering spiritual sacrifices (Ex 29:19, 35–36; see Ex 39:1 and Lv 8:12; 9:22).
> —The Day of Atonement and the sweet spices prefigure Christ and the sweet savor of his sacrifice (Ex. 30:10, 34; see Eph 5:2).
> —Moses' intercession prefigures Christ's (Ex 33:12–17).
> —The burnt offering, its regulations, and the entrance to the tent of meeting prefigure Christ (Lv 1:2–14; 3:17).
> —The frankincense of grain offering typifies Christ's satisfaction and intercession (Lv 2:1).
> —Washing clothes after being pronounced clean signifies Christ's cleansing with blood (Lv 13:6).

53. Lawrence C. Landini, "The Role of Self-Offering in the Understanding of the Eucharist as Sacrifice," *Josephinum Journal of Theology* 1, no. (1994): 21.

54. See his *OT Notes*, Ex 29:35; see *HLS* 46:2, associating Aaron and Melchizedek with Christ.

55. See Wesley's *OT Notes* for the following verses.

—Two birds and a crimson thread after being healed of leprosy signifies Christ's dying and rising and his blood (Lv 14:4).

—The two goats of the Day of Atonement signify Christ's death and resurrection; the scapegoat prefigures Christ's forsakenness; the Day of Atonement signifies "the two great gospel privileges: remission of sins, and access to God, both of which we owe to the mediation of the Lord Jesus" (Lv 16:8, 21, 34).

—The Jubilee and the Day of Atonement signify spiritual liberty, repentance, and atonement (Lv 25:9).

Second, not only do Israel's priests and sacrifices (both ceremonial and sin offerings) prefigure Christ, but whatever efficacy they have to expiate sin and make atonement with God comes, in fact, from Christ's unique sacrifice on the cross, the virtue of which was operative within Israel's sin offerings. The guilt offering (Wesley calls it a trespass offering), for example, serves partially "to make them sensible of their spiritual diseases, that they might fly to God in Christ for the cure of them."[56] Moreover, when the priest laid hands on the goat, confessed Israel's sins, and sent it into the wilderness, he was, in effect, laying their sins upon Christ: "Charging all their sins and the punishments to them upon the goat, which tho' only a ceremony, yet being done according to God's appointment and manifestly pointing at Christ upon whom their iniquities and punishments were laid, Isa 53:5, 6."[57] His comments on Hebrews' exposition of the Levitical cult are illustrative. When Hebrews 9:22 asserts that the forgiveness of sins requires the shedding of blood, he says, "All this pointed to the blood of Christ, effectually cleansing from all sin, and intimated there can be no purification from it by any other means."[58] Likewise, when Hebrews 9:26 writes that Christ's atoning sacrifice was "once for all," he writes, "The sacrifice of Christ divides the whole age or duration of the world into two parts, and extends its virtue backward and forward, from this middle point wherein they meet, to abolish both the guilt and power of sin."

O thou whose offering on the tree the legal offerings all foreshew'd,
Borrow'd their whole effect from thee, and drew their virtue from thy
    blood;
The blood of goats and bullocks slain could never for one sin atone;
To purge the guilty offerer's stain thine was the work, and *thine* alone.[59]

---

56. *OT Notes*, Lv 14:12; see Lv 4:4; 10:17.

57. *OT Notes*, Lv 16:21; see Lv 16:14; Nm 6:14; 1 Sm 1:10; 1 Kgs 3:15.

58. Heb 9:22 refers to Lv 17:11; see Lv 17:4.

59. *HLS*, 123:1. See Wainwright, "Our Elder Brethren Join," 16; Nichols, "Theology of Christ's Sacrifice and Presence," 22–23; Tyson, "Charles Wesley's Theology of Redemption," 13–14; Stevick, *Altar's Fire*, 158–59, 181–82. See *HLS* 4, 27, 36, 44, 46, 113, 123:2–3, 126:2, 127:2.

Wesley's theology of Old Testament sacrifices in relation to Christ's sacrifice has much in common with patristic and medieval theology, including that of Thomas Aquinas. His understanding of Christ's "eternal now," which allows him to assert Christ's priestly office in the eucharist, functions here with respect to Christ's efficacious sacrifice: namely, if in the order of knowing, Israel's sacrifices precede Christ's, nevertheless, in the order of being, his passion is the true cause of their atoning effects. Wesley's Christology suggests also how he relates Christ's passion—which was infinite and complete—to the daily sacrifice of the eucharist.

Wesley then turns to address the relationship between the eucharistic sacrifice and the unique, infinite sacrifice of Christ's passion. He relates the two in the way that a "commemoration" relates to the "real" event: Christ's "real" sacrifice was offered only once, yet the eucharistic sacrifice, "by a devout and thankful commemoration," is offered daily.[60] To offer up the eucharistic sacrifice as a commemoration of Christ's real sacrifice is what Paul calls "To set forth the death of the Lord," both before humankind *and* before God.[61] Thus Wesley uses *commemoration* in this instance as a synonym for *sacramental,* in much the same way that Aquinas uses the language of *representation.* This becomes more clear when he lists the three ways in which the "flesh of Jesus" is sacrificed: (1) the "prefiguring sacrifices" of the law; (2) the "real deed upon the cross," and (3) this "commemorative sacrifice" by which "we present before God the Father that precious oblation of his Son once offered. And thus do we every day offer unto God the meritorious sufferings of our Lord, as the one sure ground whereon God may give, and we obtain, the blessings we pray for."[62] The Catholic response to *BEM* regrets that the text "does not *say* unambiguously that the eucharist is in itself a *real sacrifice, the memorial* of the sacrifice of Christ on the cross," but Wesley unequivocally does, referring to the Lord's Supper as the Christian Sacrifice, the daily Sacrifice, and a commemorative sacrifice.

> To us thou hast redemption sent; and we again to thee present
> The blood that speaks our sins forgiven, that sprinkles all the nations
>   round;
> And now thou hear'st the solemn sound loud-echoing thro' the courts
>   of heaven.

60. *CSS,* VI.2.
61. See *NT Notes,* 1 Cor 11:26.
62. *CSS,* VI.2.

Father, the grand oblation see, the death as present now with thee,
As when he gasp'd on earth—"Forgive!" Answer, and shew the
    curse remov'd,
Accept us in the well-belov'd, and bid thy world of rebels live.[63]

Stevick and Rattenbury both note the sacrificial reciprocity between Christ's sacrifice and the eucharist. Like the former on which it depends, the latter is neither simply a memorial nor a sacrifice of praise. It is at least these things, but it is also its own proper, corporate, liturgical sacrifice, and this liturgical sacrifice corresponds to the self-offering of those who are incorporated into Christ at baptism and who are strengthened in the eucharist. Rattenbury comments, "The broken bread and the poured-out wine, the tokens of the passion of Christ, plead that passion. When Brevint calls it a kind of sacrifice, he does not mean that it is no sacrifice, but that it is a sacrifice of a different kind from that of Calvary . . . the whole content of it is what happens in heaven and is symbolized on earth."[64]

> Memorial of thy sacrifice this eucharistick mystery
> The full atoning grace supplies, and sanctifies our gifts in thee:
> Our persons and performance please, while God in thee look down
>   from heaven,
> Our acceptable service sees, and whispers all our sins forgiven.[65]

> With solemn faith we offer up, and spread before thy glorious eyes
> That only ground of all our hope, that precious, bleeding sacrifice,
> Which brings thy grace on sinners down, and perfects all our souls in
>   one.[66]

Wesley's affirmation that the church does in fact offer the sacrifice of Christ is highly significant, since it clearly moves beyond the idea of intercession. The church sacramentally unites itself to Christ by offering to God the eucharist, which represents Christ's sacrifice, thereby participating in Christ's self-offering of his body and blood to the Father. The whole congregation— and not the minister alone[67]—offers the sacrifice of Christ to God: "And to God it is an altar, whereon men mystically present to him the same sacrifice

---

63. *HLS*, 121:1b, 2b. Charles's thought aligns closely with John's; Stevick, *Altar's Fire*, 152–53.

64. Rattenbury, *Eucharistic Hymns*, 122; Stevick, *Altar's Fire*, 164–65.

65. *HLS*, 123:4.

66. *HLS*, 125:2.

67. Bowmer, *Sacrament of the Lord's Supper in Early Methodism*, 163–65, 180–83. See the following section on Priesthood.

as still bleeding and suing for mercy."[68] Wesley's facility with biblical imagery from both testaments reinforces that the eucharist is a sacrifice: Jesus is the Paschal Lamb, and his sacrifice on the cross was the "True Passover."[69] Owing to this, Wesley calls the sacrifice of the eucharist wine-offerings, burnt-offerings, and peace-offerings—a sacrificial offering that relies on Christ's atoning work, to be sure, but a necessary sacrifice all the same. It is in this manner that Jesus' disciples continue the sacrificial meal he inaugurated in which they "set forth the death of Christ" (1 Cor 11:26).[70]

> Victim Divine, thy grace we claim
> While thus thy precious death we shew,
> Once offer'd up a spotless Lamb in thy great temple here below,
> Thou didst for all mankind atone, and standest now before the throne.[71]

> Father let the sinner go, the Lamb did once atone,
> Lo! We to thy justice shew the Passion of thy Son;
> Thus to thee we set it forth: he the dying precept gave,
> He, who hath sufficient worth a thousand worlds to save.[72]

Cummings cites the Catholic Catechism (1362, 1366) and says, "Given the contemporary Catholic understanding of the eucharist as the sacramental representation of the unique sacrifice of Christ on the cross, Wesley's position would seem to be not far distant." Significantly, Louis Bouyer's critique of Cranmer at precisely this point—i.e., his disavowal of the sacramental presence of Christ's sacrifice in the eucharist—reinforces Cummings's remark. Wesley, however, does not align with Cranmer or "so many other Protestants"; rather, he affirms the eucharist as a sacrifice: the repetition of the Last Supper, the sacramental memorial of the cross, which entails the sacramental presence of Christ's sacrifice and which conveys to believers the reconciling grace of his passion.[73]

With respect to the agency of Christ, Wesley once again stresses that his person (and his office) is the controlling factor in the sacrifice: Jesus Christ,

---

68. *CSS*, VI.2.

69. Borgen, *John Wesley on the Sacraments*, 186.

70. Borgen, *John Wesley on the Sacraments*, 241.

71. *HLS*, 116:1. Steven Hoskins shows how this celebrated hymn brings together the themes of sacrifice, presence, memorial, experience of deliverance, assurance, and eschatology; Hoskins, "Eucharist and Eschatology in the Writing of the Wesleys," 76.

72. *HLS*, 122:1.

73. Cummings, "John Wesley and Eucharistic Ecclesiology," 149–50; Louis Bouyer, "Cranmer and the Anglican Eucharist," in *Primary Readings on the Eucharist*, ed. Thomas Fisch (Collegeville, MN: Liturgical Press, 2004), 122–24.

"the High Priest himself," has "set up both this table and the altar, for the communication of his body and his blood to men, and for the representation of both to God; it cannot be doubted but that the [table] is most profitable to the penitent sinner, and the [altar] most acceptable to his gracious Father."[74] The offering to the Father of Jesus' body and blood in the eucharist is done by the One who is both priest and victim: Jesus himself "is gone up into the true sanctuary, and doth there continually present both his own body and blood before God."[75] In his resurrected and glorified humanity, Jesus makes an offering of himself to the Father on behalf of all humanity. For Wesley (and Trent), Christ's eternal heavenly intercession is inseparable from his historic passion and from the church's eucharistic sacrifice.

Priesthood

The risen Christ's self-offering grounds the sacrifice of the eucharist in its anthropological dimension. In fact, many of the sacrificial hymns refer to the nexus of the divine-human encounter as it occurs through the elements and the eucharistic prayer, and the twofold agency between God and the faithful at the eucharistic mystery finds its focal point in the use and reception of the elements. Wesley singles out the agency of the ordained minister, the whole congregation, and Christ, each in crucial ways. Like *BEM* and the Catholic position in *The Grace Given You in Christ*, the ordained has a representative function on the part of Christ before the people: "To men it is a sacred table where God's minister is ordered to represent from God his master the passion of his dear Son, as still fresh, and still powerful for their eternal salvation." Wesley distinguishes himself from Trent by not differentiating between the offering of the priest and the offering of the faithful, although throughout his life he maintained the necessity among Methodists of the ordained priesthood in order to celebrate the eucharist.[76]

In correspondence on these matters, Wesley writes, "We believe there is, and always was, in every Christian Church . . . an outward priesthood, ordained by Jesus Christ, and an outward sacrifice offered therein."[77] Space does not permit a full-blown discussion of Wesley's theology of priesthood, but Borgen makes the case (contra Rattenbury) that despite Wesley's affirmation of priesthood, he distances himself from any conception of a sacerdotal priesthood that makes an "outward sacrifice." Borgen looks carefully and more broadly

74. *CSS*, VI.2.
75. *CSS*, VI.3.
76. See Wesley's sermon "Prophets and Priests" (no. 121, vol. IV).
77. Rattenbury, *Eucharistic Hymns*, 84.

than Rattenbury at some key points: (1) the context of Wesley's language and his use of words such as priest, pastor, minister, royal priesthood; (2) the corporate and individual context of sacrifice; and (3) Wesley's omission of Brevint's language of "sacrificing priesthood" and "sacerdotal priesthood."[78]

As with transubstantiation, it is unclear whether Wesley (or many of his interpreters) properly understood the Catholic theology of priesthood and sacrifice, since what he seems to be reacting against is the mistaken Protestant idea that the priestly sacrifice at the eucharist is a sacrifice additional to and independent of the cross and thus bearing its own meritorious and expiatory efficacy. However, the Council of Trent does not teach this idea. It might explain, though, Wesley's omission of the word "expiation" from the line in this section (VI.2) of presenting Christ's sacrifice to God on the altar "as still bleeding and still suing for expiation and mercy."[79] Perhaps this omission implies that Wesley does not wish to suggest that at the hands of the priest the eucharist—which is itself legitimately a sacrifice—adds any expiation to our forgiveness that Christ's did not. (The hymns make this point unambiguously, and again, Trent does not teach this.) Significantly, though, what Trent and Wesley both teach is that the infinite, once for all, and all sufficient expiation of Christ's sacrifice is applied to believers in the eucharistic sacrifice by means of which they receive God's forgiveness. Wesley is careful to suggest that all expiation for sin moves from Christ to humanity, and his teaching that Jesus is the priest of the eucharist who extends his forgiveness to those who receive him there secures this affirmation. Thus he distinguishes between the cause of sin's expiation, the cross, and its application to believers in the eucharist, both through the agency of Christ's priestly office.[80]

Notice that for both the minister and the faithful in the eucharistic sacrifice, Wesley holds together the interiority of faith with the need for an external signification. The minister contributes in representing the passion of Christ to the people who in turn demonstrate their desire to be united to Christ by offering to God the same sacrifice of Christ. In addition to the forgiveness and sanctification that those who are "under the shadow of his cross" hope to obtain by presenting to God the "figure of his sacrifice," the goal of human agency in uniting to the cross is to "present ourselves in very deed before him."[81]

78. Borgen, *John Wesley on the Sacraments*, 244–46, 265–69. Wesley critiques the Mass as a repetition of Christ's sacrifice on the cross. See his "Reply to a Roman Catechism," in Jackson, *Works of John Wesley*, X:121; Cummings, "John Wesley and Eucharistic Ecclesiology," 148.

79. Borgen, *John Wesley on the Sacraments*, 243, 268.

80. See *NT Notes*: Heb 10:14. Stevick interprets Charles similarly: *Altar's Fire*, 159–60.

81. Wesley, *CSS*, VI.3.

> Ye royal priests of Jesus, rise, and join the daily sacrifice,
> Join all believers in his name to offer up the spotless Lamb.[82]

Sacrifice of Ourselves

Wesley's affirmation, therefore, that the church offers the same sacrifice of Christ through the priesthood of its head already suggests a commonality with Trent's formulation, and it brings the previously suggested idea of participation to the foreground in Section VII. He is clear that although the cross has brought an end to those sacrifices "that atone for sin," Christians are still under the obligation to make a sacrifice. Nor is this sacrifice incidental to a life of faith in communion with Christ; rather it "is absolutely necessary to our having a share in that redemption. So that though the sacrifice of ourselves cannot procure salvation, yet it is altogether needful to our receiving it."[83] Creaturely cooperation in God's act of salvation is far from a rallying cry of the Reformation, yet, based on his anthropology and epistemology, it is at the center of Wesley's doctrine of salvation.[84]

This anthropology, for which offering the sacrifice of Christ is "altogether needful" for procuring salvation, again demonstrates Wesley's refusal to reduce faith simply to an interior disposition. On the one hand it attests to the nature of faith as a fully embodied act that shows forth corporately as the church's liturgy, and on the other hand it means that Wesley cannot view the eucharist as merely a symbolic or tangential ritual that the church can cut from its worship of God. From Wesley's perspective, the necessity of the eucharistic sacrifice does not thereby render it a good work above and beyond the saving work of Christ; rather, it is the way believers receive Christ's work.

The church cannot take lightly its participation in the work of its Lord, since Christ himself does not: "Jesus Christ does nothing without his church, insomuch that sometimes they are represented as only one person."[85] The eucharistic sacrifice, as the act of the body's union with its head, entails a complete commitment on the part of its members to follow Christ in the movement of his passion. "This conformity to Christ, which is the grand principle of the whole Christian religion, relates first to our duty about his sufferings, and then to our happiness about his exaltation, presupposing his sufferings." The faithful cannot expect to enjoy "com-

---

82. Wesley, *HLS*, 137:1.

83. Wesley, *CSS*, VII.1.

84. See "Grace and Response—the Nature of Human Salvation" (141–56), and the subsection "The Co-Operant Character of Salvation" (147–51), in Maddox, *Responsible Grace*.

85. *CSS*, VII.2.

munion" with Christ in glory unless they "have conformity with him here in his sufferings."[86]

> Would the Saviour of mankind without his people die?
> No, to him we all are join'd as more than standers by.
> Freely as the victim came to the altar of his cross,
> We attend the slaughter'd Lamb, and suffer for his cause.[87]

> While faith th'atoning blood applies, ourselves a living sacrifice
> We freely offer up to God: and none but those his glory share
> Who crucified with Jesus are, and follow where their Saviour trod.

> Saviour, to thee our lives we give, our meanest sacrifice receive,
> And to thy own oblation join, our suffering and triumphant head,
> Thro' all thy states thy members lead, and seat us on the throne divine.[88]

In general, Wesley locates ecclesiology under soteriology, which is a systematization that may be debated. Raymond George argues that the Wesleys did not have a strong theology of incorporation and that Wesley spoke more frequently of Christ the Head leading his members rather than his body; however, emphasis on the language of *member* evidently begs the question: to whom do these members belong?[89] Eucharistic theology will always provoke ecclesial questions, and these hymns show that Wesley locates his anthropology of sacrifice under his doctrine of Christology and Jesus' incarnation, a systematization that is entirely appropriate. His eucharistic theology brings these themes together, and Paul Chilcote notes the individual and communal aspects of sacrifice: the eucharist "establishes a cruciform pattern of life in the faithful disciple and draws all the followers of Jesus into a community shaped by the cross and resurrection as well."[90] All the hymns of oblation are sung in the plural, thereby suggesting a corporate incorporation of the eucharistic sacrifice with Christ's: "The Church can do nothing apart from Christ and out of union with Him."[91] The unity between Christ's passion and his eternal sacrifice, and this unity on which the church's eucharistic sacrifice

86. *CSS*, VII.4.

87. *HLS*, 131:1.

88. *HLS*, 128:3. Stevick remarks on this idea in Charles's thought as well; *Altar's Fire*, 157.

89. Raymond George, "The Lord's Supper," in *Doctrine of the Church*, ed. Dow Kirkpatrick (New York: Abingdon, 1964), 157.

90. Paul Chilcote, "Eucharist and Formation," in *A Wesleyan Theology of the Eucharist: The Presence of God for Christian Life and Ministry*, ed. Jason E. Vickers (Nashville: General Board of Higher Education and Ministry, 2016), 192.

91. Rattenbury, *Eucharistic Hymns*, 132; see Stevick, *Altar's Fire*, 171.

depends, demands a unity between the church's sacrifice and Christ's. The eucharist is not two complementary and simultaneous sacrifices: because Christ is really the Guest and Host, the eucharistic is, therefore, the one sacrifice of Christ.

> Whate'er we cast on him alone is with his great oblation one,
> His sacrifice doth ours sustain, and favour and acceptance gain.
>
> Mixt with the sacred smoke we rise, the smoke of his burnt sacrifice,
> By the eternal Spirit driven from earth, in Christ we mount to heaven.[92]
>
> With him the corner stone the living stones conjoin,
> Christ and his church are one, one body and one vine,
> For us he uses all his powers, and all he has, or is, is ours.
>
> The motions of our head the members all pursue,
> By his good Spirit led to act, and suffer too
> Whate'er he did on earth sustain, 'till glorious all like him we reign.[93]

Conformity to Christ's sacrifice in the eucharistic sacrifice stands in anthropological and soteriological continuity with the sacrifices of Israel's cult. Just as Israel and the priest identified with the sacrificial victim who was offered to God in order to represent them and by which they offered themselves to God, so also Christians in the eucharist—who are not crucified "in the same manner"—identify with Christ their priest and representative so that "their whole body of sin" is crucified to the extent that the life that remains they offer to God in service. "The Saviour thus offering himself, and the saved so united to him by faith, so partaking of his sufferings, and so given up to his will, are accounted before God one and the same sacrifice."[94] Bowmer summarizes nicely: "In the eucharist, the Church, as the corporate body of worshipping Christians, re-presents the sacrifice so that its effects become a present reality. It is His Body offering His Body."[95]

The consequence of communion with Christ's sacrifice in the eucharist, then, is nothing short of a complete transformation from sin and guilt to atonement and pardon, the crucifixion of the sinful body in order to offer oneself as a holy and living sacrifice to God. Because the eucharistic sacrifice unites the self-offering of believers to the sacrifice of Christ, it is perhaps not

---

92. *HLS*, 137: 3,7.
93. *HLS*, 129: 2–3.
94. *CSS*, VII.7.
95. Bowmer, *Sacrament of the Lord's Supper in Early Methodism*, 186.

surprising that Wesley takes the next step of placing the words of Christ in his sacrifice in the mouths of the faithful. Just as Christ spoke to God the words of self-offering in Psalm 40 to describe the true nature of sacrifice, so Christians can speak those same words now: "Lo, I come! if this soul and body may be useful to anything, to do thy will," and no matter what "agonies may trouble my spirit, O Father, into thy hand will I commend my life."[96]

> Yet in this ordinance divine we still the sacred load may bear;
> And now we in thy offering join, thy sacramental Passion share.
>
> Thou art with all thy members here, in this tremendous mystery
> We jointly before God appear to offer up ourselves with thee.
>
> True followers of our bleeding Lamb now on thy daily cross we die,
> And mingled in a common flame ascend triumphant to the skie.[97]
>
> Thy sacrifice with heavenly powers replete, all holy, all-divine,
> Human and weak, and sinful ours; how can the two oblations join?
>
> Our mean imperfect sacrifice on thine is as a burden thrown,
> Both in a common flame arise, and both in God's account are one.[98]

Sacrifice of Our Goods

Wesley concludes his text with a brief section that in his mind follows straightforwardly and uncontroversially from what has gone before—namely, that the eucharist also entails the "sacrifice of our goods." This sacrificial dimension of the eucharist has consequences for the faithful both with respect to the neighbor and before God. Wesley's position is that the altar is the proper place where believers can come penitently and renew their vows and promises to God so that whatever "good, moral works" they may do might become

96. *CSS*, VII.11; see Heb 10:5–9; Lk 23:46.

97. *HLS*, 141:5, 7, 8. On the central idea in Charles Wesley's hymns of "seeing" Christ's passion and identifying with it, see Joanna Cruickshank, "'Appear as Crucified for Me': Sight, Suffering, and Spiritual Transformation in the Hymns of Charles Wesley," *Journal of Religious History* 30, no. 3 (2006): 311–30. James Gordon makes a similar comment with respect to the hymn Victim Divine, cited earlier; Gordon, "'Impassive He Suffers; Immortal He Dies': Rhetoric and Polemic in Charles Wesley's Portrayal of the Atonement," *Scottish Bulletin of Evangelical Theology* 18, no. 1 (2000): 57–60. See, too, Stevick's section, "Theology and Feeling," in *Altar's Fire* (208–13), and John R. Tyson, "Charles Wesley and the Language of Evangelical Experience: The Poetical Hermeneutic Revisited," *Asbury Journal* 61, no. 1 (2006): 25–46.

98. *HLS*, 147: 2, 4. For an outlying Methodist position that rejects almost any notion of offering, see Franz Hildebrandt, *I Offered Christ: A Protestant Study of the Mass* (Philadelphia: Fortress, 1967), 169–70, 203–6.

"religious sacrifices."[99] If the faithful can offer their whole selves to God in sacrifice in the eucharist, then an act of charity and mercy toward the neighbor and the church's struggle for justice in the world are simply extensions of this personal and corporate self-sacrifice (see Heb 13:6).

In a complementary fashion, Wesley also contends not only that eucharistic sacrifice entails sacrificial living for the sake of the neighbor, but that Christians should bring the "freewill offering of their goods" to Holy Communion.[100] With this comment Wesley ventures toward what has been historically—and what remains—highly contentious ground vis à vis the appropriate use of the elements in the eucharistic rite.[101] Following the Passover sacrifice, from which the eucharist at least partially derives, and the practice of the early church, Thurian urges churches to incorporate the offering of bread and wine into the eucharistic rite as a way of holding together the orders of creation and redemption. Protestant churches historically have not embraced this idea under the suspicion that a sacrifice of any kind would detract from and diminish the unique sacrifice of Christ. So, for example, although *BEM* avoids the language of offering, it nonetheless says that bread and wine are presented to the Father in thanksgiving for the goodness of creation, and while the United Methodist response receives it approvingly, the German Methodist churches do not.

> Father, our sacrifice receive, our souls and bodies we present,
> Our goods, and vows, and praises give, whate'er thy bounteous love
>   hath lent.
> Thou can'st not now our gift despise, cast on that all-atoning Lamb,
> Mixt with that bleeding sacrifice, and offer'd up thro' Jesu's name.[102]

Wesley only addresses this obliquely—just enough to provoke contrasting interpretations—although he was familiar with how the different versions of Anglican prayer books had sought to deal with this question.[103] At points, he

99. *CSS*, VIII.5.

100. *CSS*, VIII.1. For a historical treatment on this topic in Methodism, see L. Edward Phillips, "Eucharist and Money," in Vickers, *Wesleyan Theology of the Eucharist*, 223–38.

101. Stevenson, "Eucharistic Sacrifice—an Insoluble Liturgical Problem," 469–92.

102. *HLS*, 153:2.

103. Alexander, "With Eloquence in Speech and Song," 256; Bowmer, *Sacrament of the Lord's Supper in Early Methodism*, 85–101, esp. 93; G. J. Cuming, *A History of Anglican Liturgy*, 2nd ed. (London: Macmillan, 1982), 77–81; Maddox, *Responsible Grace*, 198–99; see chapters 34, 35, 40 on *The Book of Common Prayer*, in Ronald Claud Dudley Jasper and G. J. Cuming, *Prayers of the Eucharist: Early and Reformed*, 3rd ed. (Collegeville, MN: Liturgical Press, 1992); McAdoo and Stevenson, *Mystery of the Eucharist*, 112; J. Brian Selleck, "The Book of Common Prayer in the Theology of John Wesley" (Ph.D. diss., Drew University, 1983). With respect to the influence of patristic and Anglican liturgies on Charles's hymns, see Wainwright, "Our Elder Brethren Join," 6–9; Nichols, "Charles Wesley's Eucharistic Hymns," 13–21.

can speak generally that in addition to a self-offering, "all that we have, all that we can do" must also be "dedicated to the glory of God" and "surrendered into his hands."[104] It is hard to know here whether or not Wesley has in view the thank offering (or oblation) of the elements; consequently, Borgen and Rattenbury engage in heated debate over the precise status of the bread and wine in Wesley's eucharistic theology. Borgen (along with George) denies any suggestion that the elements are offered to God as a sacrifice. Rattenbury, however, who personally disagrees with Wesley on the nature of priesthood, nevertheless interprets him more in the Anglo-Catholic tradition and in continuity with the offertory of the early church: "The offering on the Altar is not only an historical memorial of what once happened but a counterpart of what is eternally taking place in Heaven; with which our oblation of ourselves is identified."[105] To be sure, Wesley is elusive on these matters, but a hermeneutic that adopts Lutheran concerns as normative—as Borgen and Franz Hildebrandt are in danger of doing—remains unsatisfying.[106] A hermeneutic that places eucharistic sacrifice as a function of Wesley's understanding of the mystery of divine-human agency is more faithful to his theology of God's way of salvation. Three observations are entailed here.

First, Wesley is clear that the eucharist is a sacrifice, and he does not delimit the definition to one of praise and thanksgiving; instead, the sacrifice is a complete offering of the self (a holy and living sacrifice) at the same time that it is a sacrifice of all that believers have—not just a sacrifice of self, but one of possessions and goods as well. Following Israel's example of offering cattle and goods to the Lord at the Exodus, he says, "It behooves every sinner at conversion to God, and whenever he approaches his Table, to consecrate all he has to Jesus Christ. . . . All things are his, as he is sovereign Lord and God. But all that we have is his by a further title, because we have given them, with our own persons, by our own act and deed."[107] In this citation, Wesley incorporates the returning of God's good gifts back to God as a worshipful action within the eucharistic celebration.[108] To whom does the bread and wine belong before it is offered to God if not the church; and what other word can describe its change of ownership from creature to Creator and its change of function from fruits of creation to body and blood of Christ if not *offering*? Consequently, the bread and wine become an offering to the Father that, by

104. *CSS*, VIII.1.

105. Rattenbury, *Eucharistic Hymns*, 134.

106. Borgen's comments are interspersed in his chapter on eucharistic sacrifice in *John Wesley on the Sacraments*, mainly pages 241–69.

107. *CSS*, VIII.2.

108. See *OT Notes*, 1 Chr 29:14.

concomitance, then becomes the body and blood of Christ in the power of the Holy Spirit. The elements once belonged to God, who gave them to the church; the church receives it as good food and drink, and in return offers it back to God to do with it what the risen Lord always does with it—use it as the means of communion with him. The offering is made not because God needs it, but because the church does. In fact, Wainwright finds in some hymns "an exact equivalent of the ancient anamnesis-oblation."[109]

> He reads, while we beneath present our Saviour's death,
> Do as Jesus bids us do, signify his flesh and blood,
> Him in a memorial shew, offer up the Lamb to God.[110]

> Father to him we turn our face who did for all atone,
> And worship tow'rd thy holy place, and seek thee in thy Son.

> To thee his Passion we present, who for our ransom dyes,
> We reach by this great instrument th' eternal sacrifice.

> The Lamb as crucified afresh is here held out to men,
> The tokens of his blood and flesh are on this table seen.[111]

Second, the eucharistic elements are rich in signification. We have already seen how, for example, they proclaim the Lord's death by signifying his body and blood, convey Christ's sacrificial presence and apply the atonement to believers, and unite the orders of redemption and creation. What is more, because the eucharist is the place where humanity and God come together to meet one another, the offering of the elements not only refers to God's divine self-gift in Christ, but also signifies the church's offering of itself to God. Acts of mercy and love toward the neighbor attest to the believer's sacrificial love, but how does the church, in a corporate and liturgical setting, demonstrate its sacrificial love to God? Wesley's comments on Israel's sacrifices indicates that he sees them not only as divinely appointed instruments of atonement, but also as the means by which Israel signified its self-offering to God.[112] The eucharistic elements also serve this function as the way in which the church unites with Christ in worship. In short, offering the elements to God is how the church offers itself, liturgically, to God in Christ. Stevick calls attention to a series of hymns that emphasize the church's display of the eucharistic sacrifice before the Father: "spread before thy glorious eyes"

109. Wainwright, "Our Elder Brethren Join," 9–10.
110. *HLS*, 118:4.
111. *HLS*, 126:1, 3, 4.
112. *OT Notes*, Ex 29:15; Lv 1:3–5; 4:4; 5:11; 8:18; 14:12.

(125:2); "see here!—It on the altar lies" (121:2); "image of his sacrifice" (118:5); "here exhibited [to God] beneath" (119:3). He notes that "in the same act" of the eucharistic sacrifice the church presents Christ's sacrifice to the world and to the Father, and in this same act, Christ presents himself to God (and, we could add, to the church).[113] By allowing the oblation of elements to carry a plurality of signification, Stevick succeeds at conceptualizing eucharistic sacrifice without false dichotomies. The intention of the display, though, is not, of course, to remind the Father of the Son's death or to effect any change in God; rather, it is for the sake of the church: "We beneath in the Church present to God his body and blood in a memorial, that under the shadow of his cross, and figure of his sacrifice, we may present ourselves in very deed before him."[114]

> Yet may we celebrate below, and daily thus thine offering shew
> Expos'd before thy Father's eyes; in this tremendous mystery
> Present thee bleeding on the tree our everlasting sacrifice.[115]
>
> The sheaf and harvest is but one accepted sacrifice,
> And we who have thy sufferings known shall in thy life arise.
>
> Still all-involv'd in God we are, and offer'd with the Lamb,
> Till all in heaven with Christ appear eternally the same.[116]

Third, Wesley's notion of a freewill offering—which is not a sacrifice for sin—may not be the same as Thurian's thank offering, but it comes awfully close. Wesley has already spoken of the eucharist as a peace offering and a thank offering, nor does he have any angst that the sacrifice of goods—when rightly united to the sacrifice of one's whole self and subordinated to the cross—threatens the singular atoning work of Christ. In fact, just the opposite: it is Christ's sacrifice once and for all that makes possible the acts of self-giving, works of mercy and justice, and the sacrifice of goods.

> Your meat and your drink-offerings throw on him who suffer'd once
>   below,
> But ever lives with God above, to plead for us his dying love.
>
> Mean are our noblest offerings, poor feeble unsubstantial things;
> But when to him our souls we lift, the altar sanctifies the gift.[117]

---

113. Stevick, *Altar's Fire*, 161–63.
114. *CSS*, VI.3.
115. *HLS*, 124:2a.
116. *HLS*, 134:3–4.
117. *HLS*, 137:2, 5.

Borgen relates the debates associated with justification, participation, and the *ordo salutis* to the same facets in Wesley's theological anthropology that I have highlighted, but he does not make the move to the eucharistic elements. He notes that only through active reception on the part of the believer can justification occur, and that only in actively receiving the means of grace can sanctification and perfection ensue. But he does not see that in order for believers actively to receive the grace that God gives through the means, the elements must first be offered up so that God can use them as means. Alternatively, Wainwright refers to the church's reception of grace and its work of the eucharistic celebration, thus: "There is room and need, therefore, for human acceptance of the gift and human obedience to the command [of Jesus to 'do this']."[118] To offer the elements is not to initiate any saving action (as George fears) if it is Jesus' presence that makes the feast—that is, if he is the Host. No creaturely salvific work is being claimed in offering up the elements and the whole rite as a sacrifice (*All hail, thou mighty to atone! To expiate is thine alone* [128:1]). On the contrary, the church must make just the opposite assertion: namely, that only when they are used of God can any saving work take place. This "logical inference" is all the more logical when Wesley's anthropology is explicitly integrated into his sacramental theology, and especially when Methodists realize that his theology of sacrifice in no way threatens the doctrine of justification by faith(ful reception). The church does not profess its faith to the Father by putting its trust in bread and wine, but in the Son's body and blood; likewise, no *anamnesis* or *epiclesis* occurs, no kerygma or evangelism, and thus no sanctification or deification can transpire, unless the materials are sacrificed to God so they can become divine means.

> Angel and Son of God come down, thy sacramental banquet crown,
> Thy power into the means infuse, and give them now their sacred use.[119]

> Come, Holy Ghost, thine influence shed, and realize the sign,
> Thy life infuse into the bread, thy power into the wine.[120]

Indeed, Wesley brings his text to an end along these lines.

> I dare appear before the Lord, with all my sins and my sorrows. It is just also that I should appear with these few blessings. Having received them of Thy hand, now do I offer them to Thee again. Forgive, I beseech Thee, my sins, deliver me from my sorrows, and accept of this my sac-

---

118. Wainwright, "Eucharist in the Churches' Responses to the Lima Text," 65.
119. *HLS*, 58:4.
120. *HLS*, 72:1; see Wainwright, "Our Elder Brethren Join," 27.
121. *CSS*, VIII.6.

rifice: or rather look, in my behalf, on that only true sacrifice, whereof here is the sacrament; the sacrifice of Thy well-beloved Son, proceeding from Thee, to die for me.[121]

Conclusion: Participation

Aquinas would agree with Wesley's comment: "There never was on earth a true religion without some kind of sacrifices. . . . The Holy Communion alone brings together these two great ends, atonement of sins, and acceptable duty to God, of which all the sacrifices of old were no more than weak shadows."[122] The sacrificial dimension of Wesley's eucharistic theology is utterly Christological, for Jesus is both priest and victim, the giver and the gift, the host of the banquet and the feast itself. The fruit of Jesus' atonement, divine grace, is the forgiving and sanctifying work that God imparts to the believer in the eucharist. Yet these words may mask, by their familiarity as theological jargon, the nature of sanctification and atonement that these hymns envision. These hymns remind the believer that even while salvation begins on earth as a pledge of heaven, *sanctification* inadequately expresses Wesley's sense of communion with God, without the conviction that sanctification entails conformity with Christ. In short, sanctification is sacrificial discipleship.

> We would, we would partake thy every state below,
> And suffer all things for thy sake, and to thy glory go.[123]

> First-born of many sons his blood for us atones,
> Saves us from the mortal pain, if we by his cross abide,
> If we in the house remain where our elder brother died.[124]

> O what a killing thought is this, a sword to pierce the faithful heart!
> Our sins have slain the Prince of Peace; our sins, which caus'd his
>   mortal smart,
> With him we vow to crucify; our sins which murder'd God shall die![125]

Wesley's theology of eucharistic sacrifice is rich and complex and consists of numerous, interrelated facets that we can summarize here.

- Genuine religion requires sacrifice on the part of God's creatures, and the eucharistic sacrifice satisfies humankind's needs for the right worship of

122. *CSS*, VI.1.
123. *HLS*, 130:1b.
124. *HLS*, 132:3.
125. *HLS*, 133:3.

God. Furthermore, it is only by making a sacrifice that the church is able to receive the fruits of Christ's sacrifice.

- The eucharist is a sacrifice that encompasses the past, present, and future because it remembers, shares in, and proclaims the one, atoning sacrifice of Christ. As such, the eucharist is a transcendent act of the Triune God that takes place in history.
- The same Christ who made atonement on the cross is both host and gift in the eucharist. Christ the great high priest eternally intercedes for the church before the Father on the basis of the redeeming work of his passion.
- Thus, the glorified and resurrected Christ is really present in the eucharist, but always as one who still bears the scars of his passion. Therefore, Christ is really present sacrificially, offering the grace of his sacrifice to the church, which consists of the pardon of Christ and the power of the Holy Spirit to pursue holiness.
- The church is always united to its head, and the Lord never does anything without his body, the church.[126] Thus, the eucharist is the same sacrifice as the cross because it is the sacramental presence of Christ's sacrifice. In the eucharistic sacrifice Christ offers his body and blood to the Father and to the church for the forgiveness of sins.
- By the signs of the eucharistic elements the church corporately unites itself sacrificially to the eternal self-offering of its head before the Father as a holy and living sacrifice. In this self-offering, it not only offers itself, but also its goods, which the bread and wine also represent, and it intercedes for God's justice for the sake of the world.

Wesley's eucharistic theology is a consistent extension of his theology of the *ordo salutis*.[127] The creature responsively cooperates in God's saving work, and this cooperation takes the form of sacrifice. Wesley does not explicitly use the language of participation that has become so prominent in current parlance, but the concept encompasses ideas that thoroughly characterize his theology—namely, communion, sanctification, and the unity of the church's sacrifice with Christ's. Because the sacrifice of the believer and of the church relies on Christ's eternal sacrifice, and because the eucharistic celebration relies on Christ's saving sacrifice in history, the idea of participation operates implicitly throughout Wesley's eucharistic theology. The ecclesial and human sacrifices, therefore, become acceptable to God only in their union with Christ's heavenly sacrifice.[128] Indeed, Stevick rightly notes that a theology of participation accurately describes the intimacy with which Wesley

126. Stevick, *Altar's Fire*: "Christ is in the Christians' sacrifice, and they are in his" (164).
127. Borgen, "No End Without the Means," 63, 78–80.
128. Borgen, *John Wesley on the Sacraments*, 256.

conceives of the church's union with Christ.[129] He likens the church's sacrifice to prayer because it relies on God to accomplish the work that it does: "The Holy Communion, like prayer, is essentially God-given; but it, like prayer, is effective on God, because God in grace wills it so."[130] Through communion with Christ the Holy Spirit bestows the fruits of his atonement—i.e., the pardon of Christ to become children of God and the power of his Spirit to go on to perfection.

> This eucharistic feast our every want supplies,
> And still we by his death are blest, and share his sacrifice.
> By faith his flesh we eat, who here his Passion shew,
> And God out of his holy seat shall all his gifts bestow.[131]

> Come Holy Ghost, set to thy seal, thine inward witness give,
> To all our waiting souls reveal the death by which we live.[132]

> Father, on us the Spirit bestow, thro' which thine everlasting Son
> Offer'd himself for man below, that *we*, ev'n *we* before thy throne
> Our souls and bodies may present, and pay thee all thy grace hath lent.[133]

129. Stevick, *Altar's Fire*, 160.
130. Stevick, *Altar's Fire*, 165.
131. *HLS*, 4:2.
132. *HLS*, 7:1.
133. *HLS*, 150:1.

CHAPTER 5

Eucharistic Sacrifice in the Teaching of the Catholic Church

What is the teaching of the Catholic Church concerning eucharistic sacrifice? This is the organizing question for the next two chapters. In two concise paragraphs, the Code of Canon Law skillfully encapsulates the central dogmatic teaching of the Catholic Church on eucharistic sacrifice. It is profitable simply to state them up front, since the issues raised in these paragraphs set the stage for the subsequent exposition of this chapter.

> No. 897. The eucharistic sacrifice, the memorial of the death and resurrection of the Lord, in which the sacrifice of the cross is perpetuated through the ages is the summit and source of all worship and Christian life, which signifies and effects the unity of the People of God and brings about the building up of the body of Christ. . . .

> No. 899. The eucharistic celebration is the action of Christ himself and the Church. In it, Christ the Lord, through the ministry of the priest, offers himself, substantially present under the species of bread and wine, to God the Father and gives himself as spiritual food to the faithful united with this offering.[1]

The language of paragraph 897 is significant in at least two places. The first is the teaching that the eucharist "perpetuates" the sacrifice of the cross. Historically, this language has, at the very least, caught the attention of Protestants, including Methodists. Just how Catholic teaching understands the perpetuation of the once-for-all sacrifice of the cross is explored in detail in certain sections to follow. The second is the affirmation that the eucharist "signifies and effects" Christian unity. This phrase is derived from Innocent III, and in the current ecumenical climate, its usage raises important ecumenical questions. While many churches would agree that the eucharist signifies and effects unity, there remains at the moment a lack of clarity among

---

1. Unless otherwise cited, magisterial texts are from the Vatican website, retrievable at http://www.vatican.va/. Citations are referenced by paragraph.

churches as to the precise relationship between eucharistic communion and ecclesial communion. Citing Innocent III, Geoffrey Wainwright asks, "How far do we have to be advanced in the unity which the celebration of the eucharist 'signifies' before we can draw on the sacramental grace to 'effect' the fullness of that unity?"[2]

Initially, we are reminded of the sacramental, theological, liturgical, and ethical centrality of the eucharist: it is the "summit and source" of the church's worship and life, which accomplishes what it signifies—namely, the unity and sanctification of the church. The teachings of *BEM*, Aquinas, and Wesley, as we have seen, resonate deeply with this affirmation of the eucharist. As to the question of eucharistic sacrifice, many issues raised in these paragraphs propose a systematic investigation of the church's teaching. What are these issues?

First and foremost, paragraph 897 brings together the language of sacrifice, memorial, and the cross, such that the sacrifice of the eucharist is the memorial of Christ's passion in which Christ's redemptive work is perpetuated "through the ages." Far from seeing the ideas of memorial and perpetuation as disjunctive, these two concepts are used mutually to explicate the doctrine of sacrifice. Second, in paragraph 899, emphasis is placed on the agency of Christ in his priestly office. The living Lord—crucified, resurrected, and ascended—does not remain far off from his church. His substantial presence in the species of bread and wine is of a distinctly priestly nature—that is to say, one of offering. In the eucharist—the focal point of which is the canon and the words of consecration—Christ gives himself to the Father; he gives himself to his body, the church; and in doing so he incorporates the church into his offering to God. Third, therefore, the church's incorporation into Christ's priestly action means that it does more than simply receive Christ as "spiritual food"; the faithful are "united" with Christ's offering, and they participate with Christ in offering himself to God. Thus, the eucharist is "the action of Christ himself and the Church."

These, then, are the issues: sacrifice, memorial, perpetuation of the cross, Christ's priestly office, his offering (of himself to God and to the church), and the church's offering (of Christ and of itself to God). What the Code of Canon Law provides by way of concision, though, it lacks by way of detailed interpretation. What, for example, is the relationship between memorial and perpetuation; what, specifically, does Christ's offering entail; and how is his substantial presence in the eucharist related to his heavenly presence?

---

2. Innocent III: the eucharist "significat et efficit unitatem ecclesiasticam" (*De sacro altaris mysterio libri sex*, book IV, chapter 36 [PL 217:87]). Geoffrey Wainwright, "Ecclesia de eucharistia vivit: An Ecumenical Reading," *Ecumenical Trends* 33, no. 9 (October 2004): 8–9.

After having reviewed the relevant ecumenical dialogues in chapter 1 and provided the theological context through the traditioning voices of Aquinas and Wesley, it is now time to consider the official teaching of the Catholic Church. Furthermore, because the objective of this project is to engage systematically the teachings on eucharistic sacrifice of the Roman Catholic and Methodist churches as they are expressed in contemporary and official ecclesial documents, those texts that enjoy the highest level of authority and that serve to speak for the whole church and to direct its life and faith will, therefore, receive the most attention in this chapter. Chief among them include the *Catechism*, the documents of Vatican II, papal encyclicals, and in chapter 6, the eucharistic prayers.[3] The insights of individual theologians are by no means ignored, but they are used in their ecclesiologically appropriate manner—that is to say, as subordinate and complementary expressions of the church's faith and worship.[4]

In the first section, I look retrospectively at the crucial teachings of the Council of Trent. In the second section, I attend to the *Catechism* and key texts from Vatican II, letting them—like the Code of Canon Law—put eucharistic sacrifice within the broader context of the liturgy. In the third section, I listen chiefly to four important papal encyclicals: Leo XIII's *Mirae Caritatis*, Paul VI's *Mysterium Fidei*, Pius XII's *Mediator Dei*, and John Paul II's *Ecclesia de Eucharistia*, each of which deepens the discussion on the sacrificial nature of the eucharist with careful doctrinal specificity. In light of these liturgical and doctrinal insights, in chapter 6 I consider how the church makes its sacrifice in Eucharistic Prayers I–IV. From this approach we will discern a nuanced, yet clear presentation of the church's faith and teaching. This method effectively inverts the ancient slogan *lex orandi, lex credendi*, not because it is invalid, but for the sake of the doctrinal clarity demanded in this chapter. Pius XII makes this point when he asserts that the liturgy is not "some proving ground for truths" and "does not decide or determine independently and of itself what is of the Catholic faith."[5] We will see that, for the purposes of this chapter, to hear Catholicism's teaching on eucharistic sacrifice first will enable us more faithfully to understand its eucharistic prayers.

---

3. For an introduction to the types, purpose, and status of different magisterial texts, see Francis G. Morrisey and Michel Thériault, *Papal and Curial Pronouncements: Their Canonical Significance in Light of the Code of Canon Law*, 2nd ed. (Ottawa: Faculty of Canon Law, Saint Paul University, 2001).

4. The work of Charles Journet in his important book *The Mass: The Presence of the Sacrifice of the Cross* (South Bend, IN: St. Augustine's Press, 2008), translated from the 1958 original by Victor Szczurek, exemplifies this approach, as does James B. Collins, *The Mass as Sacrifice: Theological Reflections on the Sacrificial Elements of the Mass* (Staten Island, NY: St. Paul's, 2008).

5. Pius XII, *Mediator Dei* (MD), 46–48.

The Council of Trent

The Council of Trent was not an ecumenical dialogue, at least not as dialogues are conventionally organized today. But that is not to suggest that the council's teachings are without ecumenical import. Some Protestants did attend portions of the council, and some on the Catholic side were already familiar with their grievances. The idea that Trent would achieve reconciliation between divided Christians proved unrealistic and infeasible; indeed, just conducting and completing the council proved quite a feat. The council, though, was more successful at implementing its other goals—namely, instituting reforms within the church and promulgating doctrine and refuting heresy.[6] Nonetheless, the council did take seriously the Protestant arguments against the sacrifice of the Mass, which required a careful and nuanced reply from the bishops.

If the council was unsuccessful at restoring unity with Protestants, it was nevertheless successful at maintaining unity among Catholics, and the Catholicism that emerged from the council was strongly sacramentalist in theology and praxis.[7] Moreover, because Trent's teaching remained the primary doctrine on eucharistic sacrifice until well into the modern era and because it is often quoted in the twentieth-century papal encyclicals that address sacrifice, it will be important here to assess the theology advanced by the council. Contrary to how the council has historically been interpreted by both Catholics and Protestants, with respect to eucharistic sacrifice, its teaching is rich with ecumenical potential.

The account of the bishops' deliberations on sacrifice is a fascinating one.[8] On the one hand, they agreed that in responding to the critiques of the Reformers, the sacrificial quality of the Mass needed to be upheld. Furthermore, the ministry of the priest in offering the Mass was, in their eyes, a fundamental aspect of its sacrificial quality, such that in upholding the Mass they were also upholding the tradition of priestly presidency in the Mass as it had developed throughout the medieval period.[9] On the other hand, when precise explanations were required in response to key questions, the bishops offered an array of interpretations, making the final text noteworthy both for what it

6. John C. Olin, *Catholic Reform: From Cardinal Ximenes to the Council of Trent, 1495–1563* (New York: Fordham University Press, 1990), 28.

7. John W. O'Malley, *Trent: What Happened at the Council* (Cambridge, MA: Harvard University Press, 2013), 250, 255.

8. Gerard Kelly, "Eucharistic Sacrifice in the Council of Trent," *Irish Theological Quarterly* 51, no. 4 (1985): 268–88; Joseph F. Kelly, *The Ecumenical Councils of the Catholic Church: A History* (Collegeville, MN: Liturgical Press, 2009), 142–46.

9. Power, *Sacrifice We Offer*, 125–32.

leaves out and for its nuanced wording, which does not state too much and remains open to different interpretations.

Session XXII treats the "Doctrine Concerning the Sacrifice of the Mass," where canons one through four encapsulate the dispute with the Reformers, and chapters one and two give the doctrine. Canon one affirms the Mass as a "true and real sacrifice."[10] Canon two (somewhat contentiously) states that at the Supper Christ instituted the apostles as priests to offer his body and blood ("do this," with the doctrine of Christ's real presence being treated earlier). Canon three states that the Mass is more than a sacrifice of praise and thanksgiving and a "mere commemoration" of the cross, but is a propitiatory sacrifice offered for "sins, punishments, satisfactions, and other necessities." Canon four denies that the sacrifice of the Mass detracts from the "sacrifice of Christ consummated on the cross."[11] If these charges are what the Council finds anathema, then what, constructively, does it teach regarding eucharistic sacrifice?

The institution of the sacrifice of the Mass (chapter 1) derives dominically from the Supper, and the propitiatory effects (chapter 2) derive from Christ's death on the cross. The text, therefore, clearly locates the sacrificial quality of the Mass in the person and work of Christ. In chapter 1, Christ is seen as the perfection of prominent Old Testament sacrificial motifs: Melchizedek, Malachi, and the sacrifices under the law and nature. Christ offered himself on "the altar of the cross to God the Father" in order to "accomplish an eternal redemption," and his sacrificial words and actions at the Supper depend upon this unique sacrifice. At the Supper Christ offered himself to the Father and gave himself to the apostles "under the form of bread and wine," and he did so for several reasons: (a) human nature ordinarily needs a visible sign ("sacrifice") when communicating with God; (b) this sacrifice "represented" the cross and "applied" its saving work; (c) by giving himself sacramentally to the apostles he constituted them as priests and instructed them to repeat what he had done within the church (*Do this in commemoration of me*).[12]

In terms of sacrifice, it is important to note, first, that there is nothing new in the Supper that would either supplement or detract from the unique work of the cross. Nothing beyond Christ's self-offering is envisioned here. And second, Christ's command to the apostles is to repeat his words and

---

10. H. J. Schroeder, *Canons and Decrees of the Council of Trent: Original Text with English Translation* (St. Louis: B. Herder, 1941), 144–50. On the Council's "exact reproduction" of Aquinas's theology, see Vonier's chapter, "Saint Thomas and the Council of Trent on the Oneness of the Christian Sacrifice," 145–57.

11. Power, *Sacrifice We Offer*, 127–28; see Schroeder, *Canons and Decrees*, 149.

12. Schroeder, *Canons and Decrees*, 144–45.

132 CHAPTER 5

actions at the Supper and not on the cross: both the Supper and the Mass are an efficacious representation of the cross, not an addition to it or a repetition of it. Chapter 1 offers this summary statement, once again stressing the centrality of the cross: "He instituted a new Passover, namely, Himself, to be immolated under visible signs by the Church through the priests in memory of His own passage from the world to the Father, when by the shedding of His blood he redeemed [us]."[13]

Chapter 2 treats the propitiatory work of the cross communicated to the believer in the mass. Genuine faith—a rallying cry of the Reformers—is an essential element for believers to approach God (*contrite, penitent, sincere heart, upright faith, fear, reverence*). Because "the same Christ" is sacramentally present ("in an unbloody manner") as he was at the cross, the "fruits" of the cross are communicated to the faithful in the Mass. The "fruits" of the mass are the same as the fruits of the cross: grace, mercy, and pardon for sins. Of course, the Mass is "truly propitiatory" because the cross is propitiatory, and the grace of forgiveness in the Mass comes solely from Christ and his redemption on the cross: "For the victim is one and the same, the same now offering by the ministry of priests who then offered Himself on the cross, the manner alone of offering being different."[14]

The text is careful to leave some key questions unspecified—for example, the effects of Christ's self-offering at the Supper and whether it was expiatory. Similarly, while reference is made to Christ's priestly office and to his offering in the Mass, it leaves open an array of interpretations relating Christ's priesthood in the Supper, the cross, and heavenly intercession. "In other words, one sees the whole sequence of the debate reflected in the finesse of the final statement, which leaves the way open to theologians to retain their various explanations . . . provided it is clearly held that the sacrifice of the mass is totally dependent on the cross and that its efficacy for sinners is totally from the power and merit of Christ."[15]

The Mass is, fundamentally, a sharing in the body and blood of Christ and a sacramental participation in the saving work of the cross. Far from stifling ecumenical convergence on eucharistic sacrifice, the Christological focus of this teaching should encourage Methodist theologians to look for commonality with Wesley's theology of sacrament and sacrifice.

13. Schroeder, *Canons and Decrees*, 145.
14. Schroeder, *Canons and Decrees*, 145–46.
15. Power, *Sacrifice We Offer*, 120.

The Liturgical Context of Eucharistic Sacrifice

The Father and the Holy Spirit

The liturgy is the heart of the church's life—"the summit toward which the activity of the Church is directed; at the same time it is the font from which all her power flows"[16]—at the very center of which is the eucharist: "the whole liturgical life of the Church revolves around the eucharistic sacrifice and the sacraments."[17] The ordered actions of the church's members in their different roles, along with the signs and symbols of its rites, attest to the "dual dimension" and agency of the liturgy—namely, the sacrificial "response of faith and love to the spiritual blessings the Father bestows." But these spiritual blessings are nothing short of "the Gift that contains all gifts, the Holy Spirit" and the presence of Christ himself;[18] thus, the liturgy reveals the saving work of the Triune God enacted in the church's midst: "As often as the sacrifice of the cross in which Christ our Passover was sacrificed, is celebrated on the altar, the work of our redemption is carried on."[19]

In the dual dimension of the liturgy, both God and the church act, but not in an equal manner. The primary work resides with God, in which each divine person acts in a differentiated manner to fulfill the unified work of the Trinity: "The Father accomplishes the 'mystery of his will' by giving his beloved Son and his Holy Spirit for the salvation of the world and for the glory of his name."[20] The Triune work of redemption originates in the "free and hidden plan of [the Father's] own wisdom and goodness" and is directed toward the Father's goal: "to raise men to a participation of the divine life."[21]

The Holy Spirit animates God's people, vivifies the liturgy, and works preveniently to prepare and gather God's people to celebrate the eucharist. The Spirit both "arouses faith" and brings about "genuine cooperation," so that

16. *Sacrosanctum Concilium (SC)*, 10.

17. *CCC*, 1113.

18. *CCC*, 1082–83; see *SC*, 6: "[Christ's] purpose was that they might accomplish the work of salvation which they had proclaimed, by means of sacrifice and sacraments, around which the entire liturgical life revolves."

19. *LG*, 3, "*opus nostrae redemptionis exercetur*"; see *LG*, 7: "Really partaking of the body of the Lord in the breaking of the eucharistic bread, we are taken up into communion with Him and with one another." David Fagerberg makes an important distinction between ritual and liturgy: "Divine Liturgy, Divine Love: Toward a New Understanding of Sacrifice in Christian Worship," in *Letter and Spirit: The Hermeneutic of Continuity: Christ, Kingdom, and Creation*, ed. Scott Hahn (Steubenville, Ohio: St. Paul Center for Biblical Theology, 2007), 3:95–97.

20. *CCC*, 1066.

21. *LG*, 2. In *Lumen gentium*, the trinitarian dimensions of the plan of salvation come through powerfully in chapter 1, "The Mystery of the Church."

the "liturgy becomes the common work of the Holy Spirit and the Church."[22] At the same time, the Spirit bears witness to another; the faith that the Spirit arouses and deepens is always directed toward Christ. The Spirit "prepares for the reception of Christ," "recalls the mystery of Christ," "prepares the Church to encounter her Lord," and makes "the mystery of Christ present" in the liturgy.[23] What is more, the "mystery of Christ" can be further specified: the Spirit directs the church's faith and devotion to the Paschal mystery, to Christ's passion, to its Passover Lamb, and as the "Church's living memory," the Spirit inspires the church's *anamnesis* in the liturgy.[24]

> Christian liturgy not only recalls the events that saved us but actualizes them, makes them present. The Paschal mystery of Christ is celebrated, not repeated. It is the celebrations that are repeated, and in each celebration there is an outpouring of the Holy Spirit that makes the unique mystery present.[25]

How does Catholic teaching understand the Holy Spirit to make present Christ's saving events in such a way that the Paschal mystery of Christ is celebrated but not repeated?

Christ the High Priest

What the Holy Spirit works to provoke, deepen, and perfect in the faith of the believer and the church perfectly unites with the person and work of Christ in the liturgy. Traditionally understood as the "participation of the people of God in 'the work of God,'" Christ works as "redeemer and high priest" to carry out the "work of redemption in, with, and through his Church."[26] Christ presides in the liturgy, and the church celebrates its part in the liturgy knowing by faith that "where two or three are gathered" he is among them, calling, teaching, and incorporating his body into his liturgical acts. In the sacraments, Christ is the primary agent. When the church proclaims his word, he is speaking, and the liturgy, in short, is "Christ's own prayer addressed to the Father in the Holy Spirit."[27] "Rightly, then, the liturgy is considered as an exercise of the priestly office of Jesus Christ . . . in the liturgy the whole

---

22. *CCC*, 1091.

23. *CCC*, 1092, 1098. On the Spirit's work more broadly in salvation and the life of the church, see *LG*, 4.

24. *CCC*, 1099, 1103; see Nichols's "pneumatological conclusion" in "Holy Oblation," 271–72.

25. *CCC*, 1104.

26. *CCC*, 1069.

27. *CCC*, 1073; see *SC*, 7.

public worship is performed by the Mystical Body of Jesus Christ, that is, by the Head and His members."[28] The Mystical Body refers to more than the visible church and its liturgical celebration, though; it is the "whole Christ," or "*Christus totus*," that also includes those saints who celebrate "without signs" in the "heavenly liturgy, where celebration is wholly communion and feast."[29] Notice two important differences—ones that Wesley also maintains—between the heavenly and the earthly liturgies: the worship of those now with Christ, the church triumphant, occurs without sacraments and without sacrifice. But this distinction between the heavenly and earthly liturgies, along with the conviction of Christ's *priestly* actions, only serves to highlight all the more the sacramental sacrifice at the heart of the church's worship here below.[30]

Lumen gentium makes another closely related Christological affirmation. Like Aquinas, it applies an instrumental causality to Jesus' humanity that it extends, in fact, to the sacramental character of the church: "the Church is in Christ like a sacrament or as a sign and instrument," and as a result of its "hierarchical organs," its "visible delineation," and its "spiritual community," therefore, "by no weak analogy, it is compared to the mystery of the incarnate Word."[31] While the telos of the church's union to Christ in the Spirit is sanctification and glorification, which these paragraphs also confess, in order to achieve this end the Spirit must lead the church in its imitation of Christ: "In that [mystical] Body the life of Christ is poured into believers who, through the sacraments, are united in a hidden and real way to Christ who suffered and was glorified."[32] To be sure, the priestly office of Christ does predominate in eucharistic doctrine, but *Lumen gentium* richly proclaims Christ "in all his offices" (as Wesley exhorted his preachers to do): Christ is the Head of the church and the Holy Spirit the soul; the one Mediator; as king he "reigns in glory in heaven"; his "prophetic office" is a "life of faith and charity"; he is "the one Mediator and the unique way of salvation"; he is the "source of salvation for the whole world"; he is the "great Prophet, who proclaimed the

<hr>

28. *SC*, 7.

29. *CCC*, 1136; see especially *LG*, chapter VII: "The Eschatological Nature of the Pilgrim Church and Its Union with the Church in Heaven."

30. Cyprian Vagaggini develops these ideas thoroughly in his chapter "The *Kyrios*—The Paschal Mystery: The One Liturgist and the One Liturgy," in *Theological Dimensions of the Liturgy: A General Treatise on the Theology of the Liturgy*, trans. L. J. Doyle and W. A. Jurgens, 4th ed. (Collegeville, MN: Liturgical Press, 1976), 247–72; and in his section "Jesus' corporeity in his work of mediation and communication of the divine life to the world after his resurrection," in *The Flesh: Instrument of Salvation; A Theology of the Human Body* (Staten Island, NY: Society of St. Paul, 1969), 42–45.

31. *LG*, 1, 8.

32. *LG*, 7.

Kingdom of His Father"; as "Fountain and Head, [he] issues every grace and the very life of the people of God"; "the Lord Jesus, the divine Teacher and Model of all perfection" is also the Victim, the "Lamb who was slain."[33] In keeping with our hermeneutics of charity, these unambiguous affirmations should allow Methodists to put aside any lingering Reformation controversy that the eucharistic sacrifice detracts from the uniqueness of Christ, and instead encourage them to consider *how*—in light of Christ's "once for all" sacrifice—Catholicism understands the eucharist to be a sacrifice.

The church's sacraments, therefore, are a "divine pedagogy of salvation" that realize what they signify because Christ, in his Spirit, is the one who administers them. They are signs of the goodness of creation, human work, and divine blessing; God sanctifies them to bless humankind, who in turn uses them to worship God. At the same time that Christ used the signs from Israel's covenant with God (especially from the Exodus and the Passover), he fulfilled and transformed them because "he himself is the meaning of all these signs."[34] In the church's eucharistic liturgy, then, what Christ signifies and effects is his own saving passion, his Paschal mystery.[35]

The Sacramental Sacrifice

In its discussion of the Trinity's and the church's actions in the liturgy (and especially of Christ's priestly office), the *Catechism* has prepared us for its discussion of the eucharist proper. In unpacking how the eucharist is a sacramental sacrifice, it speaks carefully and clearly, explaining key concepts on the one hand and reiterating the dual nature of divine and human interaction on the other. Throughout these paragraphs, the *Catechism* stresses the essential unity between the Last Supper, the cross, and eucharist. The church calls this rite the Holy Sacrifice because it "makes present" Christ's sacrifice, it "includes the Church's offering," and it "completes and surpasses" the sacrifices of the Old Covenant.[36]

At the outset, it becomes clear that eucharistic sacrifice is shaped by the anamnetic nature of Christ's actions and command, and furthermore, that the concept of memorial means much more than remembrance. Christ himself instituted the eucharistic memorial at the Last Supper in order to provide a means of incorporating his church into his death and resurrection;[37] indeed,

---

33. *LG*, 7, 9, 12, 14, 17, 35, 50, 40, 51.
34. *CCC*, 1145–53; see 1127.
35. *CCC*, 1084–85.
36. *CCC*, 1330.
37. *CCC*, 1337. See Paul's reflection on this matter in 1 Cor 10:16–18.

as we have seen, his priestly work in the eucharist continues in the liturgy: "At its head is Christ himself, the principal agent of the eucharist. He is high priest of the New Covenant; it is he himself who presides invisibly over every eucharistic celebration."[38] In its liturgical celebration, therefore, the church—as Christ's body indissolubly united to its head in the Spirit—understands itself obediently to be repeating what the Lord commanded: "Do this in remembrance of me." Once again, *remembrance* cannot mean a particular state of mind—i.e., simply recalling a past event. Rather, the eucharistic memorial consists of a dominically instituted liturgical action.[39] How does the liturgy (including and in addition to the ordained priesthood) signify and effect this reality? The sacrifice of the eucharist comes to its fullest expression in the apex of the anaphora, the consecration, the *anamnesis*, and the offering.[40]

Replete with the memory of God's covenant faithfulness from Melchizedek to the wedding at Cana, the bread and wine are presented and joyfully offered to the Father with thanksgiving for all the good gifts of creation that the Creator has bestowed.[41] "The eucharist is also the sacrifice of praise by which the church sings the glory of God in the name of all creation. This sacrifice is possible only through Christ: he unites the faithful to his person, to his praise, and to his intercession, so that the sacrifice of praise to the Father is offered through Christ and with him, to be accepted in him."[42] At the heart of the anaphora, the priest offers the bread and wine in the name of Christ and "commits the Creator's gifts into the hands of Christ who, in his sacrifice, brings to perfection all human attempts to offer sacrifices." This action of relinquishing the bread and wine to the agency of Christ further signifies Christ's presidency and repeats "the very action of Christ at the Last Supper—'taking the bread and a cup.'"[43]

In the institution narrative, human and divine actions are most closely related, and the eucharistic sacrifice is fully realized. The priest speaks the words of institution *in persona Christi*, and by the power of the Holy Spirit and by the very words of Christ, the bread and wine become the body and blood

---

38. *CCC*, 1348. The single-most-important Christological affirmation from Trent is one of immense ecumenical import, as it is upheld, for example, both by *BEM* and Wesley: "For the victim [Christ] is one and the same, the same now offering by the ministry of priests, who then offered Himself on the cross, the manner alone of offering being different"; Session XXII, Chapter II.

39. *CCC*, 1333, 1341.

40. Josef A. Jungmann, *The Eucharistic Prayer*, rev. ed. (Wheathampstead: A. Clarke, 1978), 3.

41. *CCC*, 1333–35.

42. *CCC*, 1361.

43. *CCC*, 1350.

of Christ, and "Christ is thus really and mysteriously made present."[44] The words of institution bear manifold sacrificial significance. First, Jesus' arrest and death is not simply an execution. It is a sacrificial act of self-giving, the gift of himself on behalf of others: "This is my body *which is given for you.*"[45] Second, in Israel's history, sacrifice, blood, and covenant bind together God and God's people. Christ not only enfolds the history of God's covenant faithfulness into the Supper, but also brings about Israel's eschatological New Covenant that Jeremiah had prophesied. "This cup which is poured out for you is the New Covenant in my blood." Third, in his sacrifice Christ realizes a divine mercy that God alone can work: he pours out his blood "for many for the forgiveness of sins."[46]

By associating Israel's Passover sacrifice with his passion, he fulfills and transforms it, providing its "definitive meaning."[47] The one who was Priest and Victim on the cross was also Priest and Victim at the Supper, giving himself to God and to the apostles in an unbloody sacrifice as a means of incorporating them into his death and resurrection. Trent notes: "He instituted the new Passover, (to wit) Himself to be immolated, under the visible signs, by the Church through the ministry of priests."[48] In his real and substantial presence in the eucharist, Christ continues to preside as Priest and Victim in the liturgy, so that "the sacrifice of Christ and the sacrifice of the eucharist are one single sacrifice."[49] Just as Christ incorporated his apostles into his redemption through the sacramental sacrifice of the Supper, so he continues to do in the liturgy. The eucharist is the sacramental sacrifice by which he incorporates the church on earth into his redemption. Thus, the *Catechism* enumerates, "The eucharist is thus a sacrifice because it re-presents (makes present) the sacrifice of the cross, because it is its memorial and because it applies its fruit."[50]

44. *CCC*, 1357; Trent, session XIII, chapter I.

45. *CCC*, 1365; Lk 22:19; see Jn 10:17–18.

46. Matthew 26:28. See Avery Dulles, "The Eucharist as Sacrifice," in *Rediscovering the Eucharist: Ecumenical Conversations*, ed. Roch A. Kereszty (New York: Paulist Press, 2003), 175–77.

47. *CCC*, 1340; see, Lk 22:20 and 1 Cor 11:25.

48. Trent, session XXII, chapter I.

49. *CCC*, 1367.

50. *CCC*, 1366; see 1362. This is a precise reiteration of Trent, session XXII, chapter I. See the chapter "The Wellspring of Life from the Side of the Lord, Opened in Loving Sacrifice: The Eucharist, Heart of the Church," in Pope Benedict XVI, *God Is Near Us: The Eucharist, the Heart of Life* (San Francisco: Ignatius Press, 2003), 42–55; Dulles, "Eucharist as Sacrifice," 179–81. Dulles is following Trent, session XXII, chapter II. For an explanation of eucharistic sacrifice as a propitiatory sacrifice that seeks to assuage historic Protestant concerns, see Roch Kereszty, "The Eucharist of the Church," 255–56.

In addition to the institution-consecration, the sacrificial dimension of the eucharist is concentrated in the *anamnesis*-offering, which follows the Institution immediately and seamlessly. The simplicity with which Catholicism interprets Jesus' words—when the dust clouds of disputation and controversy subside—is striking. Jesus offered his body and blood—*my body given for you, my blood poured out for you for the forgiveness of sins*—and said, "do this," that is, offer his body and blood for the forgiveness of sins. This is how the Catholic Church has understood Jesus' words and what, as the *totus Christus*, it understands itself to be doing in the eucharist.

> The eucharist is also the sacrifice of the Church. The Church which is the Body of Christ participates in the offering of her Head. With him, she herself is offered whole and entire. She unites herself to his intercession with the Father for all men.[51] In the eucharist the sacrifice of Christ becomes also the sacrifice of the members of his Body; the lives of the faithful, their praise, sufferings, prayer, and work are united with those of Christ and with his total offering and so acquire a new value. Christ's sacrifice present on the altar makes it possible for all generations of Christians to be united with his offering.[52]

Relatedly, neither for Catholics nor Wesley is there a problem with the idea that Christ can be present to his people while being present in glory in heaven.[53] The theology expounded here is, in many respects, an extended reflection on Paul's teaching of eucharist and sacrifice in 1 Corinthians 10–11. Commenting on 1 Cor 11:27–34, Hans Urs von Balthasar remarks, "The community is the bride of Christ, which will take part in the body eucharistically and has its own fruitfulness only by that body."[54] This exposition also goes a long way to answering the question raised at the beginning of this section as to how Catholic teaching understands the Holy Spirit to make present Christ's saving events in such a way that the Paschal mystery of Christ is celebrated but not repeated. The eucharistic memorial in all its trinitarian, Christological, priestly, liturgical, sacramental, and sacrificial richness is "not merely the recollection of past events but the proclamation of the mighty works

51. With respect to intercession, it cites *LG*, 48, *SC*, 7, and Rom 8:34; see also *CCC*, 1373; *LG*, 48. With respect to the application of the fruit of the cross, see *CCC*, 1391–97.

52. *CCC*, 1368; see 1354: "In the anamnesis that follows, the Church calls to mind the Passion, resurrection, and glorious return of Christ Jesus; she presents to the Father the offering of his Son which reconciles us with him." For a treatment of the different roles of the bishop, priest, and laity in the eucharist, see *LG*, 10–11, 21, 28, 34; see Dulles, "Eucharist as Sacrifice," 183.

53. *LG*, 21; Trent, session XIII, chapter I.

54. Hans Urs von Balthasar, "The Holy Church and the Eucharistic Sacrifice," *Communio* 12 (Summer 1985): 144.

wrought by God," but is made "in a certain way present and real."[55] It is by way of Christ's humanity, united to his divinity and in his Spirit, that his redemption is made present and real; likewise, it is by way of giving his humanity in the sacrificial meal that he incorporates his church into his redemption. Christ's Paschal mystery, which extends from the Supper through to his enthronement at the right hand of the Father, is an unrepeatable historic event; however, it is also the eschatological event that directs history toward its end. "All that Christ is—all that he did and suffered for all men—participates in the divine eternity, and so transcends all times while being made present in them all. The event of the cross and resurrection abides and draws everything toward life."[56]

The union of the church with its Lord in the eucharist means that the church learns to offer itself as a holy and living sacrifice in the way of holiness. It is to be perfect, "even as your heavenly Father is perfect," and to strive for the fruit of the Holy Spirit. Christians are called to the "fullness of the Christian life and to the perfection of charity . . . they must follow in his footsteps and conform themselves to his image . . . [and to] the service of their neighbor." This imitation of Christ—modeled by many saints—is possible "not because of their works," but by the gift of the Spirit of Christ. Thus, through baptism and a life of self-sacrifice represented and strengthened in the eucharist, Christians are "really made holy" and become "sharers in the divine nature." This emphasis on sanctification grounded in the sacrament resonates deeply with Methodism's history of personal piety and social justice, along with the exhortation to go on to perfection: "Then, too, by God's gift, they must hold on to and complete in their lives this holiness they have received."[57]

Papal Encyclicals

In this section, we consider four encyclicals: Leo XIII, *Mirae Caritatis* (1902), Pius XII, *Mediator Dei* (1947), Paul VI, *Mysterium Fidei* (1965), and John Paul II, *Ecclesia de Eucharistia* (2003). A central doctrinal concern of these encyclicals is eucharistic sacrifice; consequently, they are able to develop further the principal teachings considered earlier. Because each encyclical develops different facets of sacrifice, albeit in complementary ways, it is helpful to hear the distinctive teaching of each pope in turn. This approach will also yield significant ecumenical insights as well.

---

55. *CCC*, 1363.
56. *CCC*, 1085; see 1382.
57. *LG*, 40; see *LG*, 8.

Leo XIII, Mirae Caritatis *(1902)*

Leo XIII's encyclical is a brief yet vigorous appeal for the church to orient itself around the eucharist. He is less concerned with giving a thoroughgoing account of eucharistic sacrifice than with encouraging the church to refocus its devotion on Christ, the "the source of life," who gives himself in the eucharist.[58] This sacrament, above all others, comes from Christ himself, and it is "a gift most admirably adapted to be the means whereby the salutary fruits of His redemption may be distributed."[59]

His tone takes on a sense of urgency when he characterizes the spiritual state of individuals and societies. Talented people "flatter themselves" by leading others to value "the possession of commodities" and the "love of comfort and display," and the society that values "prosperity" above all else never finds "peace" because "it is pursuing an object that ever escapes it." In a word, the pope is concerned with justice—i.e., rightly ordered relationships between Creator and creatures. Individuals and societies "have their being from God," yet modern secular states seek to relocate the "dignity of man" to such an extent that "the seat of war has since been enlarged and extended, until it has come to this, that men deny altogether that there is anything above and beyond nature." The proper end of both the individual and society, however, is in communion with God in the eucharist. The "entire supernatural order" is contained in the "mystery of faith" by which Christ unites humanity to himself and makes them "sharers and partakers in the divine nature."[60]

How does this elevation of the creature take place, more specifically? It happens through the sacrifice of Christ. Leo XIII develops an analogy between the nourishment of food and Christ, the Bread of Life. Jesus' activities surrounding food attest to his life-giving ministry, which culminates in the gift of himself, his sacrifice: "the bread which I give is my flesh, for the life of the world . . . amen, amen I say to you, unless you shall eat the flesh of the Son of Man and drink His blood, you shall not have life in you" (Jn 6:52, 54).[61] The goodness that food gives to the body compares to the gift of Christ to the soul, with the exception that whereas the body turns food into itself, in the eucharist the faithful are made alike to Christ.[62] Because the "immortal body of Christ" is contained in the Host, the Christian hope of the resurrection of the body is contained also in the eucharist: "He that eateth my flesh

58. *Mirae Caritatis (MC),* 4.
59. *MC,* 1.
60. *MC,* 6–7.
61. *MC,* 4–5.
62. *MC,* 6.

and drinketh my blood hath everlasting life; and I will raise him up at the last day" (Jn 6:55).

In his discussion of eucharistic sacrifice directly, the pope touches on several noteworthy topics. First, he notes that eucharistic sacrifice transpires within the modality of a sacrament. From the Catholic perspective, of course, this point is obvious; yet in the case of ecumenical dialogue with Methodists—even in a context where no history of direct division exists—it is worth keeping this observation front and center. The eucharist, for Leo XIII, is an efficacious sign: it is "no mere empty commemoration" of Christ's death; rather, it is a "bloodless and mystical renewal of it."[63] Catholic teaching has, from the patristic period, used the language of the unbloody and mystical to denote the sacramental modality of the church's sacrifice. Despite its ancient usage, it is a point that continually bears mentioning. Additionally, as the *Catechism* teaches and as we will consider more, the sacramental modality of the eucharist does not in any way impede it from being a real and proper sacrifice.

Second, his thoughts on eucharistic sacrifice are deepened by his understanding of memorial, and his language of the "renewal" of Calvary should be taken to occur within the modality of a sacramental memorial. He touches briefly on familiar Catholic teaching on the topic. While he does not underscore the theology of Christ's priestly office, he is clear that in the eucharist it is Christ who gives himself and that this self-giving is decidedly paschal: "He may impart to them of His own inexhaustible abundance the benefits of that redemption which He has accomplished."[64] Jesus' Last Supper was also the first memorial of his sacrifice.[65] His command to "Do this in memory of me" is sacrificial, referring to Jesus' "pains, sorrows, afflictions, and death" on the cross, from which the eucharist derives its sacrificial quality, making it a "perpetual memorial of His passion."[66] In affirming Jesus' real presence he affirms transubstantiation and the establishment of the priesthood.[67]

Third, the redeeming work that Christ accomplishes in the sacrifice of the eucharist is inseparable from the work that he accomplished in his humanity in his sacrifice of the cross. Indeed, it is the same work, because the eucharist is "in a manner a continuation and extension of the Incarnation." The "manner" in which it is a continuation is by way of the sacrament, the mystery of faith, and although the language of Christ's priesthood is absent, the theological content is present: "For in and by it the substance of the incarnate

---

63. *MC*, 18.
64. *MC*, 4.
65. *MC*, 2.
66. *MC*, 10.
67. *MC*, 4, 7. 10.

Word is united with individual men, and the supreme Sacrifice offered on Calvary is in a wondrous manner renewed."[68] Furthermore, in keeping with Christ's covenantal promise that in his blood is the forgiveness of sins, Christ communicates the fullness of his atoning work in the eucharist: "And Christ has willed that the whole virtue of His death, alike for expiation and impetration, should abide in the eucharist."[69]

Lastly, eucharistic sacrifice, by necessity, entails the participation of the whole church. On the one hand, the eucharist signifies the "gratitude" of the church—i.e., the spiritual sacrifice and self-offering that true worship entails; on the other hand the worship that God is due is "infinite," and only in the presentation of the Father's only-begotten Son can the church "make an adequate return."[70] In joining with the offering of Christ, the "exile" church on earth is strengthened in both unity and charity, giving itself here and now in service to one another and uniting to those who have died, to those heavenly saints and to those "detained" in purgatory.[71] Because the eucharist is the "centre," the "soul," and the "source" of the Christian life, it is the primary instrument by which the faithful are "engrafted on the divine nature," which is also the *telos* of the Christian life.[72]

Pius XII, Mediator Dei *(1947)*

In *Mediator Dei*, Pius XII treats what are by now familiar teachings, yet at nearly forty pages, he takes the time to enter into sufficient detail such that he is able to bring out new facets of these doctrines. As the title suggests, his orientation is utterly Christological and soteriological, and his explanations of the liturgy, sacraments, eucharist, priesthood should be understood from this perspective. "Sin had disturbed the right relationship between man and his Creator; the Son of God would restore it."[73]

Christ's Priesthood and the Liturgy

Toward the end of his encyclical, Pius XII offers a remark that, for our purposes, will be more helpful to highlight at the beginning. "By assuming human nature, the Divine Word introduced into this earthly exile a hymn which is sung in heaven for all eternity. He unites to Himself the whole human race

---

68. *MC*, 7.
69. *MC*, 18.
70. *MC*, 17.
71. *MC*, 12.
72. *MC*, 7, 14–15.
73. *MD*, 1.

and with it sings this hymn to the praise of God."[74] This comment encapsulates the pope's whole theology of liturgy, sacrament, and priesthood. In addition to underscoring the centrality and interrelatedness of Jesus' humanity and his priestly office as he exercises it in heaven for our salvation, it also recalls a principal idea from the *Catechism*—namely, the divine eternity of the Godhead that transcends the created order and into which humanity's creaturely nature is nonetheless incorporated as a result of Jesus' divine humanity.

Pius XII begins his discussion of the eucharist by following Aquinas and noting that humanity's life is to be directed toward God and that this is achieved by offering "worship to the One True God by practicing the virtue of religion." This is a "fundamental duty" for both individuals and communities.[75] The function of sacrifice and the priesthood in the Old Testament served this end, along with foreshadowing Christ's sacrifice, his priesthood, and the New Covenant.[76] Christ's incarnation—just like his death, resurrection, and ascension—is nothing short of a demonstration in time of the "priestly office" that he holds "uninterruptedly" forever. Christ consummated his life, which he lived obediently to the Father by his sacrifice on the cross, and by the liturgy of the Last Supper—the "new Pasch"—he established its memorial. Christ's "single aim" is to glorify God and continually to sanctify humankind, and he accomplishes this through his presence in the sacraments and his "unfailing intercession" before the Father.[77] Recall Trent's teaching that Christ's sacramental presence is not to be juxtaposed with his heavenly intercession; rather, his redemptive presence in the eucharist is precisely the sacramental modality of his heavenly intercession. And this aim is realized when "Christ lives and thrives" in the hearts of men and women. The participatory nature of the church in Christ's priestly office is therefore unmistakable: the eucharist is "the public worship which our Redeemer as Head of the Church renders to the Father, as well as the worship which the community of the faithful renders to its Founder, and through Him to the heavenly Father." In sum, it is the worship of the *totus Christus*.[78]

The visible sacrifice that Christ instituted at the Supper requires that the church also make a visible sacrifice for other reasons as well. Human nature is composed of body and soul, so human worship must be both exterior and interior. Pius XII likens the church—itself a social organism—to the body. Just as individuals learn through visible, created means to direct their intellect

---

74. *MD*, 144.
75. *MD*, 13; see Aquinas, *ST* II-II, q. 81, a. 1.
76. *MD*, 16.
77. *MD*, 17.
78. *MD*, 20.

and devotion to the invisible God, so also the ecclesial body must do, and "this obviously it cannot [do] unless religious activity is also organized and manifested outwardly. Exterior worship, finally, reveals and emphasizes the unity of the mystical body."[79] The church's worship through signs and symbols in the liturgy and especially through the sacraments functions as a divine pedagogy for both the individual and the community. While the church's rites "can claim no perfection or sanctity in their own right," and while the "chief element of divine worship must be interior," the composite nature of the body nonetheless requires the external in service of the internal.[80] "It should be clear to all, then, that God cannot be honored worthily unless the mind and heart turn to Him in quest of the perfect life, and that the worship rendered to God by the Church in union with her divine Head is the most efficacious means of achieving sanctity."[81]

The dual dimension of the church's liturgy consists, therefore, not only in the participation of human agency with Christ's, but also in the dual dimension of interior and exterior worship. Christians simply cannot offer a sacrifice of praise and cannot offer themselves as holy and living sacrifices unless they participate with their body and their senses in the visible sacrifice of the church, nor can the church do so as a corporate body without a visible sacrifice that signifies its corporate self-offering. The outward sacrifice signifies the interior, which is more important, yet for the interior sacrifice to deepen and grow, it needs the outward.[82] To be sure, the eucharist, as a work of Christ himself, has the power "objectively" of "conveying and dispensing grace," but at the same time, the pope stresses that in order for the eucharist to "produce [its] proper effect" and to prevent it from being reduced to "mere formalism," the heart must be "properly disposed" to receive it. "Emphatically, therefore, the work of redemption, which in itself is independent of our will, requires a serious interior effort on our part if we are to achieve eternal salvation."[83] Pius XII brings to a close this opening section of the encyclical—focused broadly on sacrifice and the liturgy—with these words: "In the spiritual life, consequently, there can be no opposition between the action of God, who pours forth His grace into men's hearts so that the work of the redemption may always abide, and the tireless collaboration of man, who must not render vain the gift of God."[84]

---

79. *MD*, 23; see Trent, session XXII, chapter I.

80. *MD*, 23–24.

81. *MD*, 26; see Jungmann, *Eucharistic Prayer*, 17.

82. Pius XII follows Aquinas (*ST* II-II, q. 82, a. 1) on the relationship of the intellect and the will in the "virtue of religion" and in the role of making sacrifice; 32–35.

83. *MD*, 24, 29, 31.

84. *MD*, 36. Pius XII then moves into a discussion of the centrality of the priesthood, the mutuality of *lex orandi* and *lex credendi*, and of liturgical development; 37–65.

Eucharistic Sacrifice: Commemorative Representation and Intercession

In the second third of his encyclical, Pius XII emphasizes the Christological and soteriological focus of his text with his discussion of eucharistic sacrifice proper. The Lord's Supper, which Christ instituted, is the "culmination and center" of the Christian faith, and it is "continually renewed" in the eucharistic anaphora. The church unites itself to Christ's eternal intercession before the Father by remembering, representing, and sharing in his passion.[85] His comments here go deeper than those of the previous encyclicals.

The eucharist is a "true and proper act of sacrifice" because the same Christ is present as priest and victim. Represented by the ordained priest, Christ presides at the eucharist by offering himself to the Father.[86] The sacrificial aspect also consists in the fact that the "divine Redeemer" is present in his "human nature with His true body and blood." Moreover, Christ's sacramental presence conveys the transcendent aspect of the eucharist as it participates in the divine eternity of the Godhead. That is, on the cross, his immolation occurred through his "bloody death." But Christ is now resurrected, ascended, and his humanity is glorified and imperishable, thus "the shedding of His blood is impossible." At the same time, the Lord's passion "is shown forth in an admirable manner by external signs which are the symbols of His death." The separation of the eucharistic species symbolizes the historic separation of his body and blood on the cross. Therefore, "the commemorative representation of His death, which actually took place on Calvary, is repeated in every sacrifice of the altar, seeing that Jesus Christ is symbolically shown by separate symbols to be in a state of victimhood."[87]

Among the many terms used to describe eucharistic sacrifice, the language of "commemorative representation" is the most theologically precise, and Pius XII further deepens his analysis by reflecting on the nature of Christ's priestly office, his self-offering, and on what, in particular, he effects by way of his commemorative representation. In other words, the *Catechism* uses the language of Christ's "intercession" more or less synonymously with the language of his "presence." Linguistically speaking, while Catholic theology uses words such as *perpetuate, reenact, commemorative representation, sign/symbol, re-present, sacrament, memorial/anamnesis, intercession, application,* etc., somewhat interchangeably to describe the work of the eucharist with respect to the cross, the one

85. *MD*, 66.
86. *MD*, 68.
87. *MD*, 70. On the state of Christ's presence in the sacrament, see Journet, *Mass*, 62–63.

word it does not use in this same fashion is *repeat*: that is, the eucharist does not repeat Christ's passion—it repeats his Supper, but not his cross.[88]

Here Pius XII offers a more detailed explanation, and his teaching on this matter consists of some closely interrelated theological considerations. The instrumentality of the sacraments coincides integrally with the instrumentality of Christ's humanity. Concerning the sacraments, they effect what they signify, and with the eucharist, then, this is Christ's passion. In Pius XII's terms, "the appointed ends are the same":[89] just as on the cross Christ realizes redemption for humankind, so also in the eucharist does Christ give himself—in his own words—for the "forgiveness of sins." This unity derives from the person and work of Jesus, the incarnate Word, who as "the God-Man is the priest and victim."[90] In what, therefore, does this redemption, or forgiveness, consist; what, specifically, is Christ doing when he is interceding?

Pius XII identifies four "ends" of both Christ's passion and the eucharist. First, he glorifies the Father: his whole life, culminating in the sacrifice of the cross as an "odor of sweetness" (Eph. 5:2) and incorporating all worship on heaven and earth, is directed to the "Father Almighty."[91] Second, he gives thanks to God: he gave thanks at the Supper, and the offering of his life on the cross was, likewise, "eucharistic"; only Jesus is capable of offering to God "a worthy return of gratitude."[92] Third, he makes "expiation, propitiation, and reconciliation": Christ's incarnation and his cross were the most fitting means for him to be immolated as a propitiation for sins (1 Jn 2:2).[93] Fourth: he entreats the Father for blessings on our behalf. On earth, he was heard for his obedience (Heb 5:7), and in the eucharist he is our mediator before God and obtains our "every blessing and grace."[94]

By specifying what Catholic teaching intends the language of "intercession" to entail Christologically, Pius XII makes an important contribution to the church's reflection on eucharistic sacrifice. There is no sacrifice in heaven; therefore, in Charles Journet's words, "The intercession of the heavenly Christ consists in presenting to the Father the unique sacrificial act by which is

---

88. *CCC*, 1368. See the important article by Jean M. R. Tillard, "Vocabulaire sacrificiel et eucharistie," *Irénikon* 53, no. 2 (1980): 145–74. Karl Rahner and Angelus Häussling also emphasize the *repraesentatio sacrificii crucis* as constitutive of the visible liturgical rite that makes the Mass a *sacrificium visibile*; Rahner and Häussling, *The Celebration of the* Eucharist, trans. W. J. O'Hara (Montreal: Palm, 1966), 18–29.

89. *MD*, 71.

90. *MD*, 76; see 79.

91. *MD*, 71.

92. *MD*, 72.

93. *MD*, 73.

94. *MD*, 74.

accomplished one time the redemption and salvation of the entire world."[95] Historically, the Letter to the Hebrews chiefly informs the church's theology behind Christ's heavenly intercession and his eternal priestly office: "Consequently, he is able for all time to save those who approach God through him, since he always lives to make intercession for them" (7:25; see also Heb 9–10). Without careful reflection, Hebrews' insistence in chapters 9–10 on the uniqueness and the once for all nature of Christ's sacrifice may appear to stand in tension with (or even in contradiction to) Christ's command to repeat the Lord's Supper "for the forgiveness of sins."[96]

To be sure, the teachings considered earlier on Christ's presidency in the eucharist, along with the incorporation into the divine eternity of the sacrament itself, *suggest* how to read Hebrews in concert with the Supper narrative. By bringing this reading of Hebrews into conversation with eucharistic sacrifice, however, Pius XII models how to think through Christ's institution narrative and Hebrews' Christology in a synthetic, rather than dichotomous, fashion. Christ's presence in the eucharist is not passive. His sacramental presence corresponds to his heavenly intercession, in which—as priest, victim, and mediator—he glorifies, thanks, atones, and entreats the Father on our behalf. Hence, with a soteriological focus, the pope says, "Its daily immolation reminds us that there is no salvation except in the cross of our Lord Jesus Christ and that God himself wishes that there should be a continuation of this sacrifice"; and likewise with a Christological focus, "It is quite true that Christ is a priest; but He is a priest not for Himself but for us, when in the name of the whole human race He offers our prayers and religious homage to the eternal Father; He is also a victim and for us since He substitutes Himself for sinful man."[97]

Eucharistic Sacrifice and Self-Sacrifice

The numerous affinities that Methodists should discern between Wesley and Pius XII on this matter is confirmed by his unambiguous teaching that salvation comes solely from the cross and the unique, priestly mediation of Christ. What is more, because participation in the eucharist essentially means participation in Christ's passion, both see in the church's communal sacrifice the impetus for self-sacrifice as well. While Christ's redeeming work is at once both universal and efficacious in and of itself (since it is a divine action), it is

95. Journet, *Mass*, 63–64. This is precisely the work that Wesley attributes to Christ in his eternal and heavenly ministry as high priest.

96. Pius XII cites Heb 10:14 on this very point; 76. For a detailed reading of Hebrews in concert with the Supper narrative, see Journet, *Mass*, 29–34.

97. *MD*, 79, 81.

still necessary that each soul "individually come into vital contact with the sacrifice of the cross"—i.e., that each person be washed in the "font" of Christ's blood.[98] God calls each person to imitate Christ: "Let this mind be in you which was also in Christ Jesus,"[99] and this imitation transpires both within the liturgy and beyond it.

In the liturgy, the faithful are called to unite themselves to Christ's offering by offering themselves in self-sacrifice. The same dynamic of the interrelation between the external rite and the internal worship of the spirit that requires the church as a body to make a visible sacrifice holds true analogously for the individual believer. The external rite should declare the interior intention, and the whole liturgy—readings, homily, rites, vestments, art—should "reproduce in our hearts the likeness of the divine Redeemer through the mystery of the cross."[100] Indeed, while offering right worship to God is the primary end of the liturgy, in doing so the church and each of its members is transformed into the one whom they worship:

> Through this active and individual participation, the members of the Mystical Body not only become daily more like to their divine Head, but the life flowing from the Head is imparted to the members, so that we can each repeat the words of St. Paul: "With Christ I am nailed to the cross: I live, now not I, but Christ liveth in me."[101]

The self-offering of those united to Christ is not, of course, "confined merely to the liturgical sacrifice"; instead, by desiring to imitate Christ and by offering themselves, believers' faith, charity, and piety are deepened and their lives are conformed to the example of their Lord. Pius XII emphasizes the double effect in the eucharist of salvation and purification, or in Wesleyan terms, sanctification. The movement in his teaching from self-offering (itself initiated by grace), to forgiveness, to union with Christ, and finally to transformation resonates closely with Wesley's teaching, especially Wesley's stress on pardon followed by power for holy living.

---

98. *MD*, 77.

99. *MD*, 80.

100. *MD*, 102; see 93, 98, 100–103.

101. *MD*, 78; see 128. Pius XII addresses in detail additional topics related to eucharistic sacrifice: (1) the difference between the priest's sacrifice and the laity's (83–97); (2) Jesus' substantial presence and the church's practice of eucharistic adoration (129–31); and (3) the distinction in the eucharist between the sacrificial rite (consecration, separation of the eucharistic species, and their oblation) and the communion (112–15).

Paul VI, Mysterium Fidei *(1965)*

Promulgated on the heels of Vatican II, *Mysterium Fidei* addresses several aspects of eucharistic doctrine, chief among them (1) eucharistic mystery, (2) Christ's sacramental presence and transubstantiation, and (3) eucharistic latria and devotion. In his introductory paragraphs, Paul VI reaffirms the centrality of the eucharist in the life of the church, the teachings of the Council of Trent, the distinction between the sacrifice and the sacrament in the eucharist, and the restoration of the liturgy through the Constitution on the Sacred Liturgy.[102] The pope's primary motivation behind the encyclical is to correct "false and disturbing opinions" associated mainly with Christ's sacramental presence. While he approves of the desire to articulate in contemporary parlance the mystery of Christ's presence in the eucharist, he does not approve of the conclusions of such efforts—namely, "transignification" or "transfinalization," which disregard or circumvent the Tridentine doctrine of transubstantiation.[103] Although *Mysterium Fidei* is longer and more detailed than *Mirae Caritatis*, it does not take up issues of sacrifice in a systematic fashion or in response to any controversy; nonetheless, important teachings are affirmed in the first two sections.

Eucharistic Mystery in the Sacrifice of the Mass: Re-enactment at the Heart of Doctrine

Paul VI starts by reiterating the threefold definition from Trent that in the eucharistic mystery the sacrifice of the cross is "re-enacted in wonderful fashion," is continually "recalled," and "its salvific power is applied to the forgiving of sins."[104] He, too, denotes the sacramental mode of sacrifice with the words "wonderful fashion," and, also with Trent, comments that Jesus' Supper in the Upper Room was in fact the first proleptic enactment, recollection, and application of Calvary. In instituting a new covenant in his body and blood for the forgiveness of sins, Jesus takes up Old Testament sacrificial actions and establishes a new and final sacrifice. This sacrifice is what Christ instructed the apostles to "repeat" in his memory. The earliest Christians in Jerusalem obeyed their Lord (Acts 2:42), just as Paul's teaching of thanksgiving, memorial, and sacrifice is also faithful to this tradition: those who partake of the Lord's table have a share in Christ's body and blood—i.e., his sacrifice.[105]

---

102. *MF,* 1–8.
103. *MF,* 10–12.
104. *MF,* 27.
105. *MF,* 28–29.

Christ's Sacramental Presence

What makes the church's participation in the body and blood of Christ more than a simple memorial is the presence of Christ himself. The church does not travel its earthly pilgrimage on its own power; instead, when the church is at work through prayer, works of mercy, preaching, governing, and all the stages of the Christian life, Christ is the one who is present, working his redemption through it.[106] When the church—obedient to his command—remembers his cross and applies its power by repeating his sacramental sacrifice, "Christ is present in His Church in a still more sublime manner." The eucharist is the same sacrifice as the Lord's Supper because Christ is present in both, presiding over his church and speaking the same words of institution; therefore, "No one is unaware that the sacraments are the actions of Christ who administers them through men."[107] More than any other action of the church, therefore, the eucharist is the work of the whole church, and because the body imitates its head and is indeed inseparable from it, the whole church "plays the role of priest and victim along with Christ, offering the Sacrifice of the Mass and itself completely offered in it."[108] The church unites with Christ's priestly office, and Paul VI highlights the dual dimension of human and divine agency, of the church's participation in the Lord's redemption.

> It is an act of Christ and of the Church. In offering this sacrifice, the Church learns to offer herself as a sacrifice for all and she applies the unique and infinite redemptive power of the sacrifice of the Cross to the salvation of the whole world. . . . The Lord is immolated in an unbloody way in the Sacrifice of the Mass and He re-presents the sacrifice of the Cross and applies its salvific power at the moment when he becomes sacramentally present—through the words of consecration—as the spiritual food of the faithful, under the appearances of bread and wine.[109]

By uniting the church ever more deeply to Christ, the eucharist increases its virtue and character, deepens its devotion and joy, strengthens its unity, and keeps it on the "paths of holiness." In short, the eucharist sanctifies the church. And this sanctification is directed outward in charity. In language that Wesley would surely embrace, Paul VI states that "unselfish love" in the soul nurtured in the eucharist acts in service of a "social love" that puts the good

106. *MF*, 35–37.
107. *MF*, 38.
108. *MF*, 31.
109. *MF*, 32, 34.

of the community ahead of oneself. In offering itself sacrificially with Christ's sacrifice, the church then learns to live sacrificially for others in the world.[110]

John Paul II, Ecclesia de Eucharistia *(2003)*

Ecclesia de Eucharistia is a powerful encyclical: "The Church draws her life from the eucharist. This truth does not simply express a daily experience of faith, but recapitulates *the heart of the mystery of the Church.*"[111] On the one hand, since it is the most significant post-conciliar magisterial document to address the topic of eucharistic sacrifice in detail, John Paul II cites not only the teaching of the Council of Trent, but the three encyclicals considered earlier (especially *Mediator Dei*) and texts from Vatican II. In doing so, it is not surprising that he reiterates and upholds all the dogmatic teaching from both councils. On the other hand, it is also the most significant post-conciliar magisterial document to address the topic of eucharistic sacrifice since the ecumenical movement, and the pope's encyclical reflects profoundly the developments in ecclesial relations that the ecumenical movement has produced.

Ecclesiological and Ecumenical Dimensions of Eucharistic Sacrifice

John Paul II's primary focus in this encyclical is the inseparable and interdependent dimension of ecclesiology and the eucharist, which was also a point of emphasis in the Catholic response to *BEM.*[112] Not only does the pope write in light of the ecumenical movement (and liturgical reform), he also writes in light of societal trends (sociological, political, economic, moral) that have changed dramatically in the latter decades of the twentieth century. In his encyclical, he places Christ's redemptive sacrifice—and therefore the eucharist—at the center of his teaching.

The pope exhorts his readers to live eucharistically by imitating the Blessed Virgin Mary, "Woman of the Eucharist." Throughout the text, he couples his strong teaching on eucharistic doctrine with personal reflection on the diverse venues where he has celebrated the eucharist and on his own eucharistic piety, and his devotion to Mary deeply shapes his eucharistic the-

110. For a reading of *MF* from a Reformed perspective that appreciates its ecumenical possibilities, see Alasdair I. C. Heron, *Table and Tradition: Towards an Ecumenical Understanding of the Eucharist* (Edinburgh: Handsel, 1983), 169–70.

111. *EE*, 1.

112. The encyclical generated many responses, among them Geoffrey Wainwright, "*Ecclesia de eucharistia vivit,*" 1–9; Thomas P. Looney, "Ecumenical 'Lights' and 'Shadows' in *Ecclesia De Eucharistia,*" *Ecumenical Trends* 32, no. 7 (2003): 1–12; Clint Le Bruyns, "*Ecclesia De Eucharistia*: On Its Ecumenical Import," *Ecumenical Trends* 32, no. 8 (2003): 8–13; and a symposium in *Pro Ecclesia* 12, no. 4 (2003).

ology.[113] Consequently, a life of Marian eucharistic devotion is sacrificial. "Mary, throughout her life at Christ's side and not only on Calvary, made her own the sacrificial dimension of the eucharist . . . the eucharist has been given to us so that our life, like that of Mary, may become completely a *Magnificat!*"[114] The saving power of Christ's redemptive sacrifice flows through the eucharist to the church: "From the perpetuation of the sacrifice of the Cross and her communion with the body and blood of Christ in the eucharist, the Church draws the spiritual power needed to carry out her mission."[115] Only a sacrificial eucharistic devotion inspired by Mary will empower the church to be faithful to this mission.

The multiple aspects of the church's mission can be mentioned only briefly, but they all derive from the eucharistic sacrifice. First and foremost is his teaching (and Vatican II's) that the church grows from the eucharist: "A causal influence of the eucharist is present at the Church's very origins," and the church is perennially strengthened by its communion with the one "who was sacrificed for our sake."[116] Because the eucharist is the treasured gift, the church must do all that it can to safeguard and maintain its truth. And from this fundamental reality comes dogmatic teaching that must be maintained on questions of apostolicity, authority, unity, ecumenism, evangelism, and sacrifice.

Apostolically, the validity of the eucharist requires a priest with valid holy orders who comes from the succession of "valid episcopal ordinations" and who are in communion with the bishop of Rome. This hierarchical order validates and demonstrates the priestly role in the eucharist: "*In persona* [*Christi*] means in specific sacramental identification with the eternal High Priest who is the author and principal subject of this sacrifice of his, a sacrifice in which, in truth, nobody can take his place."[117]

Authoritatively, the pope counters the liturgical abuses after Vatican II stemming from a "misguided sense of creativity and adaptation" that reacted against the binding liturgical norms of the Magisterium, a reaction that is "unauthorized" and "inappropriate."[118] Eucharistic abuses risk introducing confusion into liturgical practice: "Stripped of its sacrificial meaning, it is celebrated as if it were simply a fraternal banquet."[119]

In terms of unity, the eucharist witnesses and strengthens the communion of the church that already exists: "The eucharist, as the supreme sacramental

113. *EE*, 53–55.
114. *EE*, 56, 58.
115. *EE*, 22.
116. *EE*, 21.
117. *EE*, 28–29.
118. *EE*, 52.
119. *EE*, 10.

manifestation of communion in the Church, demands to be celebrated in a context where the outward bonds of communion are also intact."[120]

Ecumenically, therefore, intercommunion between separated communities is not possible. Even while the Catholic Church celebrates recent ecumenical convergences and remains committed to Christian unity, intercommunion "would result in slowing the progress being made towards full visible unity."[121] Despite the dismay expressed by many Protestants at the pope's prohibition on intercommunion, he is right to maintain Catholicism's traditional position. The lack of intercommunion keeps front and center urgent issues like the doctrine of the church and the precise nature of visible unity. Were, it to occur, the Catholic Church would immediately be reduced to one denomination among many, an option for people to "choose" just like any other—sacramental communion would then render other ecclesial differences merely bureaucratic, organizational, or institutional, and this devolution would put at risk the ecumenical hope of a truly visible church.

Evangelically, John Paul II relates the church's task of a "new evangelism" of the third millennium to the eucharist. The church does not need a "new programme"; instead, it has been given all it needs: the Gospel, Tradition, Christ, and the Trinity. "The implementation of this programme of a renewed impetus in Christian living passes through the eucharist."[122]

What, for John Paul II, does the eucharistic sacrifice have to do with the church in all its fullness? In short, everything. What the church receives in the eucharist; what builds it up and strengthens it; what propels it forward "into the deep on the sea of history"; and what unites it with the fiery love of the triune God is nothing less than Christ himself, present in the Holy Spirit by the power of his redemptive sacrifice.[123]

> Every commitment to holiness, every activity aimed at carrying out the Church's mission, every work of pastoral planning, must draw the strength it needs from the eucharistic mystery and in turn be directed to that mystery as its culmination. In the eucharist we have Jesus, we have his redemptive sacrifice, we have his resurrection, we have the gift of the Holy Spirit, we have adoration, obedience, and love of the Father. Were we to disregard the eucharist, how could we overcome our own deficiency?[124]

---

120. *EE*, 38; see 35.
121. *EE*, 30; see 44.
122. *EE*, 60.
123. *EE*, 6.
124. *EE*, 60. Wesley would heartily approve of the pope's insistence that the eucharist lies at the heart of both evangelism and holiness, which were two features at the center of the Wesleyan revival.

Eucharistic Sacrifice and the Mystery of Faith

John Paul II's discussion of Christ's redemptive sacrifice for humanity is concentrated in his introduction, which sets the theological foundation for his treatment of eucharistic sacrifice in chapter 1, "The Mystery of Faith." Christ's passion, or the *Triduum sacrum,* from the Thursday Supper to his Sunday morning resurrection, "embraces" both the *"mysterium paschale"* and the *"mysterium eucharisticum."*[125] "The Church was born of the paschal mystery," and as its sacrament, the eucharist "stands at the centre of the Church's life."[126] The origin of the church resides in the "Triduum paschale," which is "foreshadowed and 'concentrated' forever in the gift of the eucharist."[127] In the introduction, the pope is careful to prepare for his detailed account in chapter 1 by articulating the relationship between the *mysterium paschale* and the *mysterium eucharisticum.* The latter is not a repetition of the former, but a sacramental participation in it. Christ's institution of the eucharist "sacramentally anticipated" Christ's impending passion, while in all subsequent celebrations "we are spiritually brought back to the paschal Triduum."[128] This sacramental participation comes about through the soteriological participation of Christ's historic passion in God's transcendent, divine eternity. "In this gift Jesus Christ entrusted to his Church the perennial making present of the paschal mystery. With it he brought about a mysterious 'oneness in time' between that *Triduum* and the passage of the centuries."[129]

John Paul II organizes his teaching on eucharistic sacrifice in chapter 1 around Paul's account in 1 Cor 11:23–26 and around the church's acclamation in the liturgy of the mystery of faith, recited also in the United Methodist Great Thanksgiving: "Christ has died; Christ is risen; Christ will come again." This acclamation is essentially a liturgical expression of Paul's teaching: "For as often as you eat this bread and drink this cup, you proclaim the Lord's death until he comes" (v. 26).

125. *EE,* 2.
126. *EE,* 3.
127. *EE,* 5.
128. *EE,* 3.
129. *EE,* 5; see 11, where he cites the *Catechism* on this same idea. See Benedict XVI's wide-ranging Apostolic Exhortation *Sacramentum Caritatis*: "In instituting the sacrament of the eucharist, Jesus anticipates and makes present the sacrifice of the Cross and the victory of the resurrection. At the same time, he reveals that he himself is the *true* sacrificial lamb, destined in the Father's plan from the foundation of the world" (10).

Christ has Died . . .

The eucharist, however, is more than a proclamation of the cross: because Christ is present as the High Priest and because his passion "participates in the divine eternity," in the eucharist Christ is present in his humanity in the power of his cross. "It is the gift of himself, of his person in his sacred humanity, as well as the gift of his saving work." This is how the "central event of salvation becomes really present" through the church's "memorial" celebration. In addition to a proclamation, then, the eucharist is also a "means of sharing in" Christ's passion (see 1 Cor 10:14–22).[130] Indeed, because Christ is truly present, the church comes into "real contact" with Christ's saving work, "since this sacrifice is made present ever anew, sacramentally perpetuated." Sacramentally, this entails the "application" of Christ's "reconciliation won once for all" to people throughout history. Because Christ is really present in the power of his sacrifice, and because the church really shares in it in the eucharist, these two are in fact "one single sacrifice."[131] He cites from Pius XII the language of "commemorative representation":

> The Mass makes present the sacrifice of the Cross; it does not add to that sacrifice nor does it multiply it. What is repeated is its memorial celebration, its "commemorative representation" (*memorialis demonstratio*), which makes Christ's one definitive redemptive sacrifice always present in time. The sacrificial nature of the eucharistic mystery cannot therefore be understood as something separate, independent of the Cross or only indirectly referring to the sacrifice of Calvary.[132]

Having cited several authoritative sources up to this point—Trent, Vatican II, the liturgy, the *Catechism*, encyclicals—the pope defines eucharistic sacrifice in his own words, as it were. Essentially, because Christ's self-gift to the Father (and then to us) is sacrificial, our incorporation into it via his sacrificial meal is also sacrificial:

> By virtue of its close relationship to the sacrifice of Golgotha, the eucharist is a sacrifice in the strict sense, and not only in a general way, as if it were simply a matter of Christ's offering himself to the faithful as their spiritual food. The gift of his love and obedience to the point of giving his life (see Jn 10:17–18) is in the first place a gift to his Father. Certainly

---

130. *EE*, 11. George Lindbeck speaks approvingly of the pope's theology of sacrifice as carrying farther Vatican II's "*rapprochement* with the Reformation"; George A. Lindbeck, "Augsburg and the *Ecclesia De Eucharistia*," *Pro Ecclesia* 12, no. 4 (2003): 409.

131. *EE*, 12.

132. *EE*, 12.

it is a gift for our sake, and indeed that of all humanity (Mt 26:28; Mk 14:24; Lk 22:20; Jn 10:15), yet it is first and foremost a gift to the Father.[133]

Aidan Nichols interprets John Paul II's language of "sacrifice in the strict sense" to refer to *sacrum facere* (to make holy), "For this sacrament is that same sacrifice now expressed in the Church in the form of a sign. That alone warrants the Roman Liturgy calling the eucharist in its concise, sober, way, *sacramentum redemptionis*, the sign of the redemption itself."[134]

Christ Is Risen . . .

When John Paul II moves to the second affirmation of the Mystery of Faith, he emphasizes a central aspect of Catholic teaching that is often overlooked in the Protestant imagination with respect to the language of Christ's passion and his redemptive sacrifice. That is, Christ's passion, his *mysterium paschale*, encompasses the whole saving movement of his atonement. He writes, "Christ's Passover includes not only his passion and death, but also his resurrection," as the liturgy expresses.[135] In a way that fills out his careful discussion, this teaching demonstrates yet again what Catholic theology intends by the language of "sacrifice" and "perpetuating the cross." Because the resurrected (now glorified) Christ is present in the power of his redemptive sacrifice, the eucharistic sacrifice cannot be a repetition of Christ's crucifixion; instead, it is a repetition of the sacrificial rite that Christ instituted that represents his sacrifice in order to commemorate it, and by doing so to participate in it, which itself is possible because all of Christ's humanity in turn participates instrumentally in the divine eternity of the Godhead. "The eucharistic Sacrifice makes present not only the mystery of the Saviour's passion and death, but also the mystery of the resurrection which crowned his sacrifice. It is as the living and risen One that Christ can become in the eucharist the 'bread of life' (Jn 6:35, 48), and the 'living bread' (Jn 6:51)."[136]

Upon comparison, John Paul II and Aquinas demonstrate significant continuity with respect to eucharistic sacrifice, since both advance the pivotal teaching "that understanding the eucharist as cultic sacrifice illumines the reality of salvation in which we are united with Christ's Cross in order to join in the Trinitarian communion of his risen life."[137] Over against any account that wants to de-emphasize the idea of sacrifice—either Christ's or the church's—

133. *EE*, 13; see Heb 10:7; Trent, session XXII, chapter I.
134. Nichols, "Holy Oblation," 259–60.
135. *EE*, 14.
136. *EE*, 14. See *EE*, 15, on eucharistic presence and transubstantiation.
137. Levering, "John Paul II and Aquinas on the Eucharist," 638.

along "analogous or metaphorical" lines and to emphasize solely the element of fellowship and solidarity instead, John Paul II and Aquinas teach that sacrifice makes communion with Christ and salvation possible.[138] Christ's passion is the cause of our redemption, and the eucharist is the source of our communion with the Trinity.[139] Consequently the eucharist also bears an undeniable, even primary, dimension of sacrifice: "For both Aquinas and John Paul II, our communion or 'abiding in Christ' comes about through our sacramental representation of, and thus sharing in, Christ's cultic sacrifice—a sharing that conforms us to Christ's image by enabling and including our gifts of self within his sacrificial self-offering to God."[140]

The life that the resurrected Christ gives in the food and drink that are his body and blood (Jn 6:53–57) "is fully realized" in holy communion because it is by this means and to this end that the "inward union" with the Lord is "intrinsically directed." From the eucharist founded on the sacrifice of Christ, it follows that it is also a "true banquet" in which "Christ offers himself as our nourishment" and in which he gives to those united to him "the source of every other gift"—namely, his Spirit.[141]

Christ Will Come Again...

In the Mystery of Faith the church exclaims its eschatological hope that Christ will soon realize God's plan. The eucharist is a "straining towards the goal," a "foretaste," an "anticipation," a "confident waiting" precisely in that through the Spirit and with Christ it is a "pledge of future glory."[142] Here the power of Christ's humanity as an instrument of the Trinity's divine eternity is once again crucial, for just as the eucharist is a sacramental making present of Christ's death and resurrection, so also is it a sacramental participation in what the body of Christ is destined to become. "Those who feed on Christ in the eucharist need not wait until the hereafter to receive eternal life: they already possess it on earth, as the first-fruits of a future fullness which will embrace man in his totality."[143] Wesley's *Hymns on the Lord's Supper* contain a strikingly similar emphasis on God's eschatological salvation as a present reality here and now in the eucharist.

---

138. Levering, "John Paul II and Aquinas on the Eucharist," 640–42. In Levering's article, David Power's *The Eucharistic Mystery* serves as the foil to the papal encyclical.

139. Levering, "John Paul II and Aquinas on the Eucharist," 642–45.

140. Levering, "John Paul II and Aquinas on the Eucharist," 646.

141. *EE*, 16. Wainwright demonstrates the convergence between John Paul II and Wesley around this theme: "*Ecclesia de Eucharistia vivit*," 3–4.

142. *EE*, 18.

143. *EE*, 18.

John Paul II consistently draws the reader back to the source of the church's hope, however, which is Christ's sacrifice. The eucharist can only be a banquet if Christ—in his humanity—gives himself to the church, and he can only do that because he has already given himself to the Father on the cross; likewise, the eucharist can only be a foretaste of the resurrection if Christ is indeed risen and glorified, which he can only be if it is indeed the case that at one point he was not. "This pledge of the future resurrection comes from the fact that the flesh of the Son of Man, given as food, is his body in its glorious state after the resurrection. With the eucharist, we digest, as it were, the 'secret' of the resurrection."[144]

Self-Sacrifice and the Church's Sacrifice

The pope completes this chapter with the teaching that God's is not the sole agency in the eucharistic sacrifice. In response to the Holy Spirit, individuals and the community become sharers in Christ's body and blood by participating in the eucharistic sacrifice, which they do by offering themselves. The church, thus, responds to and unites with the sacrifice of its head: "In giving his sacrifice to the Church, Christ has also made his own the spiritual sacrifice of the Church."[145] Moreover, this sacrifice is, properly speaking, the sacrifice of the *totus Christus*—the whole Christ in head and body—which encompasses the church on earth as well as in heaven. The "eschatological tension" fostered by celebrating the "sacrifice of the Lamb" unites the church on earth with the "heavenly 'liturgy,'" celebrated by those saints and martyrs who have gone before and who even now give glory to God and to the Lamb. "The eucharist is truly a glimpse of heaven appearing on earth."[146]

The labor to which individual Christians are called in this life receives its strength from the church's eschatological vision. The hope of a new heaven and a new earth, though, do not foster an otherworldly orientation that distances Christians' concerns for the condition of humanity now. The "seed of living hope" that the church has even now only makes more urgent the "sense of responsibility for the world today" in the realms of justice, solidarity, human life, globalization, weakness, poverty, and despair. Eucharistic sacrifice is a call to transformation for the church and for the world. It is both the means of that transformation (since Christ himself is sacrificially present) and the goal (typified in Christ's example of foot washing). Participation in the eucharistic sacrifice means taking on the charge to live a life that is "completely eucharistic."[147]

144. *EE*, 18.
145. *EE*, 13.
146. *EE*, 19.
147. *EE*, 20.

The resources discussed in this chapter offer a rich and profound teaching on the *lex credendi* of eucharistic sacrifice, and they provide answers to our opening questions on sacrifice, memorial, perpetuation of the cross, Christ's priestly office, and the church's offering. It is significant to note that the encyclicals were promulgated as the liturgical renewal movement and the ecumenical movement were advancing, yet never do the popes consider teaching on eucharistic sacrifice in order to placate historic Reformation grievances. Even John Paul II, who was committed to the ecumenical cause, insists that the eucharist is a sacrifice because of its connection to Calvary. But does this insistence hinder Christian unity? By no means; and quite the contrary: on this side of the *Joint Declaration on the Doctrine of Justification* (to which Methodists are co-signatories), this body of consistent teaching can be received as an ecumenical gift with respect to this historically controversial doctrine. The eucharist is the sacramental sacrifice—the commemorative representation—that makes present Christ's one saving sacrifice, which is itself the mystery of faith.

CHAPTER 6

Eucharistic Sacrifice in the Worship of the Catholic Church
Eucharistic Prayers I–IV

In this chapter, the focus shifts to a consideration of how the church expresses its teaching and its faith (*lex credendi*) in its liturgy (*lex orandi*). In keeping the focus on sacrifice, we will turn our attention to that part of the liturgy where the church's sacrificial worship is concentrated, namely the eucharistic prayers (primarily EPs I–IV). The *General Instruction of the Roman Missal (GIRM)* provides a valuable explanation of the central role that eucharistic sacrifice plays in the church's liturgy and how "the liturgical norms of the Council of Trent have certainly been completed and perfected in many particulars by those of the Second Vatican Council, which has carried into effect the efforts to bring the faithful closer to the Sacred Liturgy that have been taken up these last four centuries and especially those of recent times."[1]

The history of the church's eucharistic liturgy is one of continuity and change. The introduction to the *General Instruction* is organized around three complementary themes in which eucharistic sacrifice has an essential place: (1) Testimony of an Unaltered Faith; (2) Uninterrupted Tradition; (3) Accommodation to New Conditions.[2] Not only does Jesus provide a model for the church's eucharist in his words of institution and his fourfold action of the elements at the Supper, but the church hears in Jesus' instructions to the disciples for the preparation of the meal the same command to care for the preparation of "people's minds, and of places, rites, and texts for the Celebration

---

1. United States Conference of Catholic Bishops, *General Instruction of the Roman Missal* 15 (*GIRM*), accessed April 7, 2023, https://www.usccb.org/prayer-and-worship/the-mass/general-instruction-of-the-roman-missal. See *Sacrosanctum Concilium* (21) on the "immutable" and changeable elements of the liturgy and on the need for texts and rites to express their symbolic function clearly, and "Vatican II and the Third Edition of the Roman Missal," in Christopher Carstens and Douglas Martis, *Mystical Body—Mystical Voice: Encountering Christ in the Words of the Mass* (Chicago: Liturgy Training, 2011), 89–130.

2. See, too, Margaret Mary Kelleher, "Preamble," in *A Commentary on the General Instruction of the Roman Missal: Developed under the Auspices of the Catholic Academy of Liturgy and Cosponsored by the Federation of Diocesan Liturgical Commissions*, ed. Edward Foley et al. (Collegeville, MN: Liturgical Press, 2007), 73–97.

of the Most Holy eucharist."[3] Our discussion in the previous chapter on eucharistic sacrifice in contemporary magisterial texts has engaged those dogmatic teachings that are true of Catholicism's eucharistic celebrations in all times and places and in all eucharistic prayers.[4]

From the early church and the fathers, through Trent, then reaffirmed at Vatican II, and now in the new Missal, the church teaches that the eucharistic sacrifice "perpetuates the Sacrifice of the Cross" by celebrating the "memorial of his death and resurrection." Referencing numerous texts from Vatican II and Eucharistic Prayers III and IV, the *General Instruction* summarizes the teaching that we have explored earlier.

> What is taught in this way by the Council is consistently expressed in the formulas of the Mass. Moreover, the doctrine . . . "for whenever the memorial of this sacrifice is celebrated the work of our redemption is accomplished"—is aptly and exactly expounded in the Eucharistic Prayers; for as in these the Priest enacts the anamnesis, while turned towards God likewise in the name of all the people, he renders thanks and offers the living and holy sacrifice, that is, the Church's oblation and the sacrificial Victim by whose death God himself willed to reconcile us to himself; and the Priest also prays that the Body and Blood of Christ may be a sacrifice which is acceptable to the Father and which brings salvation to the whole world.[5]

Thus, the purpose of this chapter will be to explore how the formulas of the Mass express this teaching. Even more succinctly, we read, "For this people is the People of God, purchased by Christ's Blood, gathered together by the Lord, nourished by his word, the people called to present to God the prayers of the entire human family, a people that gives thanks in Christ for the mystery of salvation by offering his Sacrifice."[6]

By addressing eucharistic sacrifice at the beginning of the Preamble and under the heading of *Testimony to an Unaltered Faith*, the *GIRM* therefore signals that the "sacrificial nature of the Mass" is a constitutive element of the eucharist because it originates from Christ's institution and his Pasch, and because it is carried forward in the church's hierarchical celebration by Christ's presidency as the High Priest.[7] These comments, along with others in the Preamble, further signal the principal object of eucharistic sacrifice that is celebrated

3. *GIRM*, 1. See Benedict XVI, *God Is Near Us*, 49.

4. Benedict XVI, *God Is Near Us*, 51.

5. *GIRM*, 2; see Kelleher, "Preamble," 76–78.

6. *GIRM*, 5.

7. *GIRM*, 2; see also 4, 11, 17, 27, and the corresponding sections in Kelleher, "Preamble."

in the *anamnesis*-offering section: namely, in its understanding of Jesus' words to "do this," the church does what Jesus did at the Supper—that is, it offers his sacrifice; in other words, the Holy Spirit unites the church to the eternal priestly intercession of Christ in offering his sacramental body and blood to the Father for the forgiveness of sins. The church's participation in the sacraments notwithstanding, the agent of salvation in the eucharist is God alone. Keith Pecklers quotes *Mediator Dei*, saying, "Christ acts each day to save us, in the sacraments and in His holy sacrifice. . . . Not from any ability of our own, but from the power of God."[8]

The *General Instruction* identifies four parts of the Mass: Introductory Rites, Liturgy of the Word, Liturgy of the Eucharist, and Concluding Rites. The Liturgy of the Eucharist itself consists of several parts: Preparation of the Gifts, Prayer Over the Gifts, Eucharistic Prayer, and the Communion Rite (Lord's Prayer, the Peace, Fraction, Communion). The eucharistic prayers are the main focus here. As if rippling out from the institution-*anamnesis*-offering, the presence and priesthood of Christ in the sacrament render sacrificial the whole eucharistic liturgy. As noted, Christ's words of institution and consecration, along with his fourfold action of taking, thanking, breaking, and giving inform the church's ritual and theology. "Hence, the Church has arranged the entire celebration of the Liturgy of the Eucharist in parts corresponding to precisely these words and actions of Christ."[9] The preparation of the gifts signifies Christ's taking of the bread and cup and entails a sacrificial posture of worship.[10] The eucharistic prayer is the act of thanksgiving by Christ and the church whereby the gifts become the body and blood of Christ. In the fraction and communion, believers receive the sacramental body and blood of Christ "in the same way that the Apostles received them from the hands of Christ himself."[11]

> Now the center and high point of the entire celebration begins, namely, the Eucharistic Prayer itself, that is, the prayer of thanksgiving and sanctification. The Priest calls upon the people to lift up their hearts towards the Lord in prayer and thanksgiving; he associates the people with himself in the Prayer that he addresses in the name of the entire community

---

8. Keith Pecklers, "Importance and Dignity of the Eucharistic Celebration," in Foley et al., *A Commentary on the General Instruction on the Roman Missal*, 100–101.

9. *GIRM*, 72.

10. "The laity's presentation of the gifts signifies its desire to give themselves to God and, along with the bread and wine, to become divinized by the power of Christ's sacrifice"; Carstens and Martis, *Mystical Body—Mystical Voice*, 162.

11. *GIRM*, 72; see Foley, "The Structure of the Mass, Its Elements and Its Parts," in Foley et al., *Commentary on the General Instruction of the Roman Missal*, 162–64.

to God the Father through Jesus Christ in the Holy Spirit. Furthermore, the meaning of this Prayer is that the whole congregation of the faithful joins with Christ in confessing the great deeds of God and in the offering of the Sacrifice.[12]

All the eucharistic prayers, despite their variety of expression and structure, share this fundamental theological purpose at the heart of the church's liturgy, and they all share the following "main elements": *thanksgiving/preface, acclamation/Sanctus, epiclesis, institution narrative and Consecration, anamnesis, oblation, intercessions*, and *concluding doxology*.[13] The structure of the Roman Canon (EP I) diverges the most from this pattern, while EPs II–IV share much in common structurally.

In the reform of the liturgy following Vatican II, the theology of offering as it was expressed in the Roman Canon became an important factor shaping the construction of Eucharistic Prayers II–IV.[14] The American bishops identified the church's "theology of offering" as it is expressed in the Roman Canon as one of many factors influencing the creation and structure of the new eucharistic prayers. They considered the dominant aspect of sacrifice to be both an asset and a detriment for the Canon. "A theology of offering is,

12. *GIRM*, 78. Foley calls attention to the primary agency of Christ in the prayer directed to the Father to which the priest and all the faithful join; Foley, "Structure of the Mass," 171–73. For more on the eucharistic prayer, see Carstens and Martis, *Mystical Body—Mystical Voice*, 169–72.

13. *GIRM*, 79.

14. The most widely cited work on the reform of the Canon and the construction of the new prayers is Cipriano Vagaggini, *The Canon of the Mass and Liturgical Reform* (Staten Island, NY: Alba House, 1967). Additionally, two books by Enrico Mazza have proved particularly valuable; Mazza, *The Celebration of the Eucharist: The Origin of the Rite and the Development of Its Interpretation* (Collegeville, MN: Liturgical Press, 1999); and *The Eucharistic Prayers of the Roman Rite* (New York: Pueblo, 1986). Among the numerous works on the history of the Canon and the new prayers, see, for example, Louis Bouyer, *Eucharist: Theology and Spirituality of the Eucharistic Prayer* (Notre Dame, IN: University of Notre Dame Press, 1968); Jasper and Cuming, *Prayers of the Eucharist*; Annibale Bugnini, *The Reform of the Liturgy, 1948–1975* (Collegeville, MN: Liturgical Press, 1990); Bernard Botte, *Le canon de la messe romaine* (Louvain: Abbaye du Mont César, 1935); Josef A. Jungmann, *The Mass of the Roman Rite: Its Origin and Development (Missarum Solemnia)* (New York: Benziger, 1951); Jeffrey Michael Kemper, "Behind the Text: A Study of the Principles and Procedures of Translation, Adaptation, and Composition of Original Texts by the International Commission on English in the Liturgy" (Ph.D. diss., University of Notre Dame, 1992). Historically, Aidan Kavanagh traces the roots of the church's eucharist in the Jewish *berakoth* and gives an overview of the central reforms of the Roman Canon; Kavanagh, "Thoughts on the Roman Anaphora," in *Living Bread, Saving Cup: Readings on the Eucharist*, ed. R. Kevin Seasoltz (Collegeville, MN: Liturgical Press, 1982), 30–59. In this same volume, Robert Ledogar treats the liturgical and theological development of the Eucharistic Prayer, with attention to the aspects of thanksgiving, *anamnesis*, and offering; Ledogar, "The Eucharistic Prayer and the Gifts Over Which It Is Spoken," 60–79.

as we have seen, one of the merits of the Roman Canon. At the same time it has a corresponding weakness. The real expression of offering in the eucharistic celebration takes place after the institutional narrative—as an essential element of the memorial." The bishops continue:

> The Roman Canon stresses the concept so frequently in its text that it obscures this fundamental truth. Moreover, the appropriate occasion for us to offer our own gifts and to ask God for his acceptance of them is in the prayer over the offerings. The present structure and wording of the Roman Canon obscures the fact that the primary gift offered at Mass is Christ Jesus himself. The concept of offering, therefore, is good and essential, but the repeated references to it in the Roman Canon exaggerate the idea and obscure its relationship to the total picture.[15]

Note that the concern expressed by the bishops regards not the theology of offering in the Canon, but the lack of clarity with which it is conveyed.[16] One of the many reasons they enthusiastically approve the new prayers is that their structure and language more clearly reveal the church's theology of offering. Foley notes that in the new prayers the "offering is intimately tied to eucharistic memorial and, therefore, to the once-and-for-all self-offering of Christ."[17] In light of this historical context, we can turn now to see how the church's eucharistic prayers express this theology of sacrifice.[18]

The Preface/Thanksgiving, Post-Sanctus, Intercessions

Eucharistic Prayer I

The theme of sacrifice in the post-Sanctus is clearly evident in several instances throughout this ancient prayer. Addressed to God the Father,

---

15. National Conference of Catholic Bishops (NCCB), *The New Eucharistic Prayers and Prefaces* (Washington, DC: Bishops' Committee on the Liturgy, 1968), 14. On the typology between Abel, Abraham, and Melchizedek, see Mazza, *Eucharistic Prayers*, 80. See also Jungmann, *Eucharistic Prayer*, 17.

16. NCCB, *New Eucharistic Prayers and Prefaces*, 14. See, for example, Mazza's discussion (following Vagaggini) on the difficult structure of the Canon and the debate around its reform; Mazza, *Eucharistic Prayers*, 53–58.

17. Foley, "Structure of the Mass," 178. For a historical perspective, see Jungmann, *Eucharistic Prayer*, 26–28. Benedict XVI defends the current liturgy in *God Is Near Us*, 66–67.

18. With the preface (at least for EPs II and IV) and post-Sanctus of EPs I–IV, the sacrificial language derives from (1) biblical references to sacrifice in the history of salvation as they prepare for Christ, (2) the Paschal mystery of Christ's once-for-all sacrifice, and (3) the offering of bread and wine. These aspects of sacrifice have a place in the United Methodist Great Thanksgiving, and they are not—either historically or currently—a point of disagreement.

the people pray that through Christ the Lord, "you accept and bless these gifts, these offerings, these holy and unblemished sacrifices, which we offer you firstly for your holy catholic Church."[19] The gifts in view here refer originally to the practice in the early church when the faithful would bring offerings (usually foodstuffs) for the church's use in addition to the bread and wine. In the Middle Ages, a monetary offering replaced the gift of food and was presented along with the bread and wine. The offertory has now been incorporated into the rite of the preparation of the gifts. When these offerings are presented, the money is to be placed away from the altar on which the bread and wine are placed and over which a prayer is said.[20]

Subsequent references pick up biblical themes that associate sacrifice with intercession and redemption: "We offer you this sacrifice of praise or they offer it for themselves and all who are dear to them: for the redemption of their souls,"[21] along with the corporate (family/ecclesial) notion of sacrifice and salvation: "Therefore, Lord, we pray: graciously accept this oblation of our service, that of your whole family."

The final prayer before the Institution/consecration asks God to "bless, acknowledge, and approve this offering in every respect; make it spiritual and acceptable, so that it may become for us the Body and Blood of your most beloved Son, our Lord Jesus Christ." While not formally an epiclesis, this prayer nonetheless serves an epicletic function of making present in the eucharist the "ontological content" of the Supper, which is the death and resurrection of Jesus.[22] Journet sees in these prayers, from the *Te igitur* through the *Quam oblationem*, not a series of separate and discrete offerings, but a movement of the church as it is pulled into the one offering of Christ: "The bread and wine are not offered except by passing immediately beyond to Christ, Who will take their place."[23]

Eucharistic Prayer II

This prayer is an adaptation from the anaphora in the *Apostolic Tradition* credited to Hippolytus, but it has been adapted to fit the Antiochene anaphora

---

19. The text cited throughout is the International Commission on English in the Liturgy (ICEL) 2010; see Mazza, *Eucharistic Prayers*, 59–60.

20. *GIRM*, 73–77. See Catherine Vincie, "The Mystagogical Implications," in *A Commentary on the Order of Mass of the Roman Missal: A New English Translation*, ed. Edward Foley et al. (Collegeville, MN: Liturgical Press, 2011), 222–25.

21. See Mazza, *Eucharistic Prayers*, 64–65.

22. Mazza, *Eucharistic Prayers*, 68–72.

23. Journet, *Mass*, 112.

pattern.[24] The brief Thanksgiving/Preface is addressed to the Father and is trinitarian in scope. According to the Father's will Christ became incarnate in the power of the Holy Spirit and was sent as "our Savior and Redeemer."[25] It concisely alludes to the Christology and soteriology of key New Testament texts in relating the Paschal mystery to the creation and new life of the People of God: "Fulfilling your will and gaining for you a holy people, he stretched out his hands as he endured his Passion, and so to break the bonds of death and manifest the resurrection."[26] The language of *redemption* and *salvation* and *holy people* evoke the biblical notions of deliverance, ransom, and exodus. Titus 2:13–14 speaks of "our great God and Savior, Jesus Christ" who "gave himself for us that he might redeem us from all iniquity and purify for himself a people of his own who are zealous for good deeds." Joyce Ann Zimmerman argues that the Preface does more than remind worshipers of Jesus' sacrifice: "It draws us into those same events and begs us to be obedient and self-giving as Jesus," with a sacrificial love that "embraces all with 'stretched out' hands and arms."[27] The text then moves quickly to the epiclesis where the Spirit is asked to come upon "these gifts," and where "they are offered as a sacrament through the grace of the Spirit that transforms them truly and sacramentally into the Body and Blood given over and shed for the holy people."[28]

Eucharistic Prayer III

The U.S. bishops comment, "The key themes in this eucharistic prayer are sacrifice and the Holy Spirit—with an obvious connection between the two. The opening section mentions the work of the Spirit in forming a worshiping community which will offer a clean sacrifice to God's glory."[29] This connection is raised in the post-Sanctus: through Christ and the "working of the Holy Spirit," God gives life to "all things" and makes them holy. The

24. For a discussion on the structural and textual changes, see Mazza, *Eucharistic Prayers*, 90–98.

25. Louis Soubigou, *A Commentary on the Prefaces and the Eucharistic Prayers of the Roman Missal* (Collegeville, MN: Liturgical Press, 1971), 263–64.

26. See Heb 2:14–15; 1 Jn 4:14. Mazza offers a rich discussion of the different Christologies between Hippolytus and EP II and the biblical themes alluded to in the Thanksgiving; *Eucharistic Prayers*, 100–108.

27. Joyce Ann Zimmerman, "The Mystagogical Implications," in Foley et al., *Commentary on the Order of Mass*, 336.

28. David Power, "Theology of the Latin Text and Rite," in Foley et al., *Commentary on the Order of Mass*, 322.

29. NCCB, *New Eucharistic Prayers and Prefaces*, 43. Vagaggini is considered the principal drafter of EPs III and IV, based on his proposals in *The Canon of the Mass and Liturgical Reform*. For the background, see Mazza, *Eucharistic Prayers*, 123–25.

Father's work for the Spirit is to "gather a people to yourself," with the intention of making a sacrifice, "so that from the rising of the sun to its setting a pure sacrifice may be offered to your name." Here the reference to Malachi 1:11 is explicit.[30] Indeed, the prayer for the Spirit's work in making a holy people is magnified in the intercessions so that they become not just capable of making a holy sacrifice, but that "he [Spirit] make of us an eternal offering to you." Finally, the intercession in this prayer is ultimately universal in scope, and the church asks, "May this Sacrifice of our reconciliation, we pray, O Lord, advance the peace and salvation of all the world."

Eucharistic Prayer IV

EP IV has the same structure as EPs II and III and the eucharistic prayers of reconciliation; it is distinctive for its fixed preface, for its length (the longest of the new prayers), and the sweep of salvation history that the prayer rehearses in the opening sections.[31] The predominant theological motif in this prayer is covenant—namely, God's covenant faithfulness—fulfilled in Christ in light of humanity's sinfulness and need of salvation. As a constituent element of divine-human covenants, the theology of sacrifice also has a prominent role. "The additional notions of blood and sacrifice, however, must be considered in connection with that covenant theme."[32] After the Sanctus, the prayer continues to glorify the Father for divine greatness, wisdom, and love. Despite humanity's disobedience, "Time and again you offered them covenants and through the prophets taught them to look forward to salvation." In response to mistaken ideas often culled from the philosophy of religions, Mazza offers this valuable corrective on the relationship between covenant and sacrifice: "Properly speaking, then, the response of the eucharist is not a repayment that cancels a debt and puts giver and recipient on the same level; that is impossible in the case of God and his creatures."[33]

The prayer then moves elegantly from the Old Testament to the New by highlighting the dynamic of sin, salvation, and covenant in God the Son. "And you so loved the world, Father most holy, that in the fullness of time you sent

---

30. See Trent, session XXII, chapter I. Christoph Cardinal Schönborn follows the text of *EP* III in his exposition of eucharistic sacrifice; Christoph von Schönborn and Hubert Philipp Weber, *The Source of Life: Exploring the Mystery of the Eucharist* (New York: Crossroad, 2007), 69–70.

31. Mazza, *Eucharistic Prayers*, 158–59. See Joseph Gelineau, "The Fourth Eucharistic Prayer," in *The New Liturgy*, ed. Lancelot Sheppard (London: Darton, Longman and Todd, 1970), 213–27; and Soubigou, *Commentary on the Prefaces and the Eucharistic Prayers*, 283–317.

32. NCCB, *New Eucharistic Prayers and Prefaces*, 48.

33. Mazza, *Eucharistic Prayers*, 159.

your Only Begotten Son to be our Savior . . . he shared our human nature in all things but sin." After summarizing the liberating nature of Jesus' ministry, the prayer turns to Christ's sacrificial and saving passion: "To accomplish your plan, he gave himself up to death, and, rising from the dead, he destroyed death and restored life." Christ's self-sacrifice proves the basis for those in him also to live a sacrificial life: "And that we might love no longer for ourselves but for him who died and rose again for us." This transition is influenced by 2 Cor 5:15: "And he died for all, so that those who live might live no longer for themselves but for him who died and was raised for them."[34]

Institution Narrative and Consecration

If the eucharistic prayer is the heart of the church's eucharistic celebration, then the institution-consecration and *anamnesis*-offering is the heart of the eucharistic prayer. "Before one can fully, consciously, and actively participate in the sacrificial act of Christ presenting himself now to the Church, that sacrifice must be sacramentalized."[35] The designation of this section of the prayer under two aspects—one historical and the other sacramental—attests to the complex and central function of this section.

The words of Christ are uniform in all four eucharistic prayers, but the description that prepares for them varies from prayer to prayer, each stressing a different aspect of Christ's sacrificial meal. Eucharistic Prayer I says, "On the day before he was to suffer, he took bread in his holy and venerable hands, and with eyes raised to heaven to you. . . ." With a Johannine allusion, Prayer II emphasizes the authority and divine sovereignty with which Jesus suffers his passion: "At the time he was betrayed and entered willingly into his Passion. . . ." Prayer III follows St. Paul: "For on the night he was betrayed he himself took bread. . . ." And Prayer IV—keeping with the Johannine themes of the Father's glory and Christ's sacrifice—begins by hinting at the ritual and covenantal aspects of the Supper that will soon be made explicit: "For when the hour had come for him to be glorified by you, Father most holy, having loved his own who were in the world, he loved them to the end." Whether at the Supper, on the cross, or in the eucharist, Christ is sovereign.

While Jesus presides over the entire liturgy as the high priest and is the one who ultimately addresses the eucharistic prayer to the Father (leading his body, the church, to be sure), it is in the words of institution that the priest speaks *in persona Christi*, lending his words—in effect—to Christ who speaks through him. For this reason, the eucharistic prayer is addressed to the Father,

---

34. This section also incorporates biblical ideas from Jn 3:16, Gal 4:4, and Heb 4:15.

35. Carstens and Martis, *Mystical Body—Mystical Voice*, 189.

because it is ultimately the prayer of the Son to the Father into which he incorporates his church by the power of his Spirit and teaches it to offer itself to the Father. The *General Instruction* underscores these words as the preeminent sacrificial moment in the prayer and enumerates several qualifications under which the eucharistic sacrifice is carried out:

> The *institution narrative and Consecration,* by which, by means of words and actions of Christ, that Sacrifice is effected which Christ himself instituted during the Last Supper, when he offered his Body and Blood under the species of bread and wine, gave them to the Apostles to eat and drink, and leaving with the latter the command to perpetuate this same mystery.[36]

First, in the power of the Holy Spirit, Christ—who is always present with his people—becomes really and substantially present in his body and blood; only the "species" of bread and wine remain. Christ says, "this is my body," and "this is the cup of my blood." The Last Supper witnessed the first transubstantiation, and for all the mystery that this dogma seeks to affirm (albeit through a glass darkly), at least one of its chief ends is to assure that the one whom the Apostles (and all subsequent generations of believers) receive in communion is none other than Christ himself, really present in the power of his unique redemptive sacrifice. As Journet writes, "Transubstantiation is, at the Last Supper, a true and real sacrifice, an unbloody sacrifice, not by multiplying the redemptive sacrifice, but by multiplying the real presence of the redemptive sacrifice."[37]

Second, this moment is also one of his self-offering—of his self-sacrifice—that John Paul II (following Trent) insisted was first and foremost an offering to the Father. "For this is my body, which will be given up for you," and "the blood of the new and eternal covenant."[38] This teaching that Christ offered himself—and therefore by concomitance his sacramental body and blood—to the Father at the Supper may not be readily apparent to Methodists: where in the ritual of taking, blessing, breaking, and giving is the action of offering? Yet the subsequent theology of *anamnesis* and offering hinges precisely on this teaching.

To understand this doctrine, consider initially that the Supper was not just the final dinner that Jesus ate with his friends. Jesus had already "set his

36. *GIRM,* 79; the formulation of Trent remains the dogmatic basis for this teaching. See Schönborn and Weber, *Source of Life,* chapters 6 and 7: "The Consecration" and "The Presence of Christ in the Eucharist."

37. Journet, *Mass,* 95.

38. On the sacrificial nature of Jesus' words *body, for you, blood,* and *covenant,* see Mazza's chapter "The Last Supper and the Church's Eucharist," in *Celebration of the Eucharist,* 297–306.

face to Jerusalem" (Lk 9:51), and the Supper was, in essence, the beginning of his passion (his obedient self-offering to the Father), as his sacrificial language (especially that of new covenant) and his words to Judas attest. Furthermore, building on his words at the Supper (*This is my body*), Christ is not only present naturally by way of his physical body "under its proper and normal appearances," but he is present sacramentally "under its foreign and borrowed or assumed appearances": "the sacramental appearance completely corresponds, primarily and immediately, to the natural presence . . . we ought to speak of the Mass as we do of the Last Supper: it is a true and proper sacrifice if it is a real presence of Christ and His one sacrifice."[39] Thus, at the Supper Christ is "present substantially twice,"[40] offering himself to the Father in the one redeeming act of his sacrifice.

Recall Aquinas's teaching, which Journet repeats, that at the Supper Christ consumed his own sacramental body and blood. This observation is a helpful point of comparison for Methodists who think they understand transubstantiation. Journet goes on to make the distinction between two types of Christ's presence, substantial and efficient: Christ was substantially present to the woman who fell at his feet (Lk 7:36–50) and efficiently present in action and power (although physically distant) in the home of the centurion whose servant he healed (Lk 7:1–10). Methodists might call this latter presence a pneumatological presence and ask whether—when this analogy is applied to eucharistic presence—it is necessary that Christ's sacramental presence also be substantial. Of course, for Catholics it is, whereas Methodists (following Wesley) have never felt compelled to decide on the nature of Christ's presence, whom they nonetheless believe to be really present as crucified and now glorified in the power of his unique redemptive sacrifice. The doctrine of how Christ is present bears directly on the nature of the *anamnesis*-offering in the following section of the prayer.

Christ's sacrificial action at the Supper transfers directly to his presidency at the Mass:

At the Mass there is, under the appearances of bread and wine, the substantial presence of Christ now glorious. And there is under the same appearances the efficient, operative presence of His one redemptive sacrifice. Not without reason does Christ, now glorious, come to us under the appearances of His Body given for us, of His Blood poured out for the remission of sins; it is in order to signify that He comes to us with the application, the contact, the power and the presence of His one redemptive sacrifice.[41]

39. Journet, *Mass*, 48–49.
40. Journet, *Mass*, 60.
41. Journet, *Mass*, 61; see also 71. Journet is following Trent, session XXII, chapter I.

Third, he gave his sacramental body and blood to his Apostles, and by doing so, he made them partakers, proleptically, in his impending passion: "Which will be poured out for you and for many for the forgiveness of sins." Less controversial than the consecration or *anamnesis*-offering, it is helpful nevertheless to remember that Christ's passion entails his crucifixion and death, along with his resurrection and ascension—in other words, the whole soteriological scope of his obedient self-offering to the Father. Similarly, *the forgiveness of sins* is a synecdoche: for Catholics and Methodists, forgiveness stands for much more than a juridical sense of being declared guilt free and (ideally) having the assurance of pardon; rather, it includes becoming adopted children of God, being made into Christ's likeness by his Spirit, and, eschatologically, sharing in the divine nature. Hence the close connection for Catholics and Methodists between eucharist and deification/sanctification.

Fourth, Christ commanded the Apostles, "Do this in memory of me." In the *anamnesis*-offering immediately following, the church demonstrates its interpretation of this command by expressing how it understands its celebration to be faithful to Christ's words. Historically, and still in ecumenical dialogues, this section of the prayer is the most sensitive. (*BEM*, for example, treated this aspect of its teaching with great care.) Christ did not say, "Remember me"; instead, he said, "Do this," and to remember him by doing, by which the *General Instruction* teaches that Christ intended for his church "to perpetuate this same mystery."[42]

Anamnesis

Following immediately after the institution-consecration and faithful to Christ's command, the church remembers its Lord, and in doing so it remembers specifically his saving passion. Power writes, "It is the action of Christ himself at the Supper and his memorial command that is the foundation and meaning of the church's sacrifice of praise, thanksgiving, and atonement."[43] Every church earnestly desires to remember Christ, and the recovery of the biblical notion of *anamnesis*—modeled after the Jewish conviction that the Passover celebration incorporates every generation into the Exodus—is one of the fruits of the ecumenical movement. *Anamnesis* "is a living reality working here and now to save [humankind]. But its effectiveness depends upon our faith. Christ would be present, of course, even if we did not believe. In fact, it is the continued presence of Jesus as Risen Lord which makes faith possible."[44]

---

42. *GIRM*, 79.

43. David Power, "Theology of the Latin Text and Rite," in Foley et al., *Commentary on the Order of Mass*, 270.

44. NCCB, *New Eucharistic Prayers and Prefaces*, 22.

The theology of *anamnesis* was the principal hermeneutic of *BEM*'s eucharist chapter, and both the Catholic and Methodist responses welcomed this theological formulation. Largely indebted to the insight of the early church, this theological recovery was successful because it found an ecumenically acceptable way of relating the actions of the worshiping community to God's saving action in the liturgy in a manner that historical Western debates surrounding sacramentality (agency, causality, efficacy) had found divisive.[45] Methodism's acceptance of this theology brings it in line with the theology of Catholicism and Orthodoxy, and—as a matter of no small importance—with the theology of Wesley as well.

In this section of the prayer the church learns to offer itself, for in praising the Father for the salvation achieved by the Son, it surely does not think that God has "forgotten" anything (Christ is always interceding [Rom 8:34]); rather, the church continually learns how to remember all the more deeply what it means to be united to the Father, through Christ, in the Spirit. Thus, *anamnesis* is fundamentally a pneumatological modality—God's people always caught up anew into Christ's redeeming sacrifice. Both theologically and syntactically, it functions as a transition between the institution and the offering, the *anamnesis* being the response to the institution and the rationale for the offering. Aidan Kavanagh puts the matter nicely: "With the Son the church maintains a communion-identity secured in the Spirit. Such a faith-response is not merely intellectual or emotional: it is total, objectively liturgical, and takes the form of an oblatory self-sacrifice that is eucharistic."[46] What is remembered is Christ's Paschal mystery, and each prayer recalls different aspects of this "living reality."

EP I: *Therefore, O Lord, as we celebrate the memorial of the blessed Passion, the Resurrection from the dead, and the glorious Ascension into heaven of Christ . . .*

EP II: *Therefore, as we celebrate the memorial of his Death and Resurrection . . .*

EP III: *Therefore, O Lord, as we celebrate the memorial of the saving Passion of your Son, his wondrous Resurrection and Ascension into heaven, and as we look forward to his second coming . . .*

EP IV: *Therefore, O Lord, as we now celebrate the memorial of our redemption, we remember Christ's Death and his descent to the realm of the dead, we proclaim his Resurrection and his Ascension to your right hand, and, as we await his coming in glory . . .*[47]

---

45. See David Power, "The *Anamnesis*: Remembering, We Offer," in *New Eucharistic Prayers: An Ecumenical Study of Their Development and Structure*, ed. Frank C. Senn (New York: Paulist Press, 1987), 146–47.

46. Aidan Kavanagh, "Thoughts on the New Eucharistic Prayers," 108. See Mazza, *Eucharistic Prayers*, 74–79.

47. On the paschal mystery as a central theme of EP IV, see Gelineau, "Fourth Eucharistic Prayer," 221–22.

While the *anamnesis* section proclaims, liturgically, Christ's Pascal mystery that the church celebrates, and while it explains, theologically, the church's participation in that mystery, the actual content and action of that participation are reserved for the oblation.

Oblation

In this section of the eucharistic prayer a sacrifice is offered to God:

The *oblation*, by which, in this very memorial, the Church, in particular the Church gathered here and now, offers the unblemished sacrificial Victim in the Holy Spirit to the Father. The Church's intention, indeed, is that the faithful not only offer this unblemished sacrificial Victim but also learn to offer their very selves, and so day by day to be brought, through the mediation of Christ, into unity with God and with each other, so that God may at last be all in all.[48]

This paragraph specifies the nature of the sacrifice—i.e., who offers what, along with the sacrifice's trinitarian dimension. In the power of the Holy Spirit and to the Father, Christ and the church offer Christ and the church. The theological doctrine of the *totus Christus* once again becomes explicit: "through the mediation of Christ," the body is led by its head. Foley notes the way in which the church participates in its head: "This respects the role of Christ as the initiator of every liturgical action (*SC*, no 7), and theologically disallows any sense that the community is making some offering on their own initiative."[49] Stressing the doctrine of the *totus Christus* with which Wesley would agree, Avery Dulles says, "The Mass may therefore be seen not only as the sacrifice of Christ but also the church's liturgical presentation of his sacrifice. In offering Christ, the church offers herself in union with him to the Father."[50]

In the offering, the church continues to perpetuate the mystery of the cross by repeating the sacrificial liturgy that Christ instituted at the Supper. The eucharistic prayer corresponds to his act of thanksgiving in which he offered his sacramental body and blood to the Father. The fraction and communion following the eucharistic prayer correspond to Christ's act of breaking and giving—a pattern also adopted by the UMC Great Thanksgiving. In the offering, the church does this: "And if He then changed the bread and wine into his Body and Blood, it was in order to permit His disciples to participate in His bloody sacrifice, to enter with Him into the offering of His bloody sac-

48. *GIRM*, 79.
49. Foley, "Structure of the Mass," 178.
50. Dulles, "The Eucharist as Sacrifice," 182.

rifice."[51] Journet's language of participation is important, for there is a correspondence in this regard between the disciples' participation in the Supper and the church's participation in the Mass, but the latter is not identical to the former. Only God can save, so "at the Last Supper, Christ acted alone, to the exclusion of the disciples": they participated in his "redemptive sacrifice" by receiving his body and blood "under sacramental signs."[52] In the eucharist, the church participates in Christ's sacrifice, but it does so by doing what Christ commanded-- offering his body and blood—in addition to receiving it. In its eucharistic sacrifice, the church can do nothing but follow its head, and it can offer nothing but what it has been given. As Karl Rahner notes, "the Church offers to God precisely the gift over which Christ himself alone has exclusive power to dispose. Others can do so only to the extent that they can act in the name of Christ."[53]

Well versed in the historical controversies of the Reformation and the current state of ecumenical dialogues and writing well after Vatican II, David Power corroborates the theology of offering expressed in the prayers. "In all the prayers," he writes, "one finds that the elements are spoken of in such a way as to designate them as Christ's body and blood, the transformation by implication being attributed to the words of the narrative." Historically he outlines the Reformation controversy and the Catholic response, and ecumenically he surveys how Catholic, Presbyterian, Anglican, Lutheran, and Methodist liturgies express the theology of offering. In his own theology, however he diverges sharply from the Catholic position.[54] Historically speaking, this section of the prayer is the most controversial, but ecumenically speaking, any confusion and misunderstanding concerning the language of offering the "unblemished sacrificial Victim" is less likely to occur when the "central act of offering" is properly integrated into the context of memorial and thanksgiving.[55] Mark Wedig remarks that EP I teaches sacrifice as a "way to pray eucharistically" and that this theology "needs to militate against understandings of sacrifice that propitiates and barters with God in order to please the divine. For Christianity there was only one sacrifice of love in Christ Jesus and therefore all other sacrifices join themselves to that one sacrifice."[56] The new eucha-

51. Journet, *Mass*, 230.

52. Journet, *Mass*, 51; Jungmann, *Eucharistic Prayer*, 15–17.

53. Rahner and Häussling, *Celebration of the Eucharist*, 27.

54. Power, *"Anamnesis,"* 150; see 165–66. Elsewhere, Power seeks to interpret sacrifice metaphorically: "Words That Crack: The Uses of 'Sacrifice' in Eucharistic Discourse," in Seasoltz, *Living Bread, Saving Cup*, 157–74.

55. Foley, "Structure of the Mass," 178. Paul Tihon develops this point carefully: "Theology of the Eucharistic Prayer," in Sheppard, *New Liturgy*, 174–93.

56. Mark Wedig, "The Mystagogical Implications," in Foley, *Commentary on the Order of Mass*, 296.

ristic prayers are structured and composed precisely to bring out this theology of offering. Each prayer expresses differently the church's offering of Christ's sacramental body and blood and its own self-offering. The language of the offering becomes progressively more explicit from EP I to EP IV.

> EP I: *We, your servants and your holy people, offer to your glorious majesty from the gifts that you have given us, this pure victim, this holy victim, this spotless victim, the holy Bread of eternal life and the Chalice of everlasting salvation . . . so that all of us, who through this participation at the altar receive the most holy Body and Blood of your Son, may be filled with every grace and heavenly blessing.*

Power notes that EP I does not capitalize *hostia*, as EPs III and IV do, and he stresses the richness with which the language of sacrifice can be interpreted here: "It is in offering that the church keeps memorial, placing before God what is taken from God's own gifts. . . . It is precisely this which is offered in remembrance: the offering of Christ, which takes on its sacramental form in the offering of the church, inclusive of its gifts and its commemorative praise and thanksgiving."[57]

> EP II: *we offer you, Lord, the Bread of life and the Chalice of salvation, giving thanks that you have held us worthy to be in your presence and minister to you. Humbly we pray that, partaking of the Body and Blood of Christ, we may be gathered into one by the Holy Spirit.*

EPs I and II refer poetically to this *pure, holy, and spotless victim, the holy Bread of eternal life and the Chalice of everlasting salvation,* and *the Bread of life and the Chalice of salvation.* Despite this liturgical circumlocution, it nevertheless remains the case "that what is offered is Jesus Christ, and that we join ourselves to him in this his sacrificial act."[58] Note the careful language here: the church offers Christ's sacramental body and blood, but it is also "his sacrificial act."

> EP III: *We offer you in thanksgiving this holy and living sacrifice. Look, we pray, upon the oblation of your Church and, recognizing the sacrificial Victim by whose death you willed to reconcile us to yourself, grant that we . . . may become one body, one spirit in Christ. . . . May he make of us an eternal offering to you. . . . May this Sacrifice of our reconciliation, we pray, O Lord, advance the peace and salvation of all the world.*[59]

57. Power, "Theology of the Latin Text and Rite," 273.

58. Alan Detscher, "The Eucharistic Prayers of the Roman Catholic Church," in *New Eucharistic Prayers*, 26.

59. For a discussion on the liturgical commission's usage of the Latin words *hostia* and *victima* and the complexities of rendering them in contemporary English, see Mazza, *Eucharistic Prayers*, 135–40. Similarly, see A. M. Roguet, OP, and Lancelot Sheppard, "Translation of the Roman Canon," in Sheppard, *New Liturgy*, 169–70. Schönborn cites Augustine that a true

Power explains the more explicit language in this prayer by connecting the eucharistic sacrifice with the propitiatory work of Christ's sacrifice: "in EP III the body and Blood of Christ in sacramental form are offered in atonement. The offering renders God propitious to sinners, and by divine power God makes of these gifts the sacramental mystery of Christ's work and atonement in which salvation is celebrated and efficacious."[60] The English translation *in thanksgiving* lends itself to multiple interpretations,[61] and the U.S. Bishops clarify that thanksgiving and memorial is the means by which the offering is made: "We do not offer in order to give thanks, but we offer by giving thanks: it is a sacrifice of thanksgiving . . . the offering is made by the memorial of the passion and glorification, by the giving thanks."[62] In EP III the *holy and living sacrifice* is further qualified as *the sacrificial Victim by whose death you willed to reconcile us to yourself.* Clearly, this designation can only refer to Christ, since he alone has reconciled humanity to the Father, and he alone can make the church into an everlasting gift and bring salvation to the whole world. As Detscher writes, "There is no question here of a new sacrifice of Christ, but only of that one saving act of Christ on the cross present before us in a sacramental manner."[63]

As we saw in chapter 3, many of Wesley's hymns address the Father in language that mirrors that of EP III, especially the ideas of reconciliation by Christ, the church's union with Christ, and the church's self-offering in Christ. Wesley did not teach Christ's substantial presence in the eucharist, but he did ask the Father to see in the church's sacrifice—and in the bread and wine— the glorified Christ really present in the power of his one redemptive sacrifice interceding on behalf of his people for their salvation and sanctification.

EP IV: *We offer you his Body and Blood, the sacrifice acceptable to you which brings salvation to the whole world. Look, O Lord, upon the Sacrifice which you yourself have provided for your Church, and grant in your loving kindness to all who partake of this one*

---

sacrifice is whatever "helps us adhere to God in a holy community" (City of God, 10.6); Schönborn and Weber, *Source of Life*, 77–78.

60. Power, "Theology of the Latin Text and Rite," 371. In the same volume, on this topic, see Tom Elich's discussion of the theological considerations of sacrifice as rendered in the English translation, "The ICEL 2010 Translation," 378–79.

61. Mazza, *Eucharistic Prayers*, 134.

62. NCCB, *New Eucharistic Prayers and Prefaces*, 46. Relatedly, see Zimmerman's reflection on sacrifice, "The Mystagogical Implications," in Foley, *Commentary on the Order of Mass*, 386–87.

63. Detscher, "Eucharistic Prayers of the Roman Catholic Church," 34. See Louis Bouyer, "The Third Eucharistic Prayer," in Sheppard, *New Liturgy*, 208–9; Schönborn and Weber, *Source of Life*: "The basic meaning of the liturgy is clear: the Church believes that she offers Christ in sacrifice to the Father" (80).

Bread and one Chalice that, gathered into one body by the Holy Spirit, they may truly become a living sacrifice in Christ to the praise of your glory.

EP IV is explicit: what is offered is *his body and blood*. This sacrifice brings *salvation to the whole world* and makes the church one *living sacrifice in Christ*. Significantly, the prayer also states that the sacramental body and blood of Christ that the church offers is not something of its own design or initiation, but is a *sacrifice that you yourself have provided for your church*. In short, "the anamnesis and offering make us contemporaries with Christ. They let us offer Jesus to the Father for the forgiveness of our sins, and give us the opportunity to become one with him in his perfect sacrifice."[64]

The liturgical precedent for the language in this section of the prayer is unclear and has provoked a variety of responses. To be sure, it is "much less traditional, being almost excessive in its theological grandeur,"[65] and Aidan Kavanagh, for example, is dismayed that EP IV replaces traditionally "ambiguous sacramental terms" with the "inadequacy" of the words *body and blood*, suggesting that this formulation revives Reformation controversies and damages recent ecumenical convergence. Yet it is unclear whether Kavanagh objects to the theology of offering expressed here or simply to the directness of the language. If it is the theology, then his own comments seem confused. On the one hand, he rightly notes that however the offering is stated, "the reality being offered is, in fact, Christ/church," and furthermore, he rightly interprets the offering of EP IV: "What is offered is understood to be the real presence of Christ's body and blood, which is the acceptable offering given to the church" through the Spirit and the words of Christ. On the other hand, he finds this "novel" approach unfortunate, and juxtaposes it with EPs I–III: "This [offering] is quite different from the other Prayers, since here we find an offering of the Blessed Sacrament rather than of the church."[66] Yet all the prayers distinguish between the offering of Christ and the church's self-offering, and EP IV likewise prays for the church to be *a living sacrifice* of praise in union with Christ.

If the directness of the language is Kavanagh's concern, then his remarks are also misguided. Liturgical language is a particular genre of corporate Christian speech, directed by the Holy Spirit, but one in which the church plays a significant constructive role as well. The liturgy must balance numerous pres-

---

64. Carstens and Martis, *Mystical Body—Mystical Voice*, 197.

65. Mazza, *Eucharistic Prayers*, 179.

66. Kavanagh, "Thoughts on the New Eucharistic Prayers," 108–9. John Baldovin, "History of the Latin Text and Rite" (406), and Power, "Theology of the Latin Text and Rite" (413) offer similar concerns.

sures: it must be concise, beautiful, and foster a sense of mystery; it should spark the imagination, the heart, and the mind; and it must also be orthodox, clear, and representative of what the church believes, teaches, and of what it does in its worship.[67] Only then can the goal of "full, active, and conscious participation" of the faithful advocated by Vatican II be achieved.[68] Not only do "ambiguous sacramental terms" hinder this goal, but they also hinder ecumenical convergence in the long run. Those who participate in the Catholic liturgy and those separated from it who seek fully to learn its theology need to be able to understand the church's *lex orandi*. Ambiguous language— however traditional—written so as not to provoke ecumenical controversy will ultimately produce a bland and vague liturgy that inspires no one, fails accurately to express the church's dogmatic teaching, obscures real doctrinal differences, and avoids exposing ecumenical differences that churches ultimately need to address. Certainly, Kavanagh does not advocate all this, but he does not acknowledge that EPs III and IV simply express more clearly the same theology of offering found in EPs I and II and taught consistently in dogmatic texts from Trent to *Ecclesia de Eucharistia*.[69]

Much more profitable is the approach taken by Detscher, who interprets EP IV in concert with the church's teaching: "This offering is none other than the sacramental participation in the one sacrificial offering of Christ accomplished for our salvation on the cross." He argues that the straightforwardness of the offertory, albeit atypical, is warranted, "for it speaks of the covenants God has made with us, and most especially of the new covenant in the blood of Christ." He follows the *General Instruction* and notes, "We join ourselves . . . to Christ's self-offering of his body and blood which inaugurates the new covenant of love."[70]

Likewise, Geoffrey Wainwright offers an irenically ecumenical and Methodist interpretation. Despite the "starkness exceptional in liturgical history" of the language with which EP IV speaks, Wainwright notes how the medieval "conceptual framework" has now shifted in light of (1) the "rediscovery" of a biblical *anamnesis*, (2) the use of "ritual phenomenology" in sacramental theology, and (3) the correction to many of the misleading and exaggerated practices of medieval piety with respect to eucharistic sacrifice. Consequently,

---

67. See Philippe Rouillard, "The Eucharistic Prayer in the Church," in Sheppard *New Liturgy*, 156.

68. *SC*, 11, 14, 19, 27, 34, 48.

69. Consider, also, Eucharistic Prayers I and II for Children. The offering of the second states, "He put himself into our hands to be the sacrifice we offer you." For an ecumenical discussion of EP IV, see Power, "*Anamnesis*," 156.

70. Detscher, "Eucharistic Prayers of the Roman Catholic Church," 40.

contemporary formulations, as we have seen, are able to explain more clearly how the Mass and the Cross are one and the same sacrifice. In a challenge to Protestant theology, he leadingly asks, "Could not the contentious 'we offer Christ' paradoxically be seen as antipelagian? It could be an acknowledgment that we have nothing else to offer."[71] He goes on to cite Wesley's *Hymns on the Lord's Supper* in line with the interpretation offered in chapter 3 and notes that in both traditions it is a question of "pleading Calvary, not repeating it." As a Protestant example, he cites the hymn: "Nothing in my hands I bring / Simply to thy cross I cling." He is certainly correct that the Catholic theology of offering Christ is intended to affirm that salvation is through Christ alone; at the same time, there is definitely something in the priest's hands when he clings to the cross. In keeping with the line of argumentation throughout these chapters, his interpretation of eucharistic sacrifice also emphasizes Christ's priestly ministry in heaven and the participation with him by the church on earth: "When in the eucharist we 'set forth' Christ's sacrifice before God, this is a sacramental action on earth corresponding to the fact that Christ is even now 'showing' himself, the once Crucified, to God in heaven on our behalf."[72]

When viewed within its eucharistic and sacramental context, the offering, in fact, is rich in ecumenical potential. "The eucharist is a sacrificial service, the blood of the Lord offered to God in sacrifice, acknowledging his absolute dominion over us and atoning for the sins of all mankind."[73] This phrase clearly witnesses to Christ's lordship, along with his unique atoning work. Moreover, it demonstrates how the church participates in Christ's lordship: it does not possess or wield the sacrament like an object in order to manipulate a distant deity. Just the opposite. By offering Christ, it submits itself to the sovereignty of its head and learns to follow him in sacrificial obedience.[74]

Conclusion

To be sure, only God can save, so Christ remains the glorified high priest who intercedes for his people and who comes to them in his Spirit in the power of his unique redemptive sacrifice, uniting his body to himself and teaching them to offer themselves as a holy and living sacrifice. Christ endured his passion for the sake of humankind, and the doctrine of eucharistic sacrifice is also intended for this purpose—that is, the church offers Christ's

71. Geoffrey Wainwright, *Doxology: The Praise of God in Worship, Doctrine, and Life; A Systematic Theology* (New York: Oxford University Press, 1980), 271–72.

72. Wainwright, *Doxology*, 273.

73. National Conference of Catholic Bishops, *New Eucharistic Prayers and Prefaces*, 48.

74. Tihon is sensitive to Protestant concerns on this point, "Theology of the Eucharistic Prayer," 189.

sacramental body and blood in order to receive him. It participates sacramentally in his redemptive sacrifice in order to be incorporated into his glorification.[75] In the eucharistic sacrifice, there are multiple agents (Christ, church, priest, and laity) engaged in multiple roles (offering, consecrating, receiving) in a twofold movement between the Lord and the church. Nevertheless, in Jesus—the great high priest and first fruit of the resurrection who ever lives to intercede on behalf of his church—the sacrifice is one, offered to the glory of the Father.

> The multiplicity of things offered, however, does not multiply the sacrifice. The Church offers the bread and the wine; she offers Christ; she offers her very self. There are not three independent offerings, three distinct sacrifices, one of bread and wine, one of Christ, and one of the Church. The bread and wine are offered only in order to be changed into the Body and Blood of Christ, Who, offering Himself, gathers around Himself His Church, which is His Body. There is but one supreme offering, that of Christ, in which the Church is engulfed along with all who depend on her.[76]

Through the sacramental priesthood, the church seeks faithfully to fulfill Christ's command to do what he instructed; additionally—as we saw with Aquinas's teaching—it places Jesus' followers here and now in the same relationship to him as he had with his Apostles at the Supper. It is the liturgical embodiment of Paul's teaching that the eucharist is both a participation in the body and blood of Christ (1 Cor 10:16–17) and a proclamation of his death until he comes (1 Cor 11:26). Moreover, when the language of *representation, sacramental renewal, perpetuating the sacrifice of the cross, memorial, commemoration,* etc.—so frequently used in dogmatic texts—is enacted liturgically, the church's teaching becomes all the more clear: (a) the eucharist is the sacramental celebration of the one sacrifice of Christ, (b) it participates in Christ's passion in the same way as the Supper, and (c) it is not a new, secondary, or derivative sacrifice that adds anything to the once-for-all atonement of the cross.

This teaching on divine action and signification in the liturgy is of considerable ecumenical importance. Upon investigation, it becomes evident that this doctrine does not jeopardize the cherished (maybe even overdetermined?) doctrine of justification by faith alone, nor does it detract from the once-for-

---

75. Journet, *Mass*, 102–3.

76. Journet, *Mass*, 111–12. See Schönborn and Weber, *Source of Life*, 71–72, and Dulles, "Eucharist as Sacrifice": "There is no need to look beyond the cross for some additional sacrifice," 183.

all nature of Christ's passion. Indeed, what the doctrine seeks to do is uphold the singular and unique redemptive work of Christ on the cross and his office of eternal high priest as head of the *totus Christus*, while at the same time taking seriously the doctrine of the church as the body of Christ united by the Spirit to its head, which is called faithfully to obey Christ's command to "do this in remembrance of me." If the United Methodist bishops commented that *BEM*'s formulation of eucharistic *anamnesis* removed the cause of past disputes between Protestants and Catholics, how much more then should a full-blown understanding of the Catholic doctrine of eucharistic sacrifice contribute to further concord and convergence with Methodists?

CHAPTER 7

Forgetfulness and Renewal

The Decline of Eucharistic Sacrifice after Wesley and Its Recovery in the Great Thanksgiving

What is contemporary Methodist doctrine and practice concerning eucharistic sacrifice? Analogous to chapters 5 and 6, this is the organizing question for these next two chapters. In keeping with the organization of this study thus far and with the nature of bilateral ecumenical dialogue, this question is one that Catholics would ask their Methodist interlocutors and one that Methodists (ideally) could answer confidently and straightforwardly. Convergence and/or agreement on a particular topic imply that both dialogue partners actually have doctrines that can be articulated, compared, and assessed. What does Methodism now believe, teach, and practice regarding the doctrine of eucharistic sacrifice? Immediately, however, Methodist theologians will recognize that this question is complex and requires some careful distinctions.

Methodism is a global and ecumenical movement of Methodist, Wesleyan, and affiliated churches relating to one another through the World Methodist Council (WMC). While united by their common Wesleyan heritage and represented ecumenically (to varying degrees) by the WMC, the WMC does not exercise doctrinal authority over its members or speak authoritatively for them. Individual churches participate both in the ecumenical endeavors of the WMC and in their own bi- and multilateral dialogues. Neither the WMC nor its member churches are organized around a unifying hierarchical office with an authoritative magisterium. Depending on the topic, this lack of doctrinal unity and authority can make answering our organizing question somewhat complicated. Indeed, Methodist churches commonly do not mandate the use of their own liturgies.[1] To be sure, on some topics—e.g., grace and free will, sanctification and Christian perfection, scriptural authority and the

---

1. Thomas Frank, *Polity, Practice, and the Mission of the United Methodist Church* (Nashville: Abingdon, 1997), 75; on the British side, see A. Raymond George, "Methodist Statements," in *Foundation Documents of the Faith*, ed. Cyril S. Rodd (Edinburgh: T & T Clark, 1987), 103.

183

role of the creeds, a zeal for preaching—Catholics would find Methodists speaking with harmonious (if not quite identical) voices.[2] At the same time, as the responses by individual Methodist churches to the Eucharist chapter of *BEM* attest in chapter 1, when it comes to eucharistic sacrifice, not all Methodist churches yet worship with one accord.

If, historically, continuity is a mark of magisterial Catholic teaching on eucharistic sacrifice, then we should recognize that from the eighteenth to the twentieth centuries discontinuity has marked Methodist teaching. Most (if not all) Methodist churches do not have an explicit teaching on eucharistic sacrifice. Neither the *Hymns on the Lord's Supper* nor the *Christian Sacrament and Sacrifice* was adopted by American and British Methodists as authoritative documents after Wesley's death, nor were they incorporated into the hymnals and catechesis with anything comparable to the fervor with which they were used during his lifetime. Thus, on the one hand, Methodist teaching on eucharistic sacrifice can be characterized as one of decline and loss. Nonetheless, as a result of their enthusiastic participation in the ecumenical and liturgical reform movements of the twentieth century, both British and United Methodism experienced a recovery of the sacrificial dimension of the eucharist as demonstrated in their current eucharistic prayers, which they constructed partly on the basis of this participation. The liturgies of these two Methodist churches, therefore, witness to a theology of eucharistic sacrifice in the *lex orandi* that still remains fully to be received in the *lex credendi*. Thus, on the other hand, teaching by these Methodist churches on eucharistic sacrifice can currently be characterized as one of initial recovery filled with potential. Indeed, acknowledging this loss and then teasing out this latent theology of sacrifice by offering a systematic interpretation of these current prayers is one of the goals of this chapter.[3]

For reasons both practical and theological, I will focus in this chapter on British and United Methodism. Theologically speaking, I focus on British

---

2. Among the many available sources, see, for example, Geoffrey Wainwright, *Methodists in Dialogue* (Nashville: Kingswood, 1995); Karen B. Westerfield Tucker, ed., *The Sunday Service of the Methodists: Twentieth-Century Worship in Worldwide Methodism; Studies in Honor of James F. White* (Nashville: Kingswood, 1996); Cracknell and White, *Introduction to World Methodism*; William J. Abraham and James E. Kirby, *Oxford Handbook of Methodist Studies* (New York: Oxford University Press, 2009); Charles Yrigoyen, ed., *T&T Clark Companion to Methodism* (New York: T & T Clark, 2010); and Daniel Castelo, ed., *Embodying Wesley's Catholic Spirit* (Eugene, OR: Pickwick, 2017).

3. For an article that traces a similar movement in American Methodist eucharistic theology and liturgy in general, see J. Robert Nelson, "Methodist Eucharistic Usage: From Constant Communion to Benign Neglect to Sacramental Recovery," *Journal of Ecumenical Studies* 13, no. 2 (Spring, 1976): 278–84.

Methodism and United Methodism in the United States because these two churches are the ones that responded most enthusiastically and constructively to *BEM* and because they have been the Methodist churches in recent years that have attempted to restore an explicitly Wesleyan vision to their eucharistic theology and celebrations. Lastly, the question of sources: nothing akin to encyclicals, the documents of Vatican II, or the Roman Missal exists for Methodists, but it does not then follow that all theological opinions among Methodists carry equal weight. While the worship books, hymnals, and some conference documents are not mandated or authoritative, they nonetheless are authorized and official and enjoy a pride of place as those texts that represent Methodist faith and worship and seek self-consciously to guide pastors and congregations in the Wesleyan-Methodist sacramental tradition. In light of the lack of magisterial texts, I will use a Methodist equivalent: namely, I will incorporate the work of those individuals who have been appointed by their churches to positions of leadership in teaching and ecumenical participation. Their individual convictions may not be authoritative, yet they are authorized to teach church doctrine and to represent the church in dialogue.

After Wesley: Eucharistic Sacrifice in the Sunday Service

James White introduces Wesley's *Sunday Service* as the "last will and testament" that he bequeathed to the Methodist people. "Until the 1970s," he writes, "material from the *Sunday Service* was American Methodism's chief link to the worship of the ancient Church, the funnel through which the whole history of Christian worship poured into local churches."[4] This is a tall order for any liturgy to fulfill. Methodists did inherit from their founder a rich eucharistic piety and practice, yet for several reasons—both liturgical and ecclesiological— they did not retain the doctrine of eucharistic sacrifice. "Despite some recovery of the connection between word and sacrament in the twentieth century, Methodists have generally understood the Lord's Supper almost to be an occasional service rather than an integral component of Sunday practice."[5]

Apart from the "necessary political, ecclesiastical, and cultural changes," White continues, Wesley's abridgement is "basically a conservative revision," and this "conservatism" is most manifest in Wesley's editing (or lack thereof)

4. James F. White, ed., *John Wesley's Sunday Service of the Methodists in North America: With an Introduction by James F. White* (Nashville: United Methodist Publishing House, 1984), 7. For a helpful treatment of Wesley's contribution to Methodist worship more broadly, see Karen B. Westerfield Tucker, "Form and Freedom: John Wesley's Legacy for Methodist Worship," in *Sunday Service of the Methodists*, 17–30.

5. Karen Westerfield Tucker, *American Methodist Worship* (New York: Oxford University Press, 2001), xiv.

of the Lord's Supper: although "the 166 eucharistic hymns of the Wesleys allowed considerable enrichment of the doctrines expressed in the Anglican rite," Wesley opted not to take advantage of this situation, and "the rite itself was changed little theologically by Wesley."[6] Bowmer's comment, at the beginning of his comparison of the *BCP* with the *Sunday Service*, that the communion office underwent "considerable modification" is somewhat misleading, since the conclusions he draws at the end are more practical than theological: "A truer judgment would be that practical motives were primary, and that much that was doctrinal was bound up with them. It is difficult to think that Wesley would have issued his own version of the Liturgy . . . had not circumstances in America forced the task upon him."[7] This is not to say that Wesley's abridgment of the *Sunday Service* overall makes no changes of theological importance, but simply that the alterations he made did not appreciably modify his eucharistic theology, especially not with respect to sacrifice.[8]

The basic shape of the liturgy in the *Sunday Service* after the Ante-Communion followed the prayer book, with these parts: offertory, collection, prayer for the church, invitation, confession, prayer for forgiveness, comfortable words, *sursum corda*, preface, *sanctus*, prayer of humble access, consecration, communion of ministers, communion of the people, Lord's prayer, Gloria, extemporaneous prayer (optional), and benediction.[9] Sacrificial themes emerge (and, likewise, are repressed) at key revealing places in the liturgy.

First, the offertory and collection occur at the beginning of the rite, and they are *placed* on the *table*, not *offered* at the *altar*.

Second, the rubric from the *BCP* where the priest quite unceremoniously "places" the bread and wine on the table for services when there is Communion is removed because Wesley pressed for weekly Communion, so presumably the bread and wine were already on the "table." In any case, there is no stipulation that the elements are offered.

Third, the confession, forgiveness, and *sursum corda* uphold both the sacramental quality of the rite (i.e., as the instrument that conveys the grace of Christ's passion to the faithful) and the graced, participatory role played by those united to Christ.

<hr>

6. White, *John Wesley's Sunday Service*, 11; see his summary of the salient alterations, 26–28.

7. John Bowmer, "Wesley's Revision of the Communion Service in the Sunday Service of the Methodists," *London Quarterly and Holborn Review* 176 (July 1951): 231, 237.

8. See Robert Webster, "The Reforming Bishop: John Wesley and the Sunday Service of 1784," *Quarterly Review* 21, no. 1 (Spring 2001): 67–80, and the lecture by A. Raymond George, "The Sunday Service 1784," *Friends of Wesley Chapel Annual Lecture* 2 (1983): 3–7.

9. Westerfield Tucker, *American Methodist Worship*, 120.

Fourth, the prayer of humble access exhibits a high notion of Christ's presence and makes explicit appeal to the application of his redemptive sacrifice to both the souls *and* bodies of the communicants: "Grant us therefore, gracious Lord, so to eat the flesh of thy dear Son Jesus Christ, and to drink his blood, that our sinful bodies may be made clean by his body, and our souls washed through his most precious blood, and that we may evermore dwell in him, and he in us. Amen."

Fifth, the consecration develops the sacrificial and redemptive theme of Christ's death:

> Almighty God, our heavenly Father, who, of thy tender mercy, didst give thine only Son Jesus Christ to suffer death upon the cross for our redemption; who made there (by his oblation of himself once offered) a full, perfect and sufficient sacrifice, and satisfaction for the sins of the whole world.

It incorporates a notion of memorial from the Protestant perspective, careful to refer to the bread and wine as "received" (and not offered) and as creatures (rather than as the substantial bodily presence of Christ):

> . . . and did institute, and in his holy Gospel command us to continue, a perpetual memory of that precious death until his coming again; hear us, O merciful Father, we most humbly beseech thee, and grant that we, receiving these thy creatures of bread and wine, according to thy Son our Saviour Jesus Christ's holy institution, in remembrance of his death and passion, may be partakers of his most blessed Body and Blood. . . .

The memorial is incorporated into the consecration, and therefore it precedes the words of institution, an arrangement that further reinforces the theology that neither the elements nor the substantial presence of Christ (which is denied in the Articles) is offered. Reference to the elements as creatures "shuts out of course Transubstantiation."[10] James White wryly puts it:

> The crowning irony is that Luther kept only the words of institution, apparently unaware that to a first-century Jew these words were about as heavily sacrificial as anything that could be spoken. Cranmer dealt with the same problem in a hardly more successful way. He gave us, instead, a prayer full of theological polemics, arguing with Roman Catholics [about Christ's one sacrifice]. . . . And so Methodists have been refuting Roman Catholics every Sunday for the last two hundred years

10. Nolan Harmon, *The Rites and Rituals of Episcopal Methodism* (Nashville: Lamar and Barton, 1926), 142–43.

though I doubt many were listening. The tragedy was that we have had
to settle for a negative statement of eucharistic sacrifice all these years.[11]

Sixth, after the minister and people receive the "Body and Blood of our
Lord Jesus Christ" in communion and say the Lord's Prayer, a note of offering
is admitted—namely, the undisputed New Testament sacrifices of praise and
thanksgiving, and of ourselves:

> O Lord and heavenly Father, we thy humble servants desire thy Fatherly
> goodness mercifully to accept this our sacrifice of praise and thanksgiv-
> ing; most humbly beseeching thee to grant that, by the merits and death
> of thy Son Jesus Christ, and through faith in his blood, we and all thy
> whole Church may obtain remission of our sins, and all other benefits
> of his passion. And here we offer and present unto thee, O Lord, our-
> selves, our souls and bodies, to be a reasonable, holy, and living sacrifice
> unto thee. . . .

Seventh, the prayer affirms the idea that worship and sacrifice (only
through Christ) are ordered by justice—i.e., the creaturely duty to offer to God
what is due: "And although we be unworthy, through our manifold sins, to
offer unto thee any sacrifice, yet we beseech thee to accept this our bounden
duty and service. . . ." The prayer concludes with a trinitarian doxology.

A theology of sacrifice is by no means absent; indeed, the prayer is book-
ended by the offertory and by self-offering. Yet by this structure, by incorporating the memorial into the consecration, and by only *receiving* the elements,
the prayer denies any theology of *anamnesis*-offering along the lines of the
Roman Canon against which it was reacting.[12]

Wesley not only revised the liturgy, but he also abridged the Anglican
Articles of Religion, and here too, his "conservatism" with respect to eucharistic sacrifice is evident. He maintained the definition from the Church of
England that sacraments are means of grace by which God works effectually
within the believer, along with the Protestant affirmation of the two sacraments of baptism and the Lord's Supper (*Church of England* [CE] XXV; *Sunday
Service* [SS] XVI). He omitted the articles on the "unworthiness of ministers"

11. James White, "Liturgy, Theology of the Laity: The Case of the 1972 United Methodist
Communion Service," *Duke Divinity School Review* 43, no. 1 (Winter 1978): 38.

12. For a treatment of the development of the eucharistic prayer in the different editions
of the BCP in their historic context, see Jasper and Cuming, *Prayers of the Eucharist*, 226–49;
Cuming, *History of Anglican Liturgy*. See, too, Harmon's rubric in his *Rites and Rituals* comparing
the different revisions of the BCP, Wesley's *Sunday Service*, and three editions of the Methodist
Ritual, 128–29.

(*CE* XXVI) and on the consumption of the Lord's Supper by the wicked (XXIX), and while his abridgment of the article on Baptism (*CE* XXVII; *SS* XVII) only served to render his theology of baptismal regeneration all the more elusive, he made no substantive alterations to the articles on the Lord's Supper (*CE* XXVIII; *SS* XVIII), of communion in Both Kinds (*CE* XXX; *SS* XIX), and on the One Oblation of Christ, Finished Upon the Cross (*CE* XXXI; *SS* XX). These articles define Anglican and Methodist eucharistic theology over against Catholic doctrine, and the latter article—the One Oblation of Christ—treats eucharistic sacrifice specifically.[13]

The article is highly polemical and does not interpret Catholic doctrine or practice with anything like the hermeneutics of charity that the ecumenical movement has helped to foster. Article XX (*SS*) does not offer any constructive doctrine, only an attack on the Mass:

> The offering of Christ, once made, is that perfect redemption, propitiation, and satisfaction for all the sins of the whole world, both original and actual; that there is none other satisfaction for sin but that alone. Wherefore the sacrifice of masses, in the which it is commonly said that the priest doth offer Christ for the quick and the dead, to have remission of pain and guilt, is a blasphemous fable and dangerous deceit.

The most striking element is the juxtaposition—indeed dichotomy—between Christ's sacrifice and the Mass. Lacking is the concept of the *totus Christus*—i.e., the priestly sacrificial *participation* of the body of Christ in the eternal mediating Priesthood of Christ—as a way of holding together the "once for all theology" of Hebrews with the "do this" dominical command from the Gospels. Although (1) Article XVIII (*SS*) speaks of the Lord's Supper as the "sacrament of our redemption by Christ's death" in which worthy communicants "receive the same," and (2) Article XX (*SS*) speaks of Christ's death sacrificially as "that perfect redemption, propitiation, and satisfaction for all the sins of the world," and (3) Wesley affirms that the believer receives forgiveness in the sacrament, his abridgment of the Articles offers no constructive teaching on how Methodists should interpret the Lord's Supper sacrificially. This is

---

13. See Nolan B. Harmon and John W. Bardsley, "John Wesley and the Articles of Religion," *Religion in Life* 22, no. 2 (Spring 1953): 280–91; Paul F. Blankenship, "The Significance of John Wesley's Abridgement of the Thirty-nine Articles as Seen from His Deletions," *Methodist History* 2, no. 3 (April 1964): 35–47. See Albert Outler's article, however, explaining United Methodism's intention to interpret its own (sometimes polemical) documents in light of its "best ecumenical insights and judgment" as a result of its dialogues with Roman Catholics; Outler, "Olive Branch to the Romans, 1970s-style: United Methodist Initiative, Roman Catholic Response," *Methodist History* 13, no. 2 (January 1975): 52–56.

unfortunate, since the theology of participation by the body in the priestly office of Christ is prominent in the *Christian Sacrament and Sacrifice* and the hymns. Moreover, the wholly negative function of Article XX gives the impression that sacrifice as a theological category should be reserved solely for interpreting Christ's atoning death.

Perhaps Wesley did not introduce a constructive theology of eucharistic sacrifice into the *Sunday Service* (which for him was essentially morning prayer followed by the Lord's Supper rite—i.e., ante-communion and communion) because he did not anticipate that the beloved *Hymns on the Lord's Supper* would fall so quickly into disuse. Be that as it may, the adoption by Methodists of the eucharistic rite from the *Sunday Service*, which they then separated from the rest of the liturgy (i.e., the separation of the eucharistic prayer from the ante-communion), coupled with the subsequent neglect of the *HLS*, constituted a situation in which the doctrine and practice of eucharistic sacrifice could easily slip into decline and loss. And this, in fact, is precisely what happened.

Eucharistic Sacrifice:
From the Sunday Service (1784) to Liturgical Renewal (1970s)

In characterizing eucharistic sacrifice among Methodists during this time period as one of decline and loss, it is important to keep in mind that we are examining only one particular aspect of the eucharist as Methodists have expressed it liturgically and theologically and not the sacrament as a whole. In the years immediately following Wesley's death, Methodists in America and England enjoyed a eucharistic practice and theology that were both vibrant and rich. Methodists in Britain clamored to receive the sacrament in their own chapels and from the hands of their own preachers, and before too long, they prevailed.[14] In his analysis of the Quarterly Meeting, Lester Ruth argues that scholars should not judge early American Methodists on the basis of insights gained from the ecumenical and liturgical renewal movements; moreover, he persuasively counters the once-popular narrative that their eucharistic practice and theology is the impoverished result of a frontier religion—i.e., a pious emotionalism lacking theological sophistication.[15]

14. John C. Bowmer, *The Lord's Supper in Methodism: 1971–1960* (London: Epworth, 1961), 22–23.

15. Lester Ruth, *A Little Heaven Below: Worship at Early Methodist Quarterly Meetings* (Nashville: Kingswood, 2000), 11–14, 212–14; as an example of scholarship that Ruth seeks to correct, see Paul S. Sanders, "The Sacraments in Early American Methodism," *Church History* 27 (1957): 355–71. Bowmer's approach is in concert with Ruth's "History of Holy Communion in Methodism," *London Quarterly and Holborn Review* 184 (April 1959): 97–102.

British Methodism

Turning first to British Methodism, Bowmer writes, "Doctrinally, no people have entered into a richer [eucharistic] legacy than the followers of John and Charles Wesley, yet never has a heritage been so lightly held."[16] Throughout the nineteenth century, the Wesleyan Methodist Conference fought a losing battle to instill in Methodists a more "conscientious attendance at the Sacrament."[17] Liturgically, the history of the various Methodist bodies in the nineteenth century is quite complex, and there is no need here to repeat the detailed accounts offered by Bowmer and David Chapman. As their accounts make clear, the role of eucharistic sacrifice—both doctrinally and liturgically—is noteworthy in its absence. Indeed, "for the greater part" of this time period, the "principal Sunday service" was congregational worship consisting of Bible readings, hymns, prayer, and a sermon. What is more, Chapman notes, is that with the exception of singing, "the congregation's active participation in worship was limited to reciting the Lord's Prayer."[18]

Several factors, liturgically and theologically, conspired to thwart eucharistic sacrifice. First, as noted previously, without the *HLS*, the communion rite allowed for only a truncated expression of sacrifice, and this tradition informed much of Methodism's eucharistic theology. As a result of the *Sunday Service*, those Methodist bodies that continued to use liturgical texts rather than extemporaneous prayers maintained a link with the Prayer Book tradition: "Communion services in early Methodism were conducted according to the Order of the Book of Common Prayer, with Wesley's 'Abridgement' as an authorized alternative."[19] Second, the liturgy and theology of the Puritan tradition (with its *Westminster Directory*) played an important role in Wesley's and Methodism's formation. The Puritan tradition is marked by congregational passivity in worship and antagonism toward a high sacramental theology and ritual practice in some parts of Anglicanism and especially Catholicism.[20] Thus, the Puritan influence in Methodism's sacramental life was to move it away from expressions of eucharistic sacrifice. Third, many Methodists were leery not only of anything that suggested transubstantiation, but of the use of prearranged liturgies and texts: "Historically, Methodists have been ambiv-

---

16. Bowmer, *Lord's Supper in Methodism*, 14. In this section I rely on Bowmer's and Chapman's work. While they treat liturgical and doctrinal developments in separate chapters, I offer a synthesis of their research with a particular focus on eucharistic sacrifice.

17. Bowmer, *Lord's Supper in Methodism*, 25; see, too, David M. Chapman, *Born in Song: Methodist Worship in Britain* (Warrington: Church in the Market Place, 2006), 18.

18. Chapman, *Born in Song*, 1.

19. Bowmer, *Lord's Supper in Methodism*, 13.

20. Chapman, *Born in Song*, 11–14.

alent in their attitude towards prescribed liturgies, many believing that use of a printed text in worship impedes the inspiration of the Holy Spirit and encourages ritualism."[21] Given how carefully liturgies have sought to express eucharistic sacrifice—in light of its controversial status—it is hardly surprising that extemporaneous eucharistic prayers failed to articulate, celebrate, and form Methodists from these bodies according to Wesley's theology.

As in America, British Methodists did not use much of the material from the *Sunday Service*, but they did use the rites for the sacraments (as did the Americans).[22] In 1835, these rites were extracted from the *Sunday Service* and organized separately as *The Order of Administration of the Sacraments and Other Services* (American Methodists had already made the same move in creating the *Ritual*). Despite numerous editions with seemingly haphazard alterations, Methodists used these two books (along with the *BCP*) until 1882. Eventually, Methodism "became ever more obsessed with the perceived threat of Roman Catholicism and the drift of the Church of England towards Rome," so much so, in fact, that the *BCP* and "even Wesley's Abridgement became a focus of suspicion." The 1874 Conference went so far as to charge the committee on liturgical revision with "the removal of all expressions" that were "fairly susceptible of a sense contrary to the principles of our Evangelical Protestantism." In this ecclesial context, it is not surprising that the *Book of Public Prayers and Services* finally authorized by the Conference in 1882 did not recover a Wesleyan doctrine of eucharistic sacrifice.[23] The 1882 service book gradually superseded previous liturgical resources and served Methodism until the Union of 1932. In sum, "despite the introduction of various amendments," this liturgy stood "within the Prayer Book tradition," such that Anglicans would have been "familiar" with its celebration; however, this liturgical tradition placed Wesleyan Methodism "out of step" with "non-Wesleyan traditions" of Methodism whose eucharistic celebrations aligned more closely with the Dissenting traditions.[24]

These Methodist bodies express a relatively low eucharistic theology. The Methodist New Connection had "no established procedure for observing the Lord's Supper"; rather than seeing the sacrament as a means of grace, it elevated the "demands of following Christ, whose presence . . . is only retrospectively discovered by the participants through their daily discipleship"; the Supper was "essentially a pious aid to devotion."[25] The Primitive Methodists

21. Chapman, *Born in Song*, 2.
22. Chapman, *Born in Song*, 17.
23. Chapman, *Born in Song*, 23–24; see Bowmer, *Lord's Supper in Methodism*, 30–32.
24. For a list of amendments to this liturgy, see Chapman, *Born in Song*, 67–68.
25. Chapman, *Born in Song*, 68–70.

understood communion as a memorial "to which the benefits of the Supper are located in the hearts of participants rather than in the 'ordinance' itself"; the 1890 revision of the eucharistic prayer even removed the words of institution.[26] The United Methodist Free Churches had a "strong sacramental theology": they upheld the real presence of Christ and the "link between the sacrament and Christian discipleship" and "valued the Lord's Supper as a means of grace."[27] The Bible Christian doctrine of the Lord's Supper serves as a good example of the lack of clarity with respect to eucharistic sacrifice. The rite is a "remembrance" of Christ's "meritorious death" that suggests a "Calvinist understanding of the real presence." It expresses the "universal dimension" of the Lord's Supper and has, overall, a "strong understanding of the sacramental efficacy"; at the same time, it reacts strongly against any notion that tends toward transubstantiation.[28]

Despite this impoverishment, however, there is one aspect of eucharistic sacrifice that Methodists maintain in their eucharistic liturgies—namely, that of self-sacrifice. Inherited from the *BCP* post-communion prayer of oblation and uncontroversially biblical, the prayer of self-oblation expresses liturgically and corporately the Wesleyan desire for holiness and perfection through sacrificial living. A prayer from the United Methodist Free Churches reads, "Accept, we beseech thee, this our sacrifice: confirm it upon our consciences, by the seal of thy Holy Spirit, and evermore increase our love to him who loved us, that with lives of holiness and zeal we may increasingly show forth his praise."[29]

Bowmer thus offers a doctrinal assessment of nineteenth-century eucharistic theology. Positively, he remarks, "Methodism accepts the sacramental principle because it believes in the Incarnation—that grace is conveyed to men through the media of material things."[30] When he compares the "salient features" of the Methodist doctrine of the Lord's Supper with nineteenth-century theology, the results are mixed. A number of prominent themes persist: a real means of grace, the duty of constant communion, a commemoration of Christ's death, a communion with Christ and with one another, and a true *sacramentum*. Negatively, some themes receive only limited attention: eucharist as spiritual nourishment, eucharist as corporate celebration, and the place of justice and eschatology in the eucharist. Other themes—*anamnesis*

---

26. Chapman, *Born in Song*, 71–73.

27. Chapman, *Born in Song*, 73–75.

28. Chapman, *Born in Song*, 75–79.

29. Chapman, *Born in Song*, 75; relatedly, see Bowmer's chapter, "The Non-Wesleyan Bodies," in *Lord's Supper in Methodism*, 34–42.

30. Bowmer, *Lord's Supper in Methodism*, 52.

and sacrifice—are lost.[31] Doctrinally, he is aware that the Wesleys went well beyond the Prayer Book tradition that limited sacrifice to "praise and thanksgiving" and to oneself. He cites, for example:

HLS 125	*HLS* 4
With solemn faith we offer up	This eucharistic feast
And spread before thy glorious eyes,	Our every want supplies,
That only ground of all our hope,	And still we by his death are blest
That precious, bleeding sacrifice.	And share his sacrifice.[32]

Referring specifically to the eucharistic hymns, he notes that their disuse is directly related to the loss of doctrine among Methodists: "*Hymns on the Lord's Supper* continued to be used until the second decade of the nineteenth century" when the 1780 hymnal (and supplement) became predominant, and "most of the great doctrinal hymns on the Lord's Supper fell into oblivion . . . [and] the main doctrinal emphasis was upon the Lord's Supper as an expression of fellowship and dedication; its sacrificial and eschatological aspects were almost entirely forgotten."[33]

Following the 1932 Union, in 1936 the Conference approved *The Book of Offices*, a prayer book that explicitly sought to harmonize the perennial tension within Methodist worship between uniformity and liturgy, on the one hand, and freedom and extemporaneous prayer, on the other. The two eucharistic rites in this book reflect significant, although somewhat inconsistent, theologies of sacrifice.

The first order of service mostly updated the 1882 Wesleyan order according to the 1928 *BCP* edition. The amendments, though, suggest a hesitancy with the language of real presence and sacrifice (even with respect to Christ's). The prayer of consecration removes the phrase "oblation and satisfaction"; the distribution of elements changes "preserve thy body and soul" to "preserve thee"; the post-communion collect changes "faith in his blood" to "faith in him"; and the manual acts are not restored (even optionally).[34]

The second prayer was an "Alternative Order of Service" and was crafted for the non-Wesleyan traditions as a "simple" and "minimal" rite not based on the Prayer Book. This prayer makes an important structural change (following the alternative order of the 1928 *BCP*). The prayer begins with the *sursum corda*, skips the proper preface, and continues with the traditional post-

---

31. Bowmer, *Lord's Supper in Methodism*, 54.

32. Bowmer, *Lord's Supper in Methodism*, 54–55.

33. John C. Bowmer, "History of Holy Communion in Methodism," *London Quarterly and Holborn Review* 184 (April 1959): 101.

34. Chapman, *Born in Song*, 80–81; Bowmer, *Lord's Supper in Methodism*, 44–45.

communion collect—i.e., the prayer of oblation. This restructuring returns the oblation to its place in the 1549 *BCP* and, in doing so, reverses the theology that sought "to distance its sacrificial language from the consecration of the elements."[35] While this move in the 1928 *BCP* edition caused "much controversy," almost "no stir" ensued in the Conference in 1936. Overall, Bowmer and others of his day do not think that either structurally or stylistically the "Alternative Order of Service" compares to the traditional liturgy; nonetheless, concerning the new location of the oblation, he admits, "It is in the correct position before Communion, not after. It is right that we should make the offering of ourselves before we communicate, to associate ourselves with the offering of Christ as commemorated in the Communion."[36] The theology alluded to in this comment will come to fuller liturgical expression in the liturgical revisions of the later twentieth century.[37]

American Methodism

In the aggregate, the history of American Methodist worship, liturgy, and theology is obviously different than British Methodism's, yet with respect to eucharistic sacrifice, the story is remarkably familiar. Karen Westerfield Tucker writes, "Despite some recovery of the connection between word and sacrament in the twentieth century, Methodists have generally understood the Lord's Supper almost to be an occasional service rather than an integral component of Sunday practice."[38] Over the course of the nineteenth century, Methodism increased greatly in numbers, acceptability, and influence; as it did so, it was likewise transformed by the culture in which it grew. As in Britain, several factors conspired to render Methodist worship distinctly non-eucharistic and therefore, non-sacrificial in shape. In the absence of regular eucharistic celebrations and accessible catechesis on the sacrament, it is not surprising that a doctrine like eucharistic sacrifice foundered.

First, liturgically, the Wesleyan style of worship—Word and Table, dynamic preaching and sacramental fervor, an ordered liturgy with room for

35. Chapman, *Born in Song*, 80–81.

36. Bowmer, *Lord's Supper in Methodism*, 45–46.

37. For an overview of Methodist worship in Britain from Wesley to 1970, see George H. Lockett, "The Methodist Tradition of Worship," in *In Church: An Introduction to Worship and Preaching*, ed. John Stacey (London: Epworth, 1971): 51–66. See, too, Raymond J. Billington, *The Liturgical Movement and Methodism* (London: Epworth, 1969).

38. Westerfield Tucker, *American Methodist Worship*, xiii–xiv; James White, *Protestant Worship: Traditions in Transition* (Louisville: Westminster John Knox, 1989), 150–70. For a helpful overview of two centuries of American Methodist worship, see James White, "Methodist Worship," in *Perspectives on American Methodism*, ed. Russell Richey, Kenneth Rowe, and Jean Miller Schmidt (Nashville: Kingswood, 1993), 460–79.

hymns and extemporaneous prayer—faced dismal prospects even before the *Sunday Service* arrived in America. Because Methodists did not have their own ordained clergy, regular communion in America was not the norm. For the twenty years prior, they had employed and grown accustomed to "a simple service of preaching," and most found Wesley's prayer book and style of liturgical worship to be unfamiliar, uncomfortable, and restrictive.[39] In 1792, large sections of the *Sunday Service* were altered or abandoned. At the same time, though, now that American Methodism was a church with ordained elders, they needed a eucharistic liturgy, and so they used Wesley's. Along with other rites (baptism, marriage, burial, and ordination), the liturgy was not incorporated into weekly worship; instead, it was collected into the *Ritual.* The sparse theology of eucharistic sacrifice from the *Sunday Service* liturgy and Articles was now codified and removed from frequent use:

> The separation of the eucharist from the pattern for regular Sunday morning worship and the transformation of the Sunday liturgy into largely an extempore service undoubtedly reflected the practice of Sunday worship for almost all Methodists. Yet by this method of revision, guidance for Methodist worship was essentially transferred from a prayer book to a piece of "canon law."[40]

The dearth of ordained clergy contributed to the inability of Methodists to fulfill their duty of constant communion. Instead, Methodists elevated the "great festival" of the quarterly meeting to celebrations not only of social, administrative, and homiletical significance, but of sacramental importance, as well. Ruth thoroughly documents that in the decades after 1792, the lack of weekly communion by no means indicated a lack of eucharistic enthusiasm and piety among Methodists. Yet he also notes that at these communal festivals—often lasting two or three days—the order of events (preaching, love feast, communion, business) was rarely fixed, and that one of the most movable elements of the quarterly meeting was the Lord's Supper.[41] There were practical reasons for this variability, yet it sowed seeds, unconsciously, about the role of the sacrament in the corporate life of the people. "It also left in doubt the continuation of the historic conjoining of word and sacrament since nowhere was it explicitly stated that a sermon must accompany Com-

39. On the lack of Wesley's influence as a theologian in America, see Randy Maddox, "Respected Founder / Neglected Guide: The Role of Wesley in American Methodist Theology," *Methodist History* 37, no. 2 (January 1999): 71–88.

40. Westerfield Tucker, *American Methodist Worship*, 9.

41. Westerfield Tucker, *American Methodist Worship*, 124–25, 128; Ruth, *Little Heaven Below*, 120–25.

munion and, according to the *Discipline* . . . the reading of Scripture lessons need not be done on Communion days."[42]

Second, culturally, was the penchant for pragmatism, followed by Protestant revivalism, as American Methodists wrestled with the perennial tension in worship "between the desire for a recognizable Methodist pattern of worship and freedom in liturgical expression."[43] Although the 1792 communion rite (either in its entirety or truncated form) predominated among the Methodist bodies for fifty years, Methodist Episcopal Church leaders allowed for the celebration of the rite in a manner "that would substantially impact eucharistic practice and theology in later Methodism." It was permitted, "if the elder be straitened for time," to excise any or all elements of the rite except the prayer of consecration. This permission encouraged "reductionism" and a "minimalist approach" toward the sacrament (hymn—consecration—distribution). Even worse, despite church legislation to the contrary, some clergy went so far as to introduce "material of their own composing even at the cost of the Prayer of Consecration itself."[44] Sometimes it was the fear of "formalism" that steered people away from prescribed liturgies. Additionally, with a focus on the "most fruitful means of winning souls," Methodists adopted the "revival style of hymn singing, ardent prayer, and fiery preaching."

Throughout the nineteenth century, this pattern of worship was reinforced. The working arrangement developed whereby "denominationally sanctioned worship orders" were circulated by the church, but "never mandated" for use by the clergy or laity.[45] As new Methodist bodies—black and white—came to be formed, they "continued or slightly altered" the forms of worship they had inherited. As Methodists increased in material prosperity and Methodism enjoyed greater societal standing, the awareness of respectability prompted a turn toward more established liturgies: "They nevertheless kept the intention apparent in the 1792 directions and reinforced by revivalism: the service was directed toward the sermon and the yield that could be obtained from evangelical preaching."[46] Thomas Frank concurs, noting how American Methodism subordinated ecclesiological issues like church order and sacraments to evangelism.[47] Moreover, "no effort was made by any of the denominations to ensure that preaching accompanied the sacrament. By

42. Westerfield Tucker, *American Methodist Worship*, 125.

43. Westerfield Tucker, *American Methodist Worship*, 10; Ruth, *Little Heaven Below*, 133–34.

44. Westerfield Tucker, *American Methodist Worship*, 126.

45. Westerfield Tucker, *American Methodist Worship*, 11.

46. Westerfield Tucker, *American Methodist Worship*, 12–14. Frank concurs, noting how American Methodism subordinated ecclesiological issues like church order and sacraments to evangelism (*Polity, Practice*, 56–59).

47. Frank, *Polity, Practice*, 56–59.

the last decades of the nineteenth century, a practice on Communion Sundays . . . was to omit preaching to save time," so that in the end, "what had already been construed as an occasional service became, wittingly or unwittingly, an irregular, special service."[48]

Third (and fourth), anthropologically (and ecclesially), Maddox underscores the significance of the "dethronement" of Wesley's moral psychology by his American heirs. "The defining goal of Wesley's heart religion was clearly this change of affections," which is a process of sanctification (and going on to perfection) that "involves both the quickening of our affections in response to the affect of God's love poured in our hearts and the tempering of these affections into holy dispositions." The means of grace, especially the eucharist, were instrumental and necessary means by which believers participated with God's transforming power. Several factors contributed to the dethronement of this anthropology, with the result that American Methodists privileged the "innate power of rational choice" apart from the means of grace, so that the graced, co-operant nature of Wesley's moral psychology was lost. The result was a moral psychology based on "decisionistic rational control" that has dominated the last two centuries. In this framework, the sacraments become duties, but not joyful means of grace.[49] Correlatively, the elevation of individual duties precipitates an "eclipse" of an ecclesiology that sees the church as a social means of grace: the church itself comes to be viewed as a body that satisfies the human need for fellowship in which participation is a "rational duty" for the Christian: "More implicit, but undeniable, is the continuing Enlightenment individualism that views the existence of the church as much more dependent upon the Christians who make it up than vice versa."[50] In this context, the doctrine of eucharistic sacrifice becomes simply unintelligible.

Fifth, theologically, American Methodists sustained most of the eucharistic theology they had inherited. In writing, preaching, and hymnody, Methodist theology evinced a rich understanding of many aspects of the eucharist: an instrumental means of grace, medicine for sin, spiritual nourishment, affirmation of Christ's real presence, epiclesis, koinonia, a sign and seal of God's covenant, the new Passover, eschatology, a sacrifice of praise and thanksgiving and of self-sacrifice, and a "dynamic remembrance (*anamnesis*)" of Christ's "sufficient satisfaction" for (all!) sin and not only a commemoration.[51] Although the sacrament set Christ's passion "mentally and sensibly" before

48. Westerfield Tucker, *American Methodist Worship*, 132.
49. Maddox, "Change of Affections," 17–23.
50. Maddox, "Social Grace," in *Methodism in Its Cultural Milieu*, ed. Tim MacQuiban (Oxford: Applied Theology Press, 1994), 143 and 146.
51. Westerfield Tucker, *American Methodist Worship*, 122–29.

the people, it appears not to have set "the meritorious passion and death" before the Father, since the affirmation of the eucharist (and not just Christ's passion) as a sacrifice is lacking. Only nine Wesleyan communion hymns circulated in an early hymnbook, and the "collection of 166 *Hymns on the Lord's Supper* [including the *Christian Sacrament and Sacrifice*] . . . appears not to have been at all widely used in America." The widely used hymnbooks from 1780 and 1784 did not have a section for sacramental hymns, and of the seven selections from the HLS that managed to make it in, none were from the section on sacrifice.[52]

Ruth's account of Methodist quarterly meetings largely corroborates this picture, while he also seeks to correct some common misunderstandings in twentieth-century scholarly literature. He notes that Methodists were knowledgeable and appreciative of Wesley's eucharistic theology and that they circulated several Wesleyan hymns, texts, and sermons, either in private or published collections. None of the hymns he lists, however, were from the *HLS* sacrificial section, and he recognizes that what "might be lacking" in Methodist eucharistic theology is "eucharistic sacrifice—both the sacrifice of Christ and that of the believing community."[53] Although the chief "discontinuity" between Wesley and American Methodists, he contends, is in the "breadth and complexity" of their theologies, Methodists did maintain several Wesleyan themes—namely, those most commensurate with the general evangelicalism of their context: a "living commemoration of Christ's redemptive suffering," the sacrament as a means of grace, and the eschatological and heavenly fellowship of the meal.[54] Another theme Methodists chose to emphasize was the "living commemoration of Christ's redemptive suffering." He argues not just that this concept is *anamnetic*, but that it should be understood as flexible enough to incorporate sacrificial aspects as well:

> Moreover, there was fluidity in Wesleyan and American Methodist spirituality about what exactly constituted a "sacramental" theme. Certain common themes in Wesleyan hymns, like the visibility of the crucified Christ and his ongoing intercession in heaven, can be found in many hymns (Wesleyan and otherwise) that are not explicitly "sacramental." Themes that appear in explicitly eucharistic material in Wesley might

52. Westerfield Tucker, *American Methodist Worship*, 122. The only two hymns from the *HLS* section on sacrifice were nos. 116 and 123, used between 1847 and 1889 (307n34).

53. Ruth, *Little Heaven Below*, 140–41.

54. Ruth, *Little Heaven Below*, 141–44; see Geoffrey C. Moore's detailed account of the hymns from the *HLS* found in different American Methodist hymnals: "Eucharistic Piety in American Methodist Hymnody (1786–1889)," in *Music and the Wesleys*, ed. Nicholas Temperley and Stephen Banfield (Urbana: University of Illinois Press, 2010): 88–102.

appear elsewhere in American Methodism, or, conversely, Wesleyan hymns like "Arise, My Soul, Arise" could be labeled as "sacramental" by American Methodists. Thus the initial hint that Americans lacked the breadth and complexity of Wesleyan eucharistic spirituality must not be overly stressed.[55]

The theological emphases and liturgical rites remained relatively consistent in the second half of the nineteenth century. Indeed, Methodists altered their eucharistic prayers very little between the 1880s and the 1960s; however, by the mid-1850s "church leaders" had grown increasingly concerned with the "growing neglect" of eucharistic practice. Those developments that did arise within Methodism's evangelical Protestant context were not congenial to a recovery of eucharistic sacrifice. From one direction, "Baptist influence" among some Methodists led them to privilege the eucharist as a "memorial and fellowship meal" and to downplay it as a "necessary and efficacious sacrament for the remission of sin." From another direction, Methodists within some churches lobbied for the removal of manual acts in the rite (as suggestive of transubstantiation) or the removal of the language of *sin, soul*, and *body* (as suggestive of a high doctrine of presence and an overly causal notion of efficacy within the elements and the rite).[56] Nolan Harmon offers a representative citation: "As the handling of the bread and wine required by the old rubrics while reciting this prayer is considered by some a mimicry of our Saviour's sacrifice—the offering of him as an unbloody sacrifice upon the altar— our Church expunges the rubrics requiring it."[57] Harmon's citation illustrates how far Methodism had strayed from Wesley, since the "mimicry" (sacramental representation) of Christ's death in the Supper is central to his notion of sacrifice. In countering arguments from either direction, any appeal to eucharistic sacrifice would have been counterproductive and highly suspect.

Well into the twentieth century, Methodism was engaged in a struggle— both from within and without—to uphold the eucharist as a sacrament that effects what it signifies. If it succeeded, it was with mixed results, and not in a fashion that was convincingly Wesleyan.[58] Ultimately, Methodists were "neither ready to strike at what they believed was the heart of the sacramental rite, nor willing as a body to continue a move in a direction of what might be construed as memorialism. They were disposed to introduce new phraseology further reinforcing that the benefits to be received from the sacrament were purely spiritual." Despite efforts to restore an order of worship closer to the 1784 liturgy,

55. Ruth, *Little Heaven Below*, 141–42.
56. Westerfield Tucker, *American Methodist Worship*, 130–33.
57. Harmon, *Rites and Rituals*, 144.
58. Westerfield Tucker, *American Methodist Worship*, 132.

revisions in the 1930s–60s attest to Methodism's double mindedness on the sacraments. In 1932, emphases on memorialism and "self-dedication to moral duties and spiritual improvement" were prominent; the 1945 *Book of Worship* offered two eucharistic prayers, one memorialist and the other sacramental; and "for Methodists and non-Methodists concerned for liturgical renewal," the two rites from 1964 "were inadequate in structure and in content."[59]

While the ecumenical movement, Vatican II, and *BEM* have been the chief catalysts behind Methodist liturgical renewal, an inkling of recovery of Wesleyan sacramental theology in America actually began in 1946 with the Order of St. Luke (OSL; originally the Brotherhood of St. Luke and a kindred spirit with the British Methodist Sacramental Fellowship). Its interests were self-consciously ecumenical, drawing from both the East and West of the ancient church. The movement does not seem to have advocated for the conception of the eucharist as an objective, corporate sacrifice; such a jump would have been too much all at once. Over against a memorialist stance, however, OSL did seek to recover the eucharist as an objective means of grace, with attention to the themes of thanksgiving, pneumatology, and self-sacrifice in union with Christ.[60] The theology behind these doctrines would need to be in place before a recovery of eucharistic sacrifice proper would be intelligible.

Eucharistic Sacrifice in Contemporary Methodism: Liturgical and Sacramental Renewal

In recent decades, Methodism in America and Britain has undergone substantial liturgical (and theological) renewal. Several factors contributed to these changes, not the least of which was Methodism's enthusiastic participation in the ecumenical movement, which was a catalyst behind the mergers of Methodist bodies in the mid-twentieth century, just as it was a chief source of inspiration and creativity behind the new worship resources that these new bodies produced. Methodist liturgical renewal and subsequent worship resources were expansive, consisting of a wide range of topics:

- Renewed interest on the form and location of the church
- Appreciation of the relationship between scripture and tradition
- Updating of language to be both culturally sensitive and biblically faithful
- Recognition of the global—and no longer uniquely Western—scope of the church

59. Westerfield Tucker, *American Methodist Worship*, 134–37; see James F. White, "The New American Methodist Communion Order," *Worship* 41, no. 9 (November 1967): 552–60.

60. Westerfield Tucker, *American Methodist Worship*, 135–36. See Romey P. Marshall and Michael J. Taylor, SJ, *Liturgy and Christian Unity* (Englewood Cliffs, NJ: Prentice-Hall, 1965).

- Recovery of trinitarian theology
- Retrieval of Word and Table as the normative shape of corporate worship
- Convergence with Anglicans, Catholics, and some Protestants on the order and form of eucharistic liturgies
- Esteem and *ressourcement* of the early church and its Wesleyan heritage
- A reconsideration of its sacramental doctrines and practices, especially the affirmation of the eucharistic elements as the instrumental means of divine grace based on Christ's incarnation and his continuing presidency in the eucharist.[61]
- Recovery of the Jewish roots of the eucharistic prayer, along with ecumenical convergence on areas such as *anamnesis* and *epiclesis*.

Ecumenical engagement with these and other topics resulted in new liturgies, hymnals, and books of worship (in that order) that express these new commitments. The revisions in United Methodism and in Britain followed similar though not identical paths. After a period of trial and consultation, British Methodism published the *Methodist Service Book* in 1975 under the leadership of A. Raymond George, followed by *Hymns and Psalms* (1983), and then the current *Methodist Worship Book* (1999). Soon after coming into existence, United Methodism began its liturgical revisions in the early 1970s, publishing its new experimental eucharistic prayer in 1972 for denominational use and commentary. The revisions went through many drafts and culminated in the current version in the *United Methodist Hymnal* (1989) and *Book of Worship* (1992). Yet more recently, both churches produced authorized documents on the eucharist that clearly reflect the use and influence of the new eucharistic prayer and include statements on sacrifice: British Methodist Church, *His Presence Makes the Feast* (2003), and UMC, *This Holy Mystery* (2004).

Although these worship resources address eucharistic sacrifice as an isolated doctrine only briefly, they do show—when looked at carefully—that eucharistic sacrifice was an important consideration in composing the new Great Thanksgivings. Not only do the prayers seek to go beyond the tradi-

---

61. Readers interested in following these topics in more detail can do so through the resources cited in this chapter. See A. Raymond George, "The Eucharist in Relation to the Total Worship of the Church," *London Quarterly and Holborn Review* 189 (July 1964): 217–23; Geoffrey Wainwright, "The Sacraments in Wesleyan Perspective," in *Worship with One Accord: Where Liturgy and Ecumenism Embrace* (New York: Oxford University Press, 1997), 105–26; Geoffrey Wainwright, "The Ecumenical Scope of Methodist Liturgical Revision," in *Liturgical Renewal as a Way to Christian Unity*, 35–60; Geoffrey Wainwright, "Word and Table: Fifty Years of Eucharistic Revisions Among English-Speaking Protestant Churches," *Archiv für Liturgiewissenschaft* 50 (2008): 332–55; and the articles by Wainwright, "Methodism and the Ecumenical Movement" (329–49); Westerfield Tucker, "Methodist Worship" (240–56); and Stookey, "Methodism and the Sacraments" (257–76), in *T&T Clark Companion to Methodism*.

tional controversies of the Reformation, but they do so by going back to the early church and by taking a strong, yet nuanced, position on sacrifice.[62] Methodist theology, therefore, expresses its doctrine of eucharistic sacrifice in these three areas: liturgy, hymnody, and conference statements.[63]

Methodist Church Eucharistic Liturgies: 1975 and 1999

The Methodist Service Book (1975)

The "Sunday Service" in the *Methodist Service Book* (1975) is, according to A. Raymond George, "the biggest change in the history of the Anglican-Methodist Communion Service since 1552."[64] The symbolic naming of the liturgy is significant: "It was a deliberate link with Wesley, but also a deliberate assertion that henceforth the official norm of Methodist worship is no longer Morning Prayer or something derived from it but the Lord's Supper or something derived from that, a service of eucharistic shape."[65] The liturgy is the result of the ecumenical recovery of the ancient order of worship and consists of four parts: the Preparation, The Ministry of the Word, The Lord's Supper, and Final Prayers.[66] As to the liturgy of the Lord's Supper, after the Peace, the Nicene Creed, and a hymn, the liturgy follows the fourfold actions of Christ: (1) the elements are brought to the minister; (2) the congregation—led by the minister—joins in The Thanksgiving; (3) the breaking of the bread is performed; and (4) the bread and wine are shared.[67] The Thanksgiving

62. White, "Methodist Worship," 478.

63. For George's account of his participation in the Joint Liturgical Group, the International Consultation on English Texts, and as an observer in the post–Vatican II Catholic revision process before his role in revising the *Methodist Service Book* (1975), see his chapter "Liturgy, National and International," in *Memoirs: Methodist and Ecumenical,* ed. Geoffrey Wainwright (Buxton: Church in the Marketplace, 2003), 206–33.

64. George, *Memoirs,* 144. Citations from the "Sunday Service" are from *The Methodist Service Book* (London: Methodist Publishing House, 1975). For an overview of the *Service Book,* see George's chapter "The Methodist Service Book," in *Memoirs,* 141–47.

65. George, "Sunday Service 1784," 9; see A. Raymond George, "The Sunday Service of the Methodists," in *Communio Sanctorum,* ed. Yves Congar et al. (Geneva: Labor et Fides, 1982), 194–203.

66. For the theological rationale behind this ordering that unites Word and Table, see A. Raymond George, "The Theology of Worship," *London Quarterly and Holborn Review* 186 (April 1961): 135–36.

67. For an explanation of the theology of the Thanksgiving prayer based on this pattern, see A. Raymond George, "The Revision of the Communion Service," *London Quarterly and Holborn Review* 187 (April 1962): 110–16. This fourfold pattern of the liturgy is based on Jesus' words and actions at the Last Supper and at the many other meals he hosted; see Gregory Dix's influential work *The Shape of the Liturgy* (Westminster: Dacre, 1945).

prayer itself follows a pattern recognizably similar to the Catholic eucharistic prayers I–III: *sursum corda*, preface, *Sanctus*, institution narrative, the mystery of faith, *anamnesis*-oblation-epiclesis, concluding prayer. The Thanksgiving prayer is characterized by several theological emphases: the sacramental (and instrumental) nature of the rite; the work of the Triune God in salvation and sanctification; a strong theology of *anamnesis, epiclesis,* and eschatology; and self-sacrifice. A theology of eucharistic sacrifice is enfolded within these emphases.

George's interpretation of the Wesleys' *Hymns on the Lord's Supper*—indeed, his correction of their theology at points—shapes his theology of eucharistic sacrifice. He finds Irenaeus's idea of offering the fruits of creation unacceptable ("a kind of harvest festival"), and he does not much embrace Augustine's theology that as the body of Christ the church's members are present and offered in the bread and cup along with Christ. He finds preferable the Wesleys' approximation of Cyprian's view: "The passion of the Lord is the sacrifice which we offer."[68] At the same time, he finds the language of "offering" with respect to our actions (and Christ's) in the liturgy to go beyond the biblical witness. The principal theological category for George is the eternal now of Christ's heavenly, priestly office. "We must regretfully admit that this way of transcending the categories of time sometimes led the Wesleys to speak of Christ still offering himself. . . . This goes beyond the scriptural notion that Christ still pleads." George does not balance the vision from Revelation of Christ as the slain lamb with his preferred imagery from Hebrews. What was offered was Christ's one historic sacrifice, which as high priest he now pleads before the Father. Neither Christ nor his people still offer (*pace* the Wesleys); both now plead Christ's one, all-sufficient sacrifice. He writes, "There never was a time when we offered Christ, whereas the statement that Christ offers himself is unscriptural only as regards its tense."[69]

He is adamant that the Wesleys are thoroughly Protestant; their rhetorical excesses serve the devotional ends of piety and do not place them in the Anglo-Catholic tradition. He laments that the ecumenical movement has accepted too uncritically the "offertory-theology" of Irenaeus and Augustine but is pleased that "Methodism has not moved in this direction and will not need to retrace its steps." He elevates the Wesleys as "ecumenical pioneers" whose "rich" doctrine he hopes has the prospect of "reconciling so-called 'catholic' and evangelical views."[70] He writes:

68. A. Raymond George, "The Lord's Supper," in *The Doctrine of the Church*, ed. Dow Kirkpatrick (New York: Abingdon, 1964), 152.

69. George, "Lord's Supper," 154.

70. George, "Lord's Supper," 158

> We may sum up these views by again saying that [the Wesleys] strongly emphasized our utter dependence on the unique sacrifice of Christ. Calvary is the atoning or propitiatory sacrifice; the sacrament of the Lord's Supper is a commemorative or eucharistic sacrifice, part of the "sacrifice of praise" (Heb 13:15) of which scripture speaks. It is a *sacrificium* which is primarily *beneficium*. They linked the sacrifice of Calvary with the heavenly intercession of Christ which is based upon it, a doctrine which some evangelicals have neglected. The series of vivid metaphors which they employed to show that Christ's death retains its efficacy or that we may view it as though it had just happened is a rich contribution to the treasury of eucharistic devotion. Never do they assert that the eucharist is an atoning sacrifice, but . . . "it implies a sacrifice."[71]

This theology of sacrifice comes across at key points in the Thanksgiving prayer.

The preface praises the Father through Christ for creation and for salvation from sin through Christ's death and resurrection and highlights Christ's priestly office in heaven: *You raised him from the dead, and exalted him to your right hand in glory, where he lives forever to pray for us.* Through Christ and the gift of the Spirit, God's people are made into *a royal priesthood*. At this point, the prayer does not describe God's priestly people as having a priestly function, but an *anamnetic* one: *to stand before you to proclaim your glory and celebrate your mighty acts.*

In turning to the fulfillment of Christ's saving work—his passion—the prayer incorporates the New Testament account of the Supper, thus recalling the sacrificial aspect of Christ's new covenant with his people and of his death on the cross. The theology here favors institution and faith in Christ's real presence over consecration and substantial change in the elements. "It is also true that the inclusion of these words in the prayer has been associated in some periods with the idea that the words themselves have consecratory force, an idea now replaced, as we have seen, by that of consecration by thanksgiving."[72]

In the *anamnesis*-oblation-*epiclesis* section that follows, the theology of sacrifice is expressed in two ways: first, through the *anamnesis* of thanks and praise; and second, through self-sacrifice in the power of the Holy Spirit:

> Therefore, Father, as he has commanded us,
> we do this in remembrance of him,
> and we ask you to accept our sacrifice of praise and thanksgiving.

71. George, "Lord's Supper,"156–57.

72. George, "Revision of the Communion Service," 114. See Arnold Clay, *What Is the Lord's Supper?* (London: Epworth, 1979), 13–14. Clay's book, written after the 1975 liturgy, is a theological explanation of the eucharist with the intention of functioning catechetically for Methodists.

> Grant that by the power of the Holy Spirit
> we who receive your gifts of bread and wine
> may share in the body and blood of Christ.
>
> Make us one body with him.
>
> Accept us as we offer ourselves to be a living sacrifice,
> and bring us with the whole creation to your heavenly kingdom.

The first notion of sacrifice as it is associated with the *anamnesis* is, of course, historically the most controversial. The ecumenical recovery of a biblical notion of *remembrance*, expressed by *BEM* and accepted in the Methodist responses, already manifests itself at this point in the prayer. Indeed, the priestly office of Christ and his eternal intercession before the Father on behalf of his people are perhaps the single most important aspect that shapes George's theology of sacrifice. He believes it is directly informed by scripture and championed by the Wesleys, and Catholics would thoroughly welcome his Christological remarks:

> If we ask how past acts can thus be effectively present or at least effective in the present, the answer lies in the Christocentric and Trinitarian character of Christian worship. Any other explanation, whether metaphysical or psychological, must start from that primary doctrine. For Christ himself is present in worship, bearing upon Himself the scars, if not the wounds, by which He wrought our redemption. And Christ said of the Spirit (Jn 16:14), "He shall take of mine and shall declare it unto you." Thus the mighty acts are present in the Spirit.[73]

The theology of sacrifice expressed in the previous section does not stop with the remembrance of Christ's historic sacrifice, or even with the eternal, heavenly intercession of his one historic sacrifice, but is qualified heavily by this Christological dimension. George is not persuaded by the "picturesque view" that the Prayer of Oblation following the communion (based on the *BCP* structure) is actually part of the eucharistic prayer and that the communion is inserted into the prayer. Instead, he notes, "traditionally the great prayer should not end here [after the institution narrative], but should go on to the remaining mighty acts, attaching them verbally to the word 'remembrance' and making a resumptive reference to Christ's death."[74]

---

73. A. Raymond George, "'Faith and Order' Work on Worship," *London Quarterly and Holborn Review* 188 (July 1963): 211.

74. George, "Revision of the Communion Service," 114.

The theology of sacrifice is further qualified in the *anamnesis* by the interpretation of Jesus' words "Do this" and his fourfold action. Rather than interpret the Lord's command to entail the offering of his body and blood (substantially present) as a priestly sacramental-sacrifice for the forgiveness of sins, his command is understood to refer to his previous instructions to "Take this and eat it," and to "Drink from it all of you." George elaborates:

> The choice of the main verb for this sentence is of decisive importance. Traditionally, it would be "We offer," though two rather different theologies are attached to this, reminiscent of Irenaeus and Cyprian respectively, according to whether it is thought that we are offering bread and wine or offering Christ. Probably neither of these theologies is exactly right in its normal form. It would be possible to say, "We make this memorial" or even "we remember," and such is the rich meaning now given to the word "*anamnesis*," that this would not at all commit us to a Zwinglian view. But it would be simpler to use a scriptural phrase which does not force the theological issue: "We do this." It also gives a neat chiasmus: ". . . Do this in remembrance of me. Therefore, having in remembrance . . . we do this."[75]

Perhaps this formulation does not "force the theological issue," but it certainly begs the theological question of the exact nature and form of the remembrance. A sacramental action is required, to be sure, and not just the mental act of remembering. The sacrificial dimension of the *anamnesis*-oblation is the commemoration of Christ's passion. As priest of the eucharist, Christ takes, blesses, breaks, and gives. As the body of Christ, believers follow suit: "We break the bread and pour out the wine just as Jesus did. By these actions we commemorate the death of Jesus";[76] then they take, eat, and drink. In the liturgy, Methodists live out this participatory dynamic of sacrifice and sacrament: *Grant that by the power of the Holy Spirit we who receive your gifts of bread and wine may share in the body and blood of Christ.*

Restricting the language of offering solely to Christ's passion restricts the degree to which offering is expressed in the Thanksgiving prayer. The emphasis in the prayer is on reception more than offering, in large part because the interpretation of the Last Supper focuses more on breaking and pouring than on offering. Arnold Clay is fully aware that the Supper's roots in the Jewish Passover make it a sacrificial meal and that in this new Passover—this new sacrificial meal—Christ institutes a new covenant with his people. The Supper points toward, interprets, and participates in Christ's death and resurrection, but

75. George, "Revision of the Communion Service," 114.
76. Clay, *What Is the Lord's Supper?*, 9.

unlike, for example, Journet or John Paul II, he does not see Christ offering himself sacrificially in the meal. "At the Last Supper, Jesus, the Lamb of God, took bread and wine, and by his actions with them, *showed forth* his death upon the Cross, and by the words he spoke, connected his own self-offering with the forgiveness of sins."[77] Christ, therefore, relates the Supper to the cross not by sacrificial participation, but by sacramental participation, by "showing forth his death" and "by the words he spoke." Throughout his account, Clay reserves the language of sacrifice to refer to the events of the cross. If nothing is offered in the Last Supper, but Christ's death is shown forth, then nothing is offered in the Lord's Supper, but his sacrifice is commemorated and pleaded. As with the Catholic liturgy, in the Thanksgiving prayer, the minister represents both Christ and the people, and the liturgy elegantly reflects the interpretation of Christ's actions and commands in the Supper *and repeats* the reconciling actions between Christ and his people. The prayer correlates entirely to Christ's action of blessing/thanksgiving and not to offering. It is precisely at this point where the theology of Christ's actions in the Supper determines the theology of the nature and function of the minister in the sacrament.

The second aspect of eucharistic sacrifice, self-sacrifice in the Spirit, follows directly from the celebration and remembrance of Christ's passion. "We must not, however, omit the biblical idea of oblation; at some point we must explicitly offer the 'sacrifice of praise' (Heb 13:15) and present our bodies 'a living sacrifice' (Rom 12:1)."[78] Hence, immediately after the *anamnesis*, the liturgy states, *we ask you to accept our sacrifice of praise and thanksgiving,* and in the *epiclesis*: *Accept us as we offer ourselves to be a living sacrifice.* On this aspect of eucharistic sacrifice, there is no confusion within Methodism or controversy with Catholics. The heart of Christian discipleship involves self-sacrifice in union with Christ and in the power of the Holy Spirit, both individually and corporately, and at the ecclesial level the church expresses its self-sacrifice corporately through the eucharistic prayer.[79]

The theology of sacrifice that the Thanksgiving prayer expresses, therefore, is one of commemorating Christ's sacrifice, of pleading his sacrifice in union with him in the Spirit, and of self-sacrifice. "When we break the bread and pour the wine, we hold up the symbols that give expression to that 'everlasting sacrifice,' and we pray that God will accept us, in Christ."[80]

If the idea of "offertory-theology" is muted in the Thanksgiving prayer, it is because the theology of sacramental participation in Christ's death and

77. Clay, *What Is the Lord's Supper?*, 10 (his emphasis).
78. George, "Revision of the Communion Service," 114.
79. George, "Theology of Worship," 130–31.
80. Clay, *What Is the Lord's Supper?*, 22.

resurrection is privileged. Does this mean, therefore, that the Catholic and Methodist eucharistic prayers are fundamentally divided over the question of sacrifice? By no means. Both Clay and George affirm what we have studied thus far in the doctrines of Aquinas, Wesley, and the Catholic tradition: "The eucharist is the making present in time of the once-for-all sacrificial act of Christ." Clay's comment is even stronger: "In the act of remembrance the past is made present and the Resurrection, so to speak, happens all over again. . . . We become present once again at the sacred and eternal moment of past history and are assured of our eternal destiny as we offer our lives to God in union with his life."[81] Consider the rich theological anthropology and the extremely strong sense of human participation in Christ that George advances:

> But here the very word "sacrifice," at first sight so dangerous and sug-gestive of a Pelagian reliance on our own effort, reminds us of the true sacrifice, the unique sacrifice of Christ; that was acceptable to God, and that was done for us. (And indeed the sacrifices of the Old Covenant in their provisional, transitory, unsatisfactory way were quite as much God's gracious provision for our salvation as our own human attempt to atone for sin.) Moreover, it is Christ who still pleads our cause and who dwells within us; and we are in Him, members of His Body, crucified and raised together with Him. Now these truths, bewildering in the rich profusion of their imagery, transform the whole situation. The one thing in the gathering which seems our own work—namely, our response—is just as much performed by Christ as was the preaching or for that matter the mighty acts themselves. It is not just that our meaner praises are joined to the worship of angels and archangels and the whole company of heaven and then joined in some way to the perfect worship and obe-dience which the Son offers to the Father, but that in some sense Christ's own worship is carried on through us.[82]

A strong theology of participation such as this ultimately renders suspect any sharp distinctions between the concepts of *anamnesis*, commemoration, pleading, offering, and sacrifice. The Thanksgiving prayer proclaims that through the bread and wine Christ is present in the power of his unique redemptive sacrifice and that through believers' communion with him—which happens by way of self-sacrifice—the saving grace of Christ's atoning work is applied to them, and they are incorporated by his Spirit and the power of his resurrection into his glorified body, the church. The prayer states, *Make us*

---

81. George, "Lord's Supper," 159; Clay, *What Is the Lord's Supper?*, 10–11.
82. George, "Theology of Worship," 138.

one body with him . . . and bring us with the whole creation to your heavenly kingdom.[83] What the Catholic liturgy affirms by way of sacrificial participation, the 1975 liturgy affirms by way of *anamnesis* and sacramental participation. In light of the sacramental and participatory teaching that affirms this soteriological reality in the eucharist, the differences between pleading and offering almost dissolve. Almost: for while the soteriological reality that both churches affirm is the same, it does not follow that the concepts of *anamnesis* and sacrifice are fully interchangeable. Doctrinal clarity relies upon linguistic and conceptual precision, and one of the main shortcomings of *BEM*, according to the Catholic response, was the document's attempt to subsume the theology of sacrifice under that of *anamnesis*. Sacrifice and *anamnesis* name interrelated, yet distinct, modalities of the church's participation in the work of Christ. I explore these differences in the following section.

The *Methodist Worship Book* (1999)

The Methodist Conference credited the eucharistic liturgy of the 1975 *Service Book* with increasing the church's understanding of eucharistic theology and with fostering a greater appreciation for the celebration of the sacrament.[84] The book begins by describing Christian worship according to 1 Peter 2:5, 9, the action of a priestly people who offer "spiritual sacrifices" acceptable to God in Christ and who proclaim God's "mighty acts." God "speaks" to the church through "symbols and sacraments," and the people respond in the Spirit through "hymns and prayer and acts of dedication."[85] It places the eucharist as "the central act of Christian worship, in which the Church responds to our Lord's command, 'Do this in remembrance of me' (1 Cor 11:24–25)." The eucharist is the sacrament that celebrates the "presence of Christ," and it "calls to mind his sacrifice and, in the power of the Holy Spirit, is united with him as the Body of Christ." The actions of Christ at the Last Supper shape the church's celebration: "At the Lord's table, Christ's disciples share bread and wine, the tokens of his dying love and the food for their earthly pilgrimage, which are also a foretaste of the heavenly banquet, pre-

83. See the Christology of Wesley's view of God's "eternal now" reiterated in David Carter, "Methodism and the Eucharist: A Discussion Article," *Epworth Review* 27, no. 2 (April 2000): 67.

84. Chapman, *Born In Song*, 84; see A. Raymond George, "From *The Sunday Service* to 'The Sunday Service': Sunday Morning Worship in British Methodism," in *Sunday Service of the Methodists*, 31–52.

85. Methodist Church, *The Methodist Worship Book* (Peterborough: Methodist Publishing House, 1999), vii; see Neil Dixon, *Wonder, Love, and Praise: A Companion to the Methodist Worship Book* (Peterborough: Epworth: 2003).

pared for all people. . . .Those who gather around the table of the Lord are empowered for mission." The interpretation of the events of the Supper continue to inform the order and theology of the rite: Christ's actions "were taken up in the Church's tradition as a fourfold shape: Taking, Giving Thanks, Breaking and Sharing. In the Great Thanksgiving, the service of praise offered by God's people on earth is joined with the praises of the heavenly host, praising God, Father, Son and Holy Spirit."[86]

The eucharistic revisions of the 1999 *Worship Book* reflect the success of the Thanksgiving prayer. The liturgy has four parts: The Gathering of the People of God, The Ministry of the Word, The Lord's Supper, Prayers and Dismissal. With some variety, the order of the Lord's Supper rite follows a similar pattern:

Peace
Offerings of the people brought to the Lord's Table
[Taking] Minister takes the bread and wine and prepares them
[Blessing] Thanksgiving prayer, led by the minister:
    Sursum corda: invitation to offer thanks and praise
    Thanksgiving for creation, God's self-revelation, salvation, the Holy Spirit
    A version of the *Sanctus*
    Institution narrative of the Lord's Supper
    Anamnesis: Christ's death and resurrection are recalled
    God is asked to receive the worshippers' self-offering
    Mystery of Faith
    Epiclesis
    Self-sacrifice in union with the whole church in heaven and on earth
    Praise and glory to the Triune God, with a congregational "Amen"
Lord's Prayer
[Breaking] Minister breaks the bread
[Giving] Minister and People receive communion

The worship book offers several new prayers for various seasons and occasions.[87] The 1999 Thanksgiving maintains a structure and a theology that follows closely the 1975 Thanksgiving prayer; at the same time, though, there are some differences worth noting.

86. *Methodist Worship Book*, 114–15.

87. For an overview of the liturgy and the different eucharistic prayers, see the chapter "Holy Communion," in Dixon, *Wonder, Love and Praise*, 72–102. Relatedly, on priesthood and ministry in the eucharist, see the document "Called to Love and Praise (1999): The Nature of the Christian Church in Methodist Experience and Practice," section IV.5, "The Priesthood of All Believers and Ministry," accessed May 10, 2023, https://www.methodist.org.uk/media/1993/fo-statement-called-to-love-and-praise-1999.pdf.

Ordinary Season (1). In the offertory prayer, the bread and wine are clearly offered to God: *Lord and Giver of every good thing, we bring to you bread and wine for our communion, lives and gifts for your kingdom. . . .* This prayer moves toward the offertory-theology of Irenaeus.[88] The *anamnesis* expresses a greater appreciation for the concept of an "eternal sacrifice" that extends beyond Christ's passion: *Remembering, therefore, his death and resurrection, and proclaiming his eternal sacrifice. . . .* Here the prayer remembers not the pleading, priestly Christology of Hebrews, but the slain Lamb of Revelation. The oblation maintains the self-offering of Christ's people: *we offer ourselves to you in praise and thanksgiving as we declare the mystery of faith.* The *epiclesis* establishes the sacramental and instrumental function of the bread and wine with respect to Christ's presence more strongly than the 1975 Thanksgiving: *Send down your Holy Spirit that these gifts of bread and wine may be for us the body and blood of Christ.*

Ordinary Season (2). Apart from addressing God as "our Father and our Mother," providing musical settings for select parts, and a strong eschatological emphasis, the distinction in this prayer with respect to sacrifice lies in the institution and oblation. The institution explicitly links the actions of the prayer with Jesus' action of the Supper: *On the night before he died, he had supper with his disciples. He took bread, thanked you, as we are thanking you, broke the bread. . . .* Despite the language in the institution of *my body, given for you* and the *new covenant in my blood*, this formula reiterates the interpretation that Jesus' words and actions at the Supper are primarily one of thanksgiving rather than offering. However, Frances Young's comments on the institution narrative as "covenant sacrifice" suggest a deeper appreciation for the sacrificial nature of the Last Supper: "It is here, of course, that we come to other notions of sacrifice affecting the reality of what we are doing: the covenant sacrifice."[89] The oblation strikes a strong note of participation with Christ: *Through his offering for us all, we offer our whole life to you in thanks and praise.*

Ordinary Season (3). This prayer emphasizes the aspects of *anamnesis*, proclamation, *epiclesis*, eschatology, and participation in Christ's priestly office, although it has no explicit oblation:

> As often as we eat this bread and drink this cup we proclaim the Lord's death until he comes.
>
> Therefore, gracious God, with this bread and this cup we remember that our Lord offered his life for us. Believing the witness of his resurrection and ascension, we look for his coming in glory, and our sharing in his great and promised feast.

88. See Frances Young, "The Great Thanksgiving Prayer," in *Living the Eucharist: Affirming Catholicism and the Liturgy*, ed. Stephen Conway (London: Darton, Longman and Todd, 2001), 86.

89. Young, "Great Thanksgiving Prayer," 90.

Amen. Come, Lord Jesus.
[traditional epiclesis]
Amen. Come, Holy Spirit.
Join our prayers and the prayers of all your people on earth and in heaven
with the intercession of Christ, our great high priest. . . .

The remaining eucharistic prayers highlight the various seasonal themes
for which they are assigned, each with its own distinctive characteristics.

Advent. The *anamnesis*-oblation uses strong sacrificial language and
includes a Wesleyan/patristic prayer for sanctification/theosis: *Recalling his
death and resurrection, and in obedience to his command, we celebrate the offering of his
eternal sacrifice, until he comes again. . . . Through him, our Priest and King, accept us as
a living sacrifice, a people for your praise. . . . Refashion us in your image that we may be
found ready at the coming of our Lord Jesus Christ.*

Christmas. The elements are again offered to God. This prayer adopts a
pattern of *anamnesis-epiclesis*-oblation and tersely states, *Through him we give ourselves to you.*

Lent and Passiontide. Themes of sacrifice and glory are appropriately
intermingled here. The post-sanctus thanks God for giving the Son *to set his
face resolutely toward Jerusalem and to be lifted high upon the cross, that he might draw all
creation to himself. When the hour of his glory came, and loving his own to the end, he sat
with them at supper.* The *anamnesis* recalls not only his resurrection, ascension,
and coming in glory, but also his *suffering and death.* The congregational prayer
at the fraction focuses on Christ's sacrifice and passion: *Jesus, Lamb of God,
have mercy on us. Jesus, bearer of our sins, have mercy on us. Jesus, redeemer of the world,
grant us peace,* while the closing prayer focuses on life, salvation, glory, love,
and asks to *see you face to face in your kingdom.*

Easter. The whole liturgy is filled with the joyful celebration of resurrection, and God's victory over sin and death in Christ is remembered throughout. The *anamnesis*-oblation takes up biblical language and beautifully weaves
together themes of sacrifice, resurrection, and priesthood: *Therefore, Father, we
celebrate this Passover of gladness; for as in Adam all die, even so in Christ shall all be
made alive. Accept, through him, our great high priest, this, our sacrifice of praise.*

As a result of the ecumenical and liturgical movements, the Great Thanksgivings in the *Worship Book* reflect a high degree of convergence on eucharistic
doctrine and celebration. With sacrifice in particular, the development of the
eucharistic prayers from the *BCP* structure and theology to the 1975–99 liturgy
is dramatic and thoroughly positive. The recovery of the ancient pattern that
reunites the *anamnesis* and the oblation also restores a theology of sacrifice as
a central doctrine of the eucharistic celebration (along with emphases such
as Trinity, creation, salvation history, *epiclesis*, eschatology, and more). Although

George was reluctant to use the language of offering and sacrifice except with respect to Christ's cross and the believer's self-sacrifice in Christ, his Wesleyan anthropology of human participation in God's work of salvation allowed for the introduction of a rich theology of sacrifice in the 1975 Thanksgiving prayer. Methodists apparently became comfortable with the theology of this eucharistic celebration, since the Great Thanksgivings of the 1999 *Worship Book* develop this theology even more: (1) the instrumental nature of the eucharistic elements is strengthened; (2) an offertory-theology that gives the bread and wine to God is introduced; (3) believers' self-offering in union with Christ's priestly office is ever-present; and (4) most significantly, the language of Christ's "eternal sacrifice" subtly expands the concept of sacrifice beyond Christ's historic passion and incorporates a Christology that draws from Revelation in addition to Hebrews.

In 2022 the Methodist Church published five alternative, authorized Thanksgiving prayers written by the Faith and Order commission. Most continue the theological position of the 1999 Worship Book, with its emphases on offering the elements, *anamnesis*, and self-sacrifice in union with Christ's saving sacrifice. One prayer in particular, however, stands out for advancing a stronger theology of presence and sacrifice, the second Thanksgiving for Ordinary time.[90] The *anamnesis* states: *Remembering therefore his death and resurrection, and proclaiming his eternal sacrifice, we praise you for the everlasting bread and mystic wine, the flesh and blood of our Saviour Christ.* Christ's *eternal sacrifice* is significantly reaffirmed, and the elements have been transformed: the bread is *everlasting* and the wine is *mystic*.

Moreover, the oblation that follows is indeed exceptional: *We offer them to you for the life of the Church and the world, for all in need, for all who hunger and thirst.* The epiclesis asks that the church's members be gathered together in unity and peace. Methodists have now become accustomed to the rich symbolism of offering the eucharistic elements to God, which signify God's gifts to us, our gifts to God, our interior sacrifice, our corporate sacrifice, the goodness of creation, and the imperative to feed the hungry. This offering goes further still—they are given for the *life of the Church and the world.* If "life" here refers to spiritual health, vitality, mission, and holiness, then Methodism is demonstrating that it has become fully comfortable with sacrifice—as an ecclesial action—as a constitutive element in its Thanksgiving prayers. In other words, the elements are offered not only to signify something, but additionally, they are offered "for" something. If "life" means new life, eternal life, salvation—which is ultimately the type of life for which the church hopes and prays in

90. Methodist Church, *Additional Orders of Holy Communion,* accessed November 30, 2023: https://www.methodist.org.uk/media/27855/additional-holy-communion-20221215.pdf.

its communion prayers—then an exceptional advance in sacrificial theology is underway.

Bread and wine cannot bring new life to the church; not even everlasting bread and mystic wine can do this, but only the flesh and blood of Jesus. The similarities with Catholicism's EP II are striking: *we offer you, Lord, the Bread of life and the Chalice of salvation. . . . Humbly we pray that, partaking of the Body and Blood of Christ, we may be gathered into one by the Holy Spirit.* One straightforward reading of this Thanksgiving is that the church offers the body and blood of Christ to the Father for the salvation of the church and the world.

Chapman seems not to appreciate these accomplishments when he writes, "It would be unwise to claim too much on the basis of convergent liturgies. . . . In particular, differences between Methodists and Roman Catholics concerning the use of sacrificial language reflect unresolved theological issues about the 'sacrifice' of the eucharist."[91] This is true, of course, hence this study. At the same time, however, these convergent liturgies both contribute to and reflect the significant theological agreement that already exists:

- a clear theology of instrumental causality in the sacrament
- the celebration of the sacrifice of Christ and the commitment to discipleship as sacrificial living (in the Spirit) in imitation of Christ
- the theological anthropology of participation in the work of Christ in the sacrament
- the conviction that the Lord's Supper should repeat the Last Supper and place believers in the same relationship to Christ—through the presidency of the minister—as were the Apostles
- the belief that in the elements Christ is really present in the saving power of his unique and eternal sacrifice, the grace of which is applied to believers (individually and corporately) for their sanctification and the church's.

From this perspective, Catholics and Methodists already hold in common an immense amount of eucharistic doctrine. Happily, in United Methodism, these commonalities also hold true.

The United Methodist Great Thanksgiving: 1970–1989

The UMC process of eucharistic liturgical revision did not produce two generations of authorized Great Thanksgivings, but the process was still similar (circulated drafts tried in the local church followed by consultation and editing), and it yielded similar results. The revision process drew on three pri-

91. Chapman, *Born in Song,* 85.

mary sources—scripture and the early church, the Wesleys' hymns on the Lord's Supper, and the ecumenical and liturgical movements—to restore corporate Sunday worship that has as its normative pattern a service of Word and Table. Although not on par with the *Missal*, for example, these texts function as analogous and near equivalents—i.e., since they are produced under the auspices of the denomination and seek to explain the history behind the creation of the church's authorized texts and the theology that they express, they are at least as authoritative as the liturgies themselves. Throughout the 1970s and 1980s, the UMC published the Supplemental Worship Resources series (eventually seventeen volumes in all) designed to educate pastors and churches on the nature of the liturgical revisions and to provide them with additional materials and ideas in keeping with the theology of these revisions. The process culminated in the authorized UMC *Book of Worship* (1992), which has become the most widely used worship resource in Methodist churches (apart from the UMC Hymnal).[92]

The Basic Pattern of Worship is the recognizable movement of Entrance, Proclamation and Response (Liturgy of the Word), Thanksgiving and Communion (Liturgy of the Eucharist), and Sending Forth. The Order of Sunday Worship Using the Basic Pattern simply expands the Basic Pattern by sug-

---

92. See, Hoyt L. Hickman, "Word and Table: The Process of Liturgical Revision in the United Methodist Church, 1964–1992," in Westerfield Tucker, *Sunday Service of the Methodists*, 117–35. See also Hoyt L. Hickman, ed., *Worship Resources of The United Methodist Hymnal* (Nashville: Abingdon, 1989), 11–19, and United Methodist Church, *Companion to the Book of Services: Introduction, Commentary, and Instructions for Using the New United Methodist Services*, Supplemental Worship Resources 17 (Nashville: Abingdon, 1988), 9–28. For a comprehensive account of the revision process for the rites of baptism, eucharist, marriage, and death and resurrection, see Robert B. Peiffer, "How Contemporary Liturgies Evolve: The Revision of United Methodist Liturgical Texts (1968–1988)" (Ph.D. diss., University of Notre Dame, 1992). See also Don E. Saliers, "'Taste and See': Sacramental Renewal Among United Methodists," in *The Eucharist in a United Methodist Perspective*, ed. Hendrik R. Pieterse (Nashville: UMC, General Board of Higher Education and Ministry, 2007), 9–19; Hoyt L. Hickman, "Worship Revision in the United Methodist Church," in *The Changing Face of Jewish and Christian Worship in North America*, ed. Paul F. Bradshaw and Lawrence A. Hoffman (Notre Dame, IN: University of Notre Dame Press, 1991), 112–24; Stookey, "Worship from the United Methodist [USA] Perspective," in *Worship Today*, ed. Thomas F. Best and Dagmar Heller (Geneva: World Council of Churches, 2004), 101–8; Don E. Saliers, "Divine Grace, Diverse Means: Sunday Worship in United Methodist Congregations," in *Sunday Service of the Methodists*, 137–56; Lester Ruth, "Word and Table: A Wesleyan Model for Balanced Worship," in *The Wesleyan Tradition: A Paradigm for Renewal*, ed. Paul W. Chilcote (Nashville: Abingdon, 2002), 136–47; Dean G. Blevins, "A Wesleyan View of the Liturgical Construction of the Self," *Wesleyan Theological Journal* 38, no. 2 (Fall 2003): 7–29; James F. White, "Sources for the Study of Protestant Worship in America," *Worship* 61, no. 6 (November 1987): 515–33; E. Byron Anderson, ed., *Worship Matters: A United Methodist Guide To Ways To Worship*, vol. 1 (Nashville: Discipleship Resources, 1999).

gesting elements appropriate for each movement in the liturgy. In this liturgy, the Invitation, Confession and Pardon, Peace, and Offering conclude the Proclamation and Response and prepare for Thanksgiving and Communion. The Great Thanksgiving of the Service of Word and Table I—the model and principal service—also follows a familiar pattern: *sursum corda*, preface, *Sanctus*, post-*Sanctus*, institution, *anamnesis*-oblation, the mystery of faith, *epiclesis*, doxology, and amen. The Lord's Prayer, fraction, communion, and closing prayer complete the section.

Like many of the eucharistic prayers coming out of churches' participation in the ecumenical movement, the text and structure of the Great Thanksgiving is based on the eucharistic prayer attributed to Hippolytus and the structure of the West-Syrian anaphora. Hoyt Hickman stresses how the three-part structure of the prayer facilitates a recovery of trinitarian theology: part one (*sursum corda* and preface) addresses the Father and gives thanks for creation and the covenant with Israel; part two (post-*Sanctus*, institution, *anamnesis*-oblation) recalls the "whole Christ event"—i.e., Jesus' sacrificial life and ministry that culminates in his Paschal Mystery (death, resurrection, and expected return); part three prominently prays for the transforming, unifying, and sanctifying work of the Holy Spirit on both the elements and the worshippers.[93] The Great Thanksgiving holds extensive catechetical resources for those Methodists who are willing to immerse themselves in its formation, which is the reason (as James White is fond of saying) the eucharistic prayer is the church's primary theological confession.[94]

The United Methodist liturgy makes the significant decision to assert the sacramental principle—based on Jesus' incarnation—as the defining hermeneutic of worship. Throughout the liturgy, and most poignantly in the Great Thanksgiving, God (in Christ and through the Spirit) reconciles the people and incorporates them into the Triune life by the grace of the saving work of Christ's passion. The worship of the earliest Christians, as informed by the book of Acts, informs this hermeneutic: "From that day [Pentecost] to this, Christian worship has been an encounter with the living God through the risen Christ in the power of the Holy Spirit."[95] Moreover, Luke's narration of the disciples' encounter with Jesus on the road to Emmaus not only unites Word and Table, but also places the resurrected Christ as the liturgical president. "When Jesus was killed, his disciples scattered; but two days later, on

93. Hoyt L. Hickman, "The Theology of the Lord's Supper in the New United Methodist Ritual," *Quarterly Review* 17, no. 4 (1997–98): 361–76.

94. James F. White, "Response to the Berakah Award: Making Changes in United Methodist Euchology," *Worship* 57, no. 4 (July 1983): 341.

95. *Companion to the Book of Services*, 31.

the first Easter, they found themselves face to face with the living, risen Christ. Ever since, Christian worship of God has been through encounter with the risen Christ. Christians have been an Easter People."[96] Admittedly, the degree of symbolism that the Methodist liturgy employs is much less developed than the Catholic liturgy; nonetheless, the hermeneutic is the same.

The Great Thanksgiving, therefore, is both the Emmaus road and the Last Supper; that is, the Spirit brings the church into communion with the risen Christ, but only by way of a sacramental participation in the sacrificial meal that itself participates in the Lord's Paschal mystery. On this point—anthropologically, sacramentally, and soteriologically—Catholics and Methodists agree fully. Because the Great Thanksgiving is the focal point of the church's saving encounter with Christ, the liturgy carefully constructs words, gestures, and symbols that convey this reality. The fourfold gesture of Christ (in obedience to Christ's command to "do this"), along with the Institution narrative, functions as the paradigm for the Great Thanksgiving.[97] "These actions," writes Hickman, "signify for us the whole ministry of Jesus and indeed all God's might acts. Moreover, they suggest a whole Christian spirituality, a pattern for a whole Christian life."[98]

> As the disciples and the risen Christ came together around the table [at Emmaus], so can we. As Jesus did the same four actions with the bread that the disciples had seen him do just three days previously [at the Supper], so in the name of the risen Christ we do these actions with the bread and cup. As "he was known to them in the breaking of the bread," so the risen and ascended Christ can be known to us in the Holy Communion.[99]

In each of the four actions that reenact the Supper, the pastor plays a key representative role, and the pastor and people together express important sacrificial aspects of the sacrament.

An important sacrificial act comes before the eucharistic liturgy, in fact, and it is the offering of the bread and wine along with any monetary or other gifts by the people out of gratitude. The offertory "is the symbolic offering to God of ourselves and all that we have. It is the corporate self-giving of God's people, in the spirit of Romans 12:1." This is Irenaeus's offertory-the-

96. Hickman, *Worship Resources*, 20.

97. White, "Function and Form of the Eucharistic Prayer," 20.

98. Hickman, "Theology of the Lord's Supper," 363. Don Saliers's book skillfully develops the relationship between worship, the sacraments, and the Christian life; Saliers, *Worship and Spirituality*.

99. Hickman, *Worship Resources*, 26.

ology, advocated strongly by Thurian (as a means of uniting the orders of creation and redemption), advanced by *BEM*, and now authorized here: "This is the mystery of giving back to God the gifts of God's creation, including signs of our labor, so that we know that all we have and are is a trust from God." Notice the corporate epistemology in this action: the congregation, as the body of Christ, gives back to God not only as a means of expressing gratitude, but as a means of learning ("so that we know") that "all" is a "trust from God." In accord with *Mediator Dei* and faithful to scripture (Rom 12:1: present your bodies [plural] as a living sacrifice [singular] to God), the corporate body needs to use tangible signs to signify back to God a corporate and interior sacrifice. United Methodism evinces no hesitation that this sacrificial offering detracts in any way from the one, saving sacrifice of Christ; indeed, if anything, it unites us closer to it.[100] J. Robert Nelson, former chair of the WCC Faith and Order Commission, puts the matter forcefully:

> Sacrifice as offering has effect in two directions, so to speak, between the risen Christ and ourselves. . . . Thanks are given; *eucharistia* is thus essentially an offering in response to the far greater gift of salvation and new life and hope in Christ . . . the rubric directing the procession of the money offering and the communion elements (gifts) connotes a theological understanding superior to what was formerly [1964] implicit . . . it may be asserted that "the whole person" is what we have to offer, not as debt but as love.[101]

Next, *Taking*: "The pastor takes the bread and cup . . . the loaf should not be broken at this time, since the breaking of the bread is an important action following the Great Thanksgiving."[102]

Then, *Blessing*: the pastor's leadership in the Great Thanksgiving corresponds to Jesus' blessing: "As Jesus gave thanks (blessed) over the bread and cup, so does the pastor, ministering in Christ's name."[103] The prayer, as the second of the four actions, is the moment where the church confesses and prays its faith verbally: "Since this prayer puts into words the Church's understanding both of God's mighty acts in Jesus Christ and of the meaning of Holy Communion, the one who leads this prayer is doing so as the authorized representative of the whole Church."[104]

---

100. Hickman, *Worship Resources*, 61.

101. J. Robert Nelson, "What Methodists Think of Eucharistic Theology," *Worship* 52, no. 5 (Spring 1978): 420–21.

102. Hickman, *Worship Resources*, 61.

103. Hickman, *Worship Resources*, 63.

104. *Hickman, Worship Resources*, 74.

Breaking: this gesture, although practically necessary, should also convey the invitation of Christ: "Breaking the bread is a gesture of invitation to the people, done in the name of the living Christ, the Head of his family and the Host at this meal." The pastor, again, plays a representative role: "It should be done in such a way that persons immediately and intuitively perceive its meaning. Preferably, the pastor stands behind the Lord's table facing the people, lifts the unbroken loaf, and breaks it by hand."[105]

In the discussion on the actions of blessing and breaking, the UMC guidelines focus primarily on the meal aspect of the Supper and on Jesus' actions with the bread and wine. They do not interpret these as a self-offering to the Father, *at this point* in Christ's passion, although the theology of his sacrificial and atoning death on the cross is expressly affirmed. Other categories are stressed: the place of scripture and proclamation, praise and thanksgiving, *anamnesis*, *epiclesis*, the participation of the congregation, and eschatology, but not sacrifice. Consequently, Christ's words of "for you" and "new covenant in my blood" do not receive the weight they deserve proportional to their place in the Institution narrative.[106]

The discussion of the final action of the liturgy, however, the *Giving*, partially corrects this imbalance by stressing the action of Christ's self-giving. Paul's theology of *koinonia* (1 Cor 10:16) is prominent here; the eucharist is nothing less than a "participation," a "sharing," and a "fellowship" in the body and blood of Christ: "This giving should be a clear and powerful acting out of the gospel. It is God's self-giving to us through another person."[107] The chief sacrificial action of the Supper, therefore, is Christ's self-giving to his disciples, both then and now. Indeed, the *Companion* not only integrates the table and the cross with each other, but it unites these two with baptism, the "renewal of church discipline," service, evangelism, and sanctification.[108] White articulates that our self-giving flows from Christ's self-giving: "Our gifts of bread and wine—one may almost say our lives—are taken, blessed, broken, and given back to us in Christ. It is a reenactment of what it means to be a Christian. Christ gives himself to us through these actions so that we can give ourselves to one another."[109]

105. Hickman, *Worship Resources*, 66.

106. Hickman, *Worship Resources*, 38–40.

107. *Companion to the Book of Services*, 68. For a developed argument on this topic, see James F. White, *Sacraments as God's Self Giving: Sacramental Practice and Faith* (Nashville: Abingdon, 1983).

108. *Companion to the Book of Services*, 46.

109. James F. White, *New Forms of Worship* (Nashville: Abingdon, 1971), 172. Paul W. Chilcote offers a nice reflection on how the fourfold action of the eucharist forms Methodists for mission and service; Chilcote, "Eucharist and Formation," in Vickers, *Wesleyan Theology of the Eucharist*, 196–201.

United Methodism's theology of eucharistic sacrifice is not limited to the fourfold liturgical reenactment of the Last Supper—that is to say, the Great Thanksgiving itself also has much to teach on this doctrine. To begin with, James White (the main author for the basic text) turned to Hippolytus and the Antiochene structure precisely to resolve some of the problems with sacrifice associated with the *BCP–Sunday Service* tradition. "The defects of the 1662 prayer—penitential obsession, the absence of the old covenant, eschatology, and pneumatology, plus a decidedly negative approach to sacrifice—could be overcome in such a structure."[110] One decisive way by which this is accomplished (and identical to the British Methodist pattern) is by bringing the oblation back into the prayer and by integrating it with the *anamnesis*. Another advantage is that the ancient structure recovers the Jewish roots of the eucharist, and since the structure and theology mutually inform each other, this *ressourcement* brings a Jewish theology of sacrifice to the fore. As White remarks, "But this point is crucial, the eucharistic prayer carries on the Jewish practice of thanking God by proclaiming God's mighty works on behalf of God's people. . . . Making memorial is our most important sacrifice because it offers God's own actions as our most precious possession." And Will Willimon's strong statement on the *anamnesis*-oblation affirms Wesley's theological anthropology: "In the offering we affirm that all our good things have come as gifts. . . . There is too much talking, listening, sitting, thinking, and too little acting and responding. The Offering is not an intrusion into our worship, it is the very core of our worship."[111]

Initially intended as a supplement to the 1964 eucharistic prayer, the 1972 Great Thanksgiving received widespread and rapid acceptance. It almost immediately supplanted the traditional version and straightaway became the foundational prayer—stylistically, structurally, and theologically—for all subsequent prayers.[112] The *anamnesis*-oblation-*epiclesis* section of the current Great Thanksgiving (1984) evidently relies upon—and improves upon—the original 1972 version.

110. White, "Berakah Award," 341.

111. White, "Liturgy, Theology of the Laity," 35–36. Relatedly, on Hippolytus's *Apostolic Confession*, see William H. Willimon, "Thanks, Papa Hippolytus," *Duke Divinity School Review* 43, no. 1 (Winter 1978): 26–27.

112. White, "Liturgy, Theology of the Laity," 39. See United Methodist Church, *At the Lord's Table: A Communion Service Book for Use by the Minister* (Nashville: Abingdon, 1981); United Methodist Church, *Holy Communion: A Service Book for Use by the Minister* (Nashville: Abingdon, 1987); Michael J. O'Donnell, OSL, *Lift Up Your Hearts: Revised and Expanded; Eucharistic Prayers Based on the "Revised Common Lectionary," Year A* (Akron, Ohio: Order of Saint Luke, 1999); Hoyt L. Hickman et al., *The New Handbook of the Christian Year* (Nashville: Abingdon, 1992). The whole of the Great Thanksgiving from 1984 is not identical with subsequent editions—the

Great Thanksgiving 1972	Great Thanksgiving 1984
When we eat this bread and drink this cup, we experience anew the presence of the Lord Jesus Christ and look forward To his coming in final victory.	Do this, as often as you drink it, in remembrance of me."
	And so, in remembrance of these your mighty acts in Jesus Christ, we offer ourselves in praise and thanksgiving as a holy and living sacrifice, in union with Christ's offering for us, as we proclaim the mystery of faith.
Christ has died, Christ is risen, Christ will come again.	Christ has died, Christ is risen, Christ will come again.
We remember and proclaim, Heavenly Father, what your Son has done for us in his life and death, in his resurrection and ascension. Accept our sacrifice of praise and thanksgiving, in union with Christ's offering for us, as a reasonable and holy surrender of ourselves.	
Send the power of you Holy Spirit on us, gathered here out of love for you, and on these gifts.	Pour out your Holy Spirit on us, gathered, here, and on these gifts of bread and wine.
Help us to know in the breaking of this bread and the drinking of this wine the presence of Christ who gave his body and blood for mankind.	Make them be for us the body and blood of Christ, that we may be for the world the body of Christ, redeemed by his blood.

Nelson offers a positive assessment of the 1972 Great Thanksgiving in its historical context. "Sacrifice," he writes, "is a concept which comprehends the wholeness of Jesus Christ. It is not limited to the cross." This insight colors the rest of his remarks. The sacrificial life of Christ—"announced at the Last Supper and consummated on the cross"—means that "each eucharist is covenantal in the sense that it takes place within the divine-human covenant

---

United Methodist Hymnal (Nashville: United Methodist Publishing House, 1989) and *Book of Worship* (1992)—but the *anamnesis*-oblation-*epiclesis* section is (except for the punctuation in the epiclesis to make it more readable).

already effected by Christ." Entailed in this *"opus operatum*, done by God in Christ," is God's forgiveness and justification. In short, the Holy Spirit applies the benefits of Christ's passion to those (individually and corporately) who appropriate them in faith.[113]

Stylistically, the current Great Thanksgiving is more concise, more poetic, and more confident, no doubt as a result of the numerous versions to which Methodists became accustomed over this twelve-year period. Structurally, the biggest change was to unite the *anamnesis* with the oblation by placing the congregational acclamation before the *epiclesis*, a move that served to enhance the trinitarian structure of the prayer as well. Theologically, "the wording of the preface, post-*sanctus*, anamnesis [and oblation] and epiclesis have all been reworked without great changes in the content" over the course of numerous additions.[114]

The offertory-theology advanced in the current Great Thanksgiving confidently integrates the church's remembrance with its offering:

And so, in remembrance of these your mighty acts in Jesus Christ, we offer ourselves in praise and thanksgiving as a holy and living sacrifice, in union with Christ's offering for us, as we proclaim the mystery of faith.

The remembrance of "these your mighty acts" refers to the whole of the Incarnation, not solely the passion, and the oblation articulates the traditional Protestant themes of sacrifice. Hickman stresses these themes:

Notice how carefully this sentence deals with the issue of eucharistic sacrifice that has so sharply divided Christians since the Reformation. It affirms with Rom 12:1 our self-offering "as a living sacrifice, holy and acceptable to God" as well as the "sacrifice of praise" commended in Heb 13:15 and the sacrifice of thanksgiving referred to in Ps 116:17, offering them "in union with Christ's offering for us," that as the Reformation insisted is "full, perfect, and sufficient," made once for all and never to be repeated.[115]

---

113. Nelson, "What Methodists Think of Eucharistic Theology," 416–19.

114. James White, "United Methodist Eucharistic Prayers: 1965–1985," in Senn, *New Eucharistic Prayers*, 86. For a discussion of the different worship resources from the 1980s and of some of these prayers' distinctive emphases, see White, "United Methodist Eucharistic Prayers," and Hickman, "Theology of the Lord's Supper." For a discussion of the Great Thanksgiving from United Methodist Church, *At the Lord's Table* regarding issues of presence, sacramental mediation of the elements, sacrifice, and atonement theology (many of which were improved in the 1984 version), see Keith Watkins, "Eucharist, American Style," *Worship* 56, no. 5 (Spring 1982): 401–11.

115. Hickman, "Theology of the Lord's Supper," 371.

His comment does not quite do justice to the oblation, however, for while he rightly stresses the positive view of our sacrifices, he does not fully appreciate the Christological richness of the phrase "in union with Christ's offering for us." To be sure, Christ's offering is "full, perfect, and sufficient," as the Reformation (and Trent) insisted, yet his words of "never to be repeated" risk temporally relegating Christ's ministry in his priestly office to the past. This historically limiting framework of understanding Christ's offering for us does not square well with the mystery of faith that immediately follows and in which the church exclaims: *Christ has died, Christ is risen, Christ will come again.* A richer approach is to integrate fully the concepts of *eucharistia, anamnesis,* and sacrifice under that of Christ's eternal and heavenly priestly office, as White demonstrates:

> [*Anamnesis*] is closely, indeed inseparably, united to *eucharistia.* What we offer is also what we proclaim. We recite what God has done both as recalling and as thanksgiving. So *anamnesis* and *eucharistia* really are one. But the new service adds another important dimension to which we have been blind. What Christ "has done for us in his life and death, in his resurrection and ascension" is all we have to offer to God. The memorial of his actions is our true sacrifice. But Christ's work is not done. He continues to be our great "high priest," "to appear now before God on our behalf" (Heb 9:24). As the worshipping Church we act "in union with Christ's offering for us." We are a priestly people through union to Jesus Christ. The language is reminiscent of Augustine, but it is more emphatically akin to Wesley who, alone of the great Reformers, stresses the importance of seeing the eucharist as sacrifice. . . . Hymn 117 reminds us, "Parts of Thy mystic body here, / By Thy Divine oblation raised, / . . . . We now with Thee in heaven appear." Recent research has made us realize just how constantly the New Testament speaks of the eucharist in sacrificial terms. Now, for the first time, United Methodism has a positive statement of eucharistic sacrifice. It is, I believe, a stronger and more biblical statement of sacrifice than any I know of in any Protestant liturgy. Once again, we find John Wesley out ahead of us.[116]

White's statement is remarkable for several reasons. First, it finally recovers a biblical, patristic, and Wesleyan Christology. Second, his conception of the church as a "priestly people" includes the classical Protestant theology of the "priesthood of all believers," yet moves beyond it: a priestly people that unites to its priestly head through a sacrificial meal that commemorates God's redeeming work in Christ needs to offer a corporate sacrifice in union with Christ himself. And the eucharist is nothing less than this. Third, and most importantly, consider what he understands the church to offer: Christ's life,

---

116. White, "Liturgy, Theology of the Laity," 41.

death, resurrection, and ascension, along with "the memorial of his actions." Nelson's theology corroborates White's and explicitly makes recourse to the key doctrine of the *totus Christus*: "If the whole Christ (*totus Christus*) is the risen Christ plus his Church, and if the whole sacrifice is what we have described, then the whole presence of Christ should be expected in the whole eucharistic action: persons, words, actions, elements."[117]

White is perhaps alone among Methodists on two related accounts: first, he perceives the relationship between *anamnesis* and sacrifice, yet distinguishes between them ("But Christ's work is not done . . . "), and second, he attributes to Methodists as a "priestly people" the corporate sacrificial action intrinsic to their office. Without recourse to the philosophical tools of substantial presence, the Great Thanksgiving embraces the offertory-theologies of Irenaeus, Augustine, and Cyprian, including the latter's comment that the *passion of the Lord is the sacrifice which we offer*. United Methodism, therefore, states its theology of eucharistic sacrifice more explicitly than British Methodism. Although the two churches are in fundamental agreement on Christology, *anamnesis*, and participation, United Methodism allows for a theology of sacrifice independent from *anamnesis*.

The *epiclesis* picks up the theology of self-offering in union with Christ. The celebration of Christ's sacrifice carries with it the duty to imitate him through Christian discipleship.

> Pour out your Holy Spirit on us gathered here, and on these gifts of bread and wine. Make them be for us the body and blood of Christ, that we may be for the world the body of Christ, redeemed by his blood.

To unite with Christ is to take on the mission of Christ; to celebrate Christ's redemption is to participate in his ongoing work. "What is sacramentally offered and received of the sacrifice of Jesus Christ and the hope for his coming and his kingdom cannot be anything but the mainspring of faithful mission."[118] To be the body of Christ in the power of his Spirit is—echoing the sacrificial language of "for you"—to be "for the world":

> By your Spirit make us one with Christ, one with each other, and one in ministry to all the world, until Christ comes in final victory and we feast at his heavenly banquet.

The emphasis on the eucharist as a source of sanctification and an impetus for justice and mission found throughout many United Methodist Great

117. Nelson, "What Methodists Think of Eucharistic Theology," 418.
118. Nelson, "What Methodists Think of Eucharistic Theology," 424.

Thanksgivings is in continuity with the early church, the Wesleyan heritage, and Roman Catholicism.

Now, for a Protestant tradition in which pragmatism has historically been the prevailing liturgical methodology, the sacrificial theology recovered in these liturgies is exceptional, and all the more so in light of the fact that the "memorial of his actions" (as White puts it) cannot simply mean our mere remembering of them. They cannot simply mean, in other words, that the ritual of Christ's fourfold actions is our offering. This offertory-theology makes profound ontological claims and transcends Methodism's historic theology that confines sacramental mediation to experiential and cognitive categories. Instead, Christ is present in the eucharist as priest and host of his sacrificial meal, a meal that shows forth, interprets, and participates in his life, death, resurrection, and ascension. Furthermore, this presence is not conceived in some passive or static fashion. Rather, by his presence Christ is active in his priestly office, and this priestly activity is described in sacrificial terms: "Christ's offering for us." The Great Thanksgiving proclaims a sacramental sacrifice that is at once patristic, Wesleyan, and ecumenical—indeed, even one that has much in common with the Catholic doctrine of "commemorative representation." Does Methodism also continue this eucharistic theology in its hymnody and authorized documents?

CHAPTER 8

Knowledge and Vital Piety

Eucharistic Sacrifice in Methodist Hymnody and Teaching

Hymn singing has always held a special place in Methodist worship, and hymns have not only been the means of joyful celebration, but a vehicle with which to transmit doctrine. Like the service books, Methodist hymnals are authorized by the Conference for use in the church; therefore, these hymns—and the theology they express—enjoy the status of officially proclaiming Methodist doctrine in a doxological mode.[1] On this note, Geoffrey Wainwright identifies the "catechetical, liturgical, and devotional" purposes of congregational hymnody associated with the celebration of the eucharist.[2] Along with the Great Thanksgiving, eucharistic hymns constitute the chief elements of Methodism's *lex orandi*.[3] Although the Wesleys' *Hymns on the Lord's Supper* are not well represented, the hymnals nonetheless offer dozens of entries under "eucharist." They touch on all aspects of eucharistic theology—chiefly its sacramental quality and Christ's redeeming presence— and many of these hymns have a sacrificial dimension of some kind.[4] Indeed, taken together, it is possible to trace nearly all the facets of eucharistic sacrifice as they appear in the course of the liturgy.

1. For example, Teresa Berger, *Theology in Hymns? A Study of the Relationship of Doxology and Theology According to a Collection of Hymns for the Use of the People Called Methodists (1780)* (Nashville: Kingswood, 1995); Paul W. Chilcote, *A Faith That Sings: Biblical Themes in the Lyrical Theology of Charles Wesley* (Eugene, OR: Cascade, 2016).

2. Charles Wesley Society, *Hymns on the Lord's Supper by John and Charles Wesley*, first edition facsimile (1745), with introduction by Geoffrey Wainwright (Madison, NJ: Charles Wesley Society, 1995), vi.

3. Four resources are considered here: Methodist Church, *Hymns and Psalms* (London: Methodist Publishing House, 1983); United Methodist Church, *The United Methodist Hymnal*; United Methodist Church, *The Faith We Sing* (Nashville: Abingdon, 2000); Methodist Church, *Singing the Faith* (London: Hymns Ancient and Modern, 2011), subsequently abbreviated as follows: *HAP, UMH, FWS, STF.*

4. Khoo gives detailed statistics in her analysis of fourteen different hymnals between Wesley and today; *Wesleyan Eucharistic Spirituality*, 255–61. See Charles Wesley, "Come, Sinners, to the Gospel Feast" (*UMH* 616) and "O Thou Who This Mysterious Bread" (*UMH* 613).

Word and Table. Although not overly sacrificial, "At the Font We Start Our Journey" is a subtle example that the liturgical recovery of Word and Table impacted the content and selection of hymns. Each stanza traces the movement of the liturgy, from baptism to the sending forth.

1. At the font we start our journey, in the Easter faith baptized . . .
2. At the pulpit we are fashioned by the Easter tale retold . . .
3. At the altar we are nourished with the Easter gift of bread;
   in our breaking it to pieces see the love of Christ outspread.
4. At the door we are commissioned, now the Easter victory's won. . . . [5]

"On the Day of Resurrection" is found in the Christological section celebrating Christ's resurrection and exaltation. All the same, this hymn recounts the repetition of the Supper through Jesus' self-giving to the disciples on the Emmaus road. Citing and paraphrasing selectively from the six stanzas. . . .

1. On the day of resurrection to Emmaus we return . . .
2. Then this stranger asks a question, "What is this which troubles you?". . .
3. [Jesus opens the scriptures, and their hearts are burning.]
4. [They ask Jesus to stay.]
5. Day of sorrow is forgotten when the guest becomes the host.
   Taking bread and blessing, breaking, Jesus is himself made known.
6. [The disciples bear witness], and Jesus is through us made known. [6]

Offertory. Significantly—and without any reservation—several hymns affirm the sacrificial symbolism of the eucharistic elements and their offering to God. "Let us Offer to the Father" highlights the corporate sacrifice with thanksgiving of the good gifts of creation.

Let us offer to the Father, with the bread and with the wine,
All our joys and all our sorrows; all our cares, Lord, all are thine.

From the country, from the city, from the riches of the land,
We bring back to our Creator many gifts of heart and hand.

All your people here together bring you offerings of love,
Joining with your whole creation, seeking liberty and peace. [7]

"Take Our Bread" combines many themes of offering, presence, self-sacrifice, witness, forgiveness, and nourishment.

5. *FWS,* 2114.
6. *UMH,* 309.
7. *FWS,* 2262:3–4.

Take our bread, we ask you; take our hearts, we love you.
Take our lives, O Father, we are yours, we are yours.

Yours as we stand at the table you set;
Yours as we eat the bread our hearts can't forget.
We are the sign of your life with us yet,
We are yours, we are yours.

Your holy people standing washed in your blood,
Spirit filled yet hungry we await your food.
We are poor, but we've brought ourselves the best we could;
We are yours, we are yours.[8]

In giving "our gifts" of bread and wine, we are "united" in belief, and through them we "belong" to God. Our gifts, in turn, become God's "gift to us" of "food" and "blood."[9] And in recognition of their spiritual poverty, the communicants offer to Christ an *empty* cup:

Fill my cup, Lord, I lift it up Lord.
Come and quench this thirsting of my soul.
Bread of heaven, feed me till I want no more;
Fill my cup, fill it up and make me whole.[10]

And they fall silent in recognition of Christ's divine self-offering to them in his incarnation: "He will give to all the faithful his own self for heavenly food."[11]

Institution and Last Supper: sacrificial meal. The four short stanzas of "Broken for Me" capture the sacrificial and covenantal nature of the Last Supper.

He offered his body; he poured out his soul; Jesus was broken that we
    might be whole.
Come to my table and with me dine; eat of my bread and drink of my
    wine.
This is my body given for you; eat it, remembering I died for you.
This is my blood I shed for you, for your forgiveness, making you new.[12]

---

8. *UMH*, 640; see also *UMH*, 636:1: "Nature's gifts of wheat and wine now are set before us; as we offer bread and wine, Christ comes to restore us."

9. *STF*, 589.

10. *UMH*, 641.

11. *UMH*, 626:2.

12. *FWS*, 2263.

The Lord's Supper is a repetition of the Last Supper, for just as Christ prepared the Upper Room, "his disciples still gather there."[13] Indeed, it can also be a repetition of Gethsemane: "Out of the Garden, Lord, you lead us."[14]

Anamnesis: Christ the Priest, Host, and Lamb. Several hymns uphold the symbolic nature of the liturgy and the sacramental conviction that Christ is actually the primary actor in the eucharist. For both the Methodist and Catholic traditions, this Christology lies at the heart of eucharistic sacrifice because it provides the hermeneutical and conceptual insight that allows the language of sacrifice to be intelligible and constructive with respect to the church's eucharistic celebration, rather than limiting sacrifice to refer only to Christ's historic passion.

He is the one who sets the Table, invites, presides, and gives. As "Come to the Table" says, "Come at the Lord's invitation; receive from his nail-scarred hand,"[15] as well as "Come, Share the Lord": "He joins us here, he breaks the bread, the Lord who pours the cup is risen from the dead; the one we love the most is now our gracious host."[16] Christ is the one who "has a table spread," and we ask him to join us in the "bread and wine which you lay down."[17]

Some eucharistic prayers tend to accentuate certain theological convictions over others (e.g., the UMC Great Thanksgiving that positively eschews any hint of penance or guilt). To some degree, this is inevitable, given that corporate prayer as a genre must be at once both confessional and catechetical, but cannot be exhaustive. The poetic quality of hymns, however, allows them to hold together the mysterious and paradoxical nature of Christ's transcendent, redeeming work in all his offices.

> Alleluia! King eternal, Thee the Lord of lords we own;
> Alleluia! Born of Mary, earth thy footstool, heaven thy throne:
> Thou within the veil hast entered, robed in flesh our great High Priest;
> Thou on earth both priest and victim in the eucharistic feast.[18]

When Christ—the eternal and great high priest (Heb 9)—presides at the eucharist, any apparent contradiction between Jesus' command to "do this" and Hebrews' teaching of "once for all" dissolves. The effects of the "once for all" passion participate in the "eternal now" of Christ's heavenly ministry:

---

13. *STF*, 569:1.

14. *STF*, 599:3.

15. *FWS*, 2264.

16. *FWS*, 2269:3. See *UMH* 617:3: "As Christ breaks bread and bids us share, each proud division ends. . . ."

17. *STF*, 572:1 and 575:5; see 580:4.

18. *HAP*, 592:4.

Lord enthroned in heavenly splendour, First-begotten from the dead,
Thou alone, our strong defender, liftest up thy people's head.
Alleluia! Jesus, true and living Bread.

Paschal Lamb, thine offering, finished once for all when thou wast slain,
In its fullness undiminished shall for evermore remain,
Alleluia! Cleansing souls from every stain.

Life-imparting, heavenly Manna, stricken Rock with streaming side,
Heaven and earth with loud hosanna worship thee, the Lamb who died.
Alleluia! Risen, ascended, glorified![19]

Christ's passion is "once for all," yet its fullness is undiminished and still cleanses
from sin. He is Manna, the Rock with streaming side, and the Lamb, but he is
also heavenly and glorified. Likewise, Christ is "Bread of life . . . broken now to
set us free," and at his table his body is "given eternally for you."[20]

The whole body of Christ in heaven and earth join in worshiping him,
and this Christology underlies the past-present-future dimension of eucharistic *anamnesis*.[21] To share in the Lord's Supper is—echoing St. Paul—to share
in Christ's "eternal sacrifice":

Spread the table of the Lord, break the bread and pour the wine;
Gathered at the sacred board, we would taste the feast divine.

Saints and martyrs of the faith to the cross have turned their eyes,
Sharing, in their life and death, that eternal sacrifice.[22]

The single-most intriguing example refers to Christ's sacrificial action at the
Last Supper:

On the night of that last supper seated with his chosen band,
He, the paschal victim eating, first fulfils the law's command
Then as food to all his brethren gives himself with his own hand.[23]

Not only is the Supper understood as a covenantal and sacrificial meal in fulfillment of Israel's Passover, but Christ's self-offering as a Paschal victim and
his self-giving to "his brethren" are explicitly affirmed. Here is the fullest sense

---

19. *HAP*, 616:1, 4, 5.

20. *STF*, 578, Refrain, and 581:2.

21. *HAP*, 600, no. 1. On the past, present, and future of the eucharist, see *STF*, 577:1
and 586:3.

22. *HAP*, 625:1–2; see *HAP*, 618:5 and *UMH*, 638:5.

23. *HAP*, 624:3.

in which Christ incorporates his apostles in his redeeming sacrifice through his sacrifice at the Supper. Such an explicit affirmation of Christ's action as sacrifice should not be surprising in light of the fact that the hymn's author is Thomas Aquinas!

Oblation. Christ's work of incorporating his body, the church, into his sacrifice is the proper context in which to understand the human response (both individual and corporate) of sacrifice. In and by the Spirit, the church as a priestly people unites its sacrifice to Christ's office of High Priest and to his intercession on its behalf.

> And now, O Father, mindful of the love that bought us, once for all, on
>   Calvary's tree,
> And having with us him that pleads above, we here present, we here
>   spread forth to thee
> That only offering perfect in thine eyes, the one true, pure, immortal
>   sacrifice.
>
> Look, Father, look on his anointed face, and only look on us as found
>   in him;
> Look not on our misusings of thy grace, our prayer so languid, and our
>   faith so dim:
> For lo! Between our sins and their reward set the passion of thy Son our
>   Lord.[24]

Pride of place must go to Charles Wesley and his hymn with the arresting opening address to the Son, "Victim Divine, thy grace we claim." In praising the risen Lord for his priestly mediation (Heb 10:12–22), the first two stanzas, especially, explain why the title "Victim Divine" is doxological (even paradoxical), but not oxymoronic.

> Victim Divine, thy grace we claim, while thus thy precious death we show;
> Once offered up, a spotless Lamb, in thy great temple here below,
> Thou didst for all mankind atone, and standest now before the throne.
>
> Thou standest in the holiest place, as now for guilty sinners slain;
> Thy blood of sprinkling speaks, and prays, all-prevalent for helpless man;
> Thy blood is still our ransom found, and spreads salvation all around.[25]

Catholics might recognize in this hymn a Christology and a theology of atonement that are quite consonant with the *Agnus Dei*, which they sing at the frac-

---

24. *HAP*, 593:1–2
25. *HAP*, 629, and *FWS*, 2259.

tion of the host.[26] Despite the modern desire to avoid sacrificial atonement theories and the belief that Christ accomplished his saving work through his blood, Mark Stamm takes Wesley (and therefore scripture) at his word: "Wesley insists that Christ the spotless Lamb of God has been offered as an atoning sacrifice—his life given in the place of ours. . . . He was slain for our guilt, just as the guilt offerings were offered on the altar of the Temple. . . . We are saved by blood."[27]

The teaching that the church's sacrifice—in the language of the preceding hymns—is a showing, presenting, and spreading forth before the Father of that same sacrifice that Christ continues to plead before the throne demonstrates that the church finds salvation solely in the one, unique passion of Christ and that its eucharistic sacrifice is a sacramental participation by faith in the cross and not a subsequent or extrinsic sacrifice to it.

Epiclesis and Self-Sacrifice. The eucharistic prayer concludes with a request for the Holy Spirit to come upon the elements and the congregation. The degree to which the bread and wine are transformed is still under debate among Catholics and Methodists, but the degree to which believers must be transformed is not. True to its heritage, contemporary Methodist hymnody sees the fruits of communion ripening in both personal holiness and social justice.

> Gracious Spirit, help us summon other guests to share that feast
> Where triumphant Love will welcome those who had been last and least.
> There no more will envy bind us nor will pride our peace destroy,
> As we join with saints and angels to repeat the sounding joy.[28]

> Now let us from this table rise renewed in body, mind, and soul;
> With Christ we die and live again, his selfless love has made us whole.[29]

Sacrificial living in imitation of Christ breeds Christian unity:

> Let us be bread, blessed by the Lord, broken and shared, life for the world.
> Let us be wine, love freely poured. Let us be one in the Lord.[30]

The goal of participation in Christ's redeeming sacrifice is a life of sacrificial discipleship in imitation of him—pardon from sin and power for holiness in

---

26. I am indebted to Geoffrey Wainwright for this observation.

27. Mark W. Stamm, *Let Every Soul Be Jesus' Guest: A Theology of the Open Table* (Nashville: Abingdon, 2006), 133.

28. *FWS*, 2268:3.

29. *UMH*, 634:1.

30. *FWS*, 2260; see also *FWS*, 2254 and 2266 for similar themes.

the Spirit. Because Christ has "come to us . . . we would come to you [and] live our lives for you."[31] Catholics and Methodists share the conviction that a eucharistic anthropology is fundamentally oriented toward sanctification.

> Because you have said: "Do this for my sake,"
> The mystical bread we gladly partake;
> We thirst for the Spirit that flows from above,
> And long to inherit your fullness of love.[32]

In organizing those hymns that treat the doctrine of eucharistic sacrifice according to the movement of the Great Thanksgiving, the intention is not to suggest that this is the criterion by which they are placed in the hymnal, and certainly not that Methodists singing these hymns would correlate a particular stanza to a line in the prayer. Rather, it is to establish that in both sacrament and song, Methodism's *lex orandi* proclaims a rich and multifaceted doctrine of eucharistic sacrifice. Although Methodism continues to overlook the *Hymns on the Lord's Supper* as the richest available resource, it does sing songs that bear witness to the sacrifice of the church in union with the one "immortal" sacrifice of Christ. These hymns celebrate the sacrificial dimension of the eucharist in manifold ways:

(1) the offering of the eucharistic elements to God
(2) the priestly agency of Christ symbolized in the actions of the liturgy
(3) the repetition of the Last Supper, with Christ as the host, the giver, and the gift
(4) the offering of the sacrifice of Christ to the Father by the bread and cup
(5) the celebration of the real presence of Christ in the sacrament
(6) the application of the work of the Paschal mystery through the elements
(7) the new life of pardon and power by Christ's eternal priestly work
(8) the self-sacrifice of believers in faithful imitation of Christ in the Spirit.

Thus, in the Spirit and by sacramental signs, Methodists offer the passion of Christ to the Father even while their Lord—the divine Victim—pleads his once-for-all sacrifice on their behalf. Methodist eucharistic hymnody exhibits a thorough doctrine of sacrifice in continuity with its eucharistic prayers.

31. *STF*, 594:3–4; see 585:4.
32. *STF*, 574:1.

Eucharistic Sacrifice in Authorized Methodist Conference Documents

Following the reception and use of their revised liturgies, both British Methodism and United Methodism have published authorized documents regarding the theology and celebration of Holy Communion in their respective churches: *Methodist Conference 2003 Report: Holy Communion in the Methodist Church:* "His Presence Makes the Feast"; and *This Holy Mystery: A United Methodist Understanding of Holy Communion.*[33] The overall design and purpose of each document is quite different, yet both share similarities characteristic to Methodism, and both offer valuable insights into the current understanding of eucharistic sacrifice in both churches.

The intention of *His Presence Makes the Feast* is to be descriptive, and its purpose, by means of a survey, is to reveal what Methodists currently believe and practice eucharistically. The text places these insights within a larger historic and ecumenical context and provides some theological resources toward the end (paragraphs 137–207). For example, "This report attempts to address the lack of a more explicit description of the Methodist position, but does not pretend to be a 'definitive,' far less 'final' word on the subject," and again, "it is not the purpose of this report to set out the limits of what is acceptable. It describes 'how things are' rather than prescribing how things 'ought' or 'ought not' to be."[34]

This Holy Mystery has a much different design and purpose: "[*THM*] was overwhelmingly approved by the 2004 General Conference. For the first time in our history, the denomination has an official, comprehensive statement of the practice and theology of the Lord's Supper."[35] *This Holy Mystery* seeks to explain, teach, and deepen (or change) current United Methodist eucharistic faith and practice. It speaks with as much authority as it is entitled in order to prescribe and to norm United Methodist eucharistic theology: "The ritual officially approved by The United Methodist Church represents the decisions of the church about the theology and practice of Holy Communion. . . . Pastors are to utilize these rituals in their leadership of the eucharist. . . . It does

---

33. Methodist Church, "His Presence Makes the Feast" (HPMF) is available through the website of the Methodist Church, and citations are given by paragraph: https://www.methodist.org.uk/downloads/conf-holy-communion-in-methodist-church-2003.pdf. Gayle Carlton Felton, *This Holy Mystery: A United Methodist Understanding of Holy Communion* (THM) (Nashville: Discipleship Resources, 2005); citations for *THM* refer to page number in the printed edition.

34. HPMF, 13–16.

35. *THM*, 6. In addition to approval by the 2004 General Conference, *THM* is included in the *Book of Resolutions*.

mean that pastors are not free to substitute their individual preferences and practices in the place of those instituted by the church."[36]

At the same time, though, these documents are not without their similarities. First, they both elucidate that the *lex credendi* of each church relies heavily on the *lex orandi* as it has been received (and continues to be received) from their eucharistic revisions. For example, the theology and liturgical practice taught in *THM* stems solely from the 1989 authorized eucharistic prayers. These texts simply could not have been written without two preceding decades of eucharistic reception through the revised liturgies. Second, both churches recognize that clear eucharistic catechesis has historically not been a priority. HPMF notes that Methodist "doctrine has received little official formulation and exists more as an undefined (or under-defined) tradition. The theology is implicit in the liturgies, hymns and the practical arrangements for Holy Communion."[37] Similarly for United Methodism, "The goal of this study is the renewal of worship in United Methodist congregations. Unfortunately, many of our churches have strayed far away from the rich liturgical and sacramental heritage of Christian tradition."[38] Third, true to their Wesleyan heritage, both believe that worship should be "effective" evangelically and should lead worshippers to "experience" the presence of Christ.[39]

Fourth, and foundational to any doctrine of eucharistic sacrifice, an ongoing task for both churches is the recovery of Methodism as a sacramental tradition: "Understanding of Holy Communion has received a new emphasis through the rediscovery of sacramental theology," and the UMC documents on baptism (1996) and eucharist reflect the "efforts to reclaim its sacramental heritage and to be in accord with ecumenical movements in sacramental theology and practice."[40] Both documents go so far as to affirm that sacramental theology derives from the incarnation, which in turn gives the church its sacramental identity.[41] The language of rediscovery and reclaiming is telling, as both churches struggle now with overcoming the modernist anthropology and the pragmatic methodology of corporate worship that shaped nineteenth- and early twentieth-century Methodism. Both documents discuss eucharistic sacrifice as an aspect of eucharistic theology that grows out of a sacramental understanding of worship—i.e., that worship brings the church into the saving presence of the crucified and risen Christ through the use of symbols, words,

---

36. *THM*, 38–39.
37. HPMF, 6.
38. *THM*, 7.
39. HPMF, 15; *THM*, 10.
40. HPMF, 9; *THM*, 8.
41. HPMF, 9; *THM*, 15–16.

gestures, and elements instituted by Christ and vivified by the Spirit. "In the Lord's Supper, the original act of saving grace remains unique and unrepeatable but the language of the service recreates in words the original drama and allows the worshipper to become both participant and beneficiary in the saving act."[42]

His Presence Makes the Feast

The report discusses eucharistic theology in light of nine "key themes" from scripture and tradition, of which eucharist, koinonia, *anamnesis*, and sacrifice are the most relevant. Its frequent references to *BEM* as a standard-bearing document attest to the influence of the ecumenical movement in Methodism.

The eucharistic dimension of the church's celebration is "inseparably linked to Christ's offering of thanks to the Father," which Jesus did at the Last Supper and at the many instances where he fed the hungry. The text notes the Old Testament relationship between sacrifice, food, and thanksgiving, where in Leviticus 7:11–18, for example, "sacrifice is offered for thanksgiving," and in Psalm 116:10–11, where "the psalmist repays the Lord for all his goodness by lifting up the cup of salvation." Jesus' "typically Jewish" action of thanking (or blessing: *eulogein*) God is picked up by the earliest Christians, including Paul, and Christians continue this tradition in the eucharistic prayer: "At the Last Supper Jesus gave thanks ('made eucharist') over the bread and cup for God's goodness and saving work. The other side of the cross and the resurrection the Church 'gives thanks' for a saving work that now includes the whole Christ event." This section emphasizes the aspect of thanksgiving at the Supper, but by linking it with sacrifices in the Old Testament, it strongly suggests that the church "makes eucharist" by means of "re-enacting" Christ's sacrificial meal.[43]

In 1 Corinthians 10–11, *koinonia* lies at the heart of how Paul relates his theology of the body of Christ with Christ's passion, and the eucharist is the means by which this fellowship and participation take place. In light of the intimacy of sharing table fellowship in the ancient world, sharing in the bread and cup is nothing less than a sharing in the body and blood of Christ, and faithful to Paul's theology, "the believer shared in Christ's humility, suffering and glory."[44] Although the text does not develop Paul's notion of sacrifice embedded in his rhetorical question—"are not those who eat the sacrifices

42. HPMF, 145.
43. HPMF, 145, 148.
44. HPMF, 152.

partners in the altar?"—it does, in a nutshell, recognize that the eucharist is a sacrifice (or is at least sacrificial) to the extent that it is the means of incorporating Christ's body into his atoning sacrifice.[45]

Anamnesis is a "highly dynamic concept" that is neither a "bare memorial" nor a "repetition" or "addition to Christ's unique work"; instead, it means "bringing into the present the continued fruitfulness and efficacy of Christ's saving work." HPMF cites "Victim Divine," *BEM*, and the UMC's favorable response to *BEM* and notes that these liturgical and ecumenical gains are "strongly reflected" in the 1975 and 1999 eucharistic prayers. As with the concept of eucharist, it notes the dependence on Judaism's celebration of the Passover:

> An Exodus or supreme act of divine delivery is at hand on the first occasion of both Jewish ritual meals—Jewish Passover and Last Supper. The gift present in the original saving event is appropriated in the subsequent repetitions of both ritual meals. Anamnesis is about renewed contact with the original source of blessing—the God who saves through the Exodus in the Passover and who saves through the death and resurrection of Christ in Holy Communion.[46]

This comment comes within a hair's breadth of referring to the eucharist as a sacrifice. If the Passover is a ritual meal, it is one because it is a sacrificial meal repeated by Israel through the generations. The Last Supper also has this sacrificial dimension, since "Christ our Passover is sacrificed" (1 Cor 5:7). In both sacrificial meals a gift of divine deliverance is present, and that gift is Christ himself, present in the saving power of his death and resurrection. This gift is then "appropriated" in "subsequent repetitions" of the sacrificial meal.

Now, it is the language of "gift" in association with the Last Supper that calls for further reflection. The gift is Christ's self-offering to his friends in the Upper Room, and this is the "saving event" appropriated by repeated meals. What, though, does Jesus' self-offering entail if it is indeed a saving event? Is it directed only toward his disciples? If this is the case, then how does his thanksgiving over the bread and wine and his identification of them with his Paschal mystery relate to his self-offering to the disciples? How do thanksgiving, Paschal meal, salvation, and self-offering relate?

Here the language of "given for you" and "new covenant in my blood" becomes unavoidable. Here is the language of sacrifice and of Christ in his humanity as the divine mediator. Christ can only give himself *to* his disciples because he also gives himself *for* them to the Father. In the Last Supper, God

---

45. *Mediator Dei* explores Paul's theology in a considerably deeper fashion, yet the interpretations of Paul's theology by both texts fundamentally agree.

46. HPMF, 157.

alone saves because in his humanity the incarnate Son effects a new covenant between the Father and humankind by way of sacrifice. To be sure, the saving power of this gift derives from the cross, but it is not the case that at the Last Supper we can speak only of thanksgiving, meal, and receiving the bread and wine. The Last Supper is a "saving event" of "divine deliverance" because it is a sacrifice of Christ: he offers himself to the Father and to the disciples and proleptically (i.e., sacramentally) incorporates them into his sacrificial passion. The Christologies of Hebrews and Revelation and the *koinonia* theology of Paul inform this theology of sacrifice. If *anamnesis* is the "renewed contact" with the God who saves through the cross in Holy Communion, then the Lord's Supper must be a sacrifice to the same extent that the Last Supper was—that is, Christ's sacramental incorporation of his body, the church, into his saving passion by means of his self-offering.

At this point, though, the concept of *anamnesis*—essentially understood as a "dynamic reality" where the events of the past are made effective once again—has been stretched too far. Eucharistic sacrifice is anamnetic, but it is also its own proper doctrine. *Anamnesis* describes a particular mode of memorial in the Spirit in which Christ and the church transcend temporal confines. Eucharistic sacrifice describes an action of offering by Christ and his church that takes place within this anamnetic mode. Admittedly, the paragraph cited earlier from HPMF does not spell out this theology of sacrifice in any detail. Indeed, was the language of "delivery," "gift," and "ritual" chosen intentionally to avoid the language of sacrifice? *BEM* employed this strategy when it sought to embed its strong offertory-theology within the concept of *anamnesis*. Whether intentional or not, HPMF's language of "gift" suggests that a theology of eucharistic sacrifice is not only unavoidable, but required.

The subsequent section in HPMF treats the theme of sacrifice directly, and it would be an ideal moment to capitalize on the idea of gift and to develop a theology of sacrifice. The section begins by highlighting New Testament exhortations for believers to offer themselves as a "living sacrifice" (Rom 12:1), to make "spiritual sacrifices" (1 Pt 2:5), and to offer up a "sacrifice of praise" (Heb 13:15). It notes the Christology of Jesus as High Priest, Lamb of God, and his "atoning sacrifice." Almost as if these acts of sacrifice were potentially in conflict with Christ's, it is careful to relate them: "The sacrifice of Christ is the one and only means whereby the Church's sacrifice of its praise and of itself can be offered. The New Testament eucharist celebrates the inseparability of Christ's sacrifice and ours."[47] HPMF notes that Israel's sacrificial system was the theological resource that helped the early Christians understand the scandal of the Lord who was yet crucified. The sacrificial

---

47. HPMF, 162–64.

system was "God's gift to them as a 'means of grace.'"[48] It also feels compelled to offer a biblical understanding of sacrifice, no doubt in an effort to counter the popular, predominant understanding of sacrifice associated with the philosophy of religion. While helpful, this demonstrates that in the Methodist imagination sacrifice is not sufficiently understood as a concept and an action proper to Christian doctrine and liturgical practice.

The document recognizes the sacrificial dimension of the institution narrative: "The association between the bread and wine and his self-offering or sacrifice is thus built into the story from the beginning. It is therefore easy to see how the understanding of Holy Communion as in some sense a sacrifice developed very early in Christian tradition." It also recognizes how this doctrine developed over the course of the church's reflection: "The bringing together of this kind of language and the understanding that the worship which is offered is itself a sacrificial act led naturally, perhaps inevitably, to the notion of 'eucharistic sacrifice.'" Unfortunately, it does not take this opportunity to affirm eucharistic sacrifice, despite these insights and the resources to do so; instead, it reduces sacrifice to a univocal term and simply asks, "Is the sacrifice the act of offering worship or specifically the offering of bread and wine?"[49]

In a few brief paragraphs, the text traces eucharistic sacrifice in the Reformers, Wesley, the Catholic-Methodist dialogues, the Catholic-Lutheran dialogues, and a comment by Outler. Building off the ideas plainly stated in scripture concerning Christ's self-offering and ours and off the idea of the whole Christ, it concludes, "In Holy Communion Methodists plead the completed and eternal sacrifice of Christ, and we offer ourselves anew in and through the eternal sacrifice, but we do not in any way offer the sacrifice again. At Holy Communion what Methodists do is to make a memorial of and participate in the offering of Christ." This comment raises similar questions as with *anamnesis* and opens itself to the same critiques. Is pleading the same as "making memorial" and "participating in"? Does not the former imply an act of offering? Christ's sacrifice is rightly (and *anamnetically*) understood as completed and at the same time eternal. The "offering of Christ" is something through which we can offer ourselves, which recalls the heavenly ministry of Christ and the Christologies of Hebrews and Revelation. At the same time, though, sacrifice is used only to refer to the cross, and the perennial fears of some re-crucifixion continue to linger: "We do not in any way offer the sacrifice again."[50] See, for example, Carter's comment: "The Christian eucharist

48. HPMF, 165.
49. HPMF, 166.
50. HPMF, 171.

is never offered for sin. It is always a celebration, and understanding that is at the heart of our liturgical revisions of 1975 and 1998."[51] The eucharist is never offered for sin as a sacrifice extrinsic to Christ's sacrifice, but Methodists do receive forgiveness from sin in the eucharist because they unite sacrificially (through worship, the elements, the rite, and themselves) to Christ's offering for our sins on our behalf. In this respect, the eucharist is always offered for sin. Ideally, HPMF would make this teaching clear. HPMF appears not to understand that the sacrifice of Christ that the Catholic Church (and the *Hymns on the Lord's Supper*) make in the eucharist is the sacrifice that Christ made at the Supper and not on the cross.

HPMF demonstrates that, catechetically, The Methodist Church remains in a doctrinally liminal position: conceptually, it speaks of sacrifice in a univ-ocal and historically limited sense, yet in the eucharistic liturgy and the concept of *anamnesis*, it has the tools to teach a doctrine of eucharistic sacrifice com-mensurate with what it already prays. Making two critical distinctions would strengthen the section on sacrifice. First, it should fully integrate the temporal with the transcendent—i.e., it should explain how the Last Supper, and not just Christ's historic passion, is in perfect continuity with his eternal priestly office and mediation. Second, it should reflect upon and affirm the sacrificial action of Christ at the Last Supper and not only in the cross. Making these two observations would reveal how human agency and sacrifice—both Christ's and ours—participate in, without detracting from, his once for all work on the cross.

This Holy Mystery

Intended as a teaching document (complete with study guide) in service of United Methodist sacramental renewal, *THM* is prescriptive rather than descriptive. It is an exposition of what the UMC intends normative eucha-ristic theology and practice to be. It is clear, concise, and accessible to a broad audience and addresses a broad range of topics, anywhere from the trinitarian nature of sacramental theology to questions such as what elements to use, who can receive communion, and how frequently. Its two main resources are the Wesleyan eucharistic heritage and the current Great Thanksgiving, both interpreted in the context of the ecumenical and liturgical renewal move-ments. In the main, it is an excellent document that is squarely on target with respect to the goals it hopes to achieve for the lay readership. Understandably, what it gains in accessibility and thoroughness it also gives up in theological depth. Considering that a continued eucharistic renewal is deeply needed

---

51. Carter, "Methodism and the Eucharist," 66.

within United Methodism, this tradeoff is the pastorally advised one.[52] Thus, eucharistic sacrifice does not receive a detailed treatment, although the trinitarian, Christological, and sacramental theology that undergirds the doctrine is firmly in place.

Christ's atoning sacrifice is the theological foundation of sacramental theology: "The grace of God is made available to us through the life, death, and resurrection of Jesus Christ and works in our lives through the presence and power of the Holy Spirit."[53] The church's eucharist is a continuation of the work of the risen Christ on the Emmaus road (Lk 24:13–35).[54] Christ is present in the eucharist by his Spirit: he is present in the congregation, through the preached Word, and through the eucharistic elements: his "divine presence is a living reality and can be experienced by participants; it is not a [mere] remembrance of the Last Supper and the Crucifixion only."[55] The words, actions, and elements of the eucharist are the means through which God conveys grace to the church, and this grace has many effects: "forgiveness, nourishment, healing, transformation, ministry and mission, and eternal life."[56] *THM* does not specifically address the idea of offering the bread and wine as a gift to God (nor

52. William McDonald and Kathy Black each submit positive responses to the question, "Will *This Holy Mystery* Serve United Methodists Well?," *Quarterly Review* 25, no. 3 (Fall 2005): 304–10. United Methodist scholarship by and large focuses on the theology of sacrament with respect to the eucharist. The following texts are excellent resources: Gayle C. Felton, *United Methodists and the Sacraments* (Nashville: Abingdon, 2007); Mark W. Stamm, *Sacraments and Discipleship: Understanding Baptism and the Lord's Supper in a United Methodist Context* (Nashville: Discipleship Resources, 1989); Scott J. Jones, *United Methodist Doctrine: the Extreme Center* (Nashville: Abingdon Press, 2002), chapter 9, "The Means of Grace"; Karen B Westerfield Tucker, "'Let Us Thy Mercy Prove': A United Methodist Understanding of the Eucharist," in Pieterse, *Eucharist in a United Methodist Perspective*, 20–33; E. Byron Anderson, *The Meaning of Holy Communion in the United Methodist Church* (Nashville: Discipleship Resources, 1996); Herchel H. Sheets, *Our Sacraments: A United Methodist View of Baptism and Communion* (Nashville: Discipleship Resources, 1996); John R. Tyson, "The Lord's Supper in the Wesleyan Tradition," in *Basic United Methodist Beliefs: An Evangelical View*, ed. James V. Heidinger II (Wilmore, KY: Good News), 80–89; J. Robert Nelson, "Eucharist, Ecumenism, Methodism," in *Wesleyan Theology Today*, ed. Theodore Runyon (Nashville: United Methodist Publishing House, 1985), 313–22; Hoyt L. Hickman, *Workbook on Communion and Baptism* (Nashville: Discipleship Resources, 1990); Kenneth M. Loyer, *Holy Communion: Celebrating God with Us* (Nashville: Abingdon, 2014); Stephen P. West, *Something Happens Here: Reclaiming the Distinctiveness of Wesley's Communion Spirituality in Times of Divisiveness* (Eugene, OR: Wipf and Stock, 2022). See also Howard A. Snyder, "The Lord's Supper in the Free Methodist Tradition," and Thomas L. McCray, "The Lord's Supper: The Perspective of the African Methodist Episcopal Church," in *The Lord's Supper: Believers Church Perspectives*, ed. Dale R. Stoffer (Eugene, OR: Wipf and Stock, 1997), 212–24.

53. *THM*, 15.

54. *THM*, 10.

55. *THM*, 23.

56. *THM*, 19.

does HPMF), probably because the action is so naturally (and now uncontroversially) integrated into the liturgy. Laurence Stookey relates the church's use of the elements with the sacrificial covenant through Christ: "Paul and the writers of the first three Gospels report that in presenting bread and wine to those in the upper room, Jesus spoke of the blood of the covenant. . . . What we eat and drink at the Table of the Lord suggests cooperation between Creator and creature as we are called responsibly to tend, prepare, and share with one another."[57] The goal of our participation in the body and blood of Christ is nothing short of our transformation into Christ's likeness: "As we encounter Christ in Holy Communion and are repeatedly touched by divine grace, we are progressively shaped into Christ's image."[58] Its emphasis that eternal life begins now, on earth, and is grounded in God's "everlasting love" accords with a similar argument by Pope Leo XIII in *Mirae Caritatis*.

The text devotes just a few sentences to each of "six major ideas" concerning the eucharist: thanksgiving, fellowship, remembrance, sacrifice, action of the Holy Spirit, and eschatology.[59] It closely associates *anamnesis* and sacrifice.

> Holy Communion is remembrance, commemoration, and memorial, but this remembrance is much more than simply intellectual recalling. "Do this in remembrance of me" (Lk 22:19; 1 Cor 11:24–25) is *anamnesis* (the biblical Greek word). This dynamic action becomes re-presentation of past gracious acts of God in the present, so powerful as to make them truly present now. Christ is risen and is alive here and now, not just remembered for what was done in the past.
>
> Holy Communion is a type of sacrifice. It is a re-presentation, not a repetition, of the sacrifice of Christ. Hebrews 9:26 makes clear that "he has appeared once for all at the end of the age to remove sin by the sacrifice of himself." Christ's atoning life, death, and resurrection make divine grace available to us. We also present ourselves as sacrifice in union with Christ (Rom 12:1; 1 Pt 2:5) to be used by God in the work of redemption, reconciliation, and justice. In the Great Thanksgiving, the church prays, "We offer ourselves in praise and thanksgiving as a holy and living sacrifice, in union with Christ's offering for us. . . ."[60]

This citation clearly shows the influence of the Wesleyan heritage ("a type of sacrifice") and the ecumenical concept of *anamnesis* (dynamic re-presentation

57. Laurence Hull Stookey, *Eucharist: Christ's Feast with the Church* (Nashville: Abingdon, 1993), 17.

58. *THM*, 19.

59. For an extended discussion of these themes plus the question of Christ's presence, see White, *Sacraments as God's Self Giving*, 53–61.

60. *THM*, 17–18.

of past events) in UMC theology. Moreover, in referring to the eucharist as a type of sacrifice in which past events are made efficacious in the present, *THM* demonstrates a willingness to reclaim an aspect of the celebration that is in line with ancient, Wesleyan, and Catholic doctrine. The concept of *anamnesis* in *THM* (as with HPMF) is stronger than that of sacrifice, and *THM*'s teaching on sacrifice could be strengthened in a few key areas.

First, the aforementioned comments reveal that, conceptually, *THM* (like HPMF) feels the need to choose between a dynamic memorial (of the cross!) on the one hand, or a re-crucifixion on the other: "It is a re-presentation, not a repetition, of the sacrifice of Christ." Faced with only these two choices, it obviously chooses the former. However, it quotes Jesus' command at the Supper to "Do this," and he obviously cannot mean, "Repeat my crucifixion"; instead, he must mean either "Offer my sacramental body and blood" or "Take, eat, and drink my body and blood." The "past gracious acts of God" that the liturgy re-presents are Jesus' actions and words at the Supper. In light of the prominence of the fourfold action of the liturgy, it is surprising that *THM* does not realize that this fourfold shape is designed to re-present Christ's passion in the same way that he did—that is, by repeating the words and actions of the Last Supper, not the crucifixion. Christ's offering at the Supper is a proleptic and anamnetic re-presentation of the cross, and the eucharist is a memorial of the cross because it is a repetition of the Supper. In general, Methodism moves too quickly in its reflections from the Institution Narrative to the cross without reflecting enough on the sacrificial dimension of the Supper itself. Willimon, however, spells out how Christ reinterprets the Passover meal to reveal the covenantal and sacrificial dimension of his own words and actions.[61]

Second, this lack of clarity reappears in chapter 6, "Setting the Table." *THM* consistently privileges the language of meal over sacrifice and of table over altar, although it allows for the use of both pairs of words. *THM* explains that Methodist pastors should stand behind the table facing the congregation to represent Christ presiding at the Supper. As part of the historical background to this explanation, it says, "Through time, the church increasingly understood the eucharist as a repetition of Christ's sacrifice on the cross, and the Table came to be seen as an altar of sacrifice." This comment is only half correct: the church did come to see the eucharist as a sacrifice occurring on an altar—the offering of Christ's substantial body and blood—but not as a "repetition of Christ's sacrifice on the cross," but as a repetition of his (proleptic and sacramental) sacrifice at the Supper.[62]

---

61. Willimon's chapter "In the Upper Room," in *Sunday Dinner: The Lord's Supper and the Christian Life* (Nashville: Upper Room, 1981), 73–79.

62. *THM*, 49.

Third, the idea of our self-offering in union with Christ's offering derives from Christ's priestly office and from believers' status as a "royal priesthood, God's own people (1 Pt 2:9)." The text's definition of priesthood is a good beginning, but incomplete: "As priests, each of us can have access to God without any human intermediary. This priesthood means, especially, that we are to be priests to each other as together we seek to live as Christians." To be sure, in Christ, Christians can address God directly, and the text rightly points out the corporate and therefore ecclesial nature of eucharist: "The whole assembly actively celebrates Holy Communion. All who are baptized into the body of Christ Jesus become servants and ministers within that body, which is the church."[63] However, priests are more than people who do not need an intermediary, nor is the priestly ministry exercised primarily between people. The priesthood is an intercessory office that mediates between God and humanity by way of sacrifice. The New Testament teaching that all Christians now share in this priestly office does not mean that mediation or sacrifice has ceased; rather, it means that all Christians as one body participate in sacrificial worship in union with their one mediator and high priest, Christ their head.

The aspect of eucharistic sacrifice where *THM* does speak strongly is with respect to believers' self-offering in sacrificial discipleship. This undisputed notion of New Testament sacrifice comes across strongly in the *UMC* Great Thanksgiving, and it resonates deeply with the Methodist tradition of social justice and the doctrine of sanctification. The eucharist feeds, heals, strengthens, inspires, and propels Christians to witness and service. Despite the presence of sin in a broken world, Christians live out their sacrificial imitation of Christ as a hopeful witness to the eschatologically renewing work begun at the resurrection: "In the midst of the personal and systemic brokenness in which we live, we yearn for everlasting fellowship with Christ and ultimate fulfillment of the divine plan. Nourished by sacramental grace, we strive to be formed into the image of Christ and to be made instruments for transformation in the world."[64] Methodists, therefore, should readily agree

63. *THM*, 35. See *THM*, chapter 5, "Serving at the Table." On the vital role of the minister, see Stookey, *Eucharist*, 120. See also Geoffrey Wainwright, "Presiding at the Lord's Table," in *Sacramental Life* 17, no. 1 (Winter 2004–5): 27–36; Richard Clutterbuck, "The Presbyter as President: Presidency at the Eucharist as the Defining Paradigm of Presbyteral Ministry," in *What Is a Minister?*, ed. Philip Luscombe and Esther Shreeve (Peterborough: Epworth, 2002), 80–90; and the contributions by John E. Harnish and Margaret Ann Crain to the question "Who Should be Allowed to Preside at the Eucharist," *Quarterly Review* 23, no. 3 (Fall 2003): 302–8.

64. *THM*, 18; see Kenneth L. Waters Sr., "Eucharist and Global Reconciliation: A Liturgical Vision of Social Transformation," in Pieterse, *The Eucharist in a United Methodist Perspective*, 34–46.

with John Paul II's exhortation that the eucharist is the source of the church's holiness and power as it sets off on the project of a new evangelism for a new millennium.

Mark Stamm develops this line of thinking more than most. Indeed, he devotes an entire chapter to discussing the sacrifice for which every person must be prepared who hears and follows the call of Christ by communing with him in the eucharist. Whereas most liturgists applauded unreservedly the eucharistic revisions that replaced the prayer's penitential theme with thanksgiving, Stamm is the exception. He worries that the lack of penitential language may unwittingly compromise our sense of God's grace and the gift of salvation, thereby diminishing our experience of being undeserving sinners to whom God has offered salvation through the costly gift of the Son. There are good reasons that United Methodists should pause before adopting too quickly his theology of the open table, but they should not critique him for advocating a theology of cheap grace. He most decidedly does not reduce the expectation of discipleship that Christ makes at the eucharist to the expectations of social pleasantries with which Christians too often settle. The eucharist of the early church, he writes, was not "primarily a means to self-fulfillment and spiritual peace, but a means for drawing them ever deeper into the Paschal mystery. The eucharistic cup is the cup that Jesus drank [Mk 10:38], and no other":

> If United Methodists insist on a radically open table, then they should (at least) proclaim this Paschal dynamic as part of their invitation. At the very least, those who eat and drink with Jesus are entering a realm where costly love is demanded, where they will be called to repent and love the unlovable. It is a converting ordinance in the deepest biblical sense, one that redefines the very meaning of happiness.[65]

THM argues that in order to make clear the call of discipleship, the eucharistic liturgy should include the rite of Confession and Pardon; otherwise, "if these are omitted, all those present may not understand either the openness of the Table of the Lord or the expectation of repentance, forgiveness, healing, and entrance into new life in Christ."[66] The text makes clear that those who respond to the invitation should receive communion, and it also stresses that communion is the covenant meal of the body of Christ, for which baptism is the sacramentally initiatory rite. Stookey notes the liturgical nature of sacrificial living with language reminiscent of Wesley's hymns: "The Lamb

---

65. Stamm, *Let Every Soul Be Jesus' Guest*, 128, 136; see chapter 6, "Open Table and the Suffering of Jesus."

66. *THM*, 26; see Stookey, *Eucharist*, 169–70.

upon the eucharistic altar is the Lamb who sits upon the throne. That Lamb is alone worthy [Rv 5:12]. . . . All of the living sacrifice of ourselves that we on earth can muster ascends to that Lamb like a fragrant offering."[67]

Conclusion

Both *His Presence Makes the Feast* and *This Holy Mystery* recognize, use, and affirm a theology of sacrifice in their teaching on the eucharist. Both texts are remarkably consonant with each other in their embrace of *anamnesis* (and *epiclesis*) as a means by which Christ's sacrifice (only on the cross and not in the supper) is applied in a saving way to the believer and by which individuals and the church offer themselves to God in self-sacrifice. The many ways in which these authorized teaching documents positively incorporate notions of sacrifice into their eucharistic theology is already an achievement considering how this topic has fared historically in Protestant theology. At the same time, though, the idea of sacrifice is not conceived with the richness and nuance that it enjoys in the Great Thanksgivings and hymnody. While these texts solidly establish that the eucharist is an instrumental means of grace grounded in Christ's unique sacrifice, Methodist liturgy and hymnody go further by establishing that the eucharist is a sacramental sacrifice that commemorates, shows forth, and participates in Christ's unique sacrifice. Methodists can conclude, therefore, that in their sacramental theology they do have a doctrine of eucharistic sacrifice. Granted, this doctrine is still in the process of being fully received, as it is more fully expressed in its *lex orandi* than it is currently taught in its *lex credendi*. Nevertheless, given the extent to which Methodists have embraced the Great Thanksgiving and the extent to which it now expresses Methodism's eucharistic theology, one can hope that the doctrine of eucharistic sacrifice found in its liturgy will continue to inform and find expression in its authorized teaching.

67. Stookey, *Eucharist*, 108.

CHAPTER 9

Eucharistic Sacrifice

Assessment and Prospects

As the result of decades of fruitful dialogue between Catholics and Methodists, both churches have come to recognize that they share a fundamental agreement on such necessary doctrines as the Triune God, the Incarnation and Lordship of Jesus, the authority of scripture, the role of tradition and the creeds, the sacramental dimension of the church, and the goal of the Christian life as directed pneumatologically toward sanctification and perfection. On other doctrines, agreement still remains a work in progress— for example, the role of the saints—especially Mary, the necessary form of the church and the ordering of its authority, the nature and function of ordination, and eucharistic sacrifice.[1] This study has been an exploration of this latter doctrine in each tradition in order to ascertain what each church actually confesses and practices and to evaluate the degree of convergence that currently exists between them. We have listened carefully to key voices within each tradition and to ecclesial documents of the highest authority from Catholicism and Methodism, and we are now in a position to offer an assessment of the current and prospective state of affairs by looking at Methodism's reception of its doctrine of eucharistic sacrifice and at its ecumenical engagement with Catholicism.

Eucharistic Sacrifice: Methodism's Reception of Its Doctrine

The revisions of the eucharistic prayers and the accompanying renewal in eucharistic theology within British and American Methodism since the 1970s have been profound; likewise, they have been widely and enthusiastically received. Methodism succeeded in looking outside its own prayer book tradi-

---

1. For a thorough assessment of Catholic-Methodist convergence on central doctrines, see the RCC-WMC report *Synthesis: Together to Holiness; 40 Years of Methodist and Roman Catholic Dialogue* (Lake Junaluska, NC: World Methodist Council, 2010). With a focus on eucharistic theology, see the two bilateral documents *Yearning to Be One: Spiritual Dialogue between Catholics and United Methodists* (Nashville: Discipleship Resources, 2000), 37–43, and "Heaven and Earth Are Full of Your Glory: A United Methodist and Roman Catholic Statement on the Eucharist and Ecology": http://www.usccb.org/beliefs-and-teachings/ecumenical-and-interreligious/ecumenical/methodist/upload/Heaven-and-Earth-are-Full-of-Your-Glory-Methodist-Catholic-Dialogue-Agreed-Statement-Round-Seven.pdf.

249

tion, and in doing so, it succeeded in (re-)discovering and appropriating the biblical, patristic, Eastern, and Wesleyan resources available to it. A chief concern throughout the process was to move beyond the controversies (and polemics) of the Reformation and to formulate a positive and constructive doctrine of eucharistic sacrifice. There should be no doubt that in this respect Methodism has succeeded thoroughly. What is more, Methodism came to embrace a doctrine of eucharistic sacrifice not by working independently of other churches or by repudiating Catholic theology, but by taking exactly the opposite approach: that is, Methodism reclaimed eucharistic sacrifice precisely by observing carefully Vatican II and Catholicism's eucharistic revisions and by participating in ecumenical dialogues with the hermeneutics of charity that it learned from John Wesley. Consequently, Methodism has recovered a doctrine of eucharistic sacrifice in its *lex orandi*, which it is still in the process of fully receiving and appropriating as its own in its *lex credendi*. Some key factors impinge directly on Methodism's reception of eucharistic sacrifice.

Sacramental theology and theological anthropology. In seeking to recover a rich appreciation and more frequent celebration of the eucharist, Methodism is right to focus on the full recovery of sacramental theology. Both *His Presence Makes the Feast* and *This Holy Mystery* stress that Methodists believe that worship should be effective and experiential. Not to be confused with emotionalism (or modern-day enthusiasm), *effectiveness* and *experiential* mean that Methodists expect that through worship they know that they have had fellowship with the risen Lord and that through this fellowship they have moved one step further by the power of the Holy Spirit on the way to holiness. Worship that does not yield the fruit of the Spirit is not effective worship. Methodism now formally teaches that eucharistic celebration lies at the heart of sanctifying worship. "Fasting, prayer, hearing His word, are all good vessels to draw water from this well of salvation; but they are not all equal"; Holy Communion "exceeds" them all.[2]

For Wesley's followers, the eucharist (and baptism) have historically taken second place to the sermon—which is received individually, notionally, and (preferably) emotionally—as the instrument of salvation. The believer hears the Word, believes, repents, and is saved. This individualistic and nonsacramental approach is quite at odds with Wesley's eucharistic theology. Christians are barraged by powerful and conflicting meta-narratives, and interior piety and fiery preaching are not enough to sustain faithful discipleship.[3] The trend

---

2. *CSS*, IV.6. A key element of Dean Blevins's article touches on this topic; "Trinity and the Means of Grace: A Sacramental Interrelationship," 231–55, especially 237–48.

3. Joshua R. Sweeden develops a similar argument; "Ordinary Practice as Ecclesial Holiness: Intersections of Work, Sacrament, and Liturgy," *Wesleyan Theological Journal* 49, no. 1 (Spring 2014): 78–92.

toward greater eucharistic participation among Methodists in recent decades (often at least monthly) should be celebrated and fostered. To feast on Christ in communal worship and to be transformed into his likeness while doing so is Wesley's method for growing in holiness in heart and life:

> But first of the celestial train benignest to the sons of men,
> The *sacramental glory* shines, and answers all our God's designs.[4]

At its best, liturgical renewal brings *effectiveness* and *experience* in line with proper sacramental theology and biblical teaching. The Catholic and Methodist appreciation for symbolism in worship and the shared conviction that the eucharistic liturgy should (effectively) show forth that Christ is the primary agent of the celebration into whose saving work believers know (experience) they have been incorporated is surely an example of theological anthropology that is faithful to scripture. An alternative model of worship is one that too easily conflates the communication of divine realities with the emotional state of the worshippers. The responsibility of the worship leader then becomes to lead congregants into a particular emotional state, and the degree to which this happens is considered the degree to which worship is effective. This model, however, trains believers out of a biblical faith (Heb 11:1) and into the idea that their feelings are the manner by which they experience God. The Spirit must be moving because they are moved, and conversely, if they are not moved emotionally, then nothing spiritual occurs. Modern American Methodist worship has too often fallen prey to this alternative model. One grave theological danger here is that it inverts the order of being and knowing with respect to divine-human agency: i.e., human actions are considered primary because that is the manner in which they are perceived. When this inverted order occurs, eucharistic sacrifice risks being perceived as a human work extrinsic to the work of Christ, and any offering that the congregation might make will be perceived to be in conflict and competition with Christ. Methodism will come to appreciate more fully the sacrificial dimension of its worship as it learns to perceive the reconciling work of Christ, the High Priest, in the fourfold action of the eucharistic liturgy.

The sacramental principle—based on the Incarnation—that Methodism inherited from the Wesleys and that it shares with Catholics is the hermeneutical key to a sacramental anthropology without which the doctrine of eucharistic sacrifice falters. The fact that Methodist scholars universally uphold the sacramental nature of the eucharist while many Methodists are still learning it points to where Methodism's catechesis should focus. *This Holy Mystery* is

---

4. HLS 62:6; see 42, 91:3.

an excellent beginning. The recovery of sacramental theology by Methodists can be facilitated by the realization that Methodists, overall, are quite comfortable with the participatory role that believers play in Wesley's *ordo salutis*. Wesley's teaching on the means of grace, to which Methodism still largely holds, entails the conviction that human and divine agency are not in competition with one another and that Christians must labor—with the aid of the Holy Spirit—if they desire to go on to perfection. Eucharistic sacrifice is the ecclesial instantiation of a corporate *ordo salutis*. In other words, eucharistic sacrifice is the means by which the church as a body participates in God's sanctifying grace. The eucharist is the church's self-sacrifice, and Methodism could make more explicit the priestly nature and function of corporate worship that is so prominent in its eucharistic prayers and yet underdeveloped in its catechesis.

Lex orandi—lex credendi. Methodism's prayers and hymnody have a more developed and explicit doctrine of eucharistic sacrifice than its authorized doctrinal statements. That is to say, Methodism does not yet fully teach what it prays, or it has not yet fully reflected on the richness of its eucharistic prayers. Doctrinally, conference documents still juxtapose the concepts of memorial, on the one hand, with the repetition of the cross, on the other, and they expound *anamnesis* (a dynamic memorial) as that concept that bridges the two. But this is simply another way of articulating sacramental theology, and it does not sufficiently address the question of *how* the church is to remember the saving work of Christ—i.e., the question of what is the relationship between "Do this" and "in remembrance of me," and what is it the church is commanded to do. Simply eating and drinking while remembering Christ's passion and believing that he is present in the midst of his people is insufficient to Wesley's understanding of eucharistic sacrifice.

Catechetically, Methodism still feels the need to clarify that it does not repeat Christ's sacrifice because in its conference texts it uses the language of sacrifice univocally. The language of Christ's sacrifice refers only to the cross; therefore, any discussion of sacrifice—either Christ's or the church's—in another context revives lingering Protestant fears. Methodist scholars, for example, speak readily of eucharistic sacrifice, but hardly at all of the eucharist as a sacrifice (except in terms of the undisputed New Testament qualifications). In its *lex orandi*, though, Methodism already confesses that its self-sacrifice occurs "in union with Christ's offering for us." This formulation expresses a Christology that sees continuity between the saving work of Christ's passion (which includes the Supper and the cross) and his heavenly, priestly intercession.

The way for Methodism to gain clarity on this oversight is for it to reflect more deeply on the significance of the words and actions of Christ at the

Last Supper. Even if the purpose of the Supper was to help the apostles interpret the cross, it was certainly also much more than that. Christ manifested his priestly office in the Upper Room just as he did on the cross and just as he continues to do in each celebration of the eucharist, and he incorporated into his death and resurrection those who communed with him then just as surely as he incorporates his church now. If participation in Christ's body and blood entails sharing in his saving sacrifice, then the means through which this participation occurs must be equally sacrificial. Indeed, Jesus' own words direct this line of thinking: he explicitly links the bread with "my body," which is "given for you," and the sharing in the cup with "the new covenant in my blood' (Lk 22:19–20). Christ establishes this new covenant with the cup at the meal (i.e., before the cross), which is a covenant of self-giving between God and humanity, and the sacrificial nature of this self-giving at the meal ("for you") serves to solidify the sacrificial quality of the Supper itself.

Once the Last Supper itself is seen as a sacrificial meal that participates sacramentally in the cross, the teaching that the eucharist is a sacrifice—indeed the same sacrifice as the cross—follows readily. The link between these two is a biblical Christology that celebrates the priesthood of Hebrews and the slain Lamb of Revelation, coupled with a doctrine of the *totus Christus* that unites the whole church in heaven and on earth to its head. Methodists can find all these elements clearly affirmed in the *Hymns on the Lord Supper*. With a continued *ressourcement* of its own heritage, Methodism in its *lex credendi* may come to affirm what it already prays—namely, that the Supper itself was a sacrifice, and therefore, so is the eucharist.

Eucharistic Sacrifice:
Methodism's Contribution and Invitation to Catholicism

At the same time, though, Wesley's theology of eucharistic sacrifice, as it is recovered in Methodism's liturgy, makes a distinctive contribution to ecumenical theology and an invitation to Catholics for assessment and reception. Protestant churches can find in Methodism a living tradition of eucharistic sacrifice rather than in a disembodied ecumenical document such as *BEM*. The *Hymns on the Lord's Supper* and the Great Thanksgiving can be appropriated as a resource and a model, respectively, of how to recover a faithful and fully biblical doctrine of sacrifice, one that goes well beyond the undisputed ideas of self-sacrifice and praise and thanksgiving. In addition, Methodism is in near complete agreement with Catholicism on this doctrine.

Following Irenaeus, the bread and wine are offered to God as a way of affirming the goodness of creation and of symbolizing the church's gratitude that all good gifts come from God. Following Cyprian, the church offers the eucharist because "the passion of the Lord is the sacrifice we offer." With the bread and wine, the church holds up before the world, before itself, and pleads before the Father the once for all redeeming sacrifice of Christ. With broad strokes, Augustine claimed that a sacrifice is anything that helps us cling to the Lord and that, through the eucharistic sacrifice, the church itself learns that it is the one being offered. In its Great Thanksgiving, Methodism roundly affirms Augustine's teaching. Wesley and Aquinas are in agreement with what makes the eucharist a sacrifice—namely, it represents Christ's passion, it contains Christ, it applies Christ's passion, and it is offered to the Father. More specifically, the communication that takes place through the sacramental signs between humanity and God is sacrificial because it signifies, on the one hand, the church's interior sacrifice of the heart that in Christ satisfies humanity's duty to worship God alone, and on the other hand, the application of the atoning grace of Christ's passion to his body, the church. Indeed, the degree of agreement between the two churches is extraordinary:

- Jesus' death was an atoning sacrifice for humanity, and he continues to intercede as our great High Priest.
- At the Last Supper, Jesus offers himself first to the Father and also to the disciples.
- The Last Supper was a sacrificial, covenantal, and sacramental proleptic sharing in the one redeeming sacrifice of the cross.
- Each eucharist is a repetition of the Last Supper based on Christ's fourfold action of taking, blessing, breaking, and giving.
- The eucharist is a sacramental and sacrificial meal because in the bread and cup Jesus is really present in the power of his unique redeeming sacrifice.
- The eucharist is a sacramental perpetuation of Christ's sacrificial meal that applies the once for all redemption of the cross.
- Christians receive this redemption not just by remembering Christ's sacrifice, but by offering it to the Father in the power of the Holy Spirit.
- The eucharistic elements are offered to God as a thank offering, uniting the orders of creation and redemption.
- The eucharistic rite is offered to God as a sacrifice of praise and thanksgiving.
- In the eucharist, we give our goods back to God in offering.
- The church, as a body, offers the eucharist as an external sacrifice to signify its interior spiritual sacrifice.
- In the eucharist, we offer ourselves as holy and living sacrifices, united to Christ's eternal offering for us.[5]

5. John Drury writes, "When we break bread together on the day that Christ was raised, we join him in his eternal act of giving thanks to God the Father"; Drury, "Christology and Eucharist," in Vickers, *Wesleyan Theology of the Eucharist*, 56.

- The Whole Christ (*totus Christus*: head and body) offers the eucharist together.

Two terms encompass the doctrine of eucharistic sacrifice in Catholicism's and Methodism's authoritative (or authorized) texts and liturgical revisions—participation and soteriology—and these terms are united by the affirmation that ultimately Jesus is the High Priest who is the chief actor in the eucharist.

Participation and Soteriology. Eucharistic sacrifice is a participation (both individual and ecclesial) in the saving sacrifice of Christ. The crucified, risen, and gloried Christ is really present in the redemptive work of the once for all sacrifice of Calvary, the grace of which is applied to believers through the bread and cup in the power of the Holy Spirit. Christ's passion—sacramentally and sacrificially celebrated at the Supper, realized at the cross, and eternally mediated by the High Priest before the Father—incorporates his body, the church, into his saving sacrifice. By this incorporation, the Holy Spirit sanctifies those united to Christ and conforms them to the cruciform image of the Lord. The church's sacrifice at the eucharist—led by the ordained minister—does not in any way detract from the cross or add to it; rather, in their doctrines of eucharistic sacrifice, both churches confess that only God can save and that salvation comes through Christ alone and his unique, once for all sacrifice. On all these fundamental convictions, both churches agree.

There is really only one aspect of eucharistic sacrifice on which Catholics and Methodists diverge. Both churches agree that by his priestly office in the eucharist Christ incorporates his body into his saving passion; thus, by his Spirit, Christ offers himself and his body—*totus Christus*—to the Father. The divergence lies only in *how* this offering takes place. For Catholics, this incorporation occurs by way of Christ placing his substantial presence into the hands of the priest who, together with the church, offers Christ to the Father (Trent: 22.2: "For the victim is one and the same, the same now offering by the ministry of priests, who then offered Himself on the cross, the manner alone of offering being different"). In this manner, for Catholics, Christ and the church offer Christ and the church. Comparatively, for Wesley, precisely because Christ is really present in the elements in the power of his eternal sacrifice offered to the Father, he does not need recourse to a sacramental priesthood or a metaphysics of substantial presence. Consequently, for Methodists, this incorporation occurs by way of the church offering the sacramental signs instituted by Christ as a means of offering Christ's passion to the Father, all of which takes place through the mediation of Christ—really present— who presides as High Priest. This offering that the church makes—inspired by the Spirit—is done by the free exercise of its own ecclesial agency without which the offering of Christ in the eucharist would not transpire. In this manner, for Methodists, Christ and the church offer Christ and the church. The offering is the same: Christ and the church offer the whole Christ in the Spirit to the Father; only the manner of this offering is different.

The difference between Catholic and Methodist doctrines of eucharistic sacrifice, therefore, resides not in who and what is offered in the eucharist; instead, the difference is instrumental—i.e., the manner in which the offering is made. This difference is not one that Methodists should find divisive. Within its own doctrinal formulations, Methodism allows for a far wider range of expression on almost every conceivable systematic topic. "Devising formal definitions of doctrine has been less pressing for United Methodists than summoning people to faith and nurturing them in the knowledge and love of God. The core Wesleyan doctrine that informed our past rightly belongs to our common heritage as Christians and remains a prime component within our continuing theological task."[6] Methodism, for example, is unlikely (at least at the moment) to be persuaded that Catholicism's teaching that Jesus offered himself at the Supper to the Father and the apostles by being substantially present twice is the one, necessary interpretation of the Supper, yet it can certainly recognize Catholicism's teaching as a perfectly appropriate one.

When Methodism sees that Catholicism essentially teaches the same doctrine and enacts the same sacramental-sacrificial liturgy, it should recognize in Catholicism a shared eucharistic Christology and a biblically faithful interpretation of the Supper and of Jesus' command to "Do this." It should recognize, in its own words, the role of the eucharist in Catholicism of "summoning people to faith and nurturing them in the knowledge and love of God." It should recognize that both offer the sacrifice of Christ not by repeating the cross, but by repeating the Supper, and it should celebrate the shared soteriology that shapes eucharistic sacrifice. Along with many steps toward Christian unity, Methodism has already committed to interpreting its own Articles and Confessions in light of its ongoing ecumenical engagements.[7] With reference to the eucharist, it states, "Within all discussion of Holy Communion, United Methodism must remain firmly anchored in its traditional sources of authority. We recognize and respect authorities that other church traditions hold dear. United Methodists remain open to greater Christian unity through the work of the Holy Spirit in response to Jesus' prayer that 'they may all be one'" (Jn 17:21).[8] With the hermeneutics of charity

---

6. *THM*, 62, quoting the United Methodist Church, *Book of Discipline* (Nashville: United Methodist Publishing House, 2004).

7. *THM*, 62.

8. *THM*, 62.

that Methodism has adopted in its ecumenical participation, it can offer a formal statement acknowledging that Catholicism's teaching faithfully proclaims the Gospel and imposes no impediment between the two churches.

In light of its contribution to the doctrine of eucharistic sacrifice, Methodism could then invite Catholicism to reciprocate. Is the Catholic doctrine of sacrifice the exclusive interpretation of the Last Supper and the sacrament, or can it recognize Methodism's witness as an alternative, commensurate, and faithful one? If not, what is lacking in Methodism's doctrine of eucharistic sacrifice (which is not, to reiterate, the same as the theology of the Mass)? After all, with only a slight modification to the wording of Trent, Methodists confess, *for the victim is one and the same, the same now offering by the ministry of the church, who then offered himself on the cross, the manner alone of offering being different.* If it can—even partially or reservedly—then a significant ecumenical milestone will be achieved. A bilateral statement, written in Christian love, could be a powerful gesture of the reconciling work of Christ and the unifying work of his Spirit among divided Christians.

Eucharistic Sacrifice: Ecclesial Sacrifice

The doctrine of eucharistic sacrifice necessarily entails a doctrine of the church because it raises the question of who are those members, specifically, and where is that body, visibly, that offers Christ and is offered by him. Catholicism clearly articulates its teaching on these matters, while Methodism continues to do so. For example, it is no accident that immediately after his chapter on the "Mystery of Faith," John Paul II turns to ecclesiology, since ecclesial holiness and unity are inextricably linked. Methodism is well aware that Wesley did not bequeath a rich ecclesiological inheritance to his followers; nonetheless, it recognizes the ecclesiological dimension of the eucharist. "Communing with others in our congregations is a sign of community and mutual love between Christians throughout the church universal. The church must offer to the world a model of genuine community grounded in God's deep love for every person."[9] Catholicism teaches that the eucharist builds the unity of the church, but that it must also express that unity; similarly, United Methodism maintains, "Holy Communion expresses our oneness in the body of Christ, anticipates Jesus' invitation to the feast at the heavenly banquet, and calls us to strive for the visible unity of the church."[10]

---

9. *THM*, 59.

10. *THM*, 59. David Chapman notes the close connection between ecclesiology and soteriology; Chapman, "Methodism and the Future of Ecumenism," in Abraham and Kirby, *Oxford Handbook of Methodist Studies*, 463–64.

In light of the ecumenical movement, Methodists—as a connectional people born in eucharistic zeal—have the resources today to advance an ecclesiology that is more developed than what Wesley bequeathed to his people. As a global church that is joined together by conferences and bishops in communion with one another, Methodism can grow into a stronger and more ancient form of community by recognizing the full work of Christ in the eucharist as the source of the holiness it longs to embody and by ordering itself more intentionally as a communion ecclesiology.[11] Indeed, in *Through Divine Love: The Church in Each Place and All Places* (2005), American Catholics and United Methodists have begun to explore their shared understanding of the church as communion. Moreover, in its 2021 round of talks, the international dialogue took up the topic of reconciliation between Catholics and Methodists. It reaffirmed the long-standing goal of *full communion in faith, mission, and sacramental life* and addressed head on how this unity might be made manifest. With respect to the eucharist, it acknowledges, "Our communion with each other remains imperfect, which motivates us toward further reconciliation."[12]

The crucified Lord who gives himself to the church in the eucharist is the source of the sacrificial love by which the church lives in the world. A sacrificial eucharist forms Christians into a sacrificial body that lives a life of sacrificial discipleship. In relation to missions and justice, Timothy Gaines argues that Wesley's eucharistic theology can redress modernity's fractured moral ontology: "The life of holiness is the life lived by participating in God's triune life, and in the Lord's Supper ethics is rendered intelligible by restoring the divine referent absent in modern ethics and by strengthening an ontology of relationality."[13] What better way than through the eucharist is there for God's people to proclaim the Lord's death until he comes?

11. See the collection of articles in *Ecclesiology* 9, no. 1 (2013): Justus H. Hunter, "Toward A Methodist Communion Ecclesiology" (9–18); Robert K. Martin, "Toward a Wesleyan Sacramental Ecclesiology," (19–38); and Kenneth Wilson, "What Is Distinctive about Methodist Ecclesiology? A Response to Papers by Miriam Haar, Justus Hunter, and Robert Martin," (66–74); and William Abraham's pneumatological communion ecclesiology in "Ecclesiology and Eucharist," in Vickers, *Wesleyan Theology of the Eucharist*, 69–85.

12. World Methodist Council–Roman Catholic Church, *God in Christ Reconciling: On the Way to Full Communion in Faith, Sacraments, and Mission* (2022), 73, http://www.christianunity.va/content/unitacristiani/en/dialoghi/sezione-occidentale/consiglio-metodista-mondiale/dialogo/documenti-di-dialogo/god-in-christ-reconciling—on-the-way-to-full-communion-in-faith.html.

13. Timothy R. Gaines, "Eucharistic Participation: Holiness as the Relational Shape of Christian Moral Theology," *Wesleyan Theological Journal* 49, no. 1 (Spring 2014): 104. See, too, Aaron Kerr's notion of "sacramental justice" in "The Lord's Supper: Food for the Journey; Wesleyan Eucharistic Piety and the Integrated Christian Life," in *Vital Christianity: Spirituality, Justice, and Christian Practice*, ed. David Weaver-Zercher (New York: T. and T. Clark, 2005), 177–87.

Convergence in eucharistic theology does, in fact, build Christian unity, and a recent development in United Methodism's ecumenical engagement exemplifies this position. United Methodism has entered into full communion with the Evangelical Lutheran Church in America, and *This Holy Mystery* was "decisive in the process of reaching the agreement . . . specifically about the 'real presence' of Jesus in the bread and wine used in the sacrament."[14] Doctrinal statements on the eucharist and ecclesial identity are inseparably united.[15] As United Methodism's eucharistic theology has played a key role in its steps toward unity with the ELCA, so Methodism's doctrine of eucharistic sacrifice could do in its dialogue with Catholics. Visible unity and full communion with Catholics will be a longer and more arduous process than with the ELCA, yet both sides should see that each other's doctrine of eucharistic sacrifice is a means to facilitating that end and not, as has heretofore been perceived, a hindrance.

14. Charles Yrigoyen Jr., John G. McEllhenney, and Kenneth E. Rowe, ed., *United Methodism at Forty: Looking Back, Looking Forward* (Nashville: Abingdon, 2008), 86–87.

15. The works of Geoffrey Wainwright and others continue to lay before Methodism the ecumenical challenge of articulating a consistent and complete ecclesiology: Wainwright, "The Sacraments," in *The Oxford Handbook of Methodist Studies*, 344–59; Wainwright, "Responsible Theology and the Ecumenism of Life? The 'Exchange of Ideas' and the 'Exchange of Gifts,'" in *Ökumene des Lebens als Herausforderung der wissenschaftlichen Theologie*, ed. Bernd Jochen Hilberath et al. (Frankfurt am Main: Otto Lembeck, 2008), 187–207; David Chapman, "Koinonia and Connexionalism," *Epworth Review* 26, no. 2 (April 1999): 82–87; Grant Sperry White, "The Recovery of the Great Eucharistic Prayer in the Wesleyan Tradition," in *Orthodox and Wesleyan Scriptural Understanding and Practice*, ed. S. T. Kimbrough Jr. (Crestwood, NY: St. Vladimir's Seminary Press, 2005), 277–92; and the related chapters in Paul D. Murray, ed., *Receptive Ecumenism and the Call to Catholic Learning: Exploring a Way for Contemporary Ecumenism* (New York: Oxford University Press, 2008).

Bibliography

Abraham, William J., and James E. Kirby, eds. *Oxford Handbook of Methodist Studies*. New York: Oxford University Press, 2009.

Alexander, J. Neil. "'With Eloquence in Speech and Song': Anglican Reflections on the Eucharistic Hymns (1745) of John and Charles Wesley." In *With Ever Joyful Hearts*, edited by J. Neil Alexander and Marion J. Hatchett, 244–60. New York: Church Pub., 1999.

Anderson, E. Byron. *The Meaning of Holy Communion in the United Methodist Church*. Nashville: Discipleship Resources, 1996.

———, ed. *Worship Matters: A United Methodist Guide to Ways to Worship*. Vol. 1. Nashville: Discipleship Resources, 1999.

Aquinas, St. Thomas. *The Summa Theologica of St. Thomas Aquinas*. Translated by Fathers of the English Dominican Province. Allen, Tex.: Christian Classics, 1948.

Balthasar, Hans Urs von. "The Holy Church and the Eucharistic Sacrifice." *Communio* 12 (Summer 1985): 139–45.

Benedict XVI. *God Is Near Us: The Eucharist, the Heart of Life*. San Francisco: Ignatius Press, 2003.

———. *Sacramentum Caritatis*. Apostolic Exhortation. February 22, 2007.

Berger, David. *Thomas Aquinas and the Liturgy*. 2nd ed. Naples, FL: Sapientia Press of Ave Maria University, 2005.

Berger, Teresa. *Theology in Hymns? A Study of the Relationship of Doxology and Theology According to a Collection of Hymns for the Use of the People Called Methodists (1780)*. Nashville: Kingswood, 1995.

———. "'Finding Echoes': *The Catechism of the Catholic Church* and the *Hymns on the Lord's Supper*." In *Hymns on the Lord's Supper: 250 Years; Papers Presented at the Sixth Annual Meeting of the Charles Wesley Society, October 1995, the Divinity School, Duke University, Durham, North Carolina*. Charles Wesley Society, 2:63–73. Madison, NJ: Society, Archives and History Center, Drew University, 1996.

Best, Thomas F., Dagmar Heller, and World Council of Churches. *Eucharistic Worship in Ecumenical Contexts: The Lima Liturgy and Beyond*. Geneva: WCC, 1998.

Billington, Raymond J. *The Liturgical Movement and Methodism*. London: Epworth, 1969.

Black, Kathy. "Will *This Holy Mystery* Serve United Methodists Well?" *Quarterly Review* 25, no. 3 (Fall 2005): 304, 308–10.

Blankenship, Paul F. "The Significance of John Wesley's Abridgement of the Thirty-nine Articles as Seen from His Deletions." *Methodist History* 2, no. 3 (April 1964): 35–47.

Blevins, Dean G. "The Trinity and the Means of Grace: A Sacramental Interrelationship." *Wesleyan Theological Journal* 36, no. 1 (Spring 2001): 231–55.

———. "A Wesleyan View of the Liturgical Construction of the Self." *Wesleyan Theological Journal* 38, no. 2 (Fall 2003): 7–29.

Borgen, Ole E. *John Wesley on the Sacraments: A Theological Study.* Nashville: Abingdon, 1972.

———. "No End without the Means: John Wesley and the Sacraments." *Asbury Theological Journal* 46 (1991): 63–85.

Botte, Bernard. *Le canon de la messe romaine.* Louvain: Abbaye du Mont César, 1935.

Bouyer, Louis. *Eucharist: Theology and Spirituality of the Eucharistic Prayer.* Notre Dame, IN: University of Notre Dame Press, 1968.

———. "Cranmer and the Anglican Eucharist." In *Primary Readings on the Eucharist,* ed. Thomas Fisch, 117–28. Collegeville, MN: Liturgical Press, 2004.

Bowmer, John C. *The Sacrament of the Lord's Supper in Early Methodism.* London: Dacre, 1951.

———. "Wesley's Revision of the Communion Service in the Sunday Service of the Methodists." *London Quarterly and Holborn Review* 176 (July 1951): 230–37.

———. "History of Holy Communion in Methodism." *London Quarterly and Holborn Review* 184 (April 1959): 97–102.

———. *The Lord's Supper in Methodism: 1791–1960.* London: Epworth, 1961.

Bugnini, Annibale. *The Reform of the Liturgy, 1948–1975.* Collegeville, MN: Liturgical Press, 1990.

Burgess, Joseph A., and Jeffrey Gros, eds. *Building Unity: Ecumenical Dialogues with Roman Catholic Participation in the United States.* Ecumenical Documents 4. New York: Paulist Press, 1989.

Busby, Jack. "The Lord's Supper: An Alternate Text for American Methodists." *Worship* 49, no. 1 (January 1975): 13–22.

Candler, Peter M. "Liturgically Trained Memory: A Reading of *Summa Theologiae* III.83." *Modern Theology* 20, no. 3 (2004): 423–45.

Carstens, Christopher, and Douglas Martis. *Mystical Body--Mystical Voice: Encountering Christ in the Words of the Mass.* Chicago: Liturgy Training, 2011.

Carter, David. "Methodism and the Eucharist: A Discussion Article." *Epworth Review* 27, no. 2 (April 2000): 61–70.

———. "Can the Roman Catholic and Methodist Churches Be Reconciled?" *Ecumenical Trends* 31, no. 1 (2002): 1–9.

Castelo, Daniel, ed. *Embodying Wesley's Catholic Spirit.* Eugene, OR: Pickwick, 2017.

Cessario, Romanus. *Christian Satisfaction in Aquinas: Towards a Personalist Understanding.* Lanham, MD: University Press of America, 1982.

Chapman, David M. "Koinonia and Connexionalism." *Epworth Review* 26, no. 2 (April 1999): 82–87.

———. *In Search of the Catholic Spirit: Methodists and Roman Catholics in Dialogue.* Peterborough: Epworth, 2004.

———. *Born in Song: Methodist Worship in Britain.* Washington, DC: Church in the Market Place, 2006.

———. "Methodism and the Future of Ecumenism." In *The Oxford Handbook of Methodist Studies*, edited by William J. Abraham and James E. Kirby. New York: Oxford University Press, 2009.

Chardonnens, Denis, OCD. "Éternité du sacerdoce du Christ et effet eschatologique de l'eucharistie." *Revue Thomiste* 99 (1999): 159–80.

Charles Wesley Society. *Hymns on the Lord's Supper by John and Charles Wesley*. First edition facsimile (1745). Introduction by Geoffrey Wainwright. Madison, NJ: Charles Wesley Society, 1995.

———. *Hymns on the Lord's Supper: 250 Years; Papers Presented at the Sixth Annual Meeting of the Charles Wesley Society, October 1995, the Divinity School, Duke University, Durham, North Carolina*. Proceedings of the Charles Wesley Society. Vol. 2. Madison, NJ: Society, Archives and History Center, Drew University, 1997.

Chauvet, Louis-Marie. *Symbol and Sacrament: A Sacramental Reinterpretation of Christian Existence*. Translated by Patrick Madigan and Madeleine Beaumont. Collegeville, MN: Liturgical Press, 1995.

Chilcote, Paul W. *A Faith That Sings: Biblical Themes in the Lyrical Theology of Charles Wesley*. Eugene, OR: Cascade, 2016.

Clark, Francis. *Eucharistic Sacrifice and the Reformation*. 2nd ed. Oxford: Blackwell, 1967.

Clay, Arnold. *What Is the Lord's Supper?* London: Epworth, 1979.

Clutterbuck, Richard. "The Presbyter as President: Presidency at the Eucharist as the Defining Paradigm of Presbyteral Ministry." In *What Is a Minister?*, edited by Philip Luscombe and Esther Shreeve, 80–90. Peterborough: Epworth, 2002.

Collins, James B. *The Mass as Sacrifice: Theological Reflections on the Sacrificial Elements of the Mass*. Staten Island, NY: St. Pauls, 2008.

Collins, Kenneth J. "John Wesley and the Means of Grace." *Drew Gateway* 56, no. 3 (1986): 26–33.

———. *The Theology of John Wesley: Holy Love and the Shape of Grace*. Nashville: Abingdon, 2007.

Cracknell, Kenneth, and Susan J. White. *An Introduction to World Methodism*. New York: Cambridge University Press, 2005.

Crain, Margaret Ann. "Who Should be Allowed to Preside at the Eucharist?" *Quarterly Review* 23, no. 3 (Fall 2003): 302, 306–8.

Cruickshank, Joanna. "'Appear as Crucified for Me': Sight, Suffering, and Spiritual Transformation in the Hymns of Charles Wesley." *Journal of Religious History* 30, no. 3 (2006): 311–30.

Cuming, G. J. *A History of Anglican Liturgy*. 2nd ed. London: Macmillan, 1982.

Cummings, Owen F. "John Wesley and Eucharistic Ecclesiology." *One in Christ* 35, no. 2 (1999): 143–51.

———. *Eucharistic Doctors: A Theological History*. Mahwah, NJ: Paulist Press, 2005.

Daly, Robert J., SJ. *Sacrifice Unveiled: The True Meaning of Christian Sacrifice*. New York: T&T Clark, 2009.

Davies, Horton, ed. *Bread of Life and Cup of Joy: Newer Ecumenical Perspectives on the Eucharist.* Grand Rapids, MI: Eerdmans, 1993.

De la Soujeoule, Benoît-Dominique. "The Importance of the Definition of Sacraments as Signs." In *Ressourcement Thomism: Sacred Doctrine, the Sacraments, and the Moral Life: Essays in Honor of Romanus Cessario,* edited by Reinhard Huetter and Matthew Levering, 127–35. Washington, DC: The Catholic University of America Press, 2010.

Deschner, John, Günther Gassmann, and World Council of Churches Commission on Faith and Order. *Baptism, Eucharist and Ministry 1982–1990: Report on the Process and Responses.* Faith and Order Paper No. 149. Geneva: WCC, 1990.

Detscher, Alan. "The Eucharistic Prayers of the Roman Catholic Church." In *New Eucharistic Prayers: An Ecumenical Study of Their Development and Structure,* edited by Frank C. Senn, 15–52. New York: Paulist Press, 1987.

Dix, Gregory. *The Shape of the Liturgy.* Westminster: Dacre, 1945.

Dixon, Neil. *Wonder, Love, and Praise: A Companion to the Methodist Worship Book.* Peterborough: Epworth, 2003.

Dulles, Avery. "The Eucharist as Sacrifice." In *Rediscovering the Eucharist: Ecumenical Conversations,* edited by Roch A. Kereszty, 175–87. New York: Paulist Press, 2003.

Emery, Gilles. *Trinity, Church, and the Human Person: Thomistic Essays.* Naples, FL: Sapientia Press of Ave Maria University, 2007.

Fagerberg, David. "Divine Liturgy, Divine Love: Toward a New Understanding of Sacrifice in Christian Worship." In *Letter and Spirit: The Hermeneutic of Continuity; Christ, Kingdom, and Creation,* edited by Scott Hahn, 3:95–113. Steubenville, OH: St. Paul Center for Biblical Theology, 2007.

Fahey, Michael A., and Catholic Theological Society of America. *Catholic Perspectives on Baptism, Eucharist and Ministry.* Lanham, MD: University Press of America, 1986.

Felton, Gayle Carlton. *This Holy Mystery: A United Methodist Understanding of Holy Communion.* Nashville: Discipleship Resources, 2005.

————. *United Methodists and the Sacraments.* Nashville: Abingdon, 2007.

Filip, Stepan Martin. "*Imago Repræsentativa Passionis Christi*: St. Thomas Aquinas on the Essence of the Sacrifice of the Mass." *Nova et Vetera* 7, no 2 (2009): 405–37.

Foley, Edward, Nathan Mitchell, Joanne M. Pierce, Catholic Academy of Liturgy, and Federation of Diocesan Liturgical Commissions. *A Commentary on the General Instruction of the Roman Missal: Developed under the Auspices of the Catholic Academy of Liturgy and Cosponsored by the Federation of Diocesan Liturgical Commissions.* Collegeville, MN: Liturgical Press, 2007.

————, ed. *A Commentary on the Order of the Mass of "The Roman Missal."* Collegeville, MN: Liturgical Press, 2011.

Frank, Thomas. *Polity, Practice, and the Mission of the United Methodist Church.* Nashville: Abingdon, 1997.

Gaines, Timothy R. "Eucharistic Participation: Holiness as the Relational Shape of Christian Moral Theology." *Wesleyan Theological Journal* 49, no. 1 (2014): 93–106.

Gavrilyuk, Paul L., Douglas M. Koskela, and Jason E. Vickers, eds. *Immersed in the Life of God: The Healing Resources of the Christian Faith; Essays in Honor of William J. Abraham.* Grand Rapids, MI: Eerdmans, 2008.

Gelardini, Gabriella. *Hebrews: Contemporary Methods, New Insights.* Biblical Interpretation Series 75. Boston: Brill, 2005.

George, A. Raymond. "The Theology of Worship." *London Quarterly and Holborn Review* 186 (April 1961): 135–36.

———. "The Revision of the Communion Service." *London Quarterly and Holborn Review* 187 (April 1962): 110–16.

———. "'Faith and Order' Work on Worship." *London Quarterly and Holborn Review* 188 (July 1963): 210–15.

———. "The Eucharist in Relation to the Total Worship of the Church." *London Quarterly and Holborn Review* 189 (July 1964): 217–23.

———. "The Lord's Supper." In *The Doctrine of the Church*, edited by Dow Kirkpatrick, 140–60. New York: Abingdon, 1964.

———. "The Sunday Service of the Methodists." In *Communio Sanctorum*, edited by Yves Congar et al., 194–203. Geneva: Labor et Fides, 1982.

———. "The Sunday Service 1784." *Friends of Wesley Chapel Annual Lecture* 2 (1983): 1–9.

———. "Methodist Statements." In *Foundation Documents of the Faith*, edited by Cyril S. Rodd, 99–110. Edinburgh: T&T Clark, 1987.

———. *Memoirs: Methodist and Ecumenical.* Edited by Geoffrey Wainwright. Buxton: Church in the Marketplace, 2003.

Gondreau, Paul. "The Humanity of Christ, the Incarnate Word." In *The Theology of Thomas Aquinas*, edited by Rik Van Nieuwenhove and Joseph Wawrykow, 252–76. Notre Dame, IN: University of Notre Dame Press, 2005.

Gordon, James G. "'Impassive He Suffers; Immortal He Dies': Rhetoric and Polemic in Charles Wesley's Portrayal of the Atonement." *Scottish Bulletin of Evangelical Theology* 18, no. 1 (2000): 56–70.

Harmon, Nolan. *The Rites and Rituals of Episcopal Methodism.* Nashville: Lamar and Barton, 1926.

Harmon, Nolan B., and John W. Bardsley. "John Wesley and the Articles of Religion." *Religion in Life* 22, no. 2 (Spring 1953): 280–91.

Harnish, John E. "Who Should Be Allowed to Preside at the Eucharist?" *Quarterly Review* 23, no. 3 (Fall 2003): 302–5.

Hart, David Bentley. *The Beauty of the Infinite: The Aesthetics of Christian Truth.* Grand Rapids, MI: Eerdmans, 2003.

Healy, Nicholas M. *Thomas Aquinas: Theologian of the Christian Life.* Great Theologians Series. Burlington, VT: Ashgate, 2003.

Heron, Alasdair I. C. *Table and Tradition: Towards an Ecumenical Understanding of the Eucharist.* Edinburgh: Handsel, 1983.

Hickman, Hoyt L. *Workbook on Communion and Baptism*. Nashville: Discipleship Resources, 1990.

———. "Worship Revision in the United Methodist Church." In *The Changing Face of Jewish and Christian Worship in North America*, edited by Paul F. Bradshaw and Lawrence A. Hoffman, 112–24. Notre Dame, IN: University of Notre Dame Press, 1991.

———. "The Theology of the Lord's Supper in the New United Methodist Ritual." *Quarterly Review* 17, no. 4 (1997–98): 361–76.

———, ed. *Worship Resources of the United Methodist Hymnal*. Nashville: Abingdon, 1989.

Hickman, Hoyt L., Don E. Saliers, Laurence H. Stookey, and James F. White, eds. *The New Handbook of the Christian Year*. Nashville: Abingdon, 1992.

Hildebrandt, Franz. *I Offered Christ: A Protestant Study of the Mass*. Philadelphia: Fortress, 1967.

Hillerbrand, Hans Joachim. *The Oxford Encyclopedia of the Reformation*. 4 vols. New York: Oxford University Press, 1996.

Hoskins, Steven T. "Eucharist and Eschatology in the Writings of the Wesleys." *Wesleyan Theological Journal* 29 (1994): 64–80.

Humbrecht, Thierry-Dominique. "L'eucharistie, 'représentation' du sacrifice du Christ, selon saint Thomas." *Revue Thomiste* 98 (Juillet–Septembre 1998): 355–86.

Hunter, Justus H. "Toward A Methodist Communion Ecclesiology." *Ecclesiology* 9, no. 1 (2013): 9–18.

Hütter, Reinhard. *Aquinas on Transubstantiation: The Real Presence of Christ in the Eucharist*. Washington, DC: The Catholic University of America Press, 2019.

Jasper, Ronald C. D., and G. J. Cuming. *Prayers of the Eucharist: Early and Reformed*. 3rd ed. Collegeville, MN: Liturgical Press, 1992.

Jenson, Robert W., and Carl E. Braaten, eds. *The Ecumenical Future: Background Papers for in One Body through the Cross; The Princeton Proposal for Christian Unity*. Grand Rapids, MI: Eerdmans, 2004.

Jeremias, Joachim. *The Eucharistic Words of Jesus*. New York: Scribner, 1966.

John Paul II. *Ecclesia de Eucharistia*. Encyclical Letter. April 17, 2003.

Johnson, Luke Timothy. *Hebrews: A Commentary*. 1st ed. Louisville: Westminster John Knox Press, 2006.

Johnson, Susanne. "John Wesley on the Duty of Constant Communion: The Eucharist as a Means of Grace for Today." In *Wesleyan Spirituality in Contemporary Theological Education*, edited by Hal Knight, Paul W. Jones, and Roberta C. Bondi, 25–46. Nashville: Division of Ordained Ministry UMC, 1987.

Jones, Scott J. *United Methodist Doctrine: The Extreme Center*. Nashville: Abingdon, 2002.

Journet, Charles. *The Mass: The Presence of the Sacrifice of the Cross*. Translated from the 1958 edition by Victor Szczurek. South Bend, IN: St. Augustine's Press, 2008.

Jungmann, Josef A. *The Mass of the Roman Rite: Its Origin and Development (Missarum Sollemnia)*. New York: Benziger, 1951.

———. *The Eucharistic Prayer*. Rev. ed. Wheathampstead: A. Clarke, 1978.

Kelly, Gerard. "Eucharistic Sacrifice in the Council of Trent." *Irish Theological Quarterly* 51, no. 4 (1985): 268–88.

Kelly, Joseph F. *The Ecumenical Councils of the Catholic Church: A History*. Collegeville, MN: Liturgical Press, 2009.

Kemper, Jeffrey Michael. "Behind the Text: A Study of the Principles and Procedures of Translation, Adaptation, and Composition of Original Texts by the International Commission on English in the Liturgy." Ph.D. diss., University of Notre Dame, 1992.

Kereszty, Roch A. *Rediscovering the Eucharist: Ecumenical Conversations*. New York: Paulist Press, 2003.

Kerr, Aaron. "The Lord's Supper: Food for the Journey; Wesleyan Eucharistic Piety and the Integrated Christian Life." In *Vital Christianity: Spirituality, Justice, and Christian Practice*, edited by David Weaver-Zercher, 177–87. New York: T&T Clark, 2005.

Khoo, Lorna. *Wesleyan Eucharistic Spirituality: Its Nature, Sources, and Future*. Adelaide: AFT, 2005.

Kilmartin, Edward J., SJ. *The Eucharist in the West: History and Theology*. Edited by Robert J. Daly, SJ. Collegeville, MN: Liturgical Press, 1998.

Knickerbocker, Waldo E., Jr. "Arminian Anglicanism and John and Charles Wesley." *Memphis Theological Seminary Journal* 29, no. 3 (1991): 79–97.

Landini, Lawrence C. "The Role of Self-Offering in the Understanding of the Eucharist as Sacrifice." *Josephinum Journal of Theology* 1 (1994): 17–25.

Le Bruyns, Clint. "*Ecclesia de Eucharistia*: On Its Ecumenical Import." *Ecumenical Trends* 32, no. 8 (2003): 120–25.

Leo XIII. *Mirae Caritatis*. Encyclical Letter. May 28, 1902.

Levering, Matthew Webb. "Aquinas on the Liturgy of the Eucharist." In *Aquinas on Doctrine: A Critical Introduction*, edited by Thomas Weinandy, Daniel Keating, and John Yocum, 183–97. New York: T&T Clark, 2004.

———. "John Paul II and Aquinas on the Eucharist." *Nova et Vetera* 3, no. 3 (2005): 637–60.

———. *Sacrifice and Community: Jewish Offering and Christian Eucharist*. Illuminations, Theory and Religion. Malden, MA: Blackwell, 2005.

Lindbeck, George A. "Augsburg and the *Ecclesia de Eucharistia*." *Pro Ecclesia* 12, no. 4 (2003): 405–14.

Lockett, George H. "The Methodist Tradition of Worship." In *In Church: An Introduction to Worship and Preaching*, edited by John Stacey, 51–66. London: Epworth, 1971.

Looney, Thomas P. "Ecumenical 'Lights' and 'Shadows' in *Ecclesia de Eucharistia*." *Ecumenical Trends* 32, no. 7 (2003): 97–108.

Loyer, Kenneth M. *Holy Communion: Celebrating God with Us*. Nashville: Abingdon, 2014.

Maddox, Randy L. *Responsible Grace: John Wesley's Practical Theology*. Nashville: Kingswood, 1994.

⸻. "Social Grace: The Eclipse of the Church as a Means of Grace in American Methodism." In *Methodism in Its Cultural Milieu*, edited by Tim MacQuiban, 131–60. Oxford: Applied Theology Press, 1994.

⸻. "Reclaiming an Inheritance: Wesley as Theologian in the History of Methodist Theology." In *Rethinking Wesley's Theology for Contemporary Methodism*, edited by Randy L. Maddox and Theodore Runyon, 213–26. Nashville: Kingswood, 1998.

⸻. "Respected Founder/Neglected Guide: The Role of Wesley in American Methodist Theology." *Methodist History* 37, no. 2 (January 1999): 71–88.

⸻. "A Change of Affections: The Development, Dynamics, and Dethronement of John Wesley's 'Heart Religion.'" In *"Heart Religion" in the Methodist Tradition and Related Movements*, edited by Richard Steele, 3–31. Metuchen, NJ: Scarecrow, 2001.

Mansini, Guy. "Representation and Agency in the Eucharist." *Thomist* 62 (1998): 499–517.

Marshall, Bruce D. "The Whole Mystery of Our Salvation: Saint Thomas Aquinas on the Eucharist as Sacrifice." In *Rediscovering Aquinas and the Sacraments: Studies in Sacramental Theology*, ed. Matthew Levering and Michael Dauphinais, 39–64. Chicago: Hillenbrand, 2009.

Marshall, Romey P., and Michael J. Taylor, SJ. *Liturgy and Christian Unity*. Englewood Cliffs, NJ: Prentice-Hall, 1965.

Martin, Robert K. "Toward a Wesleyan Sacramental Ecclesiology." *Ecclesiology* 9, no. 1 (2013): 19–38.

Martos, Joseph. *Deconstructing Sacramental Theology and Reconstructing Catholic Ritual*. Eugene, OR: Resource, 2015.

Mazza, Enrico. *The Eucharistic Prayers of the Roman Rite*. New York: Pueblo, 1986.

⸻. *The Celebration of the Eucharist: The Origin of the Rite and the Development of Its Interpretation*. Collegeville, MN: Liturgical Press, 1999.

McAdoo, Henry R. "A Theology of the Eucharist: Brevint and the Wesleys." *Theology* 97 (1994): 245–56.

McAdoo, Henry R., and Kenneth Stevenson. *The Mystery of the Eucharist in the Anglican Tradition*. Norwich: Canterbury, 1995.

McDonald, William. "Will *This Holy Mystery* Serve United Methodists Well?" *Quarterly Review* 25, no. 3 (Fall 2005): 304–7.

McDonald, William, and Kathy Black. "Will *This Holy Mystery* Serve United Methodists Well?" *Quarterly Review* 25, no. 3 (Fall 2005): 304–10.

McKenna, John H. "Eucharist and Sacrifice: An Overview." *Worship* 76, no. 5 (2002): 386–402.

Methodist Church. *The Methodist Service Book*. London: Methodist Publishing House, 1975.

⸻. *Hymns and Psalms*. London: Methodist Publishing House, 1983.

⸻. *The Methodist Worship Book*. Peterborough: Methodist Publishing House, 1999.

———. "His Presence Makes the Feast." Accessed Feb. 10, 2011. http://www.methodist.org.uk/static/news/papers/holy_communion03.htm.

———. *Singing the Faith*. London: Hymns Ancient and Modern. 2011.

———. "Called to Love and Praise (1999): The Nature of the Christian Church in Methodist Experience and Practice." Accessed Dec. 17, 2021. https://www.methodist.org.uk/media/1993/fo-statement-called-to-love-and-praise-1999.pdf.

———. "Additional Orders of Holy Communion." Accessed Nov. 30, 2023. https://www.methodist.org.uk/media/27855/additional-holy-communion-20221215.pdf.

Meyer, Harding, and Lukas Vischer, eds. *Growth in Agreement: Reports and Agreed Statements of Ecumenical Conversations on a World Level.* 2 Vols. Geneva: World Council of Churches, 1984.

Moore, Geoffrey C. "Eucharistic Piety in American Methodist Hymnody (1786–1889)." In *Music and the Wesleys*, edited by Nicholas Temperley and Stephen Banfield, 88–102. Urbana: University of Illinois Press, 2010.

Morrisey, Francis G., and Michel Thériault. *Papal and Curial Pronouncements: Their Canonical Significance in Light of the Code of Canon Law.* 2nd ed. Ottawa: Faculty of Canon Law, Saint Paul University, 2001.

Murray, Paul D., ed. *Receptive Ecumenism and the Call to Catholic Learning: Exploring a Way for Contemporary Ecumenism.* New York: Oxford University Press, 2008.

National Conference of Catholic Bishops. *The New Eucharistic Prayers and Prefaces.* Washington, DC: Bishops' Committee on the Liturgy, 1968.

Nelson, J. Robert. "Methodist Eucharistic Usage: From Constant Communion to Benign Neglect to Sacramental Recovery." *Journal of Ecumenical Studies* 13, no. 2 (Spring 1976): 278–84.

———. "What Methodists Think of Eucharistic Theology." *Worship* 52, no. 5 (Spring 1978): 409–24.

———. "Eucharist, Ecumenism, Methodism." In *Wesleyan Theology Today*, edited by Theodore Runyon, 313–22. Nashville: United Methodist Publishing House, 1985.

Nichols, Aidan. *The Holy Eucharist: From the New Testament to John Paul II.* Dublin: Veritas, 1991.

———. "The Holy Oblation: On the Primacy of Eucharistic Sacrifice." *Downside Review* 122, no. 429 (2004): 259–72.

Nichols, Kathryn. "Charles Wesley's Eucharistic Hymns: Their Relationship to the Book of Common Prayer." *Hymn* 39 (1988): 13–21.

———. "The Theology of Christ's Sacrifice and Presence in Charles Wesley's Hymns on the Lord's Supper." *Hymn* 39 (1988): 19–29.

O'Donnell, Michael J. *Lift Up Your Hearts: Revised and Expanded; Eucharistic Prayers Based on the Revised Common Lectionary, Year A.* Akron, OH: Order of Saint Luke, 1999.

Olin, John C. *Catholic Reform: From Cardinal Ximenes to the Council of Trent, 1495–1563.* New York: Fordham University Press, 1990.

O'Malley, John W. *Trent: What Happened at the Council*. Cambridge, MA: Harvard University Press, 2013.

O'Meara, Thomas F. *Thomas Aquinas, Theologian*. Notre Dame, IN: University of Notre Dame Press, 1997.

O'Neill, Colman. *Sacramental Realism: A General Theory of the Sacraments*. Chicago: Midwest Theological Forum, 1998.

Outler, Albert. "Olive Branch to the Romans, 1970's-Style: United Methodist Initiative, Roman Catholic Response." *Methodist History* 13, no. 2 (January 1975): 52–56.

Paul VI. *Mysterium Fidei*. Encyclical Letter. September 3, 1965.

Peiffer, Robert B. "How Contemporary Liturgies Evolve: The Revision of United Methodist Liturgical Texts (1968–1988)." Ph.D. diss., University of Notre Dame, 1992.

Pickstock, Catherine. *After Writing: On the Liturgical Consummation of Philosophy*. Challenges in Contemporary Theology. Malden, MA: Blackwell, 1998.

———. "Thomas Aquinas and the Quest for the Eucharist." *Modern Theology* 15, no. 2 (1999): 159–80.

Pius XII. *Mediator Dei*. Encyclical Letter. November 20, 1947.

Power, David N. *The Sacrifice We Offer: The Tridentine Dogma and Its Reinterpretation*. New York: Crossroad, 1987.

———. *The Eucharistic Mystery: Revitalizing the Tradition*. New York: Crossroad, 1992.

Rahner, Karl, and Angelus Häussling. *The Celebration of the Eucharist*. Translated by W. J. O'Hara. Montreal: Palm, 1966.

Rattenbury, J. Ernest. *The Eucharistic Hymns of John and Charles Wesley: To Which Is Appended Wesley's Preface Extracted from Brevint's Christian Sacrament and Sacrifice Together with Hymns on the Lord's Supper*. London: Epworth, 1948.

———. *The Evangelical Doctrines of Charles Wesley's Hymns*. 3rd ed. London: Epworth, 1954.

———. *Thoughts on Holy Communion*. London: Epworth, 1958.

Remy, Gérard. "Le Christ médiateur dans l'oeuvre de Saint Thomas D'aquin." *Revue Thomiste* 93 (1993): 183–233.

Reumann, John Henry Paul. *The Supper of the Lord: The New Testament, Ecumenical Dialogues, and Faith and Order on Eucharist*. Philadelphia: Fortress, 1985.

Runyon, Theodore. *The New Creation: John Wesley's Theology Today*. Nashville: Abingdon, 1998.

Ruth, Lester. *A Little Heaven Below: Worship at Early Methodist Quarterly Meetings*. Nashville: Kingswood, 2000.

———. "Word and Table: A Wesleyan Model for Balanced Worship." In *The Wesleyan Tradition: A Paradigm for Renewal*, edited by Paul W. Chilcote, 136–47. Nashville: Abingdon, 2002.

Saliers, Don E. *Worship and Spirituality*. 1st ed. Philadelphia: Westminster Press, 1984.

————. "'Taste and See': Sacramental Renewal Among United Methodists." In *The Eucharist in a United Methodist Perspective*, edited by Hendrik R. Pieterse, 9–19. Nashville: UMC, General Board of Higher Education and Ministry, 2007.

Sanders, Paul S. "The Sacraments in Early American Methodism." *Church History* 27 (1957): 355–71.

————. "Wesley's Eucharistic Faith and Practice." *Anglican Theological Review* 48, no. 2 (1966): 157–74.

Schenk, Richard. "'Verum sacrificium' as the Fullness and Limit of Sacrifice in the Sacramental Theology of Thomas Aquinas: Historical Context and Current Significance." In *Ressourcement Thomism: Sacred Doctrine, the Sacraments, and the Moral Life; Essays in Honor of Romanus Cessario*, edited by Reinhard Huetter and Matthew Levering, 169–207. Washington, DC: The Catholic University of America Press, 2010.

Schönborn, Christoph von, and Hubert Philipp Weber. *The Source of Life: Exploring the Mystery of the Eucharist*. New York: Crossroad, 2007.

Schroeder, H. J. *Canons and Decrees of the Council of Trent: Original Text with English Translation*. St. Louis: B. Herder, 1941.

Seasoltz, R. Kevin, ed. *Living Bread, Saving Cup: Readings on the Eucharist*. Collegeville, MN: Liturgical Press, 1982.

————. "Another Look at Sacrifice." *Worship* 74, no. 5 (2000): 386–413.

Selleck, J. Brian. "The Book of Common Prayer in the Theology of John Wesley." Ph.D. diss., Drew University, 1983.

Senn, Frank C., ed. *New Eucharistic Prayers: An Ecumenical Study of Their Development and Structure*. New York: Paulist Press, 1987.

Second Vatican Council. *Lumen gentium: The Dogmatic Constitution on the Church*. 1964.

Sheets, Herchel H. *Our Sacraments: A United Methodist View of Baptism and Communion*. Nashville: Discipleship Resources, 1996.

Sheppard, Lancelot C., ed. *The New Liturgy*. London: Darton, Longman and Todd, 1970.

Soubigou, Louis. *A Commentary on the Prefaces and the Eucharistic Prayers of the Roman Missal*. Collegeville, MN: Liturgical Press, 1971.

Stamm, Mark W. *Sacraments and Discipleship: Understanding Baptism and the Lord's Supper in a United Methodist Context*. Nashville: Discipleship Resources, 1989.

————. *Let Every Soul Be Jesus' Guest: A Theology of the Open Table*. Nashville: Abingdon, 2006.

Staples, Rob L. *Outward Sign and Inward Grace: The Place of Sacraments in Wesleyan Spirituality*. Kansas City: Beacon Hill Press of Kansas City, 1991.

Stevenson, Kenneth W. "Eucharistic Sacrifice—an Insoluble Liturgical Problem." *Scottish Journal of Theology* 42 no. 4 (1989): 469–92.

Stevenson, Kenneth W., and Richard Holloway. *Covenant of Grace Renewed: A Vision of the Eucharist in the Seventeenth Century*. London: Darton, Longman and Todd, 1994.

Stevick, Daniel B. *The Altar's Fire: Charles Wesley's Hymns on the Lord's Supper, 1745 Introduction and Exposition*. Peterborough: Epworth, 2004.

Stoffer, Dale R., ed. *The Lord's Supper: Believers Church Perspectives*. Scottdale, PA: Herald, 1997.

Stookey, Laurence H. *Eucharist: Christ's Feast with the Church*. Nashville: Abingdon, 1993.

————. "Worship from the United Methodist [USA] Perspective." In *Worship Today*, edited by Thomas F. Best and Dagmar Heller, 101–8. Geneva: World Council of Churches, 2004.

Sweeden, Joshua R. "Ordinary Practice as Ecclesial Holiness: Intersections of Work, Sacrament, and Liturgy." *Wesleyan Theological Journal* 49, no. 1 (Spring 2014): 78–92.

Thurian, Max. *L'Eucharistie: Mémorial du Seigneur, sacrifice d'action de grâce et d'intercession*. Neuchatel: Delachaux et Niestlé, 1959.

————, ed. *Churches Respond to BEM*. Geneva: World Council of Churches, 1986.

Thurian, Max, and World Council of Churches Commission on Faith and Order. *Ecumenical Perspectives on Baptism, Eucharist and Ministry*. Faith and Order Paper No. 116. Geneva: World Council of Churches, 1983.

Thurian, Max, and Geoffrey Wainwright. *Baptism and Eucharist: Ecumenical Convergence in Celebration*. Faith and Order Paper No. 117. Geneva: World Council of Churches, 1983.

Tillard, Jean M. R. "Vocabulaire sacrificiel et Eucharistie." *Irénikon* 53, no. 2 (1980): 145–74.

Torrell, Jean-Pierre. *Saint Thomas Aquinas*. Vol. 1, *The Person and His Work*. Washington, DC: The Catholic University of America Press, 1996.

————. *Saint Thomas D'aquin, maître spirituel: Initiation 2*. Editions Universitaires. Paris: Cerf, 1996.

————. *Aquinas's Summa: Background, Structure, and Reception*. 1st ed. Washington, DC: The Catholic University of America Press, 2005.

————. *Nouvelles recherches thomasiennes*. Paris: J. Vrin, 2008.

Tyson, John R. "Charles Wesley's Theology of Redemption: A Study in Structure and Method." *Wesleyan Theological Journal* 20, no. 2 (1985): 7–28.

————. "The Lord's Supper in the Wesleyan Tradition." In *Basic United Methodist Beliefs: An Evangelical View*, edited by James V. Heidinger II, 80–89. Wilmore, KY: Good News, 1986.

————. "Charles Wesley and the Language of Evangelical Experience: The Poetical Hermeneutic Revisited." *Asbury Journal* 61 no. 1 (2006): 25–46.

United Methodist Church. *At the Lord's Table: A Communion Service Book for Use by the Minister*. Nashville: Abingdon, 1981.

————. *Holy Communion: A Service Book for Use by the Minister*. Nashville: Abingdon, 1987.

————. *Companion to the Book of Services: Introduction, Commentary, and Instructions for Using the New United Methodist Services*. Supplemental Worship Resources 17. Nashville: Abingdon, 1988.

————. *The United Methodist Hymnal*. Nashville: United Methodist Publishing House, 1989.

———. *The Faith We Sing*. Nashville: Abingdon, 2000.

———. *The Book of Discipline*. Nashville: United Methodist Publishing House, 2016.

United Methodist Church–United States Conference of Catholic Bishops. *Eucharistic Celebration: Converging Theology—Divergent Practice* [United Methodist-Roman Catholic Dialogue, 1981]. In *Building Unity: Ecumenical Dialogues with Roman Catholic Participation in the United States*. Ecumenical Documents 4, edited by Joseph A. Burgess and Jeffrey Gros. New York: Paulist Press, 1989.

———. *Yearning to Be One: Spiritual Dialogue between Catholics and United Methodists*. Nashville: Discipleship Resources, 2000.

———. *Thirty Years of Mission and Witness*. Washington, DC: United States Catholic Conference, 2001.

———. *Through Divine Love: The Church in Each Place and All Places* (2005). https://www.usccb.org/resources/Through-Divine-Love-the-Church-in-Each-Place-and-All-Places.pdf.

———. *Heaven and Earth are Full of Your Glory: A United Methodist and Roman Catholic Statement on the Eucharist and Ecology* (2012). https://www.usccb.org/beliefs-and-teachings/ecumenical-and-interreligious/ecumenical/methodist/upload/Heaven-and-Earth-are-Full-of-Your-Glory-Methodist-Catholic-Dialogue-Agreed-Statement-Round-Seven.pdf.

United States Conference of Catholic Bishops. *General Instruction of the Roman Missal*. Accessed April 7, 2023. https://www.usccb.org/prayer-and-worship/the-mass/general-instruction-of-the-roman-missal.

Vagaggini, Cipriano. *The Canon of the Mass and Liturgical Reform*. Staten Island, NY: Alba House, 1967.

———. *The Flesh: Instrument of Salvation; A Theology of the Human Body*. Staten Island, NY: Society of St. Paul, 1969.

———. *Theological Dimensions of the Liturgy: A General Treatise on the Theology of the Liturgy*. Translated by L. J. Doyle and W. A. Jurgens. 4th ed. Collegeville, MN: Liturgical Press, 1976.

Vanhoye, Albert. *Old Testament Priests and the New Priest: According to the New Testament*. Studies in Scripture. Petersham: St. Bede's, 1986.

Van Nieuwenhove, Rik. "Bearing the Marks of Christ's Passion: Aquinas' Soteriology." In *The Theology of Thomas Aquinas*, edited by Rik Van Nieuwenhove and Joseph Wawrykow, 277–302. Notre Dame, IN: University of Notre Dame Press, 2005.

Van Nieuwenhove, Rik, and Joseph Peter Wawrykow, eds. *The Theology of Thomas Aquinas*. Notre Dame, IN: University of Notre Dame Press, 2005.

Vickers, Jason E., ed. *A Wesleyan Theology of the Eucharist: The Presence of God for Christian Life and Ministry*. Nashville: General Board of Higher Education and Ministry, 2016.

Vonier, Anscar, OSB. *A Key to the Doctrine of the Eucharist*. Westminster, MD: Newman Press, 1951.

Wainwright, Geoffrey. *Eucharist and Eschatology*. London: Epworth, 1971.

————. *Doxology: The Praise of God in Worship, Doctrine, and Life; A Systematic Theology*. New York: Oxford University Press, 1980.

————. *Baptism, Eucharist and Ministry: A Liturgical Appraisal of the Lima Text*. Rotterdam: Liturgical Ecumenical Ctr Trust, 1986.

————. "The Lima Text in the History of Faith and Order." *Studia liturgica* 16, no. 1–2 (1986): 6–21.

————. "Word and Sacrament in the Churches' Responses to the Lima Text." *One in Christ* 24, no. 4 (1988): 304–27.

————. "The Eucharist in the Churches' Responses to the Lima Text." *One in Christ* 25, no. 1 (1989): 53–74.

————. "The Roman Catholic Response to Baptism, Eucharist and Ministry: The Ecclesiological Dimension." In *A Promise of Presence*, edited by David Noel Power, Michael Downey, and Richard N. Fragomeni, 187–206. Washington, DC: Pastoral Press, 1992.

————. *Methodists in Dialogue*. Nashville: Kingswood, 1995.

————. "Methodism through the Lens of Lima." In *Sunday Service of the Methodists*, edited by Karen B. Westerfield Tucker, 305–22. Nashville: Kingswood, 1996.

————. "'Our Elder Brethren Join': The Wesleys' *Hymns on the Lord's Supper* and the Patristic Revival in England." In *Worship in Eighteenth-Century Anglicanism and Methodism: Papers presented at the Fifth Annual Meeting of the Charles Wesley Society, October, 1994, Princeton, New Jersey*. Charles Wesley Society, 1:5–31. Madison, NJ: Society, Archives and History Center, Drew University, 1996.

————. *Worship with One Accord: Where Liturgy and Ecumenism Embrace*. New York: Oxford University Press, 1997.

————. "The Ecumenical Rediscovery of the Trinity." *One in Christ* 34, no. 2 (1998): 95–124.

————. "Wesley's Trinitarian Hermeneutics." *Wesleyan Theological Journal* 36, no. 1 (2001): 7–30.

————. "*Ecclesia de Eucharistia vivit*: An Ecumenical Reading." *Ecumenical Trends* 33, no. 9 (October 2004): 1–9.

————. "Presiding at the Lord's Table." *Sacramental Life* 17, no. 1 (Winter 2004–5): 27–36.

————. "The Ecumenical Scope of Methodist Liturgical Revision." In *Liturgical Renewal as a Way to Christian Unity*, edited by James F. Puglisi and Horace T. Allen, 35–59. Collegeville, MN: Liturgical Press, 2005.

————. "Any Advance On '*BEM*'? The Lima Text at Twenty-Five." *Studia liturgica* 37, no. 1 (2007): 1–29.

————. "Responsible Theology and the Ecumenism of Life? The 'Exchange of Ideas' and the 'Exchange of Gifts.'" In *Ökumene des Lebens als Herausforderung der wissenschaftlichen Theologie*, edited by Bernd Jochen Hilberath et al., 187–207. Frankfurt am Main: Otto Lembeck, 2008.

————. "Word and Table: Fifty Years of Eucharistic Revisions Among English-Speaking Protestant Churches." *Archiv für Liturgiewissenschaft* 50 (2008): 332–55.

————. "The Healing Work of the Liturgy." In *Immersed in the Life of God: The Healing Resources of the Christian Faith; Essays in Honor of William J. Abraham*, edited by Paul Gavrilyuk, Douglas Koskela, and Jason Vickers, 63–85. Grand Rapids, MI: Eerdmans, 2008.

————. "An Ecclesiological Journey: The Way of Methodist–Roman Catholic International Dialogue." *Ecclesiology* 7 (2011): 50–70

Wainwright, Geoffrey, and Karen B. Westerfield Tucker, eds. *The Oxford History of Christian Worship*. New York: Oxford University Press, 2006.

Walsh, Liam G. "Liturgy in the Theology of St. Thomas." *Thomist* 38 (1974): 557–83.

————. *The Sacraments of Initiation: Baptism, Confirmation, Eucharist*. London: Geoffrey Chapman, 1988.

————. "The Divine and the Human in St. Thomas's Theology of Sacraments." In *Ordo Sapientiae et Amoris*, edited by Carlos Josaphat Pinto de Oliveira, 321–52. Fribourg, Switzerland: Universitatsverlag Freiburg Schweiz, 1993.

————. "Sacraments." In *The Theology of Thomas Aquinas*, edited by Rik Van Nieuwenhove and Joseph Wawrykow, 326–64. Notre Dame, IN: University of Notre Dame Press, 2005.

Waters Kenneth L., Sr. "Eucharist and Global Reconciliation: A Liturgical Vision of Social Transformation." In *The Eucharist in a United Methodist Perspective*, edited by Hendrik R. Pieterse, 34–46. Nashville: UMC, General Board of Higher Education and Ministry, 2007.

Watkins, Keith. "Eucharist, American Style." *Worship* 56, no. 5 (Spring 1982): 401–11.

Webster, Robert. "The Reforming Bishop: John Wesley and the Sunday Service of 1784." *Quarterly Review* 21, no. 1 (Spring 2001): 67–80.

Wesley, John. *Explanatory Notes upon the Old Testament*. 3 vols. Bristol: Graham and Pine, 1760–62; many later reprints.

————. *The Works of John Wesley*. 14 vols. Edited by Thomas Jackson. London, 1872; Grand Rapids, MI: Zondervan, 1958.

————. *Explanatory Notes upon the New Testament*. London: Epworth, 1976.

————. *Sunday Service of the Methodists in North America*. Edited by James F. White. Nashville: Quarterly Review, 1984.

————. *The Works of John Wesley*. Bicentennial Edition. Edited by Albert Outler et al. Nashville: Abingdon, 1984ff.

Wesley, John, and Charles Wesley. *Hymns on the Lord's Supper* [facsimile of the first edition]. Madison, NJ: Charles Wesley Society, 1995.

West, Stephen P. *Something Happens Here: Reclaiming the Distinctiveness of Wesley's Communion Spirituality in Times of Divisiveness*. Eugene, OR: Wipf and Stock, 2022.

Westerfield Tucker, Karen B., ed. *The Sunday Service of the Methodists: Twentieth-Century Worship in Worldwide Methodism; Studies in Honor of James F. White*. Nashville: Kingswood, 1996.

———. *American Methodist Worship.* New York: Oxford University Press, 2001.

———. "'Let Us Thy Mercy Prove': A United Methodist Understanding of the Eucharist." In *The Eucharist in a United Methodist Perspective,* edited by Hendrik R. Pieterse, 20–33. Nashville: UMC, General Board of Higher Education and Ministry, 2007.

White, Grant Sperry. "The Recovery of the Great Eucharistic Prayer in the Wesleyan Tradition." In *Orthodox and Wesleyan Scriptural Understanding and Practice,* edited by S. T. Kimbrough Jr., 277–92. Crestwood, NY: St. Vladimir's Seminary Press, 2005.

White, James F. "The New American Methodist Communion Order." *Worship* 41, no. 9 (November 1967): 552–60.

———. *New Forms of Worship.* Nashville: Abingdon, 1971.

———. "Liturgy, Theology of the Laity: The Case of the 1972 United Methodist Communion Service." *Duke Divinity School Review* 43, no. 1 (Winter 1978): 33–43.

———. "Function and Form of the Eucharistic Prayer." *Reformed Liturgy and Music* 16, no. 1 (Winter 1982): 18–21.

———. "Response to the Berakah Award: Making Changes in United Methodist Euchology." *Worship* 57, no. 4 (July 1983): 333–44.

———. *Sacraments as God's Self Giving: Sacramental Practice and Faith.* Nashville: Abingdon, 1983.

———, ed. *John Wesley's Sunday Service of the Methodists in North America: With an Introduction by James F. White.* Nashville: United Methodist Publishing House, 1984.

———. "Sources for the Study of Protestant Worship in America." *Worship* 61, no. 6 (November 1987): 515–33.

———. *Protestant Worship: Traditions in Transition.* Louisville: Westminster John Knox, 1989.

———. "Methodist Worship." In *Perspectives on American Methodism,* edited by Russell Richey, Kenneth Rowe, and Jean Miller Schmidt, 460–79. Nashville: Kingswood, 1993.

Willimon, William H. "Thanks, Papa Hippolytus." *Duke Divinity School Review* 43, no. 1 (Winter 1978): 20–31.

———. *Sunday Dinner: The Lord's Supper and the Christian Life.* Nashville: Upper Room, 1981.

Wilson, Kenneth. "What Is Distinctive about Methodist Ecclesiology? A Response to Papers by Miriam Haar, Justus Hunter, and Robert Martin." *Ecclesiology* 9, no. 1 (2013): 66–74.

World Council of Churches. *Baptism, Eucharist, and Ministry.* Faith and Order Paper No. 111. Geneva: 1982.

World Methodist Council–Roman Catholic Church (WMC-RCC). *Speaking the Truth in Love: Teaching Authority among Catholics and Methodists.* Lake Junaluska, N.C.: World Methodist Council, 2001.

———. *The Grace Given You in Christ: Catholics and Methodists Reflect Further on the Church.* Lake Junaluska, NC: World Methodist Council, 2006.

————. *Synthesis: Together to Holiness; 40 Years of Methodist and Roman Catholic Dialogue*. Lake Junaluska, NC: World Methodist Council, 2010.

————. *Encountering Christ the Saviour: Church and Sacraments*. Lake Junaluska, NC: World Methodist Council, 2011.

————. *God in Christ Reconciling: On the Way to Full Communion in Faith, Sacraments, and Mission* (2022). Accessed April 16, 2023. http://www.christianunity.va/content/unitacristiani/en/dialoghi/sezione-occidentale/consiglio-metodista-mondiale/dialogo/documenti-di-dialogo/god-in-christ-reconciling-on-the-way-to-full-communion-in-faith.html.

Yocum, John P. "Sacraments in Aquinas." In *Aquinas on Doctrine: A Critical Introduction*, edited by Thomas Weinandy, Daniel Keating, and John P. Yocum, 159–82. New York: T&T Clark, 2004.

Young, Frances. "The Great Thanksgiving Prayer." In *Living the Eucharist: Affirming Catholicism and the Liturgy*, edited by Stephen Conway, 79–94. London: Darton, Longman and Todd, 2001.

Yrigoyen, Charles, ed. *T&T Clark Companion to Methodism*. New York: T&T Clark, 2010.

Yrigoyen, Charles Jr., John G. McEllhenney, and Kenneth E. Rowe. *United Methodism at Forty: Looking Back, Looking Forward*. Nashville: Abingdon, 2008.

Permissions

Index

About the Author

Stephen Sours (Ph.D. Duke University, 2011) is professor of religion and chair of the department at Huntingdon College in Montgomery, Alabama, where he teaches classes in Bible and theology. Dr. Sours is a John Wesley Fellow and a member of the Alabama–West Florida Annual Conference of the United Methodist Church.